ADDITIONAL PRAISE FOR *MIDDLE MARKET M&A*

"At last we have a comprehensive body of knowledge for the M&A middle market. This anthology of contemporary thinking is very timely considering how global this market has become. Many of these insights and best practices are truly universal and will resonate with leading practitioners the world over."

—*Paul Hawkins*
Managing Director,
MergeCo International Pty Ltd, Sydney, Australia

"*Middle Market M&A* brings together the knowledge and expertise of several seasoned M&A professionals to provide an abundance of information, practice tips, and examples on the middle market, the practice of M&A, and related technical topics. From a valuation perspective, a clear and concise explanation is provided on how there can be multiple values for the same company, based on the value worlds concept. This book will serve as a fabulous reference not only to any advisor who deals with M&A issues, but also for any business owner or executive contemplating the purchase or sale of a business. A must-have for anybody involved in M&A!"

—*Chris M. Mellen, ASA, MCBA, ABAR, CM&AA*
President, Delphi Valuation Advisors, Inc.
Co-author, Valuation for M&A: Building Value in
Private Companies, *2nd edition, Wiley, 2010*

"Four talented authors combine their talents for one powerful treatise on Mergers and Acquisitions. A great educational tool for the M&A novice or professional, and a valuable referral source for both."

—*Everett H Walker, Jr.*
Chairman/President,
National Funding Association, Inc.

"Marks, Slee, and company have produced a volume that fills the void for information on a topic of crucial importance to sellers of businesses, students of finance, and those who have or wish to have a career in the world of M&A. Written in clear, precise language, the book thoroughly details the basics of the M&A process. This is an exceptional work and will be of tremendous benefit to anyone involved in buying and selling a business."

—Barry Yelton
Vice President and Business Development Officer,
TAB Bank

"There is no roadmap for banking and business consulting for middle market M&A. Each deal needs its own roadmap. The strength of the handbook is that it reflects the judgment and experience of Kenneth Marks and its other authors and equips the reader to approach each deal uniquely."

—Gerald F. Roach
Head of Corporate Group,
Smith, Anderson, Blount, Dorsett, Mitchell & Jernigan, LLP

Middle Market M&A

Founded in 1807, John Wiley & Sons is the oldest independent publishing company in the United States. With offices in North America, Europe, Australia and Asia, Wiley is globally committed to developing and marketing print and electronic products and services for our customers' professional and personal knowledge and understanding.

The Wiley Finance series contains books written specifically for finance and investment professionals as well as sophisticated individual investors and their financial advisors. Book topics range from portfolio management to e-commerce, risk management, financial engineering, valuation, and financial instrument analysis, as well as much more.

For a list of available titles, visit our Web site at www.WileyFinance.com.

Middle Market M&A

*Handbook for Investment Banking
and Business Consulting*

KENNETH H. MARKS
ROBERT T. SLEE
CHRISTIAN W. BLEES
MICHAEL R. NALL

WILEY

John Wiley & Sons, Inc.

Published by John Wiley & Sons, Inc., Hoboken, New Jersey.
Published simultaneously in Canada.

For general information on our other products and services or for technical support, please contact our Customer Care Department within the United States at (800) 762-2974, outside the United States at (317) 572-3993 or fax (317) 572-4002.

Wiley also publishes its books in a variety of electronic formats. Some content that appears in print may not be available in electronic books. For more information about Wiley products, visit our web site at www.wiley.com.

Library of Congress Cataloging-in-Publication Data:

Marks, Kenneth.
Middle market M & A : handbook for investment banking and business consulting / Kenneth Marks . . . [et al.].
    p. cm. – (Wiley finance series)
    Includes index.
    ISBN 978-0-470-90829-7 (hardback); ISBN 978-1-118-19860-5 (ebk);
    ISBN 978-1-118-19861-2 (ebk); ISBN 978-1-118-19862-9 (ebk)
    1. Consolidation and merger of corporations.   2. Small business–Mergers.
I. Marks, Kenneth, 1963–
    HG4028.M4M53 2012
    658.1′62–dc23
                                                                2011037185

Printed in the United States of America.

10   9   8   7   6   5   4   3   2   1

To our families and God

Contents

Deal markets go through cycles just as the broader economy ebbs and flows. And after a long drought of merger and acquisition (M&A) activity, the market for private companies is on the rise again. If you own, operate, or advise a middle market company, one with $5 million to $500 million in revenues, what does this mean for you and your clients when thinking about shareholder liquidity, or selling or buying a business? And how can you improve the odds of getting a deal done? *Middle Market M&A: Handbook of Investment Banking & Business Consulting* is a foundational reference for those advisors, leaders, and executives involved in the lifecycle and process of M&A transactions. It is based on the body of knowledge of the industry benchmark credential: the Certified M&A Advisor® (CM&AA) originated and led by the Alliance of Merger & Acquisition Advisors (AM&AA).

As with all industries and segments, the private capital markets continue to evolve, addressing challenges and seizing opportunities. Significant influence in the middle market over the past several years has come from private equity, regulatory reform, and the impact of aging Baby Boomers seeking eventual liquidity or transitions from their middle market businesses. Couple these drivers with a cross-border appetite for investment and growth, and you have a wealth of opportunity.

From a private equity perspective, the dollars invested in middle market companies more than doubled since 2009. Buyout and growth equity funds have record amounts of committed capital ready to invest. The challenge continues to be credit availability (especially at the lower end of the middle market) and partner time tied up in fixing existing portfolio companies. Publicly traded strategic buyers like the S&P 500 companies have unusually high levels of cash, and are seeking to deploy part of this hoard to generate significant revenue through external growth initiatives like acquisitions. While most middle market companies by themselves will not move the needle in terms of revenue for the S&P 500–sized businesses, a number of strategic acquisitions can begin to impact their overall performance. These relatively smaller, or niche, acquisitions can provide access to new customers, higher-margin product lines, new technologies, and entrepreneurial talent. The same concept applies to what private equity refers to as *tuck-in* or *bolt-on* acquisitions for larger existing portfolio companies. For buyout funds, some middle market companies provide a platform for entry into new markets and from which to add niche businesses for expansion.

On the surface, the number of transactions is increasing and appears to be rebounding; however, the character of the market and deals is different from that of the pre–Great Recession vintage. In the period from 2004 to early 2008, there was significantly less scrutiny in underwriting and financing transactions. There was an abundance of capital available to all types of companies, almost independent of operating performance. Coupled with easy credit, valuations soared. Today, the performance bar has been raised very high with a flight to quality. Transactions are being done primarily with the very best industry players within a market or segment; and these companies are able to garner valuation multiples at nearly 2008 levels. However, the average and lower performing businesses will likely find greatly depressed multiples, or worse, no interest from buyers or investors at all. Thus the quandary: the "value gap." What is the typical middle market company to do to create a partial or complete exit for its owners? This challenge creates an opportunity for resolute leaders and executives as well as for innovative and trusted advisors.

This handbook is meant to be a practical guide and reference for those practitioners and operators, buyers and sellers, and educators and students. The term *M&A advisor* is used throughout the text as a reference to the many professionals involved in the M&A process, including investment bankers, M&A intermediaries and specialists, CPAs and accountants, deal and transaction attorneys, valuation experts, wealth managers and investors, and consultants and business advisors. The intent is to provide a holistic overview and guide concerning mergers, acquisitions, divestitures, and strategic transactions for middle market companies. It covers pretransaction planning, deal execution, and post-transaction considerations, and addresses the processes and core subject areas required to successfully navigate and close deals in the private capital markets. *Middle Market M&A* and the CM&AA program can be thought of as providing a horizontal perspective for the many participants in the process, which typically bring expertise in one or more vertical subject areas.

The main content is divided into three parts, with the first being an overview of the middle market including a global view. This market perspective is heavily influenced by the work of co-author Robert Slee and his research and experiences in the private capital markets (also the title of one of his books). Keeping in sync with market trends, this section includes a high-level discussion about corporate development and its intersection with the middle market. This is particularly important given the likely impact that strategic buyers will have in shaping the exit and liquidity plans of middle market owners, and the competing pressure against private equity. As the public markets have become a less attractive alternative, these strategic buyers (represented by those in corporate development) also represent a potentially desirable exit for the same private equity buyers then selling a few years later. This section ends with a look at the global and cross-border impact of middle market M&A activity.

Part II focuses on the M&A processes and practice management. It addresses sell-side, buy-side, and merger processes and introduces a framework for professional standards and ethics. This is thought to be the first such introduction for the middle market.

Part III delves more deeply into the technical subjects. Each chapter is a stand-alone treatise on a specific topic. Together, they provide the supporting details to begin understanding the subtleties and intricacies in making a deal or transaction work. Keep in mind that this handbook is a guide. It is not intended as an endpoint in the search for understanding and clarity about M&A, but is rather a quick start to understanding the topics and processes and determining where more in-depth knowledge and experience is required.

The remainder of the text provides an epilogue for business owners; a glossary; references to a companion website (www.MiddleMarketMA.com) for tools and resources of the trade; and a brief introduction to Transaction Value, an alternative view of valuing companies based on the work and research of Mike Adhikari, a leading member, thought leader, and president of the AM&AA and the founder of Business ValueXpress™ software company.

Throughout the handbook, wherever practical, there are anecdotes and annotations that provide a global perspective: character, details, and practical advice about the subject matter as it relates to cross-border and regional differences and concepts. We expect to bolster these and make them more robust in future editions of this handbook.

The author team crafting this handbook includes Robert T. Slee, as mentioned above; Christian W. Blees, chair of the CM&AA credentialing program and a key instructor in developing its content; Michael R. Nall, CPA, founder of the AM&AA and the MidMarket Alliance; Mona Pearl, a special contributor to this work and author of *Grow Globally*; and Kenneth H. Marks, lead author of the *Handbook of Financing Growth* and also an instructor in the CM&AA program. We have endeavored to generate and capture content, knowledge, and experiences from industry and subject matter leaders to provide a holistic, practical, and balanced perspective. As you scan the list of contributors and reviewers involved in creating this edition, you will notice that the breadth and depth of experience, expertise, diversity, and backgrounds is vast.

M&A is a careful blend of art and science. On one hand it is multi-disciplinary, complex, and analytical. On the other, it is all about people, relationships, nuances, timing, and instinct. This dynamic produces opportunity coupled with conflict, ambiguity and challenges, all supporting an exhilarating business ripe for those seeking to create value.

We invite you to send your comments, questions, and observations to us at: khmarks@HighRockPartners.com, r.slee@midasnation.com, blees@biggskofford.com, mnall@amaaonline.org.

KENNETH H. MARKS
ROBERT T. SLEE
CHRISTIAN W. BLEES
MICHAEL R. NALL

www.MiddleMarketMA.com

Acknowledgments

The author team is grateful to the contributors and reviewers (listed below) who provided a wealth of time, content, shared experiences, shared expertise, and support in writing this handbook. They represent a cross-section of industry experience and subject matter expertise from the many disciplines involved in the M&A process; we extend our sincerest appreciation and acknowledgment to each. We have included their biographies in the final part of this handbook.

Special Contributor

Mona Pearl	BeyondAStrategy, Inc.	www.BeyondAStrategy.com

Contributors

Michael P. Saber, Esquire, and Amanda Keister	Smith, Anderson, Blount, Dorsett, Mitchell & Jernigan, LLP	www.SmithLaw.com
David A. Cohn	Diamond Capital Partners	www.DiamondCapital Partners.com
Michael S. Roberts	Roberts McGivney Zagotta, LLC	www.rmczlaw.com
Champ W. Davis III	Davis Capital, LLC	www.DavisCapital.com
Stephen Cazalet	Double Eagle Advisory, LLC	www.DoubleEagle Advisory.com
John C. Watts	Curtiss-Wright Corporation	www.CurtissWright.com
Allen Burchett	ABB North America	www.ABB.com
Scott Moss	Cherry, Bekaert & Holland, LLP	www.cbh.com

Reviewers

Amalie L. Tuffin	Whitmeyer Tuffin, PLLC	www.Whit-Law.com
Deirdre Patten	Patten Training & Review, LLC	www.pattentraining.com
John A. Howard	High Rock Partners, Inc.	www.HighRock Partners.com
William H. Stewart	Navigator Partners, LLC.	www.navigatorpartners .com
David G. Kostmayer	Barrett & Kostmayer, PLLC	www.BarrettKostmayer .com
Daniel A. Cotter	Korey Cotter Heather & Richardson, LLC	www.kchrlaw.com
Austin Buckett	BiggsKofford Capital, LLC	www.BiggsKofford.com
B. Graeme Frazier IV	Private Capital Research LLC	www.pcrllc.com
Mark Devine	Independent consultant	
Mike Ertel	Legacy M&A Advisors, LLC	www.legacymandaadvisors .com
Annette Mason	BAE Systems	www.baesystems.com
Brandon Clewett	McGladrey Capital Markets LLC	www.mcgladreycm.com
Darrell V. Arne	Arne & Co.	www.arne-co.com
Willis E. Eayrs	Corporate Financial Advisor	
Bruce N. Lipian	StoneCreek Capital, Inc.	www.stonecreekcapital.com

Thanks to Eric Chabinsky for his visual critique, to Carolyn Manuel and Capital IQ for their assistance in obtaining market data, and to Andy Greenberg and GF Data Resources for valuation data. We appreciate the support, patience, and direction of John DeRemigis, Jennifer MacDonald, Laura Cherkas, and the entire team at John Wiley & Sons. Lastly, special thanks go to the never-wavering support and encouragement of Diane Niederman, vice president for business development and marketing, and the operations team, both of the Alliance of M&A Advisors.

The Middle Market

CHAPTER 1

Private Capital Markets

A fundamental premise in this handbook is that there is a difference between the deals, transactions, and financings in the middle market and those in the large-company, traditional-corporate-finance public market. As indicated in the preface, the focus of this book is the middle market, primarily composed of private businesses. This chapter sets the stage for the balance of the discussion in this handbook by providing an overview and perspective of the middle market and private capital market activity.

A *capital market* is a market for securities (debt or equity) where businesses can raise long-term funds. Since the 1970s, public capital markets[1] have received much of the attention from academics in the literature and press. Since that time it has been assumed that the public and private markets are substitutes, but in recent years this assumption has been challenged by research studies showing that the two markets are different in many meaningful ways.[*]

Merger and acquisition (M&A) activity is mainly driven by capital availability, liquidity, and motives of the players, which vary in each market. Regardless of the purview of the buyer, seller, M&A advisor, investor, or lender in the middle market, it is important to understand the market differences and dynamics.

A number of factors differentiate the public and private markets:

- Risk and return are unique to each market.
- Liquidity within each market is different.

---

[*]Examples of middle market research and studies: (1) multiple industry surveys of middle market advisors by the Alliance of M&A Advisors, 2008–2011; (2) *Private Capital Markets: Valuation, Capitalization, and Transfer of Private Business Interests* (John Wiley & Sons, 2011), by Robert T. Slee; (3) *Handbook of Financing Growth: Strategies, Capital Structure and M&A Transactions, 2nd Edition* (John Wiley & Sons, 2009), by Kenneth H Marks et al.; and (4) the Pepperdine Private Capital Markets Project.

- Motives of private owners are different from those of professional managers.
- Underlying capital market theories that explain the behavior of players in each market are different.
- Private companies are priced at a point in time, while public companies are continuously priced.
- Public markets allow ready access to capital, whereas private capital is difficult to arrange.
- Public shareholders can diversify their holdings, whereas shareholders of closely held businesses have few opportunities to create liquidity or to reallocate their ownership in a private company.
- Private markets are inefficient, whereas public markets are fairly efficient.
- Market mechanisms have differing effects on each market.
- Costs of capital are substantially different for each market.
- The expected holding period for investors is different.
- The transaction costs of buying versus selling a business are different.

So, why does it matter whether large public and middle markets are different? It is important because acquisition pricing and behavior vary by market, or more specifically, by market segment. Further, much of what is taught in traditional corporate finance is not easily applied, nor appropriate to apply, to the private capital markets and to many middle market deals. And lastly, a clearer understanding of market behaviors, drivers, processes, and dynamics will ideally enable those on all sides of a transaction to put greater focus on meeting strategic objectives, creating value, and achieving owner and shareholder objectives.

SEGMENTED MARKETS

The private markets actually contain numerous marketplaces. For example, there are different submarkets for raising debt and equity and for transferring business interests. This handbook consistently uses the collective term *markets* to describe activity within the private capital markets, rather than attempting to describe particular submarkets with a confusing array of terminology. While there are no definitive size boundaries, Figure 1.1 depicts market segmentation by size of business.[2]

Small businesses with annual sales of less than $5 million are at the bottom of the ladder. There are more than 5 million small businesses in the United States and together this group generates approximately 15 percent of the U.S. gross domestic product. These businesses generally are handled

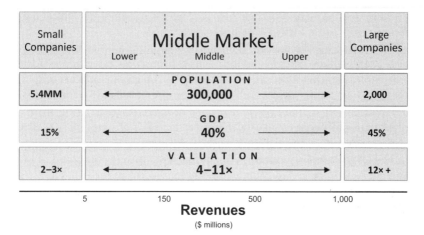

FIGURE 1.1 Segmented Capital Markets

by the business banking group of community or smaller regional banks and are almost always owner-managed. These businesses have limited access to the private capital markets beyond assistance from the Small Business Administration (SBA) and business brokers. Capital access improves as the business moves into the upper segments.

The entire middle market generates roughly 40 percent of the U.S. gross domestic product (GDP). The *lower-middle* market segment includes companies with annual sales of $5 million to $150 million. The lower-middle market is the main province of the private capital markets as described in this book. Companies in this segment have a number of unique characteristics:

- There is owner management.
- Owners have virtually unlimited liability and personally guarantee the debt.
- Owners typically have most of their personal wealth tied to the business.
- A vast majority of these businesses will not transfer to the next generation.
- Access to capital varies greatly, is situation dependent, and is difficult to prescribe.
- The enterprise value of the company can vary widely from year to year.

The *middle-middle* market includes companies with annual sales of $150 million to $500 million. They are serviced by regional investment banks and draw the attention of the bank's top lenders—their corporate bankers. Generally, capital market access and efficiency improve at this level as the sophistication and robustness of the business increase. Companies with sales over $150 million begin to have access to nearly all capital market alternatives in some form, though selective.

The *upper-middle* market is comprised of companies with sales of between $500 million and $1 billion. These companies have access to most of the capital market alternatives available to the largest public companies. This group of companies, which tend to be publicly held, attracts the secondary attention of the largest Wall Street investment banking firms; the largest regional bankers also take notice. In this tier, capital is accessible and priced to reflect the riskiness of the borrower.

The *large-company* market, which is almost entirely composed of public companies, is estimated to generate about 45 percent of the U.S. GDP. Large companies have the complete arsenal of capital alternatives at their disposal. Many use discounted-cash-flow techniques to make capital decisions because they can fund projects at their marginal cost of capital. Almost all are public, and the few that are private have most of the financial capabilities of public companies. Wall Street bankers focus primarily on these companies. This segment of the market is where the finance theory, research, and rules of traditional capital markets were developed and typically applied.

Each market segment yields information and liquidity, which form the basis for particular investor return expectations manifested by acquisition multiples paid for companies within it. Acquisition multiples based on *EBITDA* (earnings before interest, taxes, depreciation and amortization) represent capital structure decisions. The reciprocal of EBITDA multiples yields an expected return on total capital. For instance, equity investors *ordinarily* require 30 to 40 percent compounded returns from investments in the middle market, and 10 to 20 percent from investments in large companies.[3]

Markets segment by investor return expectations because players within a segment view valuation parochially. The relationship between investor return expectations and valuation is straightforward: Greater perceived risk requires greater returns to compensate for the risk. Using a capital market–determined discount rate is another way of looking at this risk/return relationship. The discount rate then is the expected rate of return required to attract capital to an investment, taking into account the rate of return available from other investments of comparable risk.

Calculating the reciprocal of a selling multiple is a shorthand method for determining the capitalization rate or, once we account for assumed long-term growth, the discount rate. EBITDA acquisition multiples for the lower-middle market typically fall between four and seven times. Expressed as a reciprocal, this roughly corresponds to a 14 to 25 percent capitalization rate, or assuming a long-term EBITDA growth rate of 2 percent, a discount rate (investor return expectation) of 16 to 27 percent. Return expectations can be expressed as discount rates and tested. Assume a buyer uses a capital structure in an acquisition with 30 percent equity, carrying 30 percent return expectation, and 70 percent debt, which costs 9 percent. The discount rate implied in this capital structure is about 15 percent, within the return range cited above. Thus, as Figure 1.1 indicates, there is a correlation between investor return expectations and pricing. Although much of Figure 1.1 is definitional, support for these findings can be found in several private company transactional databases.[4]

Since a number of factors form boundaries in the capital markets, appraisers must correctly identify the segment within which the subject will be viewed. Characteristics need to be weighed in their totality. For example, some companies have annual sales of $3 million, but meet other criteria that may allow them to be viewed as lower-middle market entities. On the contrary, companies with sales over $5 million may be viewed by the markets as small businesses if they don't have certain characteristics. An incorrect assessment will lead to improper valuation. Table 1.1 provides criteria appraisers can use to define the segment within which their subject should be viewed.[5]

Some criteria warrant further explanation. Owners significantly influence the segment in which their company will be viewed. For instance, if an owner decides to personally manage every aspect of the business and desires to achieve only a good lifestyle from the business, the market will probably view it as a small business. Conversely, owners who strive to create company value and build a functional organization may induce the markets to view the company as a lower-middle market entity.

Market players also help decide how a subject will be viewed. For example, business bankers and business brokers work with small businesses; commercial bankers and private investment bankers work with lower-middle market businesses.

Once again, market segmentation matters in M&A because segmentation (how a company is viewed by the capital markets) determines several critical issues: how that company will be valued, capital access and costs, transfer options or exit alternatives, and which professionals are likely to engage and support the business. Therefore, one element of a strategy to maximize a company's value is for management to get the company viewed in a more advantageous segment based on their objectives.

WHY ARE MARKETS SEGMENTED?

Markets, like individual firms, have a cost of capital that reflects the return expectations of capital providers in that market. But, how do capital providers determine risk and return within a market? Capital markets are

TABLE 1.1 Defining Characteristics by Segment

Characteristic	Small Market	Lower-Middle Market	Middle-Middle Market and Up
Revenue Size	<$5 million	$5–$150 million	$150–$500 million
EBITDA Size	<$500,000	$500,000–$15 million	$15–50 million
Ownership Profile	Owner-managed	Owner-managed, professionally managed	Professionally managed
Owner or Manager Capital Motives	To manage cash in business, not balance sheet	To manage the business, not the balance sheet	To manage net assets on the balance sheet
Ownership Goal	Lifestyle	Lifestyle—entity wealth creation	Entity wealth creation
Role of Key Manager	Wears all hats	Wears few hats—functional management	Functional management
Market Orientation	Service	Service—market maker	Market maker—service
Capital Access			
Debt	Business banking	Commercial banking	Corporate banking
Equity	Personal/family	Personal/private equity	Private equity
Intermediation	Business brokers	M&A advisors and local investment bankers	Regional/national investment bankers

segmented for two primary reasons. First, capital providers are the authorities that set rules and parameters. Second, owners and managers view and define risk and return differently in each market.

Capital Providers

Capital providers use what may be thought of as *credit boxes*, which depict the criteria necessary to access the specific capital. Many institutional capital providers use portfolio theory to diversify risk while optimizing return. Portfolio theory is built on the premise that the risk inherent in any single asset, when held in a group of assets, is different from the inherent risk of that asset in isolation. It is unlikely that even investments in a class, like senior middle market debt, will experience returns that co-vary. Credit boxes help capital providers filter asset quality and set return expectations. Loans or investments that meet the terms of the credit box should promise risk-adjusted returns that meet a provider's goals.

Providers also use other devices to manage portfolio risk and return. Techniques such as advance rates and loan terms enable providers to hedge risks. They manage risk with interest rate matching and hedges, and diversify investments across geography and industries. Loan covenants are a major risk/return management tool; by setting behavioral boundaries around the borrower, capital providers are better able to manage portfolios. Providers constantly monitor their portfolios, feeding back information through their credit boxes to adjust the characteristics of assets in their portfolios.

Debt providers' use of loan covenants further segments capital markets. For example, the range of senior debt multiples and the ratio of senior debt to EBITDA, is different for each segment. Small market debt providers usually will not lend more than two times EBITDA; middle market lending usually occurs in the three-to-five-times range; finally, middle-middle and large-company lenders often lend beyond five times EBITDA.

It is possible to get a general idea of acquisition multiples by knowing just a few variables. These variables are equity investment and senior lending multiples. According to recent surveys by Pepperdine University, the typical private equity group (PEG) deal employs about 48 percent equity in the capital structure.[6] This percentage, by the way, represents an all-time-high equity investment level by PEGs. The most recent Pepperdine survey indicates that senior lenders use a financial covenant of 2.5 run-rate EBITDA on total debt. This combination of debt and equity yields an equation that derives acquisition multiples as follows:

Acquisition multiple = Senior lending multiple/(1 − % Equity investment)

$$= 2.5/(1 - 0.48) = 4.8$$

Thus, when senior lenders employ a 2.5 lending multiple and equity represents almost half the capital structure, acquisition multiples fall to below 5. Many middle market owners resist selling for less than a 5 acquisition multiple, primarily because net proceeds after closing fees and taxes do not enable them to meet their financial needs. In an attempt to overcome low multiples, advisors may craft economic bridges (earnouts, seller notes) to boost purchase prices.

Markets are further segmented by the ability to accommodate perceived risk differences. In the middle market there is a distinct difference between the portfolio risk experienced by equity providers and that of debt providers. Equity risk is generally greater, due to its legal structure, and it is likely to be a larger portion of a smaller portfolio, further increasing risk. Debt tends to be less risky, due to its substantial bundle of legal rights, and it is usually a smaller portion of a larger investment portfolio, diminishing the impact of risk. Middle market equity investors generally spread their risk among relatively few investments contained in a given fund or portfolio. In contrast, debt investors spread the risk among a larger pool of investments in the portfolio. *Mezzanine investors* can assemble blended portfolios with an entirely different risk profile since they tend to make relatively smaller investments in a greater number of companies. Moreover, the debt portion of their investments diminishes mezzanine investors' risk, while the equity portion improves their return. Rounding out this discussion of the impact of portfolio risk, pity the poor business owner who has a portfolio of one company to absorb all risk.

Lenders' and investors' portfolios define the limits of their expected returns, and managing these limits creates market fluctuations. Similarly, owners manage a balance sheet with a blend of equity and debt. In other words, owners manage a portfolio of equity and debt in order to maximize utilization of capital and control exposure to risk. It is the day-to-day operation of these portfolios of investments working through market mechanisms that *defines* the market at any point in time.

Owners' and Managers' Views of Risk/Return

Appraisal attempts to estimate the balance between risk and return. The foregoing illustrates that risk and return balance by market segment. Behavior of parties in the markets reinforces this premise. For instance, when a large public company, whose stock may be trading at 30 times earnings, acquires a lower-middle market company, why does the larger company pay 4 to 7 times earnings, and not 20? Paying any multiple less than 30 would be accretive, thus adding value to the shareholders. The reason is that the larger company views investments in the lower-middle market as riskier, and therefore needs to pay less to balance risk and return.

Here is the key insight: Risk and return are viewed and defined differently by owners and managers in each market. At a minimum, both risk and return are comprised of financial, behavioral, and psychological elements. Financial risk/return indicates that the monetary results of an action must compensate for the risk of taking the action. Behavioral risk/return describes the fact that actions occur within a set of social expectations. For example, loss of face in a community may be viewed as a behavioral risk. Psychological risk/return is personal to the decision maker and accounts for an individual's or an institution's emotional investment in a course of action.

Owners of small companies view risk/return more from a personal perspective, unlike shareholders in larger-market firms. Many small and lower-middle market company owners view the business as a means to a desirable lifestyle, rather than an entity that creates purely financial value. Most small firm owners do not measure investments in the business with the tools of corporate finance. They are more likely to use a gut-feel approach in making an investment decision.

Middle-middle market owner-managers tend to balance the financial and psychological elements of risk/return. They understand that cost of capital is relatively high, so financial returns must compensate for investment risk. However, personal pride and community standing still have great importance. Middle-middle and larger-company managers are driven to realize risk-adjusted returns. This drives economic value–added approaches to managing, which have taken root only in larger companies. Behavioral and psychological decision making are less important to large-company managers, or at least they take different forms.

The combination of capital providers that balance risk/return through portfolio management and owner-managers who view risk/return differently leads to market segmentation. The behavior and perceptions of players are unique in each market. Therefore, making proper financing, appraisal, and investment decisions requires using theories and methods appropriate to the subject's market.

Buyers

Once the market segment in which a company will be viewed is ascertained, the next step is to determine which of the four types of buyers is likely to be interested in the subject company. Table 1.2 offers a brief description of each.

Many owners of mid-size companies think there is one *value* for their firm, when in fact every company has a range of values, depending on the

TABLE 1.2 Four Types of Buyers

Buyer Profile	Description
Individual	Most individual buyers are acquiring a job (or source of income) when they purchase a business. Purchase prices tend to be constrained, and are typically comprised of a relatively small down payment with the balance coming from bank financing and seller notes.
Financial	Private equity groups are the main financial buyers in the market. They typically cannot bring synergies to a deal. An institutional buyer that does not currently participate in the subject's industry or cannot leverage the subject's business is probably a financial buyer. This group includes some holding companies.
Strategic	Corporate buyers are usually the strategic buyers. They can extract or create value beyond what a financial buyer can enable, resulting in synergies. These synergies can result from a variety of acquisition scenarios. Perhaps the most quantifiable group of synergies emanate from *horizontal integrations*. A horizontal integrator can realize substantial synergies by cutting duplicate overhead and other expenses. Some of these savings *may* be shared with the seller. *Vertical integrations* also can create substantial synergies. These tend to be strategic, in that the target company helps the acquirer achieve some business goal. Synergies also can result from the different financial structures of the parties. For instance, the target may realize interest expense savings due to adopting the cheaper borrowing costs of the acquirer.
Value Investor	These acquirers seek assets or franchises that may be thought of as distressed or turnaround companies. They may seek to acquire a target company that has no defensible current or future earnings prospects, or is in an industry that does not give credit for value beyond the fair market value of its assets.

appraisal purpose and who does the valuation. For example, a perfect-fit strategic buyer will value a company one way, while a nonstrategic individual buyer will value it another.

Mid-size companies can sell to one of these four types of buyers. Each of these alternatives normally represents a different value range.

Each prospective buyer-type brings something different to the table, which directly affects its valuation. Individual buyers can use only the seller's financial statements as a basis for value. Typically, this group has a return expectation of 30 to 40 percent on its investment in the company. This means that individual buyers operate mainly in the small business segment. This was confirmed by one study comprising 10 years of data that showed that the selling price/earnings (P/E) multiples of small companies (transactions of less than $1 million) have averaged in the 2.5-to-3.0-times range. This study used the Institute of Business Appraisers database, which houses selling data for more than 10,000 small companies. Interestingly, one of the conclusions of the study was that even with inflation and varying interest costs, the average selling P/E stayed within a fairly tight range.

PEGs are financial buyers that tend to make direct investments in middle market companies and tend to pay four to seven times EBITDA for companies. They normally make control investments; however, many groups will take a minority position in the most promising deals. Private equity groups provide strategic capital for a number of activities, including recapitalizations, leveraged buildups, management buyouts, and management buy-ins. PEGs are opportunistic investors and look at many deals before making an investment. Frequently, PEGs will create investment opportunities by sponsoring an executive team to target an industry in which the team has relevant experience and a strong track record. Many PEGs are comfortable investing in family businesses.

The current view is that the optimum available alternative for most mid-sized companies is to sell to strategic corporate acquirers. The best corporate buyers are normally in the same line of business, but need the subject company's market share or production capability. These buyers use what we call the *second-spreadsheet rule* to determine value. First, they forecast the numbers for the target acquisition with no change in ownership (i.e., the stand-alone value). Next, they add the difference for the change in ownership, which should be increased investment, new business, and so on. The second spreadsheet is different for every acquirer, and this difference explains why five different corporate acquirers will value a company five different ways (six if one of the CEOs gets involved).

It should be noted that strategic buyers typically pay similar acquisition multiples as financial buyers (4–7 times) for middle market companies. The valuation may be higher than a financial buyer because the second spreadsheet increases adjusted EBITDA by the amount of synergies the strategic buyer credits to the seller. For example, if the buyer decides to "share" $500,000 in synergies with the seller, but still uses a 5 acquisition multiple, the resulting valuation will be increased by $2.5 million beyond what a financial buyer would pay.

Value investors (sometimes referred to as buyers of distressed companies) acquire the assets of the seller and value them accordingly. Earnings are not really used as the basis for the valuation. Rather, the assets are valued on either a liquidation basis or other appropriate premise of value depending on the circumstances and underlying assets.

While we have provided the foregoing as an indication of what historical multiples have been for each buyer group, it should be noted that valuation multiples vary tremendously in actuality. Differences in risk profiles, expected growth rates (particularly in the years following the one used in valuing the company), and the strategic significance of the company to the buyer all play huge roles in establishing value. What's more, there are certain industries, technology being one, where it would be highly unusual for a successful company to trade within these multiples. This is not to say that these multiples cannot be used as general guidelines, but instead, is an admonition not to take anything for granted, and that nothing takes the place of good homework, thoughtful analysis, and due diligence when establishing a company's value.

MARKET ACTIVITY

The middle market can be viewed by the sizes and quantities of transactions. Figures 1.2, 1.3, and 1.4 provide a historical context for understanding the market, particularly as it relates to M&A activity. The data in Figures 1.2 and 1.3 has been segmented by revenue of the target company in synchronization with those segments in Figure 1.1. To some degree, there is a

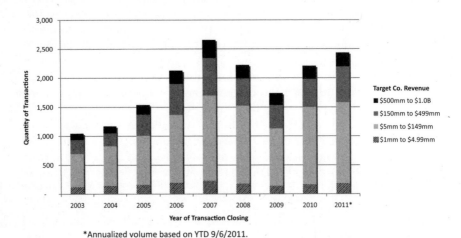

*Annualized volume based on YTD 9/6/2011.

FIGURE 1.2   Global Middle Market M&A Activity-Transaction Volumes
Data source: Copyright © Capital IQ, Inc. a Standard & Poor's business. Standard & Poor's, including its subsidiary corporations, is a division of The McGraw-Hill Companies, Inc. Reproduction of this chart in any form is prohibited without Capital IQ, Inc.'s prior written consent.

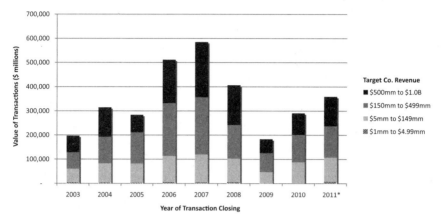

*Annualized values based on YTD 9/6/2011.

FIGURE 1.3   Global Middle Market M&A Activity-Transaction Values
Data source: Copyright © Capital IQ, Inc. a Standard & Poor's business. Standard & Poor's, including its subsidiary corporations, is a division of The McGraw-Hill Companies, Inc. Reproduction of this chart in any form is prohibited without Capital IQ, Inc.'s prior written consent.

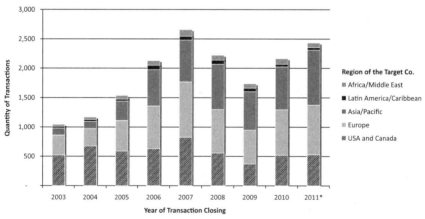

*Annualized volume based on YTD 9/6/2011.

FIGURE 1.4   Global Middle Market M&A Activity-Transactions by Region
Data source: Copyright © Capital IQ, Inc. a Standard & Poor's business. Standard & Poor's, including its subsidiary corporations, is a division of The McGraw-Hill Companies, Inc. Reproduction of this chart in any form is prohibited without Capital IQ, Inc.'s prior written consent.

blurring of definitions of private and public deals on a global basis at the company size on which this handbook focuses. The data supporting these charts includes both private and public information as appropriate. It does not include growth equity or recapitalizations, which would increase the quantity and value of the transactions significantly. These charts are meant to illustrate the pure M&A deals.

As shown in Figure 1.2, the quantity of transactions has nearly doubled over the past eight years, particularly in the lower-middle market.

Figure 1.3 highlights the escalation of investment in the middle market just prior to the Great Recession, as values and investment by private equity peaked. Note that the total value of transactions in the segment below the lower-middle market is negligible. The information on this segment in Figures 1.2, 1.3, and 1.4 is included for reported transactions that likely included institutional buyers or investors; not included are the thousands of main-street brokerage deals.

The value of global middle market transactions reached over $585 billion in 2007. About 57 percent of the target companies were privately held, representing 80 percent of the transaction dollar values. In 2011, it is estimated that about 47 percent of the target companies are privately held, representing 77 percent of the transaction dollar values. Thus the estimated global dollar value of private middle market transactions in 2011 is $276 billion.

Figure 1.4 highlights the global nature of the middle market. In 2003, the target middle market companies were primarily in the United States, Canada, and Europe, representing 82 percent of the volume. Today, the majority of the targets are in Asia, the Pacific Rim, and Europe, with the quantity of deals in the United States and Canada remaining relatively flat.

The middle market is global, vibrant and active.

CHAPTER 2

Valuation Perspectives for the Private Markets

Chapter 1 outlined the differences in the private capital markets and traditional corporate finance theory with a focus on laying the foundation for understanding middle market M&A, particularly for privately or closely held businesses. This chapter continues that theme by providing a high-level overview of valuation and how to frame the valuation analysis in the context of doing deals; it describes the fundamental concepts underlying private business valuation. Keep in mind that valuing a business is a blend of art and science, with a reasonable level of subjectivity.

Business valuation is an attempt to estimate the balance between risk and return in an entity. What exactly is risk? Most analysts view risk as the degree of uncertainty in terms of the amount and timing of realizing expected returns.

Thought of in this way, we can view risk as the capital market's assessment of the likelihood that a subject will actually achieve its expected returns. Business appraisal quantifies this risk assessment as a company's cost of capital.

An underlying principle of all valuation is that risk and return are related. With a greater perceived risk of owning an investment, a greater return is expected by investors to compensate for that risk. The desire to achieve a return that is at least equal to the corresponding risk is the primary motive for investors to bear the uncertainty of investing.

Investors *expect* to earn a certain return from any investment, and return expectations for risk-free investments are often the starting point in the valuation process. By varying the required (expected) rate of return to correctly measure risk, expected returns can be converted to a *fair market value* rate of return. This makes all investments comparable; that is, alternative investments with different risk profiles can be valued on an "apples to apples" basis.

The precise mechanism by which that risk differential is incorporated into a company's value is the discount rate. While a great deal of its level is based on the company's risk profile, it is also determined by the market itself, and in particular, the rate of return available from other investments of comparable risk.

And importantly, just as the risk for any particular investment will vary greatly, so will the risk tolerance for any particular investor, a fact that has been well documented by many researchers, including one of this book's authors. The important point to keep in mind is that required rates of return are not fixed but dynamic, varying with the changes in the risk tolerances of the market, the composition of the investors considering a particular opportunity, and the characteristics of the investment itself. Often, historical measures of return for specific classes of assets provide a "best guess" of what those required levels of return should be, but remember that required rates of return are constantly in flux based on changing conditions and the perception of risk itself.

PRIVATE BUSINESS VALUATION CAN BE VIEWED THROUGH DIFFERENT STANDARDS OF VALUE

Private securities do not have access to an active trading market and, therefore, must rely on point-in-time appraisal or be involved in a transaction (like a sale) for their value to be determined. But before we describe the process of making such a determination, it may be helpful to first discuss the concept of *value*.

There are actually many definitions of value (in appraisal terminology, these are called standards of value). That may come as a surprise to some readers who assume that the definition of value is necessarily the one historically promulgated by the Internal Revenue Service, known as *fair market value*, which, simply stated, is the price at which an asset will sell between a willing buyer and willing seller, neither of whom are under any compulsion to buy or sell and both of whom are knowledgeable of the relevant facts about the asset.

One of the factors that helps (but does not completely) determine which standard of value applies in a given situation is the purpose of the appraisal. In other words, why is the valuation being performed? For example, business owners may need to know the value of their business in order to raise equity capital. Or, they may need to know the value of the business because they want to employ an estate planning technique such as a family limited partnership to transfer shares of the company to their children. Or perhaps one of the owners is involved in an oppressive shareholder action and is litigating to enforce his or her economic claims.

The purpose can both open and close possibilities in terms of the definition of value, either based on statute or simply because it is intellectually appropriate. For instance, an estate planning motive leads to a fair market valuation, which will yield a financial, nonsynergistic value. Choosing this path limits the value of the business but may reduce taxation as well as meet other personal planning goals.

Motives also drive the importance of having a business professionally valued, as shareholders of a private business should not undertake a capitalization or ownership transfer without first knowing the value of their businesses. To do so would be the business equivalent of flying blind. Furthermore, a valuation establishes to potential buyers (or in some cases the IRS) that an independent party has opined on the value of the company, which can add credibility to the sellers' assertions of value, strengthen their negotiating leverage, and better ensure that they will not "leave money on the table." Simply put, without a current valuation, it can be very difficult to know what a business is worth, and attempting to transfer a business without this knowledge is usually an exasperating and frustrating experience.

Therefore, every private company has a number of different values simultaneously depending on both the purpose of the valuation, and for some of these purposes (particularly litigation and taxation), there are agents or agencies with the primary responsibility to develop, adopt, promulgate, and administer standards of practice within that world. An *authority* decides which purposes are acceptable in its world, sanctions its decisions, develops methodology, and provides a coherent set of rules for participants to follow. Authority derives its influence or legitimacy primarily from government action, compelling logic, or the utility of its standards.

And examples of authorities extend far beyond those like the IRS. For instance, secured lenders are the primary authority for the world of collateral value. They develop criteria for accessing this value and administering the methodology used to derive value. Lenders discourage noncompliance by withholding funds.

Another example involves the world of investment value. The investor is the authority in this case since the investor governs both the rules within the world and the methodology used to derive value. However, for these to have meaning beyond the investor's view they must be expressed in communally shared methods and standards. Again, the investor can discourage noncompliant behavior by not investing. The reverse might be true as well. Investors who require too much return for the risk may not have opportunities to invest.

Table 2.1 illustrates a number of concepts of value in terms of purposes, functions, and authorities. While this list is not all-inclusive, it indicates a universe of appraisal possibilities currently beyond the scope of most appraisers.

TABLE 2.1 Value Concept Chart

Appraisal Purpose	Value World	Appraisal Functions	Responsible Authority
To find the highest value in the open market	Market value	Sale of a minority or control interest to support a merger	Financial intermediaries
To find a value for tax matters and for some legal reasons	Fair market value	Federal estate and gift taxes, ESOPs, charitable contributions	Federal law, administrative rulings
For dissenting shareholder issues; certain accounting purposes	Fair value	Equitable distribution, financial statement presentation	Case law, FASB and other accounting authorities
Shareholder wealth measurement	Incremental business value	To create/measure management bonus plans, company performance measurement, capital allocation systems	Academic community and management consulting industry
To value the business from one investor's perspective	Investment value	Value specific to one investor, probably for purchase/investment	Investor
To value the business from an owner's perspective	Owner value	Value specific to owner, probably for sale	Owner
To determine the borrowing capacity of the business	Collateral value	To obtain a secured loan	Secured lending industry
To determine the net asset value	Book value	Value of the net assets based on cost. Sometimes used for buy/sell agreements	Generally Accepted Accounting Principles (GAAP)

Market Value

Market value can be thought of as the highest value of a business interest in the open market. While market value is typically considered the highest value for a business, it is important to note that every private company has various values based on different buyer types, which include asset buyers, financial buyers, and synergistic (strategic) buyers. There is a detailed discussion of market value in Chapter 17.

Asset buyers will generally focus on what the company will be worth if the most likely selling price is based on net asset value as opposed to the company's earnings stream. In this case, the buyer is not giving credit to the seller for goodwill beyond the possible write-up of the assets. In other words, no value is included for the operations of the subject. That also means that goodwill, which we define as the intangible asset that arises from name, reputation, customer patronage, and similar factors (which result in some economic benefit a buyer is willing to pay for beyond the company's asset value) is excluded.

Financial buyers are concerned with what an individual or nonstrategic buyer would pay for the going concern enterprise, inclusive of goodwill. A financial buyer is more concerned with the subject's income statement than the asset buyer, as the earnings stream as well as the balance sheet will be considered in structuring a deal. Since the financial buyer brings no synergies to the deal, the deal itself must supply the earnings and the collateral that enable the transaction to be financed. This effectively creates a boundary around the valuation, in that there is a definable limit of how much a financial buyer can pay for a business. This is based on capitalizing or discounting some measure of earnings (such as EBITDA or a measure of free cash flow), which is usually normalized for things like excess owner compensation. Deriving such numbers to capitalize is a process that includes not only the selling company but also (clearly) the valuation professional.

Strategic buyers are focused on the value from their specific standpoint, which many people actually refer to as investment value. Synergy is the increase in performance of the combined firm over what the two firms are already expected to accomplish as independent companies. Such synergies could include horizontal and vertical integrations or any other combination where the acquirer can leverage the capabilities of the subject.

Synergies can result from a variety of acquisition scenarios. Possibly the most quantifiable group of synergies stem from horizontal integrations, which can lead to substantial synergies through eliminating duplicate overhead. In some cases, part of these savings *may* be shared with the seller. Vertical integrations can also create substantial synergies. These tend to be strategic, where the target helps the acquirer achieve some particular business goal. Synergies also can result from the different financial structures of the parties. For instance, the target may realize interest expense savings due to adopting the cheaper borrowing costs of the acquirer.

Synergistic value is determined by capitalizing or present valuing a synergized benefit stream at an appropriate rate of return. The party most responsible for creating the synergies is usually the buyer, and buyers will not readily give these synergies away since the realization of the synergies happens while they own the business. A high level of mature judgment and experience is necessary when quantifying the synergized benefit stream.

Fair Market Value

Fair market value is a term that is often used in tax and many legal matters. The process used for determining fair market value is fairly systematic and generally follows the dictates of Revenue Ruling 59-60, which lists a number of items to consider when valuing a business interest.

If the purpose of the appraisal involves legal matters, the lawyers or courts will normally provide the choice of the standard of value, although case law and precedent do not provide a great deal of consistency, even within the same jurisdiction. For example, in North Carolina, the statutes do not require a particular standard of value for divorce valuations, nor is there a North Carolina Court of Appeals case that mandates a specific standard. This condition also exists in other states.

Fair Value

Fair value is generally used in dissenting shareholder issues and in many equitable distribution cases (such as divorce). It varies from fair market value in at least two ways. First, whereas fair market value often includes a discount for lack of marketability, fair value many times does not. Likewise, whereas fair market value often includes a discount for lack of control, fair value often does not. For example, in the case of a person who owns 25 percent of a company, the fair value will often be determined to be 25 percent of the pro rata share of the company, even though the fair market value (what someone would pay for that interest) may be considerably less. The focus here is less on what a value would be in the market and more on what is "fair." But even with this standard of value, there is still a wide range of interpretations from the courts concerning whether marketability and control issues should be considered.

Incremental Business Value

Incremental business value is the change in value that results from generating revenues beyond the corresponding economic costs. Economic costs include the opportunity cost of all employed capital. In this way, incremental business value is a measurement by which economic income exceeds, or falls short of, the required minimum rate of return that both shareholders and lenders could get by investing in other securities of comparable risk.

Investment Value

As mentioned previously, investment value is a term that is closely aligned with synergistic value (and is considered to be the same by many valuation professionals), and it describes the value of a business interest to a particular investor, given a set of specific investment criteria. It differs from market value, though, in that market value is the highest value available in the market, based on likely investor profiles. Investment value relates to a single investor, based on his or her benefit stream and specific return expectation.

Owner Value

Owner value is obviously the value of a business or business interest to the current owner. Owners tend to highly value their businesses, not only because they consider all compensation and perquisites as part of the benefit stream but also because there often exists a significant nonfinancial investment in the business. It is often difficult for an owner to turn his or her back on the exhausting late-night hours and weekend work that went into making the business successful. Additionally, there are many examples of personal items, such as business contracts, covered expenses such as insurance and business trips, and possibly even relatives on the payroll. Owners tend to capitalize this liberal benefit stream by a low return expectation, since the owner may view the equity risk as less risky than the market might perceive.

Collateral Value

Collateral value measures the amount a creditor would be willing to lend given the subject's assets serving as security for the loan. This value relates to secured lending, such as a commercial or asset-based loan, or the use of assets in some financially engineered way, such as a sales-leaseback arrangement.

Book Value

Occasionally book value is used as a benchmark in a shareholder matter, as in a buy/sell agreement. Book value is an accounting concept that simply refers to the value of an asset as reflected on the financial statements. It may or may not be consistent with GAAP, and therefore, care must be taken in relying on any representation of book value. It often is net of depreciation if it is a fixed asset, and if it is in compliance with GAAP, must follow certain procedures, such as necessarily being shown at the *lower* of cost or market. Accordingly, book value is a cost-based concept and is generally not meant to represent the actual value of an asset. Book value is also sometimes used as a term to describe the assets of a firm (as reflected on the balance sheet) less total liabilities. Care must be taken before using this interpretation of book value as a valid valuation measure in assessing private companies.

WHY THE DIFFERENT VERSIONS OF VALUE?

In some ways, these different versions of value can be thought of as residing within certain *value worlds*. The range of possible values for a business interest at any *point in time* varies widely based on which world one is operating within. An interest may be worth nearly nothing in one world, while its value could be tremendous in another. Starting off in the correct world is vital to understanding the value proposition. Keeping the worlds separate involves keeping the arguments, logic, and facts consistent in that world and separate from the other value worlds. For example, the fair market value world rotates with a fairly strict set of assumptions.

Second, with no ready market pricing for their private shares, owners must rely on point-in-time appraisals for most of their valuation decisions. Once the correct value world is chosen, a replicable valuation process is available. These processes provide relatively accurate answers to difficult questions.

Finally, value worlds may collide. For example, owners are often faced with several decisions at the same time that require knowledge of the value worlds. This "war of the worlds" is important, primarily because it often happens to unsuspecting business owners. If owners are advised that their company is worth a specific dollar value, and that all of their decisions should revolve around that value, they could suffer as a result of that advice.

The intention of the involved party precedes the purpose of an appraisal. Purposes for undertaking an appraisal are referred to as giving rise to value worlds. Value, then, is expressed only in terms consistent with a particular world. Stated differently, a private business value is relative to the *purpose* and *function* of its appraisal.

VALUATION AS A RANGE CONCEPT

Each value world is likely to yield a different value indication for a business interest. Private business valuation is a range concept. A privately held company has *at least* as many correct values at any given point in time as the number of value worlds. Within each world there are multiple functions of an appraisal calling for unique valuation methods. The range of values can be quite large between worlds.

Beyond the different values determined by world, there exist nearly as large a number of possible values *within* each world. This observation is based on four factors. First, there is latitude regarding the application of a prescribed valuation process. For instance, in the world of fair market value, appraisers decide which methods are suitable among the asset, income, and market approaches. This decision-making process causes variability among appraisers. Most value worlds require judgment regarding the application of methods.

Second, once the appropriate value world is chosen, the next important valuation issue is the calculation of a suitable benefit stream. Each value world may employ a different benefit stream to value a business interest. Examples include a synergistic benefit stream versus an owner's benefit stream. The difference in benefit stream definitions in each world is an essential reason that *value variability* exists between each value world.

Third, similar to benefit streams, risk tolerance and return expectations are determined within each value world. These expectations and required rates of return allow for a benefit stream to be converted into a present value, so they are crucial to the value equation. Value variability between worlds is increased because each world employs a unique risk tolerance and return expectation.

Finally, the probability of different value drivers occurring must be considered. For example, if a company's earnings before interest, taxes, depreciation and amortization (EBITDA) is $3 million, and this number is used in the valuation, it is assumed with 100 percent probability that the company will indeed achieve a $3 million EBITDA. What if, upon further due diligence and consideration of revenues and cost variables, it seems reasonable to presume that the company has only a 50 percent chance of achieving a $3 million EBITDA? An independent analysis might further indicate the company has a 25 percent chance of generating a $2 million EBITDA, and a 25 percent chance of earning $3.5 million.

Wouldn't each of these scenarios lead to three different values, even in the same world?

Appraisers have a good deal of latitude in interpreting the correct valuation process, calculating the proper benefit stream and private return expectation, in addition to deciding on the probability of each variable occurring. These choices cause a wide range of possible expected values.

Although most private business appraisals generate a point-in-time singular value, the foregoing demonstrates private business valuation as a range concept. On a macro level, the range is defined by a host of different values that correspond to the various value worlds. Within each world, every company has a nearly infinite number of values based on the probability of the underlying valuation variables occurring.

For an appraisal to be useful, the derivation of a single value is typically necessary. The challenge, then, is to generate point-in-time appraisals within the range concept; in other words, to derive singular values within the range of possible values.

VALUE WORLDS AND DEALS

If each of the major players in the markets has a unique view of business value, and in fact generates a different value for a business, how does an M&A deal ever happen? For instance, an owner will view value in the owner value world; investors will be in the investment value world; the bank is in the collateral value world; the government is in the fair market value world, and so on. And the values in each different world can vary substantially. It is not unusual for an owner or shareholder to believe his or her business is worth two or three times what an investor thinks. So how do the parties come to a value agreement that allows a deal to happen?

The answer can usually be found in the world of market value. More specifically, the buyer and seller need to meet in this neutral value world to work out the valuation issues. In this context, the goal of the M&A advisor is to educate buyer and seller as to market valuation principles and to facilitate reaching an agreement. The process is made more difficult because no two buyers or sellers are alike.

Chapter 17 provides more detail about market value.

AN ALTERNATIVE VALUATION APPROACH

Valuation of companies continues to be part art and part science, supported by research and new methods. Transaction Valuation is an alternative approach being used by some middle market M&A advisors. An overview of this method is presented in the appendix.

CHAPTER 3

Corporate Development

As mentioned in Chapter 1, the two major players in the private capital markets are strategic buyers (*strategics*) and private equity groups (PEGs). Strategics are corporate buyers typically seeking to acquire more than just financial results. For smaller strategics that are themselves middle market companies, an acquisition may mean a merger of equals or the purchase of a larger business. For larger strategics, including S&P 500–sized public companies, an acquisition of a middle market business is likely part of a series of transactions within an overall strategic initiative. This is of particular interest given the increased level of activity in the middle market by larger strategic buyers as they seek to deploy the record amounts of capital currently stored on their balance sheets. Teams within larger strategic buyers that lead external initiatives, including acquisitions and divestitures, are generally referred to as *corporate development* teams. In the context of this handbook, the focus on corporate development is about their acquisitions.

For middle market M&A advisors, understanding the role and motivations of those in corporate development can be valuable in navigating a sell-side engagement. Conversely, corporate development professionals active in buy-side initiatives in the middle market can benefit from understanding the process and nuances of acquiring and integrating privately held businesses; there are distinct differences between buying emerging-growth and middle market companies and closing larger, publicly traded transactions as studied and written about in traditional corporate finance.

Corporate development increasingly has broad capability and responsibilities within the strategic buyer as illustrated in the following list based on recent research by Deloitte:[1]

- Corporate strategy development
- M&A strategy and target identification
- Deal pipeline management
- Managing the internal approval process

- Valuation and analytics
- Leading negotiations
- Financial due diligence
- Postmerger integration
- Divestiture preparation, target buyer identification, and reverse due diligence

Two of the most prevalent types of strategic buyers are those seeking synergies for cost cutting and economies of scale and those that are focused on growing the top line.

While the organizational aspects will likely be very different, private equity–funded platform companies seeking strategic acquisitions share many common issues and motivations of those in corporate development. This chapter will provide a high-level overview of corporate development and the buying process from the strategics' perspective, and some practical suggestions and lessons learned to increase the likelihood of a successful deal and a value-creating investment.

WHY ACQUIRE?

In an ideal scenario, an acquisition is the result of choosing the best alternative to accomplish a strategic objective or fill a gap. It can meet a number of goals if approached and executed as part of a long-term growth strategy. Some of the typical reasons executives pursue acquisitions include:

- To accelerate revenue growth
- To enter an adjacent market space
- To expand into a new geography or obtain a physical footprint in a new location (as an alternative to a "greenfield investment" or in-house start-up)
- To capture market share
- To improve speed to market
- To access new customers
- To access technology and innovation
- To overcome IP barriers
- To strengthen the pool of talent and capabilities
- To complete or augment a product or service line
- To reduce costs
- To prevent a competitor from gaining advantages (defensive move)
- To create an opportunistic buying opportunity
- To achieve step-function growth

- To obtain other critical assets, such as contracts
- To create competitive barriers to entry

These strategic reasons or motives can make sense for middle market firms buying each other or buying smaller companies. They also apply to large Fortune 500–sized companies buying emerging-growth and middle market businesses. In linking the overall objectives (and needs created by the gaps),

> ... *those who advocate a deal should explicitly show, through a few targeted M&A themes, how it advances the overall growth strategy. A specific deal should, for example, be linked to strategic goals, such as market share and the company's ability to build a leading position. Bolder, clearer goals encourage companies to be truly proactive in sourcing deals and help to establish the scale, urgency, and valuation approach.... Certain deals, particularly those focused on raising revenues or building new capabilities, require fundamentally different approaches to sourcing, valuation, due diligence, and integration. It is therefore critical for managers not only to understand what types of deals they seek for shorter-term cost synergies or longer-term top-line synergies [see Figure 3.1], but also to assess candidly which types of deals they really know how to execute and whether a particular transaction goes against a company's traditional norms or experience.[2]*

The Dismal *D*s

Now, tie in the dynamics of the real market. Potentially as important as the reason to acquire is the reason that businesses are for sale, or that the opportunity exists to acquire a certain company. In the middle market, owners are frequently receptive to selling because of the so-called Dismal *D*s. These are reactive drivers:

- Death
- Disability of the owner
- Desire to transition to the next generation
- Divorce
- Dissention
- Downturn (debt)
- Distractions (hobbies, other use for money, owner fatigue)
- Divestment (i.e., worth more to someone else; must have capital to grow and cannot get it alone; or the market has peaked)

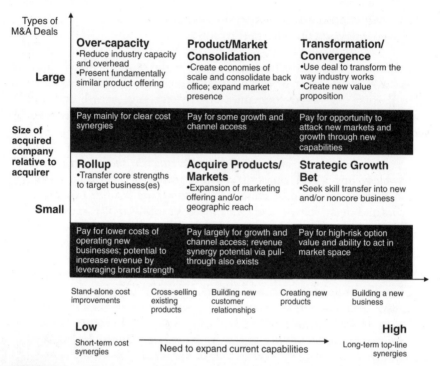

FIGURE 3.1 The Value in Different Types of Deals
Source: "Running a Winning M&A Shop," March 2008, *McKinsey Quarterly*,
www.mckinseyquarterly.com. Copyright © McKinsey & Company. All rights
reserved. Reprinted by permission.

As can be imagined, none of these Dismal *D*s means that a business for sale
is a good opportunity—it all depends. Note that downturn and divestment
can very well be market or sector driven, not just driven by the owner's
circumstances, and may fundamentally create opportunities for the aware
and astute acquirer.

Alternatives

Another dimension that needs to be considered in formulating an acquisition
strategy is assessment of the alternatives. Why not acquire? Are there better
organic options? There might be a less risky alternative that may include:[3]

- Partners, alliances, joint ventures, contracts—channels, products,
  services

- Internal R&D, contract R&D, licensing—technologies
- Outsourcing, brand labeling—products
- Internal growth—hiring, refocusing, organizational realignment, training, startup
- Investment

Coupling these perspectives and alternatives with a clear understanding of the types of deals and potential sources of value can lay the foundation for a solid acquisition strategy and plan. At the end is being able to answer the critical question: "What is the compelling strategic rationale for the deal?"[4] Being able to answer this question provides credibility for the deal. Having a solid response reduces the chance of going before the CEO or board of directors and being told "we're only interested in this deal because it is the opportunity at hand."

THE ACQUISITION PROCESS

Figure 3.2 provides a generic high-level framework from which to think about the acquisition process. The first phase typically will address finding a target company to buy; this begins with a strategic plan that should lay the foundation to determine many of the parameters and the focus of the process. The second phase of the process is to structure the deal, close the transaction, and integrate the business. The process is iterative, using lessons learned and market information to continually refine and shape the focus and plan.

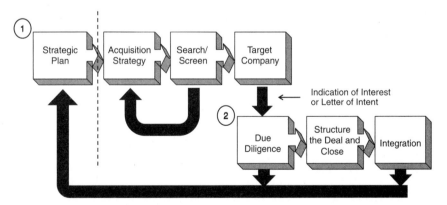

FIGURE 3.2 Acquisition Process
Source: Copyright High Rock Partners, Inc. 2011.

It is not unusual for a strategic to court a target over a period of months or years to develop a relationship with management and understand the business and its potential. However, a focused search process may identify targets within a few months. While there are always exceptions, the typical acquisition process from completion of the acquisition strategy to closing on the first target can take from six months to more than a year.

In this chapter we touch on many topics, such as valuation, structuring, and due diligence in summary. Additional detail on these topics is provided elsewhere in this handbook.

The Pipeline and Filter

Depending on the size and M&A experience of the acquiring company, there is a range of process maturities, from the very formal gated stages and approvals to the informal and possibly less disciplined progression of events—both of which might lead to consummation of a deal. Somewhere in these processes there are usually one or more filters that are defined and used to compare and test the targets against minimal criteria to meet management's objectives. Throughout the process, targets continue to get filtered in or eventually expelled as a distraction, or non-fit. While investigating and testing targets, information is gained and gleaned from the marketplace that allows the corporate development team to refine its search and plans, and focus its efforts.

The pipeline of targets is generated and maintained by a number of techniques and sources. Following are a few of the many to be considered:

- Through the strategic planning process: Potential targets will likely emerge from the market assessment and competitive analysis. Note this is not the list of "who's for sale," but rather the list of "who has what we need and how do we convince them to sell."
- Recommendations from business development and sales teams: Sales representatives are many times a valuable resource in developing a list of targets and accessing the right relationships to engage the seller. The parallel concept is to seek input from suppliers and those involved in the supply chain—particularly for strategies that involve vertical integration or expansion of capabilities tangential to the buyer's current business.
- Recommendations from customers: They may be seeking to consolidate their supply chain or "fix" a problem supplier.
- Investment bankers and M&A advisors: On a reactive and proactive basis, intermediaries can provide input and ideas to prime and fill the target pipeline—seeing businesses that are actively for sale and having insight into those that may be considering their alternatives.

- Published databases of targets seeking to be acquired.
- Professional, industry, and trade associations.

If the acquirer is a larger business with multiple divisions, one approach is to obtain both corporate and divisional buy-in to the filter criteria and acquisition process before going to market, to allow the acquisition team to focus on targets that will likely be given serious consideration as well as allow for quick response to market opportunities. A key competitive lever that private equity groups use against strategic acquirers is speed and certainty of close. Corporate development processes that build consensus and buy-in and accelerate routine approvals may make the difference between being able to seize the moment and missing the opportunity. Not to overstate the obvious, owners of emerging growth and middle market companies are usually entrepreneurial and fast acting. The acquisition process is taxing enough without adding undue drag and delay and potentially creating a deal-weary seller.

For smaller acquirers, the same concept of obtaining buy-in and early support is just as important. Have the board of directors, investors, key advisors, and other stakeholders (e.g., commercial bankers, accountants, etc.) briefed and synchronized with the objectives and plans. It is likely better to gain their feedback and address objections early so that those involved can act in unison when the time comes.

Smaller acquirers many times require outside financing to consummate a deal. Having as part of the team funding sources that have bought into the growth and acquisition strategy of the business from the outset and are ready to act quickly when the right target is found can make the difference between being considered a viable acquirer and not being taken seriously by the seller.

Approaching the Target

Approaching and engaging a target takes planning; in the case of a private company, it can take extra time and relationships to get to a receptive ear. If the target is a public company, the deal will likely be a choreographed dance involving investment bankers and corporate development leadership. The "privately owned and not for sale" target is more challenging.[5] Spend time determining how to make the approach and what the message is. Although approaching the target is a small part of the overall process, it is one of the most critical. Approaching "privately owned and for sale" targets with an M&A advisor already engaged is typically easier because the sellers have initiated the process themselves, are likely open to exploring a sale, and have a defined contact in place.

The Balance between a Deep Dive and Locking In the Deal

At some point in the process, and depending on the strength and sophistication of the seller or selling team, an indication of interest and/or letter of intent must be issued.* Conversely, and depending on the attractiveness of the target, the buyer may or may not desire to lock up the deal and gauge the seriousness of the seller. Thus the dance of the parties progresses. In this dance, the strategic will inevitably take a deep dive to understand the target and to validate the fit beyond a cursory test in the filter. This deep dive is not confirmatory due diligence of the seller, but rather a more in-depth analysis and test to see whether the acquisition may actually work and achieve the desired results. Here is an example of the steps of such a deep dive to illustrate a comprehensive screening that may lead to a firm commitment:

1. More complete understanding of the target's market
2. Fit within the existing portfolio of product lines and businesses (and an understanding of potential overlap)
3. Cultural fit between the companies
4. Strategic fit within the acquirer
5. Strengths, weaknesses, opportunities, threats (SWOT) assessment (to be validated in due diligence)
6. Identification of synergies with expected values
7. Integration strategy and expectations
8. Financial analysis and valuation

The insight developed during this deep dive should allow the corporate development team to better understand and develop a rapport with the seller and build the business case that a potential deal makes sense within the acquisition strategy, and then to circle back to the initial filter and validate the fit.

Lower-Middle Market versus Middle Market Deals

It may be helpful to keep in mind the differences between the smaller company deals and the larger middle market transactions, and the motives and factors driving each. As discussed in Chapter 1, owners' motives drive transactions. From a strategic's perspective, the likelihood of success with

---

*Assuming that a nondisclosure or confidentiality agreement has been negotiated and is in force between the parties.

lower-middle market transactions can be improved by understanding why the seller is selling (i.e., the Dismal *D*s); addressing the impact of the deal to his employees, suppliers, and customers; and being sensitive to the tax impact of the deal and structure to the seller. Couple these with certainty of close, and the potential lack of speed can be overcome. Do not discount the importance to many entrepreneurs and owners of leaving a legacy; if they think the business they started and built will essentially cease to exist, they may be much less inclined to sell.

In larger middle market deals, there will likely be a more formal M&A process with investment bankers where price and speed will rule.

Valuation from a Strategic's Perspective

Unlike a financial buyer, which is primarily driven by an internal rate of return for the capital deployed or by a minimum cash-on-cash return, the strategic buyer has a number of alternatives through which to view or financially analyze the value and potential impact of an acquisition. These options depend on the particular buyer: his acquisition strategy, his access and cost of capital, and his motivation for the deal. They often include discounted cash flow, payback period, net present value, minimal hurdle rate, market value, and (somewhat unique to the strategic buyer) an accretion/dilution analysis (particularly the public company buyer).

While the authors of this handbook may argue that some of the valuation approaches previously mentioned should not be as relevant as those academically published (and that they do not really explain what happens in the middle market in general), practical experience shows that strategic acquirers use some of these techniques and that those involved in middle market deals need to understand their application and how to bridge the difference in valuation methodologies and outcomes to be successful in negotiating and closing transactions.

Accretion/Dilution Analysis   Accretion/dilution analysis is commonly performed for strategic acquisitions or a merger of two companies with synergies, particularly where the buyer is a public company. As the name suggests, the purpose of the analysis is to determine whether the transaction is accretive (i.e., increases earnings per share—EPS) or dilutive (i.e., decreases EPS). If there is no effect on the pro forma EPS, then the transaction is earnings neutral. An important aspect of this analysis is quantifying the projected synergies between the two businesses. The analysis involves combining the pro forma financials for the merging companies and adding any synergistic gains in revenue and expenses. To quantify the synergies, the acquirer must critically analyze each segment and aspect of the target's operations. An overestimation in synergies can lead to overpaying for a company and possibly diluting shareholder value.

Other Variables   Other factors in addition to alternative valuation approaches that allow a strategic to see the value of a company differently from that of a financial buyer include:

- *Positive synergies*—a term used to describe factors that financially improve the performance of combined businesses. These generally take the form of revenue enhancement and cost savings, neither of which a financial buyer can provide outside of helping management make better decisions—the exception being "soft" synergies among portfolio companies of a financial buyer.
- *Negative synergies*—the strategic may give the target company's forecast a "haircut," discounting their sales, order input, and cash flow because they believe these are overly optimistic. Sometimes they are optimistic because of the nature of the entrepreneur and other times the buyer has more detailed information on the marketplace and therefore can generate a more accurate forecast. Additionally, some buyers may need to add cost to the target's forecast (i.e., to move the target's benefit plans into compliance with that of the buyer).
- *Longer investment horizon*—equity capital obtained by strategic buyers is typically "evergreen," meaning that there is no predefined period within which buyers must return the capital to their investors, allowing them to view an investment with a much longer time horizon. Most private equity groups (which are the main financial buyers in the middle market) must invest their money, grow it, and then return it to their limited partners within a 10-year period. From a practical view, they need to be in and then out of an investment within 3 to 7 years, depending on the lifecycle of the fund. With this said, strategics often have a defined return on invested capital hurdle within a specific time horizon (e.g., three years).
- *Cost of capital and hurdle rate*—the effective cost of capital for most large strategic investors is much lower than those of their financial competitors, so their minimum rate of return on a transaction may be lower. There is an argument that the hurdle rate applied to a particular acquisition should be based on the risk of that particular deal and not the actual cost of capital; however, in practice this is not always applied. Sometimes this apparent disconnect in cost and risk is actually accounted for, being embedded in the pro forma forecast.

Range of Values   The range of potential values that a strategic can derive for a particular target is likely broader than that of a financial buyer. Typically, the low end of the valuation range is based on the *stand-alone value* of the target. This is the value of the business based on its current capital structure, growth plans, and operating performance, and is the amount that most strategics would like to pay. At the other end of the spectrum is the value to the strategic buyer applying all of the synergies once integrated as part of the buyer. This is the amount that the seller wants to obtain. Somewhere in the middle, there may be a deal.

Structuring the Transaction

Once the acquirer determines the price of the bid for the target, it must formulate a structure that is acceptable to both parties and takes into account the risks associated with the deal. A typical transaction structure consists of some combination of cash and stock, and possibly a seller note. There are other, more creative components to a deal structure, such as earnouts and options that can be used for incentivizing the seller to accept an offer tied to future or ongoing performance. Earnouts are performance-based contingent payments awarded to owner management. Earnout structures vary greatly but often contain certain hurdles that, if met or exceeded, trigger additional considerations for the seller.

The use of an option is another way to make the purchase price contingent on the performance of the combined company, not just the seller. An option gives the owner the right to sell a security at an agreed-on strike price during a certain period of time. If the combined company is successful in its continued operations, the value of its shares would theoretically increase, making the options valuable when sold at the strike price. Conversely, if the company does not perform, the value of the option will decline and is sometimes rendered worthless. Earnouts and options are features that allow the acquirer to effectively offset some of the risk in purchasing the target. They are also attractive to the sellers due to the potential of receiving very large payouts in addition to cash at closing. Keep in mind that the value of this approach is inversely proportional to the size differential between the buyer and seller. If a $10 billion company buys a $10 million company, it is not likely the acquired company will significantly affect the future stock price of the buyer—there are always exceptions, as in the world of high-tech companies.

Many factors contribute in determining the transaction structure, including the valuation of the company, the market environment, and buyer/ seller preferences. The many different aspects of the transaction structure allow the acquirer and target several ways to bridge valuation gaps and achieve both parties' objectives.

Part III of this handbook has a number of chapters that delve into the technical details and techniques used in structuring transactions.

The Bid

Depending on the rigor, sophistication, and relative strength in the deal of the buyer versus the seller, a letter of intent (LOI) may be required earlier in the process (for a structured sale run by an investment bank in an auction) or later in the process after much due diligence (in the case of a company that is not on the market and the acquirer is the only company at the table).

In a negotiated transaction, the challenge for management is to determine a reasonable bid for purchasing the target. The predicament for the acquirer is to identify a purchase price and structure that the target will accept that will also make the investment worthwhile. This amount and the structure are included in a bid in the form of an LOI, which is extended to the board of directors and shareholders of the target company. It is not uncommon for the initial purchase price proposed in the LOI to be lower than that at which the target is willing to sell. Negotiations between the two parties either directly or through intermediaries follow and continue until the mutually agreed price and structure are determined.

In an auction process, different companies pursue different strategies in how they structure an initial bid. Some will indicate a very high price to ensure they stay in the process, and then work the price down over the course of due diligence and negotiations. Others will take more of a "down the middle" approach and convince the seller and seller's advisors they mean what they say. Bidders will usually provide a value range instead of a point estimate in an initial indication, later narrowing it to a specific number. M&A advisors will often request detailed LOIs that are effectively term sheets requesting deal terms early in the process in addition to the basic value and transaction structure. This approach provides leverage in the auction process. Bidders, on the other hand, want to provide only the minimum amount of information necessary to get them to the next stage of the process. While the end goal of completing the deal is always in mind, the practical goal of each stage is to get to the next stage.

Due Diligence

Due diligence can be thought of in two categories: traditional and strategic. Traditional due diligence tends to focus on the technical and somewhat mechanical aspects of the business to assure that a transaction can be completed, that it is priced right, and that the information provided is accurate, and to obtain information that is needed but not provided or not known. Areas of traditional due diligence include financial information, taxes, legal and regulatory compliance, environmental compliance, human resources, and contracts, among others. More information about this topic is provided in Chapter 16.

Strategic due diligence explores whether the potential of the deal is realistic by testing the rationale and seeking to answer two key questions. The first is externally focused and the second is internally focused:[6]

1. Is the deal commercially attractive?
2. Are we capable of realizing the targeted value?

Figure 3.3 illustrates an example methodology[7] to arrive at the answers to these key questions. It highlights the thought process and steps to arrive at an understanding of the market and competitive aspects of the deal, the major strategic issues to be considered, the impact to the current strategic plan, and an assessment of the reasonableness of the proposed transaction.

Due diligence is really an ongoing set of activities throughout the transaction process. In a structured sale process where the seller is a public company, the signing of the LOI allows the acquirer access to the proprietary and confidential information of the target. Prior to the signing, the acquirer has access only to information that is known to the public. A right of entry into the target's private information allows the acquirer to obtain intelligence on every detail of the company's financials, operations, contracts, intellectual property, processes, assets, and anything else deemed material to the sale. Then the acquirer will perform exhaustive due diligence on this material to enable its management to make informed decisions regarding the transaction. Sellers should also perform a due diligence analysis on the buyer to determine whether the acquirer is a good fit.

In the case of a private seller in an auction process, the seller will likely have an offering memorandum disclosing base information from which to obtain indications of interest. Then there will be some access to management through a structured interchange, eventually seeking a bid in the form of an LOI. Upon selection to be the acquirer, a deeper dive is then allowed to continue the due diligence process.

In the case of a private seller in a less structured process, a limited auction, or a negotiated sale, the deeper dive and due diligence may advance further before a bid or LOI is offered.

Regardless of the buyer or seller processes and the timing of each aspect of the due diligence analysis, comprehensive due diligence is needed both in the traditional sense and strategically to fully understand and successfully integrate a target.

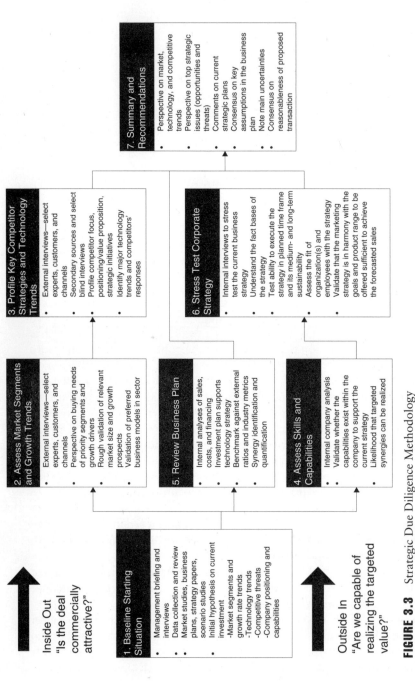

FIGURE 3.3 Strategic Due Diligence Methodology

Source: Gerald Adolph, Simon Gillies, and Joerg Krings, "Strategic Due Diligence: A Foundation for M&A Success," from www.strategy-business.com, Booz & Company, copyright 2006, and featured in *The Whole Deal: Fulfilling the Promise of Acquisitions and Mergers*, edited by Michael Sisk and Andrew Sambrook (2006, New York: strategy+business books, Booz Allen Hamilton).

Integration

Benchmarking and best practices with successful acquirers show that integration planning begins early in the acquisition process, is supported by strategic due diligence, engages many functional departments within the buyer and the seller, and most importantly is an aligning process focused on assuring progressive synchronization of the teams.

Successful integration enables companies to achieve their business case objectives for doing the acquisition. Without proper integration, the performance of the combined company will not justify the purchase price and sometimes will even destroy shareholder value. Common consequences of failed integration include loss of customers, loss of employees, slowed growth, operational difficulties, impaired brand equity, impaired reputation, and culture clash.

The process used for postmerger integration often differentiates experienced, successful acquirers from value destroyers. The key is to find the right balance between speed and thoroughness. It is important to realize the potential synergies quickly, ideally within the first 12 to 18 months. However, executives often declare victory too quickly and rush to return to business as usual, leaving synergies and planned lift (the positive impact on performance) unexploited. A disciplined and well-structured integration plan including the following steps is vital to successful acquisition strategies:

- *Communicate the vision and business logic of the deal.* Employees, customers and other pivotal stakeholders, including investors, must understand the strategic rationale, business objectives, and postmerger integration milestones and targets. Senior management should lead the implementation.
- *Separate the postmerger integration from the core business.* Postmerger integration needs its own organization, with a dedicated team of executives and faster-than-usual governance and decision-making processes. Correct allocation of resources is especially important where there are mission-critical functions.
- *Monitor core business performance.* Establish early warning systems to alert management to any falloff in revenue or profitability in the core business; minimize the distraction.
- *Proactively manage the soft issues.* Postmerger integration is not just a numbers game. The process likely involves complex organizational and cultural changes. Identify key staff and design strategies to keep them on board because they are the value of the franchise. Handle new appointments with care; take time to facilitate a transition; minimize uncertainty; show improvement in benefits, training, and working conditions (if you can); and show potential for growth.[8]

■ *Move before the close of the deal.* There are many actions that can be taken in advance (prior to the close) that enable the team to begin to realize the benefits of the transaction immediately after it is finalized. Develop and implement a very clear first-100-days plan.

■ *Challenge decisions and assess progress after completion.* During a postmerger integration, companies often make decisions on pragmatic or political grounds, resulting in inflated costs. Regularly revisit those decisions and question their contribution to the company's value-creation potential. Test those decisions against the company's strategic plan.

When integration is successful, the payoff can be striking and significant!

CASE STUDY #1

Following is an example transaction where a mid-sized publicly traded strategic buyer provided a reasonable solution for the shareholders of a lower-middle market component supplier with revenues slightly under $20 million.

The president, his spouse, and the chief engineer were the founders and sole shareholders of an S corporation providing highly engineered components into the aerospace and defense markets. All were in their late sixties or seventies and desired to monetize their hard work and investments over the prior 20 years. Their objectives were:

■ Maximize the value from the business.
■ Ensure stability for their employees.
■ Transition out of the workforce.
■ Minimize the transaction costs.

Strategic Rationale

The buyer's compelling strategic driver for the acquisition was the expansion of its technology portfolio. The target company operated in the same broad markets of aerospace and defense as the acquirer, but provided different technologies and products. It was the cornerstone of a new acquisition/consolidation strategy being implemented. The "current market/new technology" play was one the company executed well because of its industry knowledge and customer relationships that enabled it to develop accurate sales forecasts for the target companies.

Challenges

There are two challenging aspects of this example deal: accounting basis and seller's counsel. Both are reasonably typical in navigating an acquisition in the middle market.

Accounting Basis   As a public company, the buyer must be fully compliant with Generally Accepted Accounting Principles (GAAP).* The seller's books were on a modified cash basis and the balance sheets needed conversion to GAAP in order for the buyer and seller to accurately forecast future performance to the level required to have teeth in the representations and warranties of the purchase agreement; there needed to be a solid basis for measurement. It is critical that the seller represent that the financial statements are true, accurate, and complete in accordance with a set standard, that being GAAP—there are really no standards or benchmarks for a "modified cash basis" accounting. Additionally, the reference balance sheet needed to be converted to GAAP for consistency for use in calculating the working capital adjustment. The process of educating the seller's finance staff and actually making the conversion was time consuming and expensive.

Seller's Counsel   The seller resisted engaging counsel until very late in the process, even after encouragement from the buyer. When counsel was engaged, the seller chose a lawyer who had extremely limited experience in business transactions. To exacerbate the situation, the seller then restricted the time counsel could spend on the deal in an effort to control costs. As a result, due diligence and negotiation took at least a month longer than would have been considered normal. During that time, the Department of Defense announced the cancelation of a major program that was a key component of the seller's future sales. This constituted a material adverse change, and the buyer had no choice but to reduce the purchase price from $18.5 million to $17.5 million. Given the deal structure and terms, the seller would have benefited by having stronger and more engaged counsel if the deal had progressed in a timely fashion and not been delayed. In this case, attempting to save a few thousand dollars in attorney's fees cost the seller $1 million in purchase price. With that said, having a seller with inexperienced counsel can cause many other complications, including significant wasted time and resources on the part of the buyer as well as an increased risk of not closing at all.

---

*Conceptually, there is one GAAP standard; however, in practice, GAAP for private companies does not always align with GAAP for SEC or exchange regulations.

Transaction

- The buyer purchased 100 percent of the stock for $17.5 million in cash.
- A 338(h)(10) election was made.
- Fifteen percent of the purchase price was placed in escrow with a staggered release: 33 percent after 12 months and the balance after 18 months.
- There was a standard working capital adjustment.
- There was no earnout.
- There were no financing contingencies; the buyer used cash from its standing credit facility.
- The facility lease was negotiated with the purchase agreement (facility was owned by the president through an affiliated company).
- Three-month consulting agreements were negotiated with the president, the chief engineer, and the CFO, who was also retiring.

Lessons Learned

Had the buyer and the seller shared their objectives with each other early in the process, much of the frustration, delays, and painful suboptimizing of outcomes could have been avoided. A savvy buyer or M&A advisor could help educate a naive seller by suggesting the help of someone in the seller's network that has shared similar one-time liquidity events.

It would have been helpful to better educate the sellers on the overall acquisition process and the need for accurate, GAAP-compliant financial statements, early on. The sellers did not fully appreciate that they would have to make representations as to the validity and accuracy of the financial statements, and did not understand the buyer's insistence that the statements be held to a defined standard. They took a "buyer beware" attitude throughout the process. The end result was achieved, but it was more painful than it should have been.

CASE STUDY #2

Consolidated Communications (CNSL) acquires North Pittsburgh Systems, Inc. for $375.1 million.[9] Figure 3.4 provides an overview of the rationale for the deal.

- Announcement date: July 1, 2007
- Closing date: December 31, 2007 (183 days later)

Illinois and Texas market
1,100 employees
232,000 access lines
64,000 broadband connections
IPTV technology
Telemarketing services
Business services

Pennsylvania market
357 employees
63,000 access lines
Superior broadband technologies
Video service
Local brand name equity

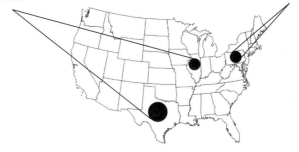

FIGURE 3.4 Acquisition Rationale
Source: Consolidated Communication, July 7, 2007; Form 8-K SEC filing.

Consolidated Communications provides communications services to residential and business customers in Illinois and Texas. It offers a range of telecommunications services, including local and long-distance service, custom calling features, private line services, dialup and high-speed Internet access, digital television, carrier access services, network capacity services over its regional fiber optic network, and directory publishing.

North Pittsburgh Systems, Inc. provides local network services, including local dial-tone service, custom calling features, and local private line services to residential and business customers; and network access services, which comprise access to its switched access facilities for the completion of interstate and intrastate long-distance toll calls and extended-area service calls, as well as access to private line network facilities for use in transporting voice and data services to interexchange carriers, cellular mobile radio service providers, and other local exchange carriers.

Following is a summary of the expected synergies of the deal:

Consolidation

- One functional organization across three markets; increase portfolio.
- Combines to have 293,400 ILEC access lines, 66,300 CLEC access line equivalents, 72,200 DSL subscribers and 1,400 employees.

- After completion of this transaction, Consolidated will be the twelfth-largest telephone company in the United States.
- The combined company obtained Verizon wireless partnership.

Provides an Advanced Network

- Ninety-nine percent DSL-capable today, at speeds up to 10 megabits per second
- Enables launch of IPTV

Leverages Scale

- Software licenses
- Maintenance contracts
- Purchasing contracts

Reduces Third-Party Costs

- Legal fees
- Audit and Sarbanes-Oxley fees
- Outsourced billing and financial system costs
- Public company fees

Figure 3.5 outlines the financial metrics of the transaction, with the results shown in Figure 3.6 charting the positive impact to shareholder value.

Transaction Values			
Total Consideration to Shareholders ($ mm)	375.13	Total Transaction Size ($ mm)	395.38
Implied Equity Value ($ mm)	375.13	Implied Enterprise Value ($ mm)	347.97
Implied Equity Value/LTM Net Income	25.0×	Implied Enterprise Value/Revenues	3.5×
Implied Equity Value/Book Value	3.8×	Implied Enterprise Value/EBITDA	7.6×
Exchange Rate	1.000	Offer per Share ($)	25.00
Consideration to Shareholders ($ mm)	375.13	Total Cash ($ mm)	300.10
Premium (1 week prior)	21.1%	Total Stock ($ mm)	75.03

FIGURE 3.5 Transaction Summary
Data source: Copyright © Capital IQ, Inc., a Standard & Poor's business. Standard & Poor's, including its subsidiary corporations, is a division of The McGraw-Hill Companies, Inc. Reproduction of this chart in any form is prohibited without Capital IQ, Inc.'s prior written consent.

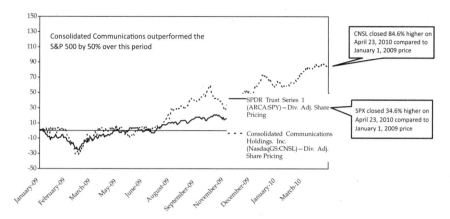

FIGURE 3.6 CNSL Relative Stock Performance One Year After Acquisition

PRACTICAL TIPS AND WHAT CAUSES DEALS TO FAIL

"M&A is a careful blend of art and science,"[10] and as much as advisors rely on spreadsheets, analysis, and process, there is no substitution for understanding the subtleties, the nuances, the relationships, the timing, and the momentum of each deal and applying the instincts that come from experience and street smarts. This section of the chapter ignores the ideal and focuses on the practicalities. To that end, following is a compilation of nuggets of wisdom captured from experienced advisors and practitioners, particularly as relates to corporate development and making strategic deals work.

What Should We Acquire?

Practically speaking, many strategic deals arise out of general knowledge of competitors, suppliers, and marketers within an industry. Key executives have met at trade shows, competed, socialized, and talked and dined together. Eventually, familiarity has a way of justifying action without rationalization. Discussions about a possible business combination begin at some point with each side having done little due diligence on the other. It can feel good and gain momentum, and in the end could be a good strategic play, but it could also be the wrong path. What should happen is a rigorous assessment of the strategies of each business as well as the alternatives to fulfill those strategies, and testing to determine whether the deal at hand is a real opportunity or a distraction for the parties. These steps should either reinforce or dampen the rationale for making an acquisition or merging the companies.

Why Are We Doing This?

A valuable exercise for the corporate development team and the sponsoring business unit to perform follows. If the buying company is a smaller strategic, try to include the board of directors. Have each team member document one major reason why this proposed acquisition or deal is good and should proceed. Collect the responses and post them, say on a virtual blackboard. Review these answers every Monday, and never on Friday. People are usually rested and visceral energy is the highest early in the week. Watch how many reasons or benefits disappear over time as the weeks pass. This simple exercise has the effect of tempering an overenthusiastic team and keeping the team in check as the deal progresses.

As an example, a major regional retailer of household goods selling big-ticket items was considering buying a smaller chain with the identical product lines. The excitement was amazing early in the process, as adding 18 locations to the company's footprint looked impressive and the numbers would be accretive. There was a long list of reasons to do the deal posted on the blackboard. As due diligence unfolded, however, it was determined that 5 of the 18 stores would need to be closed due to lack of business. The target stores were one-third the size of the acquirer's stores, and the number of offered SKUs was half. In addition, the selling model was geared to offering choice, where the target's offering was limited. Lastly, it turned out that there was a major cultural difference in floor selling techniques. As imagined, the list became shorter and it became self-evident that this was the wrong deal.

Alignment of Interests

Are you able to get into the heads of the target's stakeholders? When meeting with the sellers, it is important to know their thought process. The entrepreneurial business owners (who are quite possibly the founders) are quick to act in many business decisions and are comfortable with risk. You can bet they understand the risk factors in their industry. They are comfortable with a contract-driven business, which can have its ups and down. They need not explain that to anybody. They may have significant customer concentration, and are able to rationalize the security of that position. A successful target business is probably self-funded and does not answer to banks. Finally, many business owners think income is more important than growth, and will curtail the capital expenditures necessary for growth. That's for the next guy to worry about. The challenge is to address these traits and issues so that you can begin to take measures to get the target company to align with your goals. They are certainly going to be different and uncomfortable in the beginning for the exiting owner.

Allocate Enough Resources

Most operating personnel already have full-time responsibilities and commitments before they are asked to be part of an acquisition process. And the best people to be part of a due diligence team are likely those who do not have the time. Find a way to put them on the team rather than opting for those with free time.[11] Ensure that adequate funds are budgeted to cover the external costs of advisors and temporary support staff, allowing the right people in the company to participate when required.

If It Can Go Wrong, It Will Go Wrong

The acquisition process is complex, difficult, risky, and costly. There are always many moving parts that need to be managed at the same time. It takes focus and an interdisciplinary approach. Many skill sets are required, some of which are within the acquiring company and some external. These include business unit experts from sales, marketing, operations, and technology supported by functional and corporate staff: finance, risk, legal, human resources, and so forth. Couple the internal team with external legal, accounting, investment banking, and environmental experts and the team begins to take shape. It is essential to maintain collaboration and confidentiality across the entire team to minimize the obvious issues and allow for focus on the details and relationships required to do the deal right and get it closed.[12]

CHAPTER 4

A Global Perspective*

The globalizing economy has fueled middle market mergers and acquisitions (M&A) in the United States and abroad (see Figure 1.4 in Chapter 1). Companies are looking for new growth and survival markets as well as technology and innovation, and conducting business without borders increases the number of potential customers exponentially. Some companies, faced with continued pressure to grow profits and the added benefit of cash on the balance sheet, see these deals as virtually mandatory. However, these cross-border opportunities are substantially more complex than domestic acquisitions and require a different set of skills and a panoramic lens with which to view the transaction and its components.

Conducting strategic due diligence across borders, managing cultural differences, integrating across borders, and establishing a clear organizational structure and lines of responsibility are difficult yet critical to the success of cross-border deals. Difficult or not, it is clear that global M&A is here to stay and it is a reality business owners, corporate development teams, and dealmakers must adapt to. It is a new frame of mind, almost a new discipline, and is no longer just an option to ponder—it is the new reality. Businesses are being acquired by foreign investors, and that brings global competition to your doorstep. To some degree, it's buy or be bought. Engage or be engaged. Business leaders can't ignore opportunities abroad any more than foreign investors can ignore the opportunities in your country. But, the long-term success of M&A depends on strong leadership, a forward-thinking mind-set, thorough due-diligence, cultural awareness, and a well-planned postmerger integration process. Each step is critical to getting it right the first time. When it is done right, the advantages are numerous.

---

*Parts of this chapter are taken from *Grow Globally: Opportunities for Your Middle-Market Company Around the World* by Mona Pearl (Wiley, 2011). Reprinted with permission of John Wiley & Sons, Inc.

ADVANTAGES OF GLOBAL M&A

Companies choose M&A for a variety of strategic reasons: to obtain new technology, new brands, complementary products, and access to experienced management/workforce; to exert control over the supply chain; to gain economies of scale; to improve distribution channels; or to remove a competitor. Plus, it's a relatively safe and economical strategy when compared to other expansion options. Another significant advantage is the built-in customer base that flows naturally with the purchase of a popular brand. For some domestic businesses, M&A abroad may represent the only tangible option for growing market share in a slumped domestic economy.

Over the past decade, global M&A activity has increased substantially as this business model is a natural progression for businesses gaining experience and confidence abroad. The current global crisis is further fueling cross-border M&A with sellers generally more distressed and, therefore, more inclined to work with foreign buyers. Also, there is less competition from buyers in the seller's home country even with prices falling to attractive levels.

When contrasted to building a business abroad from scratch, consider these important benefits of expanding through M&A, assuming you conducted the due diligence on your target and have your strategy and vision aligned:

- An existing, successful business is already functioning and properly set up and may require only minor changes to meet expansion goals.
- The workforce of the business is already in place and organized. The buyer now needs to develop a relationship with the workforce and discover what motivates them.
- Marketing initiatives and contacts are already established.
- The customer base and revenue stream are established.
- An existing company can more easily access capital than a new market entrant.

The big picture issues are usually known ahead of time and can be analyzed by advisors. What usually kill deals or cause failure are the soft issues—the ones that are under the surface, that need a different perspective, and that require a high level of emotional intelligence coupled with cultural fluency and a strategic approach.

CHALLENGES TO GLOBAL M&A

Pursuing expansion and growth in the global market through M&A requires an entirely new perspective and understanding of due diligence and risk assessment that is very different than being risk averse, and that's proving to be a significant obstacle for many businesses. Acquiring or merging with a foreign company requires due diligence that extends way beyond financial numbers and reaching agreeable terms. Rather, the critical (and often overlooked) aspects of any due diligence process should be strategic and cultural in nature. These issues are more likely to cause real problems than numbers alone. Long-term success of an M&A deal is equally dependent on dealing effectively with differences in corporate cultures, maintaining employee, stakeholder, and customer loyalty in a foreign company, and gaining a workable understanding of that company's human and business values. Due diligence is much more than making sure the numbers work.

Unfortunately, the majority of due diligence, fact-finding, and investigative resources are focused solely on the fundamental hard challenges, such as infrastructure; earnings before interest, taxes, depreciation, and amortization (EBITDA); and return on investments (ROI). However, over 80 percent of the real risks associated with international M&A are derived from soft challenges. Soft challenges originate from cultural differences, corporate transparency, and systems of doing business in a new country such as legal, labor, accounting, and cultural integration issues. Understanding the corporate global growth strategy and culture, along with the culture of the country or region plays a crucial role in securing the long-term success of any M&A deal. While profits, EBITDA, and ROI are important matters, these considerations represent just the visible tip of the iceberg. Underneath the water, and hidden from view, lurk the real dangers that must be exposed through extensive research and due diligence.

Some of the issues that may appear on the surface to be of a legal nature have cultural solutions and can be resolved through relationships and by knowing how to get things done:

- Highly regulated government approval processes for noncitizens and/or nonresidents to purchase businesses and/or real estate (e.g., in India)
- Prohibited/restricted foreign ownership of certain industries (e.g., defense, energy, infrastructure, and banking industries in China)
- Industries competing with government or contrary to regional law (e.g., Sharia law prohibits gambling and certain foods)
- Industry permits and factory licenses
- Land use/zoning permits
- Corporate organizational laws
- Difficulties with entity formation
- Required corporate governance—extensive and personal liability
- Informal and cultural barriers
- Perception of contracts (e.g., U.S. freedom of contract and "a deal is a deal" mentality versus evolving relationships of the parties)

- Use of agents/distributors/representatives (definitions of terms differ in many countries by law and contract terms, financial terms, cultural and business understanding)
- Employee loyalty, ethics, and performance, which may be based on relationships and cultural norms*
- Liability for layoffs without just cause
- Liability to pay redundant employees
- Rights by law (e.g., worker's councils)
- Noncompete clauses that may not be enforceable

Years ago, Michael Porter argued that most cross-border ventures were bound to fail mainly due to cultural issues. To emphasize the cultural effect, Professor Geert Hofstede says that culture is more often a source of conflict than of synergy. Cultural differences are a nuisance at best and often a disaster. Integrating after an acquisition is difficult, and often results in failure. This is especially true since it involves emotional and personal factors that are embedded in one's cultural background and beliefs. The facts of the matter are that:

- Two years after an acquisition, the vast majority of acquisitions fail to meet pre-acquisition objectives.
- Three years after an acquisition, a mere 12 percent of companies grow more quickly than they did before.

Unsurprisingly, it has become a widely accepted belief that the rate of success in the postmerger phase remains poor because of the difficulties of culturally integrating the two companies involved. Constrained by the limited time in which it has to obtain results and by lack of planning, the acquiring company seeks to imprint its own culture on the acquired company. It seems as if the challenging issues come as a surprise, rather than being addressed during the due diligence stage.

Too often, the real difficulties and challenges of M&A surface months after deals are signed. Then, the soft questions but tough issues that should have been addressed in the front-end due diligence process start flowing. For example:

- How will this newly acquired enterprise be integrated into the existing company?
- Will it operate independently or as a department?

---

*For example, bribery and situations involving the Foreign Corrupt Practices Act that can present ethical and legal issues or issues involving gender discrimination in certain countries. The definition of performance is not universal, and in some countries, having people show up for work on time cannot be taken for granted.

- How will the integration be made smooth and seamless?
- How will the acquiring company deal with duplicate departments, systems, vendors?
- How will the new business be operated on day 1?
- Will this organization structure produce loyalty in the company, among the employees as well as among the vendors and suppliers?
- Will the employees and managers stay?
- What will the local reaction be to any proposed changes?
- What is the new competitive landscape?

The answers to these questions, and many others, come from gathering the *right* information from the *right* sources. It's easy to get misdirected or overwhelmed by the staggering quantity of available information. Stay focused on research that includes assessment of consumer demand, consumer profiles, competition, pricing, packaging, foreign regulations, shipping, and distribution (among other things). In addition, companies need to look internally at their strengths and weaknesses in relation to their action plan. That means evaluating corporate resources, human assets, internal knowledge base, and the company's own culture (perception, loyalty, motivation) in the context of the new reality and new international structure before determining whether expansion opportunities are viable and warrant penetration into new markets.

NEGOTIATIONS AND THE IMPORTANCE OF CULTURAL TUNE-IN

After months of preparation to enter the global marketplace—including extensive market analysis, identification of a target market, numerous product modifications, and the development of an elaborate market entry strategy—it's finally time to seal the deal! But not so fast. Sealing that deal successfully will require tremendous finesse in terms of international negotiation skills.

The fact is that cross-cultural negotiations can make or break even the most carefully executed global expansion efforts. Not to mention, for example, that both Asian and European countries have, as a matter of survival, developed expertise in negotiating in an international marketplace and are light-years ahead of the United States in this proficiency.

Beware: The skills required to negotiate successfully in your own country do not necessarily translate to success abroad. In fact, past strengths can be future weaknesses on the international stage. The key is to identify which skills cross over, which skills require retooling, and which skills are simply missing from the toolbox. Most importantly, businesspeople should never assume that knowledge and understanding of the business operations and finance of the target company, no matter how in-depth, will compensate for lack of cultural understanding in the negotiating process. It won't. Cultural awareness is no longer a nice skill to have; it's essential for success overseas.

For example, negotiation, as it is understood in the United States, is the process by which interested parties resolve disputes, agree on courses of action, bargain for an individual or collective advantage, and attempt to create a win-win outcome. Internationally, however, negotiating has much more to do with understanding people and their customs and developing relationships. Unfortunately, many U.S. executives are unfamiliar with this dance and mistakenly launch directly into the technical phase of negotiations. Such short-circuiting of the negotiating process will lead to frustration, disappointment, squandered resources, and lost opportunities.

STRATEGIC DUE DILIGENCE

Some of the fundamental importance of cross-border strategic due diligence lies in the following statements:

- Even the best financial and legal due diligence practices *do not uncover the whole story* for any given prospect, and certainly do not guarantee success.
- Neglecting cultural due diligence can have consequences no less disastrous than neglecting legal due diligence.
- Strategic due diligence is increasingly being demanded by boards of directors.

While all mergers and acquisitions require bridging the differences between different corporate cultures, this task becomes even more daunting when you add in the effects of national cultural differences, distance, and language barriers. In many cross-border M&A deals, the effort involved in cultural integration proves more difficult and just takes longer than expected, not to mention that the rate of failure is pretty high. Part of the problem stems from the difference in mind-set and the interpretation of business transactions and conduct, and also from local transparency practices. In the United States, people are used to very clear guidelines for the law and the ability to enforce judgments and actions. In quite a few countries, such as in the Middle East or in Latin America, there are elite groups to which the laws may not apply in regard to their actions and that expect to get a free hand in almost everything that is done.

As an example, Fellowes, Inc., based in Itasca, Illinois, confirmed in 2010 that its Chinese joint venture partner, Jiangsu Shinri Machinery Co.,

Ltd., had blocked all shipments at Fellowes's manufacturing facility in Changzhou, China.[1] Fellowes had had a successful 12-year association with its Chinese joint venture (JV) partner. The relationship evolved in late 2006 from a third-party relationship to a cooperative joint venture. At that point, Fellowes gained 100 percent control of the operation and the Chinese partner ceased to be involved in the operations. The terms entitled the Chinese partner to an annual return on its investment. Fellowes had met this obligation each year.

The shipment stoppage was unilaterally imposed in August 2010 by the Chinese partner to force Fellowes to radically change the key provisions of the contract and board resolutions with the effect of shifting power, control, and financial gain to the Chinese partner. In spite of Fellowes's efforts to negotiate a settlement with the assistance of the government, the demands from the JV partner have continued to grow with no willingness to compromise or find common ground.

Problems began in late 2009 when a dispute broke out between the two brothers of the Chinese partner company, Shinri. The dispute resulted in Fellowes's longstanding partner leaving the business and his older brother taking over. Tensions mounted over the ensuing months, but the stoppage of shipments came as a surprise to Fellowes as the shutdown dramatically undermined the Chinese partner's economic opportunity.

Fellowes continued to work with Chinese government and party officials with the help of the U.S. government. The Chinese government has assisted Fellowes in this dispute but so far has been unable to lift the blockage. In the meantime, Fellowes is diligently working to create alternative products and new supply chains to bring its affected machines back into the market.

Other problems arise from a lack of understanding of the basic rules that govern how business is conducted in different cultures. For example, when working with Japanese colleagues, failing to understand the importance of maintaining the appearance of harmony and agreement (even when neither actually exists) risks creating serious discomfort among coworkers or causing offense at meetings with behavior that would be viewed as perfectly acceptable in a Western context.[2] In the Middle East, *sharia*, or Islamic law, influences the legal code in most Muslim countries. A movement to allow sharia to govern personal status law, a set of regulations that pertain to marriage, divorce, inheritance, and custody, is even expanding into the West.

Language is the mirror to the nation's culture as well as the corporate culture and is another barrier to the successful completion of a cross-border deal. With a few exceptions, it is seldom practical for an acquirer to impose its language on the acquired company. In many cases, enforcing the acquirer's language stirs up resentment that makes cooperation even more difficult. This is especially true when the two countries represented in the deal have a long and troubled history—such a language imposition winds up opening old wounds.[3]

Also challenging is developing a team spirit post-M&A, and physical distance only complicates this important process. Without regular opportunities to meet face-to-face, misunderstandings can easily arise. This can lead one group to conclude that their remote colleagues are incompetent or, worse, not acting in line with the organization's overall strategy. Add in language differences and culturally driven behavior, perceptions, interpretation, and expectations, and the risk of misunderstandings increases, making successful cross-border cooperation even more difficult.[4]

A final area of concern is the reaction of national governments and consumers who face losing control over critical strategic assets or iconic brands. For example, when a foreign company was rumored to be considering the acquisition of Danone, the giant French company known for its yogurt, Prime Minister Dominique de Villepin declared that the government would come to "the defense of Danone's interests and the French future of Danone." The flap led to passage of a "strategic sectors" bill, dubbed "The Danone Law." A similar outcry in the United States greeted Belgian brewing giant InBev's proposed acquisition of Anheuser-Busch, makers of revered American beer Budweiser. However, that deal was finalized.[5]

Rigorous due diligence conducted by a team of people who possess a deep knowledge of the local language, customs, and legal requirements is essential. During the due diligence stage, close attention is needed to ensure that the potential value of the target is being fully captured. In particular, the transfer of rights (including intellectual property) and assets, as well as access to favorable supplier contracts, must be carefully considered in the context of the culture and the way business is conducted in that country.[6] A contract may outline certain terms, but there are other issues—unwritten rules and agreements—that can be found only when talking to local people and only after establishing a trusted working relationship. Again, anyone can see the tip of the iceberg, but it takes a trained eye to see the real danger hidden under the water.

Too often, U.S. businesses are hastily lured into specific global markets by competitors before extensive due diligence is complete. Many simply hunger for market share and quick profits and fail to do their homework. As such, they neglect to ask the right questions, do their research, gather data, and analyze that data carefully in order to establish a detailed strategy and comprehensive plan for international expansion. Erroneously, some businesses just assume they have to expand and fail to consider the long-term versus short-term implications of globalization. Consequently, over half of U.S. global ventures end in failure and valuable resources are squandered.

International due diligence requires a company to go beyond traditional M&A work and consider variables that are unfamiliar to most companies and to most businesspeople who lack cross-border experience. Because you don't know what you don't know, unintentional mistakes are made and rarely corrected in time. Avoid this by identifying the right team of experienced people—people who can obtain and interpret actionable data concerning the political, national, corporate, and human culture of the targeted company as it relates to the ongoing business operation. Ignoring or misunderstanding these issues will jeopardize a company's M&A initiative.

In emerging markets, increasing wages and social benefit obligations may not be deal breakers, but it is critical that these and other human capital costs be included and played under several scenarios for a number of years if a buyer is to get a more realistic picture of a target company's value and of future integration issues. The lack of transparency combined with the greater overlap between political, regulatory, and economic policies in emerging markets adds to the nature of unpredictability, and therefore requires more due diligence, data points, and sensitivity to cultural nuances.

The more a country falls into the category of emerging market, the more likely it is that political red tape will slow the pace of progress, and that labor laws will vary from one jurisdiction to another.

Other issues may include the limit on the number of foreign nationals who can be brought in to assume key responsibilities and the issue of local employee loyalty and how to maintain it. U.S. firms face the Sarbanes–Oxley issue, since most companies in the emerging markets are not obliged to comply with that regulation.

All of this means that from the very first stages of negotiation, and certainly before a letter of intent has been entered into, the parties in a cross-border transaction must think carefully about their legal assumptions and question whether they apply before coming to the negotiating table. Legal counsel can certainly assist in this endeavor, but it is up to the business people to raise the issues in a timely manner and ensure that their vision is satisfied. Such successful negotiations occur only when both sides understand and trust each other and are willing and able to engage in a process of meaningful information exchange. Although it may sound simple, it isn't.

POSTMERGER INTEGRATION: ARE THE ODDS IN YOUR FAVOR?

Most international acquisitions or mergers fail after closing, during integration. Initial price negotiations, while certainly important, are rarely, if ever, the primary reason for failure. Most often it is the *cultural* evaluation of a target company that creates problems. Will its employees remain loyal? What motivates them? How about the customers? How will these issues affect operations and the business's chances of future success?

A well-planned post-M&A integration enables:

- Companies to achieve business objectives
- The business to grow more rapidly

Failure at this stage causes:

- Lost customers
- Lost employees
- Lost focus on the core business
- Damaged image in the marketplace
- Reluctance to undertake future M&A deals

Companies can prevent late-stage integration issues from derailing an otherwise-sound international expansion initiative by following these additional guidelines:

- *Practice cultural due diligence.* Determine how the target company operates in a broader, human-capital sense. How will customers and employees view a foreign company moving onto their turf? What's the work ethic of its employees? How is productivity viewed, measured, and maintained? What's the management style of its executives? Who are the company's main competitors? How stable is the political environment? Are there any conflicts with the U.S. Foreign Corrupt Practices Act?
- *Make a strong commitment.* Peter Drucker once said, "Unless commitment is made, there are only promises and hopes ... but no plans." Management has to be on board 100 percent—on both sides! Developing an international market requires enormous energy, knowledge, managerial buy-in, and an understanding of business practices in other countries. Few, if any, companies have the resources to go it alone. They'll need a non-U.S. view of the world and the assistance of people experienced in global business transactions.
- *Be humble.* The brash, pushy approach of the rugged American businessperson doesn't cut it in the global arena. Successful international business leaders possess a quiet, respectful humility combined with a passion for learning, understanding, and practicing how people in other cultures live, work, and like to be rewarded. Customers in different countries have unique ways of relating to products and services. Their

lifestyles vary greatly, along with their values, priorities, and buying habits. Savvy international businesspeople blend in and adapt to the cultural norms of whatever market they're serving. In this respect, cross-cultural or intercultural diversity as a corporate principle is an absolute requirement for business survival and long-term profitability.

- *Educate your team on cross-cultural communication.* Research shows that communication between culturally different organizations is often plagued by prejudice and stereotyping on the part of the acquiring company's managers. Poor or insensitive communication between managers and the target company's employees can absolutely derail an international venture's chance for success. With proper cross-cultural training, these problems can be minimized or prevented altogether.

- *Ask for help.* Seek guidance from an experienced, hands-on international business expert—someone who thoroughly understands how to do business internationally and in that specific region. Such a professional is sensitive to the national and corporate cultures of both the client and target countries and will be able to guide you and put some of the essential policies in place. For example, what does it mean when foreign business executives become quiet at a key meeting? Are they in agreement or disagreement? Are they insulted? Are they trying to hide their laughter from you? How does the country's ethical system differ from that of the United States? Is corruption rampant? Will the U.S. entity be competing with businesses owned by relatives of the country's president? (If so, good luck!) While there are no guarantees in any business venture, the right international business expert can make a dramatic difference in and increase the chances for ultimate success.

Since almost 40 percent of corporate revenues are spent on people (salaries, benefits, hiring costs, etc.), due diligence must focus on all issues related to human capital in every phase of the M&A process—and the earlier the better. In Japan, for example, a deal that fails to demonstrate tangible benefits for target company employees, and not just the acquirer's shareholders, may not get off the ground. In China, wage inflation is becoming a serious problem for owners, and India is fast running short of technically trained people.

FROM THE START: THINK INTEGRATION

Sixty-five percent of cross-border mergers and acquisitions fail. Some deals never emerge from the initial phase of negotiations and due diligence while others fall apart in the latter stage when the acquisition is being integrated into the mission, vision, and values of the acquiring organization. For these latter failures, the cause is a lack of foresight. Too often, dealmakers are so consumed by making the numbers work that they fail to establish a front-end strategic integration plan that details how the business will operate post-M&A. Instead, consider integration at the outset of any talks. It's never too early to start thinking about integration and what issues it may trigger. Companies making their first international acquisition must realize that integrating a foreign business into an organization that has been optimized for operation in a single country will require additional resources. For example, the volume of work required to accommodate multiple currencies, reporting requirements, and local employment laws is often underestimated, leaving the acquirer poorly prepared to operate as an integrated whole.

A word of caution here: Do not rely on the CPA, the attorney, or the investment banker to perform the strategic integration plan. First, this team of dealmakers already received its payment in full (whether a lucrative commission or a hefty fee) when the transaction was officially completed and no longer has a vested interest in the success of the transaction. Second, the essential questions are strategic in nature and require the foresight of a global business expert—someone who can ask the right questions, gather the requisite data, and evaluate the information in a cross-border context.

Another reason why integration issues must be addressed early is that businesses operate very differently in other countries. For example, a business in Malaysia cannot be run the same way a business is run in the United States. In addition to cultural differences, there are environmental, political, and legal differences that need to be understood and factored into an overall assessment and the evaluation of the viability of the venture. In some countries, for example, the government has tremendous influence on how, when, where, and whether business can be conducted. The government might also reserve the right to retroactively institute changes that could result in land, buildings, or certifications being revoked. Without cause, some governments can simply eject a company from the country with no explanation. In one recent example, a mining company with operations in Africa was conducting business as usual on Monday. By Wednesday, it was shut down and management was told to leave the country. Their mining certificate was revoked and they were provided no explanation.

ACQUISITIONS THAT BUILD VALUE

The vast majority of acquisitions fail to meet the pre-acquisition objectives two years afterward. Even three years following an acquisition, only a mere 12 percent of companies report that overall growth has surpassed the pre-acquisition period. In other words, 88 percent of acquisitions are still trying to figure out what went wrong three years after the deal is complete. This failure to succeed, at least immediately, is often the result of limited time spent addressing and planning important aspects of the cultural integration of the two unique businesses. Rather, the acquiring company seeks to imprint its own culture on the acquired company and appears surprised by the issues that result—issues that should have been discovered and planned for during the due diligence phase.

But it doesn't have to be that way. Savvy businesspeople can improve the likelihood of success with a more relevant distribution of due diligence and an emphasis on post-deal integration. If 80 percent of the risk comes from the soft issues, that's where the focus of efforts should be directed. By extending the principles of traditional due diligence, businesses can make more informed decisions. Remember, even when the numbers look good, the deal can become a disastrous failure if the soft issues are not properly addressed. Learn about the culture of doing business; learn about the legal system and how it may affect your new venture; and learn about the political environment and any implications for daily business.

Although the art of cross-border postmerger integration is still evolving, there are three best practices that can be distilled from observing the most successful deal practitioners.

1. Set Clear Expectations and Invest in High-Quality, Two-Way Communication

Clear communication is the basis for post-acquisition cooperation between the two companies' management teams. When cross-border deals go wrong, lack of clarity about goals and objectives, compounded by poor and deteriorating communications, is frequently the cause. In addition, careful attention is needed to ensure that remote companies fully understand the overall corporate direction and have an opportunity to customize the strategy to local requirements.

For best results, companies should bring together management teams across borders on a regular basis, whether through face-to-face meetings, management rotation, or other methods. For example, critical factors in the successful integration of Abbey National into Banco Santander included a three-year plan with ambitious objectives, strong internal communications, and the assignment of key Santander managers to work with Abbey on a day-to-day basis.

Some best practices in this area include:

- Early integration of key leadership of the acquired company into the appropriate information and decision-making forums. This gives leaders access to the larger corporate context and ensures that local decision making is aligned with overall corporate direction.

- Selective use of headquarters management to support the leadership of acquired companies, rather than second-guessing or overruling them. These assignments should be treated as both sensitive and critically important for realizing the value of the acquisition and not as an opportunity to offload managers for whom no other obvious role is available.
- Headquarters' attention focused on critical decisions that will drive value in the acquisition, rather than micromanaging local activities or imposing rules and procedures that may not be appropriate.
- Investment in high-quality, two-way communications between the parent and the acquired company. This provides transparent visibility of performance, early warning of potential problems or changes in direction, and clear roles and responsibilities on both sides for maintaining these links.

2. Acknowledge Cultural Differences but Simultaneously Create a Common Corporate Culture with a Single Goal: Achieving High Performance

The rules of etiquette tell us that it is rude to refer to national stereotypes, profiling, and so on, or to base expectations of behavior or performance on cultural background. There are systematic differences in both values and behavior between countries that will color interactions between individuals of different backgrounds. Understanding these can be extremely useful in avoiding misunderstandings. Here are some examples:

- Germans dislike uncertainty.
- French are inclined to be skeptical and self-critical.
- Japanese place a high importance on correct form and ceremony.
- Swedes prefer decision making based on consensus.
- British have a high tolerance for ambiguity and use humor in ways that foreigners often find puzzling.
- Americans are less formal than Europeans.

One advantage of openly acknowledging cultural differences is that it sets the stage for a broader examination of the larger postmerger company culture, and creates an opportunity for the two entities to work toward a single shared culture that is more supportive of high performance. Conversely, the failure to acknowledge and adopt superior practices of the acquired company can result in lost value opportunities, usually accompanied by the departure of key individuals.

One merger in the banking industry, for example, combined two companies with very different attitudes about the organization of international teams. The smaller acquired company favored a more informal approach, while the larger acquiring company relied more on formal structures and procedures. Rather than examining these differences and evaluating their relative merits, the large company's approach dominated by default, resulting in the loss of key skills and management, and, ultimately, the closure of several international sites.

Some best practices in this area include:

- Conduct cross-cultural training workshops and one-on-one coaching sessions to raise awareness of and sensitivity to cultural differences. These should cover both national differences and those arising from different company cultures.
- Use tools such as the Accenture Culture Value Analysis to objectively assess both organizational cultures, from the macro level down to individual functions and departments. The purpose is to establish a baseline against which change can be measured and to identify potential areas where gaps are likely to create integration problems.
- Develop a clear description of the desired postmerger shared culture, one that combines the strengths of both organizations.
- Implement formal programs for cultural change sponsored and driven from the most senior levels of the organization.

3. Move to a Cross-Border Operating Model

The recent surge in cross-border mergers is part of a broader set of trends that reflect how companies are adjusting their strategies to compete in a world in which customers and suppliers are increasingly global. The best international competitors are simultaneously leveraging the benefits of global scale and configuring activities to ensure a highly tailored response to local customer needs.

For many companies embarking on a cross-border acquisition for the first time, the temptation is twofold: (1) to make as few changes as possible in the structure and management processes of the newly acquired company, and (2) to look for the most straightforward way of connecting them to an existing operating model. While this is often a safe near-term strategy, over time the failure to exploit the benefits of scale can add up to significant lost profit opportunities.

More sophisticated acquirers will move to realize the obvious cross-border synergies, such as leveraging purchasing scale or moving to shared back-office services. At the same time, the continued duplication of management structures, the inefficient distribution of assets, and the dispersion of critical skills across multiple geographies often remain as unexploited opportunities for profit improvement. Companies that develop superior skills in selecting, evaluating, and integrating cross-border acquisitions will benefit from faster growth and higher profitability. Those that struggle are more likely to become acquisition targets themselves.

The Legal Environment and the Acquisition Process

An understanding of local customs is critical to any successful venture in an international transaction. This is particularly true in the case of an acquisition transaction in an emerging market. Before sitting down to draft, an acquirer should take due note of a prevailing local custom relating to contract drafting. Some may be surprised to discover that the execution of the final acquisition documentation simply marks the beginning of the next round of negotiations. In fact, in some countries it is customary to incorporate vague language and imprecise terms in the documentation on the implicit understanding that there will be later negotiations.

An acquiring company should also have a good understanding of the enforceability of contracts in an emerging-market environment. In some countries justice delayed is not only justice denied, but it is also commonplace. Even where the court dockets are not overloaded, the quality of justice may be strained. While local arbitration is an option, foreign interests often believe that local arbitrators tend to favor local interests. If the acquirer has sufficient bargaining power to dictate governing law and a dispute resolution mechanism (e.g., arbitration in another country), the acquiring company may find enforceability of a decision problematic. Enforcement may require utilization of the same local courts that the dispute resolution process was designed to avoid. Moreover, it is particularly important to be aware of the sacred cows embedded in the public policy of a developing country. Courts in an emerging country may find that, without regard to the merits of a decision that has been rendered, a particular dispute resolution mechanism itself violates public policy.

Both developing and developed countries have laws that prohibit or limit acquisitions by foreign companies of key resources or entities operating in sensitive industries such as banking, energy, and the like. Developing countries tend to have broader restrictions and a nondomestic acquirer often confronts laws that dictate both the nature of the acquiring entity (e.g., a joint venture vehicle) and the percentage of ownership that the nondomestic acquirer may hold. An acquiring company may find that the acquisition will not be effective until one or more governmental agencies have blessed the transaction. In addition to governmental approval, local law may require that the transaction receive the imprimatur of the local labor force.

Acquisition due diligence may well encounter difficulties resulting from the local legal environment. For example, relevant public records may be incomplete, nonexistent, or difficult to find due to bureaucracy. In certain countries it is common practice to avoid formal real property transfer mechanisms because they are time consuming, expensive, and tainted by corrupt practices. This complicates the determination of something as basic as land ownership as well as the ability to determine whether there are third-party liens attaching to property of interest. Of course, it is not unusual to encounter private records that are incomplete at best and accounting that is unreliable.[7]

The Legal Environment and the Conduct of Business

It is not unusual to encounter a decidedly uncertain legal environment in emerging markets. Just as Section 1 of the U.S. Sherman Antitrust Act, with its unreasonable-restraint-of-trade language, has provided fertile ground for interpretation, so also many laws of emerging markets leave a great deal to interpretation. Some governments prefer this arrangement because it permits them the flexibility to effectively adjust their laws to changing circumstances without the necessity of amending the laws via a legislative or administrative process. Local counsel is an invaluable aid in determining which way the wind is blowing, but certainty can remain elusive.

Another hurdle to conducting business in an emerging market is often the requirement to seek governmental approval for items that would simply be a matter of contractual agreement in the United States. Sometimes a local attorney can work magic by structuring or labeling the arrangement at issue in a manner that is more likely to achieve a favorable ruling. There are also Foreign Corrupt Practices Act pitfalls to seeking government approval that are discussed later in this chapter. An acquiring company may also face the specter of ongoing governmental inspections or licensing requirements. In addition, in some countries, there are extralegal forces at work that have their own method of enforcement in the event compliance is not readily given.

Even if one is aware of the local written law, there are two factors to be aware of. First, there may well be a difference between the law as written and the law as applied. Moreover, the law may be applied inconsistently. Emerson said, "A foolish consistency is the hobgoblin of little minds," and certain developing countries have taken this to heart. The law as applied may be not only the law *du jour*, but possibly the law of the hour. Second, nations evolve and so do their laws. Businesses must be mindful of the possibility of the retroactive application of new laws. For example, whereas a business decision might be made in an environment where environmental laws are limited in scope or nonexistent, the business making that decision might in the future be subject to cleanup obligations of later-enacted laws. Particularly in developing countries, a foreign party must factor in the risk of future restraints on repatriation of funds; of expropriation; of inflation and currency devaluation; and of war, revolution, or insurrection.

Protection of intellectual property can be a major concern. Developing countries may perceive the protection of intellectual property as a form of economic taxation imposed by developing countries that own significant intellectual property. To the extent that there are laws that provide apparent protection for intellectual property, it is especially important to be aware of the differences between the law as written and the law as enforced. Many enter into transactions assuming there will be no legal protection for their intellectual property and hedge their risks in other fashions such as avoiding the transfer of crown-jewel technology to the entity located in the developing country.

TAXATION

Although there is an aversion to paying taxes in all countries, in certain emerging countries aversion has become evasion and can rise to the level of local custom. Business valuations must carefully evaluate prior tax compliance by the target company as well as the impact of full tax compliance on future operations. As with an acquisition in any country, the acquirer should structure the acquisition to minimize (but not evade) future tax obligations, paying attention to the tax on dividends and other transactions within the corporate family (e.g., royalties, commissions, and so on) as well as the potential taxes attendant to exit strategies. For example, sometimes it is tax efficient to form a holding company in a country with a favorable tax treaty with the home country of the target so that a later sale of the target will receive the benefits of that treaty.

LABOR

In and of themselves, labor relations are a critical factor to the success of any acquisition. An acquiring party should be well aware of the cultural aspects of local labor relations and the experience of other foreign entrants into the local labor markets. Many countries have laws protecting their local labor force, but in developing countries this is a particular concern. In addition to the possible right to participate in acquisition negotiations noted previously, the local labor force may have extensive rights limiting the acquirer's ability not only to terminate employees but also to change pre-acquisition employment rights and privileges, including those attendant to seniority.

FOREIGN CORRUPT PRACTICES ACT (FCPA)

Corruption, while not unique to developing countries, is more common in emerging markets. And any level of corruption will complicate compliance with FCPA rules and regulations. The FCPA prohibits payments to foreign officials for certain purposes; however, it can be difficult in certain developing countries to know whether an individual is a private businessperson or a foreign official. Regardless of local enforcement, it is a violation of the FCPA to induce foreign officials to commit any act in violation of their duty to uphold local law. The FCPA does exempt certain payments to foreign officials who "expedite or secure" the performance of routine governmental action. However, many more facilitation payments are a matter of due course in some developing countries.

When examining target companies, ensure compliance with the FCPA by asking the following questions:

- Has the target company (or its principals, directors, or key managers) been publicly sanctioned or come under suspicion for corruption?
- Have background checks and other forms of due diligence been performed on key members of management, customers, agents, and so on to identify potential government links?
- To what extent does the target company rely on third parties to conduct business?
- Consider the amounts of retainers, commissions, and expenses paid to third parties in connection with sales.
- Has the target company distributed a compliance policy to all employees and agents?
- Has the policy been assessed as to whether it is regularly enforced and records maintained?
- To what extent does the target company maintain written agreements for all international agents regarding FCPA and anticorruption clauses?

SUCCESS FACTORS

The following is a summary of success factors in M&A:

- Complete an in-depth evaluation of the M&A opportunities in terms of strategy, long-term as well as short-term.
- Perform thorough due diligence that includes cultural, strategic, financial, legal, and more.
- Interpret the information gathered within the context of the country and pay special attention to the soft skills.
- Understand the culture of the target market.
- Plan the postmerger integration process starting on day 1. Successful M&A requires forethought regarding post-integration issues, expanded due diligence, and cultural awareness.
- Be sensitive to all personnel-related issues. They won't go away and will impede on your factors for success.
- Have strong leadership and an effective cross-cultural communication plan.
- International M&A is no longer an option—it's the new reality.

There are best practices for global M&A—apply them!

PART TWO

The M&A Practice and Processes

CHAPTER 5

Practice Management

An M&A advisor takes on a number of roles for his or her client during the course of a transaction and may emerge as the lead from various disciplines within the process. Unlike large corporate finance transactions, where deals are almost exclusively led by the investment banker, middle market deals can be led or shepherded by one of the many professionals active in the process. In reality, that lead professional is routinely chosen by the client based on relationship and experience in knowing whom to trust.

Some of the obvious players whom clients reach out to are those they routinely engage, like their attorney or accountant. And many clients recognize that they need assistance with certain specialized skills for valuation, tax, accounting, and legal issues. In addition, the advisor can also be the financial strategist, the marketer of the business, the deal finder, and, when advising the buyer, the master of due diligence. Some of the less obvious roles that M&A advisors play include operational consultant to help prepare a company for sale, integration manager to assist in combining two businesses, or financial advisor to view the business within the context of the seller's overall portfolio. The successful transition of a company normally takes a multidisciplinary team where one of the members assumes the lead role or becomes the quarterback in the process—this is the M&A advisor.

The following professionals are routinely involved in the M&A team:

- Strategic advisor
- Operational consultant
- M&A intermediary
- Investment banker
- Business broker
- Valuation expert
- Tax accountant or attorney
- Audit accountant
- Deal attorney

- Financial advisor or wealth manager
- Due diligence consultant
- Integration manager

While the tasks of the advisor remain relatively constant, given the recent changes in the global economy, the historical role of an M&A advisor is not necessarily enough to get engaged with clients anymore. Today, the M&A advisor must be more of a strategic advisor to a business owner, and more than just transaction focused. It is now important to be holistic in viewing the long-term needs of clients and understanding where they are in the business cycle of their company and in the lifecycle of their ownership, and then to proactively guide them to prepare for a transition, make the needed strategic decisions, operate the company effectively to achieve their desired objectives, execute a transaction, and transition to the next phase. This value-added approach seems to be appropriate for many professional service providers as the broad economic cycle has recently put fee and price pressure on routine services and clients demand more from their relationships.

This chapter is structured to address some of the high-level issues that those assuming the role of M&A advisor may encounter or need to address in building a successful practice.

PRIMARY M&A ADVISORS

Traditionally, M&A advisors serving private business owners are one of three types: business broker, M&A intermediary, or investment banker. Each of these M&A advisors plays a role in the transfer process based on the size, market, and characteristics of the target company as shown in Table 5.1.

- *Business broker*. Business brokers generally represent small business owners, and often work with companies selling for $2 million and below in local markets. Business brokers often closely resemble their commercial real estate counterparts, and share some common practices. Like commercial real estate agents, business brokers will often provide asking prices for companies, use listing websites similar to the MLS, and may even be licensed as real estate agents. Typically the buyer of the business in a business broker transaction is an individual as opposed to an institution or strategic buyer.

   Secondarily, business brokers help individuals seeking to purchase a business, find a target, obtain bank financing, or negotiate a deal.

TABLE 5.1 Comparison of M&A Advisors

Characteristic	Business Broker	M&A Intermediary	Private Investment Banker	Public Investment Banker
1. Typical transaction size	<$2 million	$2 to $100 million	$2 to $100 million	>$50 million
2. Seller and buyer representation	Yes	Yes	Yes	Yes
3. Company valuations	Yes	Yes	Yes	Yes
4. Post an asking price	Yes	Maybe	No	No
5. Capital structure raising	No	No	Yes	Yes
6. Management buyouts	Maybe	Maybe	Yes	Yes
7. Recapitalizations	No	Maybe	Yes	Yes
8. Board advisory services	No	No	Yes	Yes
9. Reverse mergers	No	No	Maybe	Yes
10. Tenders offers	No	No	Maybe	Yes
11. Access public markets	No	No	No	Yes
12. Likely selling process	Negotiated	Negotiated/Private	Private Auction	Public Auction

- *M&A intermediary.* This is often a catchall category meant to include any number of consultants who can provide assistance with the sale of a company, merger, acquisition, recapitalization, or the like. Other professionals, such as attorneys or certified public accountants (CPAs), serve as M&A intermediaries on occasion but more frequently operate as small, boutique service providers. M&A intermediaries often work on transactions sized just above those of business brokers (greater than $2 million) and well into the middle market.
- *Investment banker.* Private investment bankers will help private companies access the private capital markets, conducting similar transactions as M&A intermediaries. However, investment bankers also offer more traditional banking services such as capital raises, debt placements, and fairness opinions. Public investment bankers conduct large company transactions focused on the public exchanges and corporate finance.

Some investment banks conduct buy-side processes to assist strategic acquirers in identifying, financing, and negotiating a deal. Others support private equity groups with similar assignments. *Investment banking* is a term generally (but not exclusively) used for those holding a license specific to the sale and exchange of company securities.

See Table 5.1 for a comparison of M&A advisors.

MARKETING THE M&A PRACTICE

One of the biggest challenges for an M&A advisor or advisory firm is identifying clients and obtaining engagements. Technical skills and ability to perform do not necessarily translate into deal flow or a paying business. It takes continuous and persistent marketing and networking to sustain a practice.

Networking

One of the most important activities for an advisor attempting to develop new business is networking. An advisor must seek out interaction and relationships with professionals in a position to refer buyers and sellers. Typical referral sources include attorneys, CPAs, other investment bankers, private equity investors, commercial bankers, friends, and previous clients. There is no substitute for referrals who have worked with your firm and had success. Good work begets good work.

While professional networking is valuable, farming existing relationships with personal contacts or contacts from a prior career can be beneficial.

Deals can come from unexpected sources and an M&A advisor should use communication with friends, neighbors, former coworkers, and even family as an opportunity to build on a network. Using Internet social networking to stay top of mind within an existing network of relationships and to reach new contacts is an excellent technique to augment face-to-face meetings.

Marketing and Advertising

In an attempt to expand a practice, advisors may employ some traditional marketing techniques; however, this should be done with caution. Advertising, publicity, cold calls, direct mail, and unrelated sponsorships may help build a trade-name and create greater market awareness but may not actually result in direct referral of clients or actual deal flow. Collateral materials that are more educational in content, such as brochures, websites, and articles describing the transaction processes or current market conditions, are often useful in selling services and informing clients of the value of the advisor and his firm. Small group seminars, articles, speeches, and proprietary research are the "First Team"[1] or most effective means of creating deal flow for professional service providers.

Offering seminars on exit planning or valuation is a good way to attract private company owners who are considering selling or transitioning their ownership. Those who take the time to attend these types of seminars, or even to respond, may be good targets. For clarification, large ballroom-type, pressure-sale seminars are not recommended. These have a tainted history in the M&A business and tend to attract the wrong clients, and will likely create the wrong image of the advisor and his firm.

Pretransaction Consulting

Offering pretransaction consulting services can enable a client to engage early with an advisor, allowing both to build a relationship. In the process, depending on the firm's skills, the advisor may provide assistance in planning for an exit or the monetization of the client's business; improving the client company's performance and hence its value; or growing the business, which may include an acquisition.

Valuation Services

Some sellers want to start the sale process by first understanding the value of their business. Others are approached with an unsolicited offer from an acquirer in their industry and seek a third-party valuation opinion. And still others, such as those who have contemplated selling their company to employees or family, start by retaining a valuation expert. All of these options can make sense.

For M&A advisors seeking to attract sell-side clients, it is helpful to offer valuation services without the opinion, which is in effect an informal market valuation. Providing a formal valuation that can be tested in court is often neither required nor appropriate for an M&A transaction (as discussed in Chapter 17, "Market Valuation"). In the event that a company owner actually needs an opinion of value (i.e., in a divorce, legal dispute, Employee Retirement Income Security Act–based reporting, etc.), the M&A advisor can refer the client to a technical valuation expert.

Other Consulting Services

Business coaches, industry specialists, financial planners, and CPAs are in a prime position to assist a company with the sale of its business or purchase of another. Often, these professionals are already trusted by the client; they know the business and may have other industry contacts to make a match and subsequently enable a transaction.

Becoming an Expert

Another effective way to build a professional network and promote services is to become known as an expert in a particular industry or segment. M&A advisors who have multiple successful transactions in a particular industry can leverage their success to attract similar deals. Coupling promotion of successful transactions with client referrals, speaking at industry events and meetings, and attendance at conferences and trade shows can result in establishing a reputation as an expert and a go-to resource for M&A services.

UNDERSTANDING THE PRIVATE BUSINESS OWNER

Success in the M&A practice is greatly influenced by understanding business owners. They may choose to participate in any number of transactions during their ownership and ultimate exit from a company. As mentioned throughout this handbook, it is their motives that drive the market. The M&A advisor must understand these motives to recommend and ultimately assist sellers with the transactions that best meet their needs and objectives.

The motives of company owners dictate what type of transaction or transfer channel they wish to pursue. There are seven from which to choose: employees, family, charitable trusts, co-owners, outside-retire, outside-continue, and public. In an outside-retire transaction, an owner who wishes to retire and cash in his chips may choose to sell entirely to an outside party. In an outside-continue transaction, an owner looking to diversify risk but remain in control of her company may choose to pursue a minority recapitalization. While the motives that drive each transfer channel may differ, a company owner should benefit from the advice and guidance provided by an experienced M&A advisor.

Company owners and shareholders will often ask the M&A advisor if it is the right time to sell their company. Most of the time the owner is asking in an attempt to time the ideal valuation from the market. However, unlike in the public markets, timing the valuations in the market is only one part of the equation. A successful transition or transfer comes together when three conditions are in sync: (1) the business is ready for external scrutiny, (2) the owner is personally ready for a transition, and (3) the timing of the markets (capital markets and the selling company's market) is favorable. These combine to provide the key to maximizing value. Table 5.2 provides a matrix of the most basic preparation steps that pulls the concepts together.

First, owners must be personally prepared to sell. This includes mentally accepting the idea that they will no longer own and control their professional destiny. This is sometimes a great hurdle for private business owners, regardless of their age. Owners who do not properly prepare to accept these personal issues can find themselves selling at less-than-optimal terms and conditions (i.e., when they become sick, or even having the business sold after death).

Second, the business must be well positioned to maximize the value to buyers. This means having a well-defined strategy, a solid management team (independent of the owner/operator), scalable systems and profitability, and, ideally, a strong positive trend as the personal and market timing components are inline.

Last is the market. Few companies operate in industries that are not impacted by the valuation influences of the broader markets. When the broad stock market is doing well, valuations tend to rise in the private markets. The opposite also holds. Therefore, it is desirable if a private company can time the business and personal readiness to sell when the broader market is also rewarding owners with overall higher valuations.

CLIENT ACCEPTANCE

A client may wish to engage you, and she may even be willing to pay you. But, are her goals realistic? Take time to assess a potential client, her needs and her expectations. As an advisor, time is a key resource in assuring success

TABLE 5.2 Basic Preparation Steps for Business Transition or Transfer

Personal	Business	Market
Reduce Dependence of Owner. The owner should not be central to the operations of the business. The sales team should handle key customer accounts. The management team should be able to manage the business. The owner spends most of his or her time on strategic issues.	**Improve the Financial Records.** Audited financial statements may be expensive but they more than pay for themselves in the transfer process. Audited statements reduce risk from a buyer's perspective. Companies should also clean up all legal issues such as lawsuits and environmental issues prior to marketing a business.	**Ride the Wave.** Peak selling cycles in the overall private capital markets tend to happen every 5 to 7 years. Normally, the crest of this merger wave occurs in the final 18 to 24 months of the cycle. Various investment banking organizations track these cycles.
Continue to Take Out Money. The owner can continue to take money out of the company, as these items will be recast. The key here is good record keeping so a buyer can trace all owner compensation.	**Defined and Documented Systems.** Financial and management systems should be upgraded, documented, and used. Companies should be able to track product line profitability, capacity requirements, sales forecasts by SKU, etc.	**Consolidators May be Watching.** Many industries continue to consolidate, in some cases, on a global basis. Typically there are a handful of consolidating companies that intend to grow through acquisition. Often private equity groups control these acquirers. Owners should monitor the activities of consolidators, usually through trade associations and the media.
Get the Estate in Order. Estate planning can require years to effect. The best plans are proactive, not reactive. Owners wishing to implement sophisticated techniques should seek professional help.	**Clean up the Place.** Clean and organized facilities make a positive difference. In some cases, it makes sense for the owner to have Phase I or II environmental audits performed before the selling process begins.	**Keep an Eye Open.** The market may present itself at a moment's notice. Special one-off opportunities may knock on the owner's door.

and high-performing advisors do not waste time on unrealistic opportunities. Common areas of disconnect between the advisor and the client exist regarding valuation and timeline, as discussed below. Before those discussions, it might make sense to educate the client or ensure that the client understands the types of transactions available to her. Some are listed here along with questions to consider. The implications for the advisor are that some analysis and preparatory work are required before the engagement to facilitate a meaningful discussion and to provide some initial recommendations and observation.

Types of Transactions

- 100 percent sale with exit of old owner/operator
- Management buy-in
- Management buyout
- Partner buyout
- Recapitalization (with debt only)
- Minority recapitalization (equity)
- Majority recapitalization (equity)
- Raise preferred stock investment
- Merger
- Family transfer
- IPO
- Structured liquidation

Questions for a Seller to Consider

- Is the company properly positioned to sell now, or should the seller consider waiting to complete certain strategic initiatives or changes (e.g., replace key managers, open a new location, launch a new product line, meet certain earnings or revenue milestones, etc.)?
- Does the seller understand the types of transactions available to her and their implications (e.g., control, time horizon, cash-out, etc.)?
- Does the seller understand who are the likely buyers of her business?
- What is the minimum after-tax cash amount that the seller needs to accept an offer?
- Are all of the selling shareholders or owners on board with the valuation and committed to selling?

Having these strategic discussions with a potential client up front will ensure the M&A project undertaken is appropriate for the circumstances and has a chance to be successful. This can save both the advisor and the client time and money.

INITIAL FINANCIAL ANALYSIS

As mentioned earlier, some preliminary financial analysis is needed to gain a basic understanding of the business and the implications for a transaction. It allows the advisor to begin to understand the management, operations, and capital structure of the potential client's business. The advisor should review preliminary financial information and perform basic industry research. In doing so, he should keep in mind valuation metrics, the appeal to active buyers, and the impact of economic volatility. This research will allow the advisor to develop an estimated valuation range for discussion purposes. If the engagement is for a recapitalization or acquisition, the same information is required to assess the likely financing alternatives and constraints.

VALUE DISCUSSIONS

The most significant cause of frustration between an M&A advisor and his client can be created when a client has unrealistic expectations of value. Often, sellers will create value expectations based on sensational media reports or "country club multiples," comparing their company to a data point without consideration for the health and performance of their business. Having a valuation discussion with the client early, based on analysis and supporting data, can save both parties time and disappointment and in many cases start the aligning process if the engagement is to move forward.

Prepare for these discussions by compiling industry research with empirical knowledge of recent M&A trends and transactions in the industry. Be prepared to discuss facts and figures, and try not to fall into the trap of believing the stories that begin with "I heard my competitor sold for . . . "

Present the valuations in a range, because that's what they are. Be careful not to be the consummate pessimist, always delivering bad news. It generally will not win favor with clients thinking that hedging may likely cap the upside for their value. One way to address the optimistic values is to show that the process will uncover the maximum value. Also, keep in mind that the terms of the deal are often as important as the valuation. It is the advisor's role to get the best overall transaction for the client.

PROCESS DISCUSSIONS

Just as setting expectations is important with regard to valuation, so is establishing a reasonable understanding with the seller (or buyer in the case of an acquisition) of the process, terms, and timeline of a transaction. Take time to document and educate clients about key steps and then keep them updated as the process progresses.

Advisors should create a process checklist that can be reviewed with a seller or buyer. This might include a generic timeline that shows key milestones and identifies responsibilities and deadlines that will occur during the process. It also enables discussion about terms of a transaction that may later be a surprise to clients, such as:

- Exclusivity provisions in the letter of intent
- Representations and warranties they may be expected to sign in a purchase agreement
- Indemnification provisions
- Earnout expectations
- Escrows and holdbacks

Early disclosure of the known negatives of the deal is always in the best interest of all parties to reduce surprises and proactively address issues. Reviewing the process with a seller may uncover issues that will likely be revealed (or should be revealed) later:

- What are the transferability issues?
- What is the impact (either way) on key people?
- What are the market vulnerabilities?
- Examine the last three or four disruptive events and ask why they occurred.
- Assess the risk of capital deployed verses other assets currently owned.
- What do I do after I sell?
- What skeletons are in the closet?

Remember, surprises kill deals!

CONFIDENTIALITY

Confidentiality may not come naturally to clients but is necessary for a successful transaction. Untimely disclosure of the seller's intent to employees, customers, vendors, and the open market could all have negative impacts on the business, which therefore could be detrimental to the deal. An M&A advisor should stress that he will do his best to keep the deal quiet. However, sellers need to be advised on the importance of keeping their own plans strictly confidential. Studies have shown that most confidentiality leaks can be traced to the sellers themselves. In the case of an acquisition, the same issue exists.

Advisors should also discuss the confidentiality rules of the road with their clients. Is sending e-mails or faxes to the president of the company acceptable? Or should the client establish a secure e-mail address? What about phone calls and voice messages? Too many phone calls and messages from Joe Investment Banker will soon leave the receptionist with little doubt as to the company's plans. Create agreeable methods of communication and the rationale for why the advisor will be asking for so much information from the company's employees. Some M&A advisors will be introduced to the company's employees as consultant, auditor, banker, or insurance/bonding agent.

Finally, the advisor should discuss the inevitable question that a seller will be asked by a friend or colleague sometime during the process: "I heard that you were selling your company ... ?" The seller has likely been asked this question a few times before, but has never been sensitive to the issue until now. Of course, a startled response, such as, "Where did you hear that?" is mere confirmation for the inquisitive friend. Therefore, prepare the seller with a response along these lines: "Of course, we are always for sale—why, are you interested in buying?"

CLIENT ENGAGEMENT

An engagement letter or agreement is usually drafted after arriving at a mutual understanding of realistic expectations regarding value, timeline, and goals. This engagement letter should set forth the understanding of services and fees between the client and the M&A advisor. A typical engagement letter will include the following provisions:*

- Identification of the parties
- Scope of services
- Limitations and disclosures
- Fees
- Termination provisions and tails

---

*Neither this handbook nor the authors or contributors thereof are providing legal advice to the reader. We recommend engaging legal counsel to establish template engagement agreements and other legal documents used in operating the M&A practice.

Identification of the Parties

It may seem obvious, but the first question an M&A advisor should ask is, "Who is my client?" Is it the company? Is it the shareholder(s)? What if there are multiple shareholders with different goals and objectives? In some cases, these are straightforward, as in a single-shareholder company looking to sell. However, in other cases (like partner buyouts or disputed sales) the answer may be a little opaque. In an acquisition where the advisor is on the buy-side, the client is typically the company.

The second question to ask when identifying the client is: "Who is authorized to engage me on behalf of the company?" Again, often it is obvious, but some situations (such as a divisional vice president asking you to help divest his part of the company) may not be as straightforward.

M&A advisors may want to engage their own contract attorney to help them understand the nuances of contracting their services in these more complicated situations.

Scope of Service

The engagement letter should set forth the actions that the advisor is intending to do for the client, and define some expected timelines. In some cases, the advisor may want to specify which services will *not* be provided. For example, it might be appropriate to disclose that the advisor will not be responsible for preparing financial statements, schedules, or forecasts that need to be generated by management. The engagement letter should also spell out the role and responsibilities of the client, such as what information will be made available to the advisor and when that information should be expected.

When describing the timeline it is generally best to reference the steps in the process, rather than hard dates. For example, "M&A Advisor will provide Seller a draft of the marketing book within 30 days of receiving the information requested from Client."

Here are some example timelines and defined milestones for a sell-side engagement:

- 30 days for data gathering
- 30 days to draft the book or deck
- 45 days to search and identify target buyers
- 60 days to have initial management meetings with buyers
- 30 days to collect and negotiate LOIs
- 90 days to process the due diligence cycle up to the closing

Limitations and Disclosures

As with any legal contract, there should be provisions to protect the advisor from liability. Typically, these include specific limitations or exclusions of services being performed by the advisor as well as indemnification by the client in favor of the advisor in the event of third-party claims that arise from things other than the advisor's own negligence.

Again, it is advisable for M&A advisors to consult with their own contract attorney in developing the standard language they will use in engagement letters.

Fees

Most middle market M&A advisors will structure a selling engagement with a mix of fees as follows:

- Up-front fee for initial work such as valuation, seller memo, consulting, and so on
- Success fee as a percentage of the price paid

The "up-front" fee charged by advisors is sometimes referred to as a *retainer*; the implication is that this is to be applied against the ultimate success fee paid at closing. Some advisors have begun to refer to the up-front fee as an *advisory fee* instead of a retainer to send the message that this is a separate fee for services and is therefore not applied against the later success fee. As an alternative to the up-front fee, it is now rather common to obtain a monthly fee for the duration of the engagement plus a success fee.

Buy-side engagements tend to have monthly fees for services coupled with a smaller success fee based on closing an acquisition. Chapter 7 contains additional information about buy-side engagements.

Some advisors use milestones defined in the scope of their engagement to cause up-front fees or retainers to be paid. For example, fees might be staged and paid upon completion of the following events:

- Upon signing of the engagement letter
- Upon completion of the first draft of the book or deck
- Upon production of a target list
- When meeting event deadlines such as management meetings
- Upon bilateral execution of an LOI
- At the introduction of the first draft of the purchase agreement by either side

The success fee can be calculated in any number of ways, but typically is a percentage of the selling price (or purchase price in the case of an acquisition) upon consummation of the transaction. The percentage used will vary based primarily on two factors:

1. Size of the transaction
2. Nature of the work being performed by the M&A advisor

For example, business brokers will often charge 8 to 10 percent for selling a business with a value under $2 million. A broker working purely as a "finder" to a buying client might charge a 1 to 5 percent fee for transactions ranging from $5 million to $20 million. Investment bankers typically charge 3 to 6 percent for lower-middle market transactions of $5 million to $20 million. And, those same investment banking firms may charge 2 to 3 percent on transactions of $20 million to $75 million.

Double Lehman Formula

M&A advisors and business brokers in smaller transactions have used a formula known as the Double Lehman, named by doubling the original formula created by the former investment banking firm Lehman Brothers in the early 1970s:

- 10 percent of the first million dollars of the purchase price
- 8 percent of the second million
- 6 percent of the third million
- 4 percent of the fourth million
- 3 percent of anything over $4 million

Most middle market advisors will establish their success fee based on a *total value amount* (TVA) percentage or aggregate consideration. TVA success fees are set as a fixed percentage based on the expected valuation or sale price. Middle market advisors' success fees approximate the following:

- 5 to 7 percent for transactions estimated around $5 million to $10 million
- 4 to 5 percent for transactions estimated around $10 million to $15 million
- 3 to 4 percent for transactions estimated around $15 million to $20 million
- 1 to 3 percent for transactions over $20 million

Other fee structures have become popular with M&A advisors and are often used to enhance, or in place of, more traditional fixed percentage success fees. Some other structures to consider include:

- *Minimum fee clause.* For smaller transactions or distressed deals, an advisor may consider having a minimum fee clause to ensure at least a reasonable fee is received, regardless of the final price.

- *Fixed-amount success fee.* These can be used for buy-side work, or raising debt and equity, when maximizing value is not applicable or may actually be counterproductive.
- *Value kicker.* These are used as additional incentive compensation when a client is rather certain that a minimum amount can be obtained with little effort, and wants the advisor to focus on the higher end of the potential deal value. An example might be 4 percent of selling price up to $10 million, plus 8 percent over $10 million.
- *Fixed rates plus closing bonus.* This structure is common for a client that is expecting only pure mechanical assistance, but wants to provide an incentive for getting the deal closed.
- *Timing bonus.* A bonus is paid for closing the transaction within a certain time frame.

Termination and Tail

Engagement letters should also include termination provisions that allow both parties to terminate the services of the advisor. In most cases, the client would be the one requesting the termination, either because he is unhappy with the performance of the advisor or because he no longer wishes to proceed with a transaction. Most termination clauses require advanced written notice.

To prevent clients from terminating an engagement letter with an advisor purely as a means to avoid paying a success fee, so-called tail provisions are generally negotiated into the terms of the agreement. Tail provisions indicate that the advisor is entitled to his success fee if a transaction is completed within a certain time after termination. Normal tail provisions continue for 12 to 24 months following termination, and may apply either to any transaction or only to transactions with parties identified at the time of termination.

Licensure Issues in the M&A Business*

In some instances, individuals who are active in certain types of M&A transactions need to be licensed as broker-dealers according to the federal laws,

---

*The comments in this chapter about the securities laws are broad generalities and need to be investigated and understood in the context of establishing and conducting the operations of the M&A practice and defining the types of services to be offered. The content of this handbook is for informational purposes only. The publisher, authors, contributors and reviewers of this handbook are not providing legal advice or opinions regarding any topic, including the licensing requirements of an M&A business.

including the Securities Exchange Act of 1934 and certain state securities laws. See the "SEC Provisions for Broker-Dealers" and "FINRA Provisions for Broker-Dealers" sections in Chapter 14 for additional discussions about this topic.

According to informal surveys within the industry, 70 to 80 percent of M&A advisors in the lower-middle market are not securities licensed. Conceptually, this makes sense given that many small transactions are asset sales that generally do not involve the exchange of securities. The percentage of deals structured as asset sales diminishes as the size of transactions increases beyond an estimated $100 million. These larger deals are more likely to involve stock sales and other consideration that may be considered a security and clearly require securities-licensed investment bankers to facilitate the transaction.

Within the business of mergers and acquisitions, there are varying opinions about the actual licensing requirements given that the securities laws were originally written during the 1930s to protect public investors in the publicly traded stock markets. Over the past decade there have been a number of initiatives to provide clarity and reduce the ambiguity regarding the law and its application within the M&A business. In some instances the SEC has issued no-action letters, and in general there is very little case law to rely on.

To some degree, there are benefits of being licensed even if the transaction does not require it. For example, in the eyes of some clients the status of broker-dealer implies a level of credibility greater than that of an unlicensed intermediary (though in practice this is not necessarily true). States business licensing requirements vary for consideration beyond securities compliance; the state level securities laws are referred to as Blue Sky Laws (see Chapter 14). There are some relatively serious penalties for noncompliance with federal and state laws depending upon the situation and state. For the M&A advisor, some of the potential hazards of noncompliance include denial of compensation, fines and penalties, rescission of the transaction, and personal liability for associated costs in the event of rescission. For the client company, noncompliance risks include potential rescission of a transaction and denial of a clean legal opinion on future securities transactions.

The list below provides a few strategies for complying with the current securities laws.[2]

- Lead only pure "asset sale" transactions—there is generally no jurisdiction under securities laws if no securities are involved.
- Structure sell-side engagements (and associated transaction terms and structure) per the Country Business No-Action letter.[3]

- Individually register with an existing broker-dealer firm to manage the deal, subject to the Financial Industry Regulatory Authority (FINRA) regulation.
- Register your firm as a broker-dealer (or form a new affiliated firm), subject to FINRA regulation.

For additional information on the topic you may find updated articles at www.amaaonline.com. We also suggest that you read the SEC's *Guide to Broker-Dealer Registration* at www.sec.gov/divisions/marketreg/bdguide.htm.

CHAPTER 6

Sell-Side Representation
and Process

Mergers and acquisitions (M&A) transactions in the middle market are completed much more frequently than larger publicly traded transactions. However, because there is no required regulatory or public disclosure of these transactions, the process and details of these transactions are never fully captured or reported. To be sure, there are many different ways in which these private transactions come together. This chapter will step through the processes used by many M&A advisors to assist a closely held or private company to complete a sale transaction.

Chapter 5, "Practice Management," discusses many of the issues involved with M&A advisors marketing their services and engaging with clients considering the sale of or transition out of their business. This chapter examines the selling process, assuming that there have been successful preliminary discussions with the client, that some diligence is done by the advisor, and that the engagement of the M&A advisor by the client is finalized.

SELLING PROCESS OVERVIEW

This chapter covers the selling process in 10 steps, illustrating and explaining the various issues and concepts that will likely be encountered as an M&A advisor assists a company to closing:

1. Collect data.
2. Research industry and identify buyer types.
3. Prepare the marketing book.
4. Drive the marketing process.
5. Negotiate price and terms with buyers.

6. Structure the transaction.
7. Receive letters of intent/term sheets from buyers.
8. Respond to due diligence requests.
9. Negotiate definitive agreements.
10. Facilitate the closing process and support postclose integration.

Step 1: Data Collection

The M&A advisor will have obtained some information from the company prior to engagement, as would be necessary to have discussions about value and process and to perform some initial research about the industry. These initial information requests may be the most difficult since the seller and the advisor are still getting to know and trust one another. In some cases it helps if the advisor offers to sign and deliver a nondisclosure agreement before any information is exchanged. It is important for the seller to know that these early information gathering stages are for preliminary analysis only. The advisor should ask simple questions about the seller's business and be respectful in not asking for too much information at first. Part of the preliminary process is determining what critical information is not available so that gaps can be filled later in the process.

After being formally engaged by a seller, the M&A advisor will need to begin accumulating a more comprehensive level of company information. However, care should be taken when requesting this initial batch for a few reasons:

- The advisor is still building trust with his client. Large generic information requests can send the wrong message to clients and may overwhelm them. Care should be taken to prepare customized request lists, rather than blindly sending checklists asking for information that is not applicable.
- The seller will likely not want to involve his entire team in the process at this stage. Perhaps one or two key personnel will know the advisor is gathering data to assist with the marketing and sale of the company, or perhaps only the owner will be responding. Either way, these early information requests will likely be filled without the administrative support the company normally relies upon.
- This initial data request is intended to merely provide you with the necessary information to assemble the marketing book. There is no need to accumulate the detailed level of information that will ultimately become part of a buyer's diligence requests. It is better to wait until a specific request comes from actual buyers, rather than trying to anticipate and build a diligence war chest at this stage.

With the above guidance, it is important to uncover likely deal killers (or skeletons) early in the process to proactively address these and develop mitigation plans. As an advisor, your reputation is on the line if you get deep into a process engaged with buyers or investors and they discover issues that you should have known about. From the client's perspective, the advisor needs to ask the obvious tough questions and help the seller gauge the reality of a likely sale, so as not to waste their time and money. In many cases, addressing the tough issues up front and developing mitigation strategies can make the difference between a successful and a failed process.

Typical information requests at this stage include the following:

- Historical financial statements and tax returns
- Forecasted financials and budgets
- Organizational charts
- Marketing and advertising information
- Corporate legal formation and shareholder documents
- Lender information
- Leases
- Industry or market research reports to which management has access
- Contact information of other professionals on the M&A team

In addition to basic data requests from the company, it is often helpful to schedule interviews with the owners and key management to discuss the following:

- History of the company
- Products and services
- Competitor analysis
- Industry trends
- Management team abilities and shortfalls
- Customer analysis and/or concentration issues
- Previous offers or negotiations to see the company

During the interview process, ask questions to ferret out the potential deal-killers or items that could become surprises later in the process. Here is a partial list of topics to address (some of which really pertain more to a recapitalization or to situations where the owners remain engaged after the sale):

- Lawsuits (employee, supplier, customer, or otherwise)
- History of bankruptcy of the company or of any of the go-forward management team

- Partner or shareholder disputes
- Any governmental action that has been taken against the company (environmental, censuring, disbarment, etc.)
- Whether they have paid their taxes (payroll, corporate, state, etc.)
- Any specialized government filings or licenses that they have ignored or taken aggressive exemption from
- Any under-the-table deals or anomalies in financial reporting that will not be evident in the financial statements
- For certain industries, such as software, whether revenue has been recognized as in compliance with Generally Accepted Accounting Principles (GAAP)
- Any prior failed attempts to sell the company or enter into strategic deals that fell apart

It may be helpful to review a typical buyer due diligence list with the seller to give the seller a sense of the level of detail that will later be required in the process and to set expectations.

Eventually, the advisor will need to accumulate information to build a "due diligence data room." This is an online file storage and transfer area for secure delivery of documents and information about the client company. Whereas much of the detailed diligence information can be requested later, some of the information will be obtained in the initial requests. Some advisors begin to build the basic data room structure with these initial items, if for no other reason than to keep themselves organized.

Step 2: Industry Research and Identifying Buyer Types

Prior to developing the marketing book, it is wise to gather industry data to establish what types of buyers most likely will be interested. Basic marketing and advertising logic tells us to understand and research the target market before creating an advertising or marketing campaign. The same can be said for marketing a company for sale. Know the target market before developing the marketing book.

The best way to narrow down the target market is to create lists of different buyer types. This is not necessarily down to the level of specific buyer names, but certainly the advisor should identify likely categories of buyers: competitors, vendors, similar industries, financial buyers, strategic rollups, and employees or management.

Then, along with the seller, rank which types of buyers are most likely, and identify issues that each buyer type may have with the business. What strengths and weaknesses will be important to the likely buyer groups? What are the key and important metrics the targeted buyer types will want to see?

These highlighted issues will help create and prioritize the outline for the marketing book, and may help in customizing the book and future presentations for the specific groups.

Step 3: The Marketing Book

There are generally two or three substeps used by advisors in delivering the company information to prospective buyers in order to capture a buyer's attention and maintain some control over the release of confidential information.

- *Blind summary or teaser.* Generally, an advisor will prepare a summary page or executive summary with company highlights. This summary is prepared "blind," meaning it does not identify the seller. Rather, it generally provides a basic explanation of the industry, its location and size, and high-level information. The intent is to broadly distribute the blind summary to capture the attention of prospective buyers and have them request more information. (*Note:* Most advisors will require a buyer to sign a nondisclosure agreement [NDA] prior to receiving any information beyond the blind summary.)
- *Book summary (optional).* Some advisors have begun to prepare a short slideshow or bullet-point presentation that accompanies the complete marketing book. While the marketing book will contain a lot of detailed information, sometimes it can be overwhelming for a buyer to pick out the key points of interest. A quick PowerPoint presentation or set of bullet-points to highlight key facts can be helpful in capturing the attention of potential buyers.
- *Complete marketing book.* The marketing book is used to provide a buyer with enough information to allow him to make an initial assessment to pursue the transaction or not. Rarely will a buyer make an offer based solely on reviewing the book, but the book should attempt to get the buyer 90 percent there.

Different advisors use different names for the marketing book, such as:

- Offering memorandum
- Prospectus
- Confidential business report (CBR)
- Book
- Confidential information memorandum

- Business plan
- Company profile

Advisors may want to be cautious using terms like *offering memorandum* or *prospectus*, especially if they are not licensed security representatives, as these names may have specific legal implications within the securities laws. Even if an advisor is securities licensed, staying away from these offering terms can avoid additional compliance concerns from the broker-dealer.

Preparation Regardless of the format or sequence of the contents, it is key to tell the story of the business—how it creates value and why it is going to be relevant in the future. There are variations in assembling the materials for the book, but most contain the following common sections, in roughly a similar order:

- Executive summary
- Business overview or history
- Organization structure (corporate structure, parent/sub, brother/sister)
- Description of products, services, processes, and so on
- Sales, marketing, and growth opportunities
- Competitive landscape
- Risks and limitations
- Financial discussion (summary and recast)
- Exhibit A: Pro forma financials
- Exhibit B: Historical financials
- Exhibit C: Other supplemental information

Advisors will want to highlight different issues and objectives for each company within the book, although buyers are often looking for some common points to be made. Consider these typical key points:

- What is the desired transaction?
- Differentiating qualities of the business
- Competitive advantages
- Growth opportunities
- Profitability

In addition to highlighting the positive elements of the company, an advisor is wise to share some negative points as well. This is done for a few reasons. Proactively sharing negative attributes allows the advisor to put these in as favorable a light as possible. Sharing some of the challenges and weaknesses of the company will allow the advisor to explain why these represent an opportunity for the buyer. No company is perfect. Therefore, revealing the negative elements shows that the company is real and may actually help to explain why the seller wants to sell. Typical negative issues include:

- Limitations/gaps in management
- Customer concentration
- Reasons for lack of growth
- Sales-team/sales-channel limitations

Seller Motivation   When marketing a closely held company, perhaps one of the most important facts to cover is the seller's motivation for selling. Whether consciously or subconsciously, buyers often wonder if the seller's motivation is based on certain negative facts not known by the buyer. Such a belief can greatly increase the risk that the deal will not proceed smoothly to a successful closing. Therefore, in almost every closely held company sale, the advisor should openly explain the seller's motivation and rationale.

Motives that will resonate with buyers include:

- *Undercapitalization.* Private equity groups especially like to hear that sellers are looking to sell or recapitalize because they just do not have the financial horsepower to carry on with their vision for the company's future or the need of the business to grow as fast as required to stay relevant.
- *Need for additional management strength.* Many strategic buyers take pride in the management team they have developed and therefore are looking for companies to acquire that are seeking to strengthen management to improve operating results.
- *Retirement due to age.* Assuming the seller is at a reasonable age to retire, this explanation may be a natural driver. A related rationale can be that the seller is aging and needs to diversify his financial risk personally as the needs of his business continue. This can create an ideal scenario for a private equity group, particularly if the seller desires to stay with the business for some time.
- *Management wants to buy out owner.* Some private equity groups like funding management buyouts, and therefore this motivation matches their desire to invest in these situations.

Financial Disclosures   The financial statement analysis section of the book is clearly an important section, since the economics of the deal are often of primary significance to a buyer. A clear and concise presentation of the financial story is important.

Most financial disclosures will begin with a summary of the historical (and perhaps forecasted) earnings before interest, taxes, depreciation, and amortization (EBITDA). This will generally include a three- to five-year historical analysis, plus information for the current year and a forecasted year or two. EBITDA calculations should be shown (including add-backs), so that presented EBITDA can be reconciled back to net income from the financial statements. In addition, it generally makes sense to summarize the significant elements of the income statement such as revenue, gross margin, net income, and so on. This provides context to the EBITDA levels presented (i.e., EBITDA is growing at a similar rate as gross margin, etc.).

One-off situations or extraordinary add-backs should be footnoted or explained when presenting normalized EBITDA as is described in Chapter 10, "Financial Analysis and Modeling."

Specific EBITDA Presentations   In some situations, a special book presentation can be made for a specific buyer or investor. The EBITDA presentation can be normalized to highlight special synergies or add-backs that exist only with that specific buyer. See Chapter 10 for a detailed discussion of normalized EBITDA.

Balance Sheet Presentation   Some M&A advisors include a normalized or postclosing balance sheet in the financial disclosures section of the marketing book. This can give buyers a better sense of the balance sheet–related issues and questions they may have, such as:

- What is the normal or average working capital to be included in the transaction?
- Which assets are included in the sale? Which are not?
- Which liabilities does the seller expect to be assumed by the buyer?

Other Financial Disclosures   Depending on the circumstances, other financial elements of the company should be disclosed and explained to provide buyers with a solid understanding of the financial picture of the company and prepare them to make an educated and complete offer. Here are some other financial disclosures to consider:

- Maintenance versus growth capital expenditures
- Working capital needs
- Seasonality trends
- Cyclical trends

Prospective Financial Presentation In most situations, advisors want to present forecasted or prospective financial statements as a part of the marketing book. However, presenting these future statements (or parts of them) requires some special considerations:

- Be careful to explain that these are management's forecasts—not the advisor's.
- Use footnotes to explain the key assumptions being made in generating the forecast.
- Tie the forecasts to specific key assumptions and metrics, which can then be explained and further supported in other parts of the book.
- Present forecasted statements and summaries in the same format as historical statements.
- Make sure they are believable—avoid hockey-stick forecasts or unrealistic growth patterns.

Step 4: Marketing Process

The process for marketing a closely held company in the middle market is unique. In most cases the M&A advisor will want to identify specifically targeted buyers, rather than market to a mass audience. In addition, the M&A advisor is trying to create a "limited auction" competitive bidding environment, as will be discussed further in this chapter. To balance these demands, most M&A advisors will use the following steps when marketing a selling company:

1. Research market buyers.
2. Clear the target list with seller/client.
3. Make initial contact with buyers.
4. Obtain nondisclosure.
5. Distribute the marketing book.
6. Follow up and discuss.

Research Market Buyers To research and identify buyers in the market, the M&A advisor should begin by understanding the selling company's strategy and business operations, and then research and understand the industry of the company. With this information, the following questions can be asked:

- Who are the most likely buyers?
- Are there related industries that might be a strategic fit for this company?
- Who has been actively buying in this industry?

- What private equity groups are buying in this industry or express an interest in this market?
- Has the seller been approached with any unsolicited offers?

There are many tools and databases that can be used to research the industry and help in accumulating a potential list of buyers. The appendix provides direction to a companion website that has a directory. When researching buyers, the advisor should attempt to identify the right person in the organization to contact. In the case of corporate buyers, it is common for larger companies to have a specific corporate development team or lead that is responsible for acquisitions. For smaller corporate buyers, it is likely to be the chief executive officer or chief financial officer. Many private equity groups have a partner dedicated to evaluating or filtering new opportunities, or it is possible that one of the partners has experience in the specific industry of the client company. Therefore it is critical to research the exact individual who will be receiving the seller's marketing materials so that the book is sent to the right person.

Clear the List with the Seller   Before any information is sent to the list of targeted buyers, the M&A advisor should share the compiled list with the seller for review. It is possible that the seller may know something about these companies that you didn't learn in your research, which would make them off limits for the seller. In some cases, the seller will not want certain buyer targets to learn that the company is for sale. These situations should be discussed with the seller to determine who will be included on the marketing distribution list.

M&A advisors may disagree with the removal of certain buyer targets from the list. They may debate the need to provide this buyer target with the company's information, because that buyer target may be a prime candidate to acquire the company. However, the decision is ultimately the seller's to make. An M&A advisor should respect the seller's wishes, and if the seller does not want any materials being sent to a particular party, then that party should be removed from the list.

Initiate Contact with Buyers   Once the seller has given authority to contact each buyer target, the M&A advisor will generally send a blind summary or teaser to the targeted buyers. As noted previously, care should be given to address the information to the appropriate individual at the specific organization so that the teaser is actually received and reviewed.

Most M&A advisors create and maintain their own databases of buyer targets for each transaction, to track who has been contacted, when information was sent, and other research information. Some tools help the M&A

advisor to remember when to follow up and can track notes made by associates or others working with the advisor. In addition, some database tools even rank buyers according to likelihood of acquisition. Those ranked at the top will be given more attention, with more follow-up phone calls, e-mails, and so on.

Seldom is sending a single e-mail with a blind summary enough to capture a buyer's attention. Even the best and most likely buyer targets will often need follow-up phone calls to specifically point out the benefits of the potential company acquisition being marketed.

Keep in mind that there are cases where it is better for management to reach out and contact potential buyers because of existing relationships or access.

Obtain Nondisclosure   If a buyer target receives the teaser information and is interested in the concept, the buyer will want to learn more about the company. Of course, this is why the full marketing book has been prepared and is ready to be distributed. But, before distribution of the marketing book, the buyer is requested to sign a nondisclosure agreement (NDA).

Some M&A advisors maintain their own template NDA that can be sent to buyers when they show interest in the company. Standard NDAs for employee matters or customer relationships are usually insufficient to cover an M&A transaction, so regardless of whose NDA is being used, ensure that it is tailored for deals. In some cases, the NDA may even be sent with the teaser in the initial e-mail, along with a comment such as, "If you are interested in the company described in the attached Executive Summary, please sign and return the attached NDA to receive more information."

The seller's attorney may want to review and comment on the completeness of the template NDA, especially if the seller has particular confidentiality concerns. Although M&A advisors may send their template NDA, many buyers will send back their own template NDA or make edits to the original NDA. These situations should be discussed with the seller or his attorney, to ensure the changes are acceptable.

Distribute the Marketing Book   After an NDA has been signed and accepted, the full book can be distributed to the buyer target. In some cases the M&A advisor may want to tailor the book, to specifically address issues important to the buyer. In addition, a separate "book summary" might be sent along with the marketing book, as discussed earlier in the chapter.

M&A advisors may serialize and track the distribution of the marketing books. This will provide evidence that only those who have signed acceptable NDAs have been provided copies of the book. Although today's books are generally sent electronically and digital numbering of the books is still possible, it sometimes may be impossible to track copies and forwarding of the materials. With the use of a data room, book downloads or viewing can be traced and controlled.

Follow Up and Discuss M&A advisors should maintain regular contact with those who have been provided the full marketing book. The goal is to determine which of the buyer targets are interested and capable of making an offer to purchase. In most cases, buyers will want additional information, questions answered, and even an opportunity to visit the company and meet and interview key personnel before an offer is submitted. Depending on the number of interested buyers, balancing the many requests, following up with multiple buyer targets, and coordinating these efforts successfully can be very time consuming. The M&A advisor's role is critical in shielding the seller from this fray and allowing the seller to stay focused on the continuing operations of his business.

Step 5: Negotiating Price and Terms

Marketing the company and negotiating the transaction are linked inextricably. Table 6.1 provides a comparison of marketing approaches, factors, and impacts as they relate to the desired outcome and implied risks. In an M&A transaction, perhaps more important than good hand-to-hand-combat negotiating techniques is following a process that gives the seller an ability to maximize value and the buyers the confidence that they are being treated fairly and that expectations are controlled along the way. In private middle market M&A transactions, value is driven by assuring that the right process is chosen to match the needs and circumstances of the owner coupled with a thoroughly prepared company and team.

Negotiated Sale A negotiated sale is where there is only one buyer in discussions with the seller at a time. The advantage of this process is that it allows the seller to maintain maximum confidentiality. The seller can engage with only one buyer at a time and therefore keep announcement that the company is being sold confidential. The negative side of a negotiated sale is the lack of leverage with the single buyer. The main negotiating point is that the seller maintains an ability to walk away and potentially find another buyer, or retain ownership. Figure 6.1 shows the key steps of a negotiated transaction.

Private Auction A private auction (sometimes called a *limited auction*) is the ideal negotiating process for most private market M&A transactions. A

TABLE 6.1 Marketing Process and Approach Comparison

Characteristic	Negotiation	Private Auction	Public Auction
Best to use when:	There is one "perfect-fit" prospect. Confidentiality is at a premium.	A select group of buyers is identified. This may be consolidators or other synergistic players in the market.	Confidentiality is not important. This may involve troubled or public companies.
Summarized Process:	The parties work out a highly customized deal. Investment value and owner value must be aligned for a deal to work. There may be simultaneous due diligence and contract negotiations.	The buyer group is managed in an auction setting. Buyers receive information at the same time and are herded toward an offer at the same point. This works best if synergy value is quantifiable. Can be one or two steps.	Public announcements are made regarding the sale. The market is completely explored. General offering materials are provided. Buyers are quickly sorted. Can be one or two steps.
Seller Perspective:	Seller controls the process. Information is tailored to the buyer's needs while maintaining strict confidentiality.	Seller still maintains control of the process but there is some risk of a confidentiality break. The final result of the process may or may not yield the highest market price available in the broader market.	An intermediary directs traffic. The seller oversees the process and should believe that the highest market price has been achieved.
Buyer Perspective:	Offer may preempt discussions with other prospects. Normally the buyer can learn enough about the subject to measure cash flow and risk.	Buyers believe they have one shot to perform or the competition may prevail in the acquisition.	Buyers believe the business will be sold, usually in a short period of time. The seller may dictate terms and conditions of the sale.

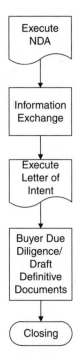

FIGURE 6.1 Negotiated Transaction

limited auction is created when a small group of buyers compete with the knowledge that others are also interested. Unlike a traditional auction, there is a limited group of buyers who know of the deal and can have assurance that the deal is not being shopped and disclosed industry-wide. It allows for the benefit of competition while keeping the process relatively quiet within a small group of suitors. There are some challenges faced by an M&A advisor in this situation.

The M&A advisor must attempt to identify and bring offers from a variety of different targeted buyers at nearly the same time. This is especially a challenge when the reaction times of buyers can differ greatly. In general, private equity groups react and bring offers quicker than strategic corporate buyers, who may be waiting for the proper operating conditions or seasonality, or who have a longer decision process. For these reasons, experienced M&A advisors learn to approach slower groups first and purposely delay the solicitation of an offer from quicker groups. Some M&A advisors set offer deadlines to encourage bidders to bring an offer by a specified date. There needs to be a realistic timeline to bring multiple offers to the seller within a tight window of opportunity for the process to work.

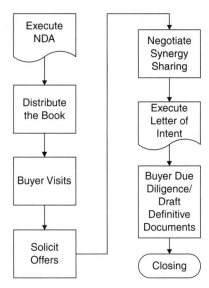

FIGURE 6.2 Private Auction

Because most offers are solicited under the terms of mutual nondisclosure, the names and exact terms being offered should not be disclosed to other buyers. However, the limited auction is successful only when buyers know there are other offers and other bidders involved. Therefore, the M&A advisor must delicately negotiate with buyers to inform them that other bidders exist, and to encourage better price and terms, without disclosing who the others are or the exact terms of their offers.

Figure 6.2 shows the key steps of a private or limited auction.

Public Auction Although most private market transactions attempt to use the limited auction as their process for driving value, there are certain situations where a public auction (sometimes referred to as a *formal* or *broad auction*) is used to solicit offers. In a broad auction the seller uses stages and deadlines to manage a large group of potential buyers. Generally all diligence materials are made available to the buyers via an electronic data room in advance of receiving offers. In addition, parameters for the terms of the offers are generally limited to a few variables (price, escrow amounts, etc.). The buyers are given a deadline to submit offers, which are then generally binding on both buyer and seller at the conclusion of the auction. Broad auctions are not very common but can be quite useful in certain situations, such as the sale of specific intellectual property (patents, software licenses, etc.). Among the downsides of this type of auction are the negatives of putting a "For Sale" sign on the company and the open awareness and flow of information within the industry and community. No matter how tightly nondisclosures are managed, in a broad auction, seller information tends to leak. Accordingly, it takes a company that has significant market opportunity and very strong buyer demand to enable a formal or broad auction to work.

Step 6: Structuring the Transaction

The negotiation of an M&A transaction is never as black and white as merely maximizing price. There are many other terms and structural differences that need to be compared, all of which collectively make up the total value of the transaction to the seller. In addition to price, the following elements should be considered to evaluate the total value (and risk) of the deal to the seller:

- Asset versus stock structure
- Tax deferral structures
- Nonstandard representations and warranties
- Deferred payment terms (holdbacks, escrows, deferred payments)
- Buyer's financing issues
- Alternative purchase price consideration
- Earnouts

Asset versus Stock Structure   The most fundamental question when beginning the structure of a business purchase is whether the deal will be structured as an asset or stock sale. The same price can have drastically different tax and legal impacts on the seller under each structure. Therefore, this primary issue should be addressed up front in any offer. Without addressing the specific tax or legal issues to be discussed in other chapters (particularly Chapters 11 and 12), here are the general "business" advantages and disadvantages comparing the two:

Primary Motivations for Stock Transactions
- Seller's tax motivation—single taxation and capital gains.
- Buyer is allowed assumption of seller's contracts, rights, and so on, without assignment.

Primary Motivations for Asset Transactions
- Buyer avoids unintended liability transfer.
- Buyer receives step-up basis in assets to tax depreciation advantage.

Other Tax Deferral Techniques In addition to the decision to structure as an asset versus a stock transaction, there are other structural alternatives that may save or defer taxes for the seller. If some of these tax-saving structures can be identified in advance at the offer stage, they may represent additional value in the offer. These are some tax-motivated structuring methods that could be identified in an offer:

- Section 1031 (like-kind) exchanges
- Statutory mergers
- Favorable allocation of purchase price
- Installment sale treatment

Nonstandard Representations and Warranties Although most offers include a provision that merely references "Standard Representations, Warranties, and Indemnifications," some offers specify certain elements that are known for being contentious. One such example is to identify the time and dollar caps that will be used in the seller's indemnification. This may help a seller evaluate one buyer's offer over another, if these commonly debated issues are agreed on well in advance of the closing documentation being drafted. This topic is discussed further in Chapter 11.

Deferred Payment Terms Most M&A transactions include some kind of deferred payment, such as escrowed funds or holdback of the purchase price. These deferred payments are generally subject to continued risk of forfeiture by the seller under certain conditions (e.g., breach of representations and warranties). These deferral terms can cause two problems for sellers. First, there is continued risk that the funds will not be paid at all or the buyer will attempt to withhold payment as leverage to get additional value, whether legitimately or not. Second, the seller may have cash demands at closing that cannot be met if the holdbacks or escrows are too large, such as paying off debt. Therefore, the terms of these deferred payments should be made known as part of any offer.

Buyer's Financing An offer should be evaluated to determine the buyer's ability to perform at closing, including the buyer's ability to obtain the necessary financing to pay the purchase price. All too often, buyers are selected based on their offer of the best price and/or terms, only to find they are unable to raise the capital necessary to close the transaction. Therefore, the buyer's financing contingencies should be determined and weighed as part of the overall offer value.

Alternative Consideration Many M&A transactions are paid in cash. However, if other consideration is being proposed, that, too, must be weighed when considering the overall value of an offer. A common non-cash consideration is the *seller note*. Seller notes should be accompanied by the proposed terms and collateral position. In most cases, seller notes are subordinate to other lenders providing capital to the transaction; arguably many are unsecured, making them relatively risky, for which the interest rate and repayment terms rarely compensate adequately. Common forms of purchase price consideration are:

- Cash
- Escrowed funds
- Debt (seller note)
- Stock of the buyer
- Other assets
- Consulting and employment contracts
- Royalty and license agreements
- Earnouts

Earnouts Earnouts are generally defined as contingent deferred payment terms used to bolster value in a transaction and ensure that the seller works to make the acquisition successful for the buyer. Earnouts are frequently used to bridge value gaps between buyer and seller when a particular asset or company operation has yet to demonstrate value to a buyer's satisfaction, yet the seller remains confident that such value will materialize.

Here is an example where an earnout might be proposed: A new product line is launched just before closing, yet it has not produced any profits. The seller has invested time and money in developing the new product and desires to realize a return. However, the buyer is not confident in the level of profitability or market acceptance of the new product line and is reluctant to consider paying anything.

In this situation, perhaps an earnout could be structured where the buyer will pay the seller 50 percent of the gross profit from the new product line for two years following closing. The seller might be happy with this, as she is confident that the new product will produce nice gross margins. And, the buyer is comfortable because she pays only if the value of the new product line materializes.

Earnouts can be structured with a variety of provisions as to the metrics by which they are calculated. When structuring an earnout, these basic issues should be addressed:

- What the earnout is based on: whose financial performance (the old company's, the new company's, or the combined company's), which nonrevenue measures, and so on
- Which financial measure is appropriate (revenue, gross profit, net income, etc.)
- The duration of the earnout
- How the earnout is measured: GAAP, modified GAAP, with or without bad debts, and so on
- Ability of seller to impact and manipulate earnout metrics
- How the earnout dispute (if any) will be resolved

In general, the higher the metric is in the hierarchy of the income statement, the better the measure for the seller. For example, it tends to be cleaner to measure revenue or gross profit than net income or EBITDA, both of which are subject to manipulation by the buyer.

There may also be alternative earnout approaches based on the specifics of the actual deal. These might include structuring an earnout based on:

- Retention of key customer volume
- Level of gross margin
- Retention of key employees
- Increases in overall revenue
- Reduction in specific customer concentration
- Maintenance of service levels

Step 7: Receiving Letters of Intent or Term Sheets

When offers are obtained from buyer targets, they are usually given to the seller in the form of a term sheet, letter of interest, or letter of intent. Each of these expressions of interest contains different levels of detail and is used in different situations.

Term Sheets   Term sheets are often used in capital-raising projects, such as angel investments, venture capital, or bank credit facilities. Occasionally, a term sheet will be used to express interest and basic terms between a buyer and seller in a full acquisition transaction. Although a term sheet can be useful for negotiating basic elements of the deal, such as price or payment terms, they are generally structured in a bullet-point format and often lack major components of the deal that might be critical in making a decision to accept the offer.

Letters of Interest   Sometimes buyers will want to perform more due diligence or conduct meetings with the company's management in advance of preparing a full letter of intent. At the same time, the seller may be reluctant to invest time meeting with buyers without knowing they are serious and are at least reasonably close with regard to their assessment of value. In these situations, the buyer may draft a letter of interest to the seller to show this interest and set expectations for future discussions.

Letters of Intent   A complete letter of intent (LOI) is used to establish a written framework for the transaction to establish a mutual understanding of the deal points between the buyer and seller. Buyers will generally draft the initial letter of intent, although it is not uncommon for various redlined versions to be passed back and forth as part of the negotiation process. When completed and agreed on, a good letter of intent will provide a road map and highlight the major elements of the deal to be documented in a definitive agreement. One philosophy in drafting the LOI is to negotiate as many of the key deal points as possible. This takes additional time, but keeps from locking up the company with exclusivity and ensures that both parties are aligned before embarking on due diligence. The alternative is to negotiate a rather broad or loose LOI that leaves some of the terms of the deal undefined, to be negotiated when the definitive documents are drafted. The risk is that the company will have invested time and money in due diligence and likely will have become emotionally tied to the deal, thus having less leverage to get what it wants. It is a balance to achieve the right level of detail in the letter of intent while maintaining momentum in the deal and keeping all parties focused. In general, the deal terms do not get better nor does price go up for the seller after signing the LOI.

Most LOIs will include both binding and nonbinding provisions. The major deal terms will generally be expressed in the nonbinding sections with issues such as confidentiality and exclusivity as the most common binding provisions.

Typical Nonbinding Provisions of an LOI
- Nature of the deal (stock versus asset deal)
- Price and terms (type and timing of consideration)
- Other significant requests in the deal (employment agreements, non-competes, closing time and place, etc.)
- Definition of the working capital position and how it is to be calculated
- Clear understanding of what will happen with key employees
- Definition of the CEO's role postclosing

- Key dates or timelines for the deal to progress (when financial and legal due diligence will be completed, when a first draft of the purchase agreement will be provided, etc.)
- Basic understanding of the representations, warranties, and indemnity caps

Typical Binding Provisions of an LOI

- Exclusivity (no-shop provision)
- Confidentiality
- Due diligence expectations
- Deposits (and whether they are refundable)
- Breakup fees (very rare)
- Expenses (both buyer and seller are responsible for themselves)

Because letters of intent have both binding and nonbinding provisions, they can create contentious situations between the buyer and seller. The most common cause for friction in a letter of intent is generally the exclusivity granted to the buyer. It is reasonable for buyers to want to lock up the seller for a period of time so they have assurance that the seller will not continue to shop for better offers while they are legitimately completing their due diligence and investing in the process. However, sellers need to be cautious to avoid lengthy lockup periods that might allow the buyer to leverage the price down unfairly and keep the seller off the market. To avoid this situation, sellers may want to insert language in the exclusivity section of the letter of intent that allows them to terminate the buyer's exclusivity, should the buyer propose a significant change in price or terms.

Step 8: Due Diligence

Due diligence is an ongoing process that begins as soon as a two parties begin discussing the concept of an acquisition, recapitalization, or sale. But, the formal process of due diligence is generally referred to as the stage of a deal following an accepted offer (or signing the LOI) but prior to closing. During this stage the buyer performs in-depth investigations to confirm the assumptions used prior to making and negotiating the deal.

Due diligence is addressed in more detail in Chapter 16, "Due Diligence, Alignment, and Integration." During the negotiation stage of the selling process the seller attempts to maximize value while during the due diligence phase the seller attempts to preserve value. Responding to a buyer's requests must be done effectively, timely, and strategically to make sure that value is best preserved. Here are some tips for sellers to keep in mind:

- *Maintain a data room.* Buyers generally submit a lengthy due diligence request list that outlines numerous documents to be reviewed by the buyer's diligence team, such as contracts, legal documents, tax documents, and so on. Having the documents indexed in the order of the request list provided by the buyer often helps streamline the process. Before electronic document systems were prevalent, these documents were accumulated in binders and placed in a room, referred to as a *data room*, to accommodate visiting buyer diligence teams. Today, most of these documents are saved, indexed, and made available through online-accessible portals that bear the same data-room name as their physical counterparts. Intermediaries and attorneys often provide sophisticated data room tools as a part of their services.
- *Identify and resolve discrepancies.* When accumulating information to support diligence requests, the seller or M&A advisor should compare documents to information previously given or expectations of buyers. If differences exist, then reconciliations can be prepared to save the buyer time and allow easier conclusion of the due diligence process.
- *Respond quickly.* Time is the ultimate deal killer. Therefore, the faster the seller can provide requested information to the buyer and his diligence teams, the sooner issues can be resolved and the buyer can move forward. To keep buyers from stalling deals, the time to start and complete due diligence should be defined in the letter of intent.
- *Create schedules.* Many of the requested items will need to be scheduled in the final definitive agreements. As items are being accumulated and provided to the buyer, they can be indexed and put in a format that converts easily into a schedule. Common items that are required in schedules to the purchase agreement are lists of contracts, assumed liabilities, excluded liabilities, fixed assets, excluded assets, and so on.

Step 9: Definitive Agreements

While due diligence is being completed the definitive agreements will likely be drafted and circulated between the legal teams of the buyer and seller. It is customary for the buyer's legal team to initiate the first draft of the definitive agreements in a traditional sale transaction. However, the final documents will generally have been redlined multiple times and therefore comprise input and language from both sides.

In addition to the definitive asset or stock purchase agreement, there are generally other related documents. Following is a list of various transaction documents that are commonly included in an M&A transaction:

- Purchase agreement
- Disclosure schedules (these usually take longer to complete than any other document)
- Noncompete agreement
- Employment agreement
- Escrow agreement
- Promissory note (seller note)
- Third-party consents (e.g., leases and contract assignments)
- Seller corporate consents
- Buyer corporate consents

Although the attorneys for buyer and seller will generally negotiate many of the finer points in these agreements, the M&A advisor should monitor the disputed issues and help to provide reconciliation, if possible. The M&A advisor doesn't need to be a legal expert to understand and help resolve typically disputed items. Try to keep the business issues between the businesspeople and the legal issues between only the attorneys. The M&A advisor often serves as mediator, and can act as a buffer, particularly during intense negotiations.

In some transactions, the attorneys will claim the provisions they are advocating are typical or standard in similar transactions. To help in compromising or settling differing opinions as to what is standard in these transactions, the M&A advisor might want to reference an annual survey produced by the American Bar Association's (ABA) M&A Practice Section. Each year, the ABA compiles statistical data related to both public and private company M&A transactions. Typical disputed terms are surveyed and the results published. For example, the survey might show that indemnification caps of 50 percent or less of the purchase price were common in 80 percent of transactions surveyed. Attorneys and M&A advisors may find this study helpful in demonstrating that the terms they are seeking are in fact standard or market.

Typical Disputed Provisions

- Employment/consulting terms for sellers
- Escrow size and period
- Postclosing purchase price adjustments
- Survival periods

- Earnouts
- Seller's representations and warranties
- Seller's indemnifications (limitations: time, caps, and baskets)
- Definitions of knowledge and material adverse effects

Step 10: Closing Process

Getting to the closing table is the finish line for many M&A advisors and the seller. Often, final small changes and negotiations are being made right up to the eleventh hour. However, major issues need to be resolved and concluded early, or closing can be delayed, which is never a good thing. Time kills deals! Delayed closings just provide an opportunity for new issues to be identified, for financing to fall through, or for either side to renegotiate some provision that everyone thought was settled. Therefore, keeping the deal on track in the weeks and days leading up to closing should be the M&A advisor's number-one job.

Common Deal Killers

- Price and valuation changes
- Terms and condition changes
- Third-party challenges
- Allocation of risk issues
- Other preclosing mistakes

Price and Valuation Changes   Because the price or valuation is generally a nonbinding provision in the letter of intent, it is subject to last-minute changes until a definitive agreement is signed (typically at the closing table). This is one reason why time kills deals. Over time, either side's expectation of value might change. The seller's perspective of value might begin to increase if performance is improving since the LOI was signed. And, of course, buyers are watching for negative signs right up to the closing date. Again, keeping a deal moving forward and maintaining momentum is the best cure for this deal killer.

Terms and Conditions Changes   Similar to price and valuation, key terms of the deal are also generally nonbinding until closing. In addition, business conditions that are outside the control of either party (such as the economy, lending terms, industry trends, etc.) can affect a transaction at any time leading up to the close. Many transactions scheduled to close in the fall of 2008 were indefinitely delayed due to the meltdown of the financial and lending markets. Again, momentum and speed to closing are the best prevention for this deal killer.

Third-Party Challenges   There are often third parties that hold the keys to a transaction getting completed. These can include: lender approval, governmental approval, lease and contract assignments, union approvals, minority shareholders, and key employee agreements. The key to avoiding these becoming deal killers is advance identification and monitoring of the needed approvals to make sure that they do not wait until the last minute if possible. Third parties generally have nothing substantial to gain or lose and are therefore not as motivated to act as the buyer or seller.

Allocation of Risk   Sellers wish to leave the business with no continued risk. Buyers generally do not want to take on any risk for issues that may have been created before they purchase or take control of the company—therein lies a natural dilemma. Most of the time this deal killer can be prevented if both parties are reasonable and are using experienced legal counsel who have similar definitions of "reasonable and customary" allocation of risk. Hopefully, level heads can prevail to prevent these issues from killing a deal.

Other Preclosing Mistakes   Common issues that cause deals to derail or fail include:

- Being impatient and indecisive
- Telling others at the wrong time (early disclosure to employees, vendors, customers, etc.)
- Leaving loose ends (failing to buy out minority shareholders or settle options or bonuses before closing)
- Failing to own up to problems or issues (leaving them to be uncovered the day before closing)
- Failing to run the business up to the last day (short-timers syndrome)
- Failing to disclose intentions to compete or retain certain assets otherwise considered standard

Postsale Integration   While the closing table may be the finish line for seller, it represents a new starting line for the buyer. Integration can refer to the process of combining the recently acquired company into a buyer's organization or integration of new management styles for a financial buyer. Either way, many transactions fail, not because of bad terms or pricing, but because of failed integration.

Buyers sometimes separate the diligence process from the integration process. This is a mistake, as great ideas, strategies, problems, and planning opportunities are identified during due diligence that could provide a perfect launching pad for the integration process. M&A deal teams should attempt to accumulate notes and ideas that can be passed along to those involved in the integration process.

There are considerations before closing that can improve the odds of successful integration and that can be critical in structuring the earnout language. Integration is discussed in more detail in Chapter 16, "Due Diligence, Alignment, and Integration."

CHAPTER 7

Buy-Side Representation and Process

Chapter 3 provides an overview of corporate development and the buy-side from the perspective of the strategic buyer. While conceptually similar, this chapter looks at the buy-side through the lens of M&A advisors and emphasizes certain details relevant to them. We will use Figure 7.1 as the baseline process for this chapter, keeping in mind that there are many variations. This chapter is meant to augment the content of Chapter 3.

STRATEGY

As introduced earlier in this handbook, an acquisition is ideally the result of choosing the best alternative to accomplish a strategic objective or fill a gap; in reality it can meet a number of goals if approached and executed as part of a long-term growth strategy. The maturity of the strategy of the client company, the stage of the business, and where the M&A advisor enters the process with the client somewhat dictate the scope of the M&A advisor's engagement and what needs to be done.

To be effective in leading a search process, there needs to be a defined set of criteria that can be agreed on by management, the board, and the acquisition team. There are many ways of getting to this set of criteria, keeping in mind that the following are typically part of the planning and preparation:

- Clearly understand the current shareholder objectives.
- Define the future market position of the client company (3-to-5-year horizon).
- Develop a consensus around the current status and position of the client company.

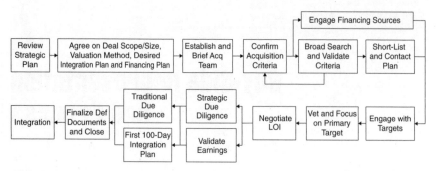

FIGURE 7.1   Buy-Side Process

- Determine the gap or missing capabilities, resources, and so on, to get to the future position.
- Agree on the size of acquisition that is practical.
- Agree on the valuation approach.
- Agree on the desired (ideal) integration method.
- Develop a financing strategy.

If the buy-side assignment is on behalf of a buyout private equity group (PEG), the criteria are likely already established based on the investment thesis (or theme) of the fund. Below are sample investment criteria for a PEG seeking acquisitions in the lower-middle market:

- Niche manufacturers of industrial products or specialty services companies (B2B)
- Revenues: $5 million to $50 million
- EBITDA: $2 million to $8 million
- Companies that are leaders in their industries and have a high regional or national market share
- Diverse and stable customer base (customer concentration <20%)
- Strong management
- Geographical focus within the continental United States

Most of the process in Figure 7.1 will be the same for a PEG search, but there will not likely be a 100-day integration plan.

If the search project is for a PEG and the target is a bolt-on acquisition for an existing portfolio company, the process will be the same as illustrated in Figure 7.1 and discussed in Chapter 3.

ENGAGEMENT AND FEES

Understanding the maturity and status of the client's strategy allows the M&A advisor to scope the engagement and estimate the amount of time and resources required to get to a credible set of criteria—and to some degree determine whether the M&A advisor is willing to assist in developing those criteria or whether others need to be engaged.

The outcome of a buy-side engagement for an M&A advisor is typically less predictable than that of a sell-side engagement. Conceptually, it is difficult to predict whether a client will actually make an investment even when presented with the ideal target. This is unlike a seller who makes a decision to transition from his business, where there is usually a significant emotional commitment that builds as the deal progresses and seems to increase the likelihood of closing as the potential to sell manifests itself. Accordingly, buy-side engagements typically have significant monthly retainers with some form of success fee to be awarded based on achieving the client's objectives. Out-of-pocket expenses are paid as incurred.

The buy-side engagement is fraught with difficulties in getting to a close (and therefore requires a retainer to entice most M&A advisors to help the buyer). This is mostly because the advisor may (or may not) be exclusive to the buyer, if not exclusive to the deal. Whereas the advisor gets paid if anyone buys the target or any deal is done in a sell-side engagement, in a buy-side engagement, there is often a lot of activity, but no deal to show for it at the end of the work. These deals tend to die near the goal line.

Some M&A advisors, especially those who source platforms for private equity groups, have learned that they can garner co-investment rights in deals. There are a lot of pluses to negotiating for and exercising these co-investment rights. First of all, there are no fees associated with them. Second, it endears the advisor to the client and creates the basis for an ongoing relationship. Third, if the investment works out, it can significantly enhance the advisor's income over time.

THE FILTER

The criteria for the target acquisition can be embedded in a decision matrix that allows the team to test various targets for fit. This decision matrix is sometimes called the *filter* or *screen*. One approach is to begin with a broad filter using market feedback and the vetting of a few actual deals to more clearly define the desired target, and then narrow the criteria and develop a short-list of companies to be approached.

From the M&A advisor's perspective, this two-step method allows him to ensure that the client's expectations are aligned and that there are no missing or underlying assumptions that did not get documented in the first iteration. It helps prevent wasted time for the M&A advisor and can improve responsiveness to the client.

FINANCING

When financing is required, it takes time. Financing sources, both debt and equity, can be approached once a coherent growth strategy can be articulated with a defined filter. The objectives are to:

- Broadly determine the level of interest by the source.
- Validate the financing strategy being contemplated.
- Build a relationship with management of the client and the funding sources seeking an acceptable fit.
- Develop a short-list of potential funding sources that will be accessible and support the acquisition process, providing feedback into the vetting of targets.

Combined, these actions allow the client and the funding sources to filter in (or out) what works for them and to buy into the eventual transaction being shaped by those who are likely to be the check-writers, and align expectations along the way.

In some instances, it will be necessary to obtain a *soft commitment letter* (or *comfort letter*) before signing the letter of intent (LOI) to provide the seller with evidence that financing is available for funding the acquisition. Obtaining a commitment letter in short order is practical only if the funding source has been part of the process long enough to be comfortable with the acquirer's management, strategy, and plans; thus this is another reason to engage the lenders and investors as early in the process as is practical.

Chapter 15 provides information on financing strategies and how to fund an acquisition.

QUALITY OF EARNINGS

Audited financial statements primarily focus on the balance sheet to ensure that the beginning balances and the ending balances of all the assets and liabilities are materially correct. This is not to imply that there is not scrutiny of the income statement by the target's auditors, but that is generally at a much higher level than is needed to adequately understand a target's business model. In most cases, there can be period-to-period changes in earnings and other fluctuations that are not revealed by an audit and may be of significance to a deal. Business valuations and some transaction financing are predicated on a certain level of available cash flow based on the core earnings of the underlying business. Although a review of audit working papers is often a part of a quality-of-earnings assessment, it is only used as a starting point for further, more forward-looking analysis.

A quality-of-earnings assessment is conducted to fully understand the historical revenues, cash flow, and earnings. Although one benefit of such an assessment includes the clarification of any accounting anomalies, a thorough assessment should result in a number of other benefits, including the following:

- Identification of concentrations of risk, including reliance on large customers, sole-source vendors, or key employees
- Quantification of the effect of trends in product pricing, volume, and sales mix on the target company's revenues and gross margins
- Analysis of the working capital needs of the business to better understand operating cash flows
- Identification of unusual and nonrecurring items of income and expense that need to be removed to assess the underlying cash flows of the target going forward
- Comparison of accounting policies used by the target with those of the acquirer to better understand the effect of the acquisition

Even though a quality-of-earnings assessment focuses on the historical performance of the target, its true purpose is to gain insight into the target's future operating results and cash flows. This is seldom the focus of an audit, except when there is an indication that the target will not be able to continue as a going concern.

One strategy to manage the professional fees associated with an acquisition is to have a quality-of-earnings assessment done quickly after signing the LOI, providing insight into what can be a deal-breaker if the expected trailing 12-months EBITDA is materially different from what was presented by the target, or if the risks associated with repeating and growing those earnings are much higher than those assumed when the LOI was signed.

From the perspective of the M&A advisor, eliminating potential deal-breakers quickly can help keep the pipeline full with other targets and increase the likelihood of achieving the client's objectives and timelines.

Chapter 16 has additional discussion about the quality of earnings and due diligence.

COORDINATION

As in the sell-side process, the M&A advisor in the buy-side process needs to manage the process, manage the timelines, coordinate activities, and assure that momentum is built and sustained. This is particularly true after the LOI is signed and where the activities are clearly in the hands of other team members and third parties.

INTEGRATION

For acquirers, closing the transaction is only the beginning of the next chapter in the life of their business. For some M&A advisors, the closing will be the end of their involvement. For others, their involvement may continue by supporting the client during integration and/or seeking the next target or investing in the target company.

Best practices show that integration planning needs to begin early in the acquisition process, even before due diligence. As indicated in Figure 7.1, it is valuable, and increases the likelihood of success, to have discussed integration and the potential impact of a deal at the outset of the initiative and to establish a framework from which to act as the acquisition process unfolds. The key is to continually align the decisions, actions, communications, and incentives with the long-term strategy and objectives, keeping everyone in the process on the same page, eliminating surprises, and setting realistic expectations.

CHAPTER 8

Mergers

For purposes of this chapter, a merger is a transaction in which two entities come together to form a combined entity that will continue as one and have combined ownership. It is often thought of when two equal-sized businesses join to create a combined business. This is unlike a sale or acquisition, in which one party will in essence take control of the other party, which may or may not continue on afterward. As a practical matter, a merger as we describe it in this chapter does not necessarily need to be structured as such for legal or tax purposes. (Chapter 13 discusses the mechanics of a legal merger.) In fact, many so-called mergers are technically structured similarly to acquisitions. The concept of a merger as we describe it here is meant to include any transaction in which the management and owners of both companies agree to join arms and combine their businesses. Another distinguishing factor of the merger for the private middle market is that the entities' owners are rarely cashed out; rather, all owners end up with common ownership in the remaining business.

Figure 8.1 provides a rough outline of the process of a merger and sets the stage for the rest of the chapter.

INITIAL ANALYSIS OF BOTH ENTITIES

Initial analysis of both entities is the first stage of any merger. It is important to start by understanding the different structures and the goals of each party, and to begin to identify any deal hurdles, such as:

- What are the current growth and operating strategies of both companies?
- How are both companies structured for legal and tax purposes?
- How are employees and, in particular, executives compensated?
- What types of third-party contracts and joint ventures are present?

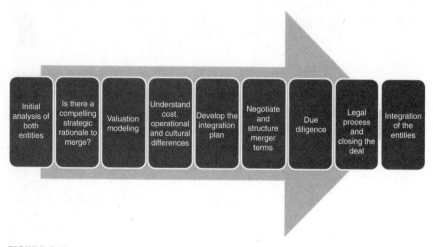

FIGURE 8.1 Merger Process

- What is the mix of products and services offered?
- How do the current buy-sell and retirement agreements work?
- What types of marketing or business development are conducted?
- What are the operational processes of each service offered?

This initial investigation process will set the stage for a proper evaluation of merger structure, valuation, deal terms, and postclosing integration, which become the next steps. In addition to these facts it is also important to ask questions that help each party better understand the cultural and administrative characteristics of the other. Generally, this initial analysis commences after the signing of a mutual nondisclosure agreement (NDA) allowing each entity to review the documents and information of the other entity.

STRATEGIC RATIONALE

Management needs to identify and document the investment thesis or compelling argument for why the two businesses are better off together than apart. It is likely that the parties have had numerous meetings and can answer this question qualitatively by the time discussions have progressed to the point of signing an NDA. It is advisable for the deal teams to document the strategic rationale for the merger (or at least the initial thinking) and what the expected benefits are as a benchmark to use throughout the merger process.

VALUATION MODELING

Valuation is a subjective topic in any acquisition or sale. However, in non-merger transactions, valuation is generally a negotiated process where the market can set the value. Both parties have direct monetary motivations to negotiate a fair value (i.e., the seller wants to maximize the value while the buyer wants to minimize the value). In contrast, a merger transaction has no buyer or seller. There is likely not a liquidity event for either party; thus the negotiation of value creates a different dynamic. Rather than allowing the market to establish the value, the parties in a merger must rely on more theoretical valuation methods.

There are numerous methods of calculating values for any company; however, when discussing value for a merger it is more important to identify the relative value (i.e., the value of the companies relative to each other) as this relative value is what determines the ownership of the combined entity. Therefore, the valuation method and process become more important than the actual dollar amounts. The first step in this process is generating a comprehensive financial model that compares the financial performance of both entities and then models the combined results. Producing this comprehensive financial model accomplishes the following goals:

- It clearly spells out the *value proposition* for each entity (i.e., WIIFM—"What's In It for Me?").
- It calculates and balances *relative value*—the value of each entity relative to the combined total.
- It sets the stage for structural considerations in defining the actual deal terms (highlighted later).
- It becomes a platform to build an operating forecast and budget that can be used to measure, manage, and capture the anticipated merger benefits.

UNDERSTAND COST, OPERATIONAL, AND CULTURAL DIFFERENCES

Inevitably, many aspects of cost structure, operations, and culture will be different in each entity. The combined entity will need to have a uniform and mutually accepted structure that addresses these differences. This is where the initial idea of a merger can potentially fall apart as both parties will need to start showing each other their inner workings and come to agreement on a common way forward. The extent of the differences will significantly affect the likelihood of success in the merger. In order to understand the differences and design a plan going forward, the following tasks need to be performed:

- Review each entity's operations to determine whether there are any overlaps in services offered to customers and whether these overlaps can be combined, or whether there are particular operations that need to be terminated and specific ones to be adopted throughout the combined operation. Also, consider whether there are gaps in services that need to be addressed after the merger.

- Undertake a detailed review of each entity's profit and loss accounts to determine where their costs are derived and highlight the differences in costs on a line-item basis. For example, what are their respective property costs and how does this relate to their useable space? What terms remain on any lease agreements? What would be the ideal property use going forward?

- Review compensation levels and agreements, especially commission plans, to determine the gaps in employee cost structures between the entities. This is especially critical as it will play a significant role in the ongoing culture and employee buy-in on the merger. It will also determine whether there are likely to be significant cost increases as part of the merger; this is a very difficult expense to reduce without eliminating positions. Rarely can either be done without damaging morale.

- Evaluate compensation, benefits, and operating authorities and roles for each set of owners, separate from employee compensation discussed above. This is a critical step found only in merger transactions, as both sets of owners will likely continue working together and managing the new combined company. However, both sets of owners are also accustomed to being 100 percent in control of their company, so the need to work together on a going forward basis represents quite a change. This is a unique cultural challenge found only in private company mergers.

- Address any other cultural differences. Again, the cultural evaluation is more important in a merger than in a true acquisition. In a true acquisition the acquired party is expected to integrate, while the acquiring party is generally allowed to continue its culture. In a merger, both parties expect to keep parts of their culture, which can create greater integration challenges. This cultural assessment is a qualitative, rather than a quantitative, exercise. Many mergers fail because the cultural differences have not been addressed sufficiently prior to the transaction.

DEVELOP THE INTEGRATION PLAN

This may sound like putting the horse before the cart, but starting with the end in mind is a very effective technique for creating alignment and providing for a filter or benchmark in making key decisions. Lead the teams to develop a straw man (or initial draft) of an integration plan based on the long-term strategy of the combined entities supported by the analysis done earlier. As management continues to move through the process, the deal structure, financial decisions, and operational tradeoffs can be tested against what is required to enable the company to be successful post-transaction.

DEAL STRUCTURE AND NEGOTIATIONS

There are multiple ways to structure a merger. Although hard to balance, an ideal structure is mutually beneficial to both parties, tax efficient, administratively feasible to operate, and as legally simple as possible.

In addition to deal structure, there will be many other related issues that need to be resolved or negotiated as a part of the transaction. Each of these will need to be driven to conclusion, seeking solutions or compromises to ensure the deal does not get derailed because of immaterial ancillary issues. In order to solve problems it will be important to offer unique structural solutions by combining the following and leveraging the work done earlier in the process:

- *Updating the strategic rationale and creating an initial merger plan* that documents the key reasons for the merger. Include the integration plan generated in the prior step. This can provide clarity in the face of disagreement between the parties by ensuring the path chosen best meets the overall merger objectives.
- *Creation of and reliance on the comprehensive financial model* to support decision making. This allows for a relative-value approach, which helps prevent unnecessary arguments over valuation.
- *Understanding and documenting the tax considerations for both parties,* which will ensure there are no surprises in the after-tax results.
- *Working closely with the attorneys drafting the documents* to ensure the documentation reflects the intent of the parties entering into the transaction.

The IRS defines a variety of merger transaction structures relevant to corporations in Internal Revenue Code Section 368 and related regulations, which are covered in more detail in Chapter 13, "Tax Provisions used in M&A"; other tax law provisions apply to transactions involving limited liability companies or other noncorporate entities. However, as discussed, the legal structure of a "merger" for privately held companies does not define the concept when we are discussing the combining of two businesses into a single whole, to be owned and operated by both parties to the transaction. Rather, there are numerous tax and legal methods to accomplish this "merger" concept. Here are a few combination structures that can be utilized, depending on the parties' existing structures and circumstances:

- *Statutory merger:* Best used with two corporations, when stock in one company is exchanged for stock in the other. (See "Type A Mergers" in Chapter 13.)
- *Asset merger:* Also used with two corporations, when stock in one company is exchanged for the assets of the other. (See "Type C Mergers" in Chapter 13.)
- *Contribution agreement:* Two companies form a new corporation by contributing their assets in exchange for stock in the new company. (See "Contributions to Corporations" in Chapter 13.)
- *LLC joint venture:* Two companies form a new limited liability company (LLC)/partnership by contributing their assets in exchange for partnership interest in the new LLC.

DUE DILIGENCE

Due diligence is really a continuous process that begins with the initial interviews and discussions between companies. Therefore, it is important to gather information along the way that will later become part of the formal due diligence process. Details of due diligence are more fully discussed in Chapter 16.

Due diligence for a merger transaction requires the concept of mutual diligence. It becomes equally important for both parties to become familiar and comfortable with each other. Although one entity will likely be eliminated during the process, any legacy legal issues will most likely impact the combined entity after the merger. Therefore, many of the technical due diligence steps that generally are performed only on the target in a traditional acquisition should be performed on both parties in a merger (i.e., historical tax compliance, pending lawsuits, human resource exposure, and environmental issues).

The due diligence phase is also the chance to ensure that all changes that are expected to be implemented can be and that the differences between entities are identified. It is also critical to confirm that all the assumptions used in the financial modeling are accurate.

LEGAL PROCESS AND CLOSING

Once a deal has been appropriately investigated, structured, and scrutinized it is important to bring the deal to a close as quickly as possible to limit the exposure and damage that can occur when a deal stalls (e.g., employee doubts, loss of focus, the "legal meter," etc.). It is not possible to list all the issues that might arise throughout the process up to and through closing. One question that must be addressed is whether the merger requires any notifications to, or approvals by, any regulatory body or governmental agency. The M&A advisor can help things run smoothly by preparing documents in appropriate formats, managing the data-gathering process, and anticipating problems before they grow out of control. Here are specific steps to help control the process:

- Provide a central driving force to keep all parties on track through the closing process.
- Work with the attorneys to deal with closing issues as they arise and elevate issues to the client level only as needed.
- Ensure all closing documents are in line with the deal structure and intent.
- Ensure all documentation is in line with tax planning efforts that will occur after closing.
- Assist with all necessary schedules and third-party approvals required prior to closing.
- As with the deal negotiation and structuring, maintain the role of buffer to limit the impact of any closing issues on the clients' working relationship with one another.

In addition to the documents necessary to effect the transaction itself, the parties may need to consider additional documentation related to the ongoing operation of the newly merged company. These might include:

- Revised shareholder/partnership agreements
- New executive compensation agreements
- Consolidated retirement plans
- New incentive stock option plans

POSTCLOSING INTEGRATION

Closing a merger transaction is never the end—it's the beginning. Statistics show that mergers and acquisitions that are considered to be unsuccessful are generally such because of poor integration following the transaction. The best way to ensure a successful transaction is to capture the ideas and benefits that are identified during the initial discussions, modeling, negotiations, structuring, and diligence stages of a deal and put those ideas to work after the close.

Creating "living" models and structures to provide a road map to measure, manage, and capture the anticipated merger benefits should assist you through the postclosing integration:

- The *valuation model* can become an ongoing financial forecasting tool that can be used to compare operations against forecasted results going forward.
- *Buy-sell provisions* for all the owners should reduce the likelihood of disputes in the future.
- Detailed *operating efficiencies* and best practices from both organizations, highlighted during the due diligence stage, can be used as key performance indicators and measurements going forward.

Chapter 16, "Due Diligence, Alignment, and Integration," provides some additional insights and direction regarding postclosing activities.

CHAPTER 9

Professional Standards and Ethics

The mergers and acquisitions (M&A) marketplace is somewhat chaotic, highly fragmented, and often fails to capture any substantial efficiency in scale, particularly in the lower end of the middle market with private companies valued at less than $150 million.

Without significant regard for the very special personal financial planning needs of the business owner, this market is now served by numerous advisors and intermediaries ranging broadly from accountants and management consultants to investment bankers to small business brokers. Unfortunately, some of these current market participants are less than fully qualified or reputable. Investment bankers tend to concentrate on the larger deals only and may take on a middle market business client only as an accommodation or fill-in activity. For reasons of economics, they primarily focus on servicing publicly traded companies and financing engagements, rather than the full-service corporate financial advisory needs of small to midsized private business clients. Because of these current market realities, many business owners often lack a knowledgeable and trustworthy M&A advisor.

America's private, family-owned businesses represent a market sector ideally suited to the services of the M&A advisor. The greatest part of America's wealth lies with these private, family-owned businesses. Currently, 7 million of the 29 million business establishments in the United States have one or more employees.[1] The larger companies in this sector, having 50 or more employees, are the primary "middle market" target segment established by the Alliance of M&A Advisors for this handbook.

The highly fragmented marketplace for middle market corporate financial advisory services offers a very opportunistic scenario for growth and profitability. With a growing number of small businesses, revolutionary technology, and a rapidly changing professional environment, this specific marketplace is now in the midst of an extraordinary transformation.

- With the significant increase in the sheer number of private businesses in the 1980s and 1990s, the middle market has become enormous but remains highly fragmented and very disorganized. Hence there exists a substantial need for adequate professional training and meaningful standards of ethical and professional conduct. A large part of America's wealth lies with family-owned businesses. Family firms comprise over 90 percent of all business enterprises in North America.
- Businesses account for 62 percent of the U.S. workforce, 64 percent of the nation's employment, and 50 percent of the gross domestic product (GDP), and are responsible for 78 percent of all new job creation.[2] Additionally, family businesses create an estimated 70 to 90 percent of the total global GDP annually.[3]
- Post–World War II entrepreneurs, having built this great wealth, are at the age when they must decide the manner in which to transfer accumulated wealth secured primarily in the value of their family businesses. In the next five years, 39 percent of family-owned firms will experience a change in leadership due to retirement or semiretirement. According to a recent national survey, 25 percent of senior-generation family business shareholders have not completed any estate planning other than writing a will; 81 percent want the business to stay in the family; and 20 percent are not confident of the next generation's commitment to their business.

The cumulative effect of this landmark "succession event" will be the largest intergenerational transfer of wealth in U.S. history. Cornell economist Robert Avery estimates that approximately $10.4 trillion of net worth will be transferred by the year 2040, with $4.8 trillion being transferred in the next 20 years.[4]

ROLE OF THE M&A ADVISOR IN THE ECONOMY

M&A advisors provide essential liquidity to small and private businesses. Large businesses have the option of going public to seek growth capital and get liquidity to their entrepreneurial efforts. However, access to public market capital and liquidity options is not available to small and midsize companies. Also, entrepreneurs are by nature creative and free-spirited. Not all are motivated to go public or want to face the scrutiny of external oversight. They rely on the services of intermediaries for capital access and liquidity. The M&A advisor facilitates that liquidity by creating a marketplace exchange process.

Business brokers and M&A intermediaries, two subgroups of the overall M&A advisor group, have been functioning for 50 to 100 years, but the profession has become organized only over the past few decades. In every economy and in every profession, as the profession gets organized, marketplace efficiency increases. In the M&A profession, this means higher valuations for the entrepreneur, faster growth through efficient capital access, fewer bankruptcies, and more revenues for the government through higher income taxes, gift taxes, and estate taxes.

A WHOLE NEW WAY

Today, most financial advisory professionals focus on just one or two specialized services (e.g., business valuation, legal, accounting, tax, M&A, etc.). Many fail to completely understand the owner's fundamental personal needs or comprehensively evaluate their client's overall business performance and potential. Because the needs of the middle market private business owner and the company are inextricably intertwined, higher-performing M&A advisors focus on the whole and not just the individual parts.

The most highly valued advisors are those who combine the expertise of deep specialty know-how with broad generalist knowledge across many strategically critical and diverse disciplines. They create extraordinary value by synergistically managing the delivery of all of the following types of interrelated business and financial advisory services:

- Business valuation
- Strategic growth planning
- Business performance improvement
- Corporate finance
- Merger and acquisition advising
- Personal financial planning
- Wealth management
- Accounting and tax
- Legal
- Estate planning

The best M&A advisors also build relationships with other professionals to help clients establish investment goals and objectives that are consistent with their risk tolerances, unique circumstances, and needs. While maintaining high ethical standards and adhering to the fiduciary duty due the client, all professionals working with private company owners should use a holistic framework to consider a client's total portfolio, which includes both financial and nonfinancial assets.

THE MIDDLE MARKET STANDARD

The Alliance of Merger & Acquisition Advisors (AM&AA), a Chicago-based international professional trade association, provides information, education, and extensive behind-the-scenes assistance to other qualified business professionals seeking to better position themselves to serve the many transactional advisory needs of small to midsized private business clients—all with the goal of providing greater value to middle market business owners.

To support the needs of the market, the AM&AA established the first industry certification for middle market advisors, called the Certified M&A Advisor (CM&AA), offered in conjunction with leading business schools. It has become the standard credential for those involved in M&A transactions in the middle market, on both the buy side and the sell side.

The CM&AA designation serves to maintain the highest recognized standards of professional excellence for middle market M&A advisors and to provide a benchmark for professional achievement within that overall industry and body of knowledge.

ETHICAL AND PROFESSIONAL STANDARDS

As with other more mature professions such as accounting and legal professional associations, M&A and corporate financial advisory service professionals have an obligation to the public, their profession, the organization they serve, and themselves, to maintain the highest standards of ethical and professional conduct. In recognition of this obligation, the following standards of conduct have been established by the AM&AA as proposed standards of conduct and best practice for this emerging profession. It is the desire of AM&AA that these standards will serve to form the basis for discussion and ultimate adoption for M&A advisory professionals worldwide.

Competence and Professionalism (Reputation)

M&A advisory professionals have a responsibility to:

- Maintain an appropriate level of professional competence by an ongoing commitment to development of their knowledge and skills
- Perform duties in accordance with relevant laws, regulations, and technical standards
- Refrain from either actively or passively subverting the attainment of the organization's legitimate and ethical objectives

- Recognize and communicate professional limitations or other constraints that would impede responsible judgment or successful performance of an activity
- Refrain from engaging in or supporting any activity that would discredit the profession

Best Practices (Activities)

M&A advisory professionals have a responsibility to:

- Communicate information fairly and objectively.
- Prepare complete and clear reports and recommendations after appropriate analyses of relevant and reliable information.
- Provide fair value for fees charged.
- Gain a client's knowledge and consent before holding, receiving, bargaining for, becoming entitled to, or acquiring any fee, remuneration, or benefit from the client.
- Refrain from disclosing confidential information acquired in the course of their work except when authorized, unless legally obligated to do so.
- Inform subordinates as appropriate regarding the confidentiality of information acquired in the course of their work and monitor their activities to assure the maintenance of that confidentiality.
- Refrain from using or appearing to use confidential information acquired in the course of their work for unethical or illegal advantage, either personally or through third parties.
- Not withdraw their services except for good cause and upon such notice as is appropriate for the circumstances. Upon discharge or withdrawal, the professional should transition the matter, including all papers and property to which the client is entitled, to the client or the client's designee, give the client all information that may be required in connection with the matter, and promptly render an account for outstanding fees and disbursements.
- Have a written engagement agreement or contract between the professional and client, covering the nature of the assignment, the subject matter of the assignment, scope of work, and amount or basis for the fees.

Ethics (Behavioral Boundaries)

M&A advisory professionals have a responsibility to:

- Disassociate themselves from any person, letter, report, statement, or representation that they know, or should know, is false or misleading, regardless of whether such letter, report, statement, or representation is subject to a disclaimer of responsibility.

- Refrain from making any oral report, statement, or representation that they know, or should know, is false or misleading.
- Uphold normal professional courtesy in all dealings.
- Take appropriate steps to ensure that they do not accept engagements on behalf of a current client that result or could be perceived to result in a conflict of interest with another current client.
- Disclose to the client any influence, interest, or relationship they have with the other parties that, in respect to the engagement, would reasonably be perceived to affect their professional judgment.
- Refrain from engaging in any activity that would prejudice their ability to carry out their duties ethically.

Country Specific (Customs)

Each country shall exclude any clauses above that are either illegal or considered unethical in their jurisdictions. Further, each country's M&A association shall add specific tenets that are deemed important to their constituents and the profession at large.

M&A Technical Discussions

CHAPTER 10

Financial Analysis

One of the first deep-dive steps in the deal process, whether on the buy side or the sell side, is to understand the real financial performance of the target company. In the public capital markets, companies have audited financial statements, and the reporting of their financial performance and making disclosures about assumptions and risk factors is mandated to comply with Generally Accepted Accounting Principles (GAAP), and, in some cases, International Financial Reporting Standards (IFRS) and certain rules of the Securities and Exchange Commission (SEC). In the private capital markets, this uniform approach of reporting business performance does not exist—or at least not at the level of rigor of the public environment. Private businesses report financial performance in a number of ways dependent on their size, industry, and, once again, the motivations of the owners.

This chapter addresses the practical analysis of private company financial performance as it relates to M&A and financing transactions.

FINANCIAL REPORTING MOTIVATION

One primary difference in understanding financial performance of a privately held company as opposed to that of a public company is the motivation and purpose for maintaining and disseminating financial statements. In a public company the mandate of management is to increase shareholder value, which should be largely impacted by increasing earnings per share and paying dividends. Their financial statements are maintained to report that performance to the public shareholders along with sharing material information to allow for an educated assessment of the risk of ownership (debt or equity).

As mentioned many times in this handbook, the motivations of owners of privately held businesses vary. One of the common motivations tends to be minimizing taxable income while meeting certain cash-flow objectives. As a result, it is common for privately held companies to attempt to defer revenues, mix personal assets and expenses with company assets, and incur expenses that enhance the owner's lifestyle or other ambitions. These motivations make the analysis of private company financials unique and require that they be *normalized*, or adjusted to a common basis for comparison.

In addition to owner motives, there is some flexibility in selection in the conventions used to report the financial performance. For example, some businesses use cash-based tax reporting and use the same approach for financial reporting and decision making. Companies that are required to file accrual-based tax reporting may also keep their financial reporting the same. GAAP financial reporting does not always match accrual-based tax reporting, so the expenses and profits for taxes are not necessarily the same as for calculating operating performance when comparing to an industry or another business. To further complicate the analysis, GAAP for privately held companies does not always match the requirements for SEC reporting.

In general, the concept is to translate the reported financial information (however presented) to GAAP, removing the owner-specific expenses and nuances to allow for analysis and comparison of the financial performance of the business as a stand-alone entity.

EBITDA

Valuation and analysis in middle market M&A often begin by deriving earnings before interest, taxes, depreciation, and amortization (EBITDA). EBITDA is used as a proxy for the cash flow of the business, eliminating the influences of the current capital structure. Adding back interest in the EBITDA calculation is meant to allow evaluation of the earning ability of a debt-free company. Income taxes are generally added back, as taxes are specific to a particular owner's circumstances. Depreciation and amortization are added back in arriving at EBITDA as EBITDA is intended to represent operating cash flow and these are noncash deductions, or merely paper cost allocations of historical expenditures. Although EBITDA by itself is generally used in evaluating the operating profits of companies, there are other adjustments often found in closely held businesses. Both positive and negative adjustments can be further applied to arrive at a normalized EBITDA.

Positive Adjustments (Increase in EBITDA)

- *Excess owner compensation.* In some situations, the owners pay themselves more (or less) than would be considered market for the role or position compared to what it would cost to hire their replacement. For the analysis, their compensation should be adjusted to a market rate.

If their compensation is below market rate, this becomes a negative adjustment.

- *Owner's discretionary expenses.* Most closely held businesses have expenses related to the owner that can be deemed discretionary and that would not likely continue under new ownership. Examples include personal auto expenses, travel and entertainment, employing family members, and so forth.

- *One-time events.* A company may have a one-time or extraordinary event that can be reasonably added back if it is unlikely to occur again. Although there are legitimate one-time expenses that can be added back, this category can also be abused. There is a balance between trying to properly normalize the EBITDA and creating suspicion as to the legitimacy of the entire normalizing process. As a general rule, add-backs in this category should be legitimately defended as truly extraordinary items.

- *Discontinued operations.* If a company has discontinued a division or product line due to operating losses, and the losses created by that division can be fairly measured, then it is acceptable to show this as a normalizing adjustment. However, similar to the one-time events previously noted, this can be a slippery slope if add-backs for discontinued operations are abused. Regular changes in business strategy and failed initiatives are not normally accepted.

Negative Adjustments (Reduction of EBITDA)

- *Capital expenditures.* Capital expenditures (often abbreviated as CapEx) is a term used to represent the average annual capital asset purchases that are needed by the business to maintain operations. Depreciation is initially added back in arriving EBITDA because it is a noncash deduction included in the income statement and does not necessarily match the real CapEx level in a particular period. EBITDA is intended to estimate the cash flow from operations, so the purchase of replacement equipment is accounted for with this adjustment. In some companies, assets have very long lives and depreciation can reasonably be added back without a need for a CapEx reduction. However, in the case of assets that need to be replaced every few years, there is likely a cash-flow impact that is not accounted for if all depreciation is added back in the EBITDA calculation.

  Although CapEx can become a reasonable negative adjustment to EBITDA, care should be taken to subtract only maintenance CapEx and not growth CapEx. Since normalizations are being applied to historical EBITDA, it is only reasonable to provide for capital expenditures necessary to maintain and replace existing assets. It is not generally appropriate to deduct CapEx for planned growth or expansion from historical EBITDA.

- *Income from unrelated assets.* Just as interest expense is added back because EBITDA assumes operations from a debt-free company, normalized EBITDA should deduct income from assets not considered to be a part of normal operations or part of the transaction. An example would be adjusting dividend income from an unrelated investment account that is excess capital being held in the business.
- *Below-market compensation for related parties.* As mentioned earlier, excess compensation paid to owners for tax-motivated reasons can become a normalizing add-back. However, a negative normalization adjustment of owner/executive compensation is made if such is below market rates or less than required to hire their replacements. Also, compensation is adjusted for relatives of the owners who are working in the business in an unpaid capacity.

Figure 10.1 shows a simple income statement for a privately held company. Figure 10.2 illustrates the basic adjustments to obtain EBITDA. Figure 10.3 shows the adjustments to derive normalized EBITDA:

- Owner/officer compensation is excessive—replacement cost is $200,000.
- Owner's discretionary expenses (travel, personal auto, etc.) paid by the company are $25,000.
- Maintenance CapEx is $50,000.
- A factoring loan will remain in place and transfer with the company.

BALANCE SHEET ANALYSIS

In most M&A transactions, valuations are established based on the income and cash flow of the company. However, the character and makeup of the balance sheet need to be assessed when evaluating a company for a transaction. There are important balance sheet considerations that impact value, finance ability, and cash to sellers.

Working Capital

Working capital is generally defined as the current assets less current liabilities of a company. For purposes of an M&A transaction, understanding

Example Income Statement

Sales	$8,000,000
Total Cost of Goods Sold	(3,500,000)
Gross Margin	4,500,000

Expenses:

Advertising	100,000
Officer Compensation	300,000
Administrative Salaries	500,000
Sales Salaries	200,000
Payroll Taxes	100,000
Pension Expense	100,000
Office Expense	220,000
Accounting Expense	100,000
Legal	200,000
Shipping	100,000
Rent	300,000
Interest Expense (LOC)	30,000
Interest Expense (A/R Factor)	50,000
Interest Expense (SH Debt)	100,000
Interest Expense (LT Debt)	100,000
Depreciation Expense	400,000
Amortization Expense	100,000
Total Expenses	3,000,000
Net Income	$1,500,000

FIGURE 10.1 Typical Income Statement

and establishing a "normal" level of working capital is important, as it is generally included in the purchase price.

Defining working capital for an ongoing company is slightly different from determining transactional working capital for purposes of an acquisition. Generally, working capital for an acquisition will include only those

Net Income	$1,500,000
Interest	280,000
Taxes	—
Depreciation	400,000
Amortization	100,000
EBITDA	$2,280,000

FIGURE 10.2 Basic EBITDA Calculation

EBITDA	$2,280,000
Officer Wages	300,000
Replacement Wages	(200,000)
Discretionary Expenses	25,000
AR Factoring Interest	(50,000)
CapEx	(50,000)
Normalized EBITDA	$2,305,000

FIGURE 10.3   Normalized EBITDA Calculation

assets and liabilities that are going to be acquired or assumed as part of the deal. Figure 10.4 is a calculation of transactional working capital from a sample balance sheet. Note that cash and the credit line are not included in the calculation of working capital—this is typical.

Cash is usually not included in the calculation of transactional working capital, nor is the seller's cash balance transferred in the sale. This is the case in most transactions for a few reasons:

- In the case of an asset sale, the seller's cash accounts are generally not included. It does not make sense to inflate the price of the company by paying cash for cash. The buyer usually establishes his or her own bank account and the cash balances are not transferred.

Assets	From the Balance Sheet	For the Working Capital Calculations
Cash	$ 250,000	$ —
Accounts Receivable	1,240,000	1,240,000
Inventory	2,030,000	2,030,000
Prepaid Expenses	175,000	175,000
Total Current Assets	3,695,000	3,445,000
Liabilities		
Accounts Payable	650,000	650,000
Accrued Expenses	550,000	550,000
Line of Credit	1,250,000	
Current Portion of Long-Term Debt	250,000	
Total Current Liabilities	2,700,000	1,200,000
Net Working Capital		**$2,245,000**

FIGURE 10.4   Working Capital Calculation

- Most closely held companies do not have distribution policies outside of those for taxes. Rather, many closely held business owners merely consider their company bank account as an extension of their personal savings or keep excess cash or excess working capital in reserve within their business. Therefore, cash balances maintained by a closely held company are likely arbitrary and don't reflect the actual needs for operating purposes.

Similar to cash balances, lines of credit or other funded portions of working capital are often omitted from the calculation of transactional working capital even though they are considered part of an operating company's working capital from a traditional accounting definition. Buyers will generally establish their own credit facilities or will finance working capital as part of the overall transaction financing.

The Peg or Target   The purpose of evaluating working capital in an M&A transaction is to determine the "normal" level that should be included as part of the deal. One of the issues in determining the appropriate level of working capital is caused by the daily change in the underlying components: receivables, inventory, payables, accrued liabilities, and so on. Buyers typically want to ensure that the amount of working capital included in the company on the closing date is sufficient to maintain the company's operation or is at least at some level that they considered when negotiating the overall transaction. A shortfall in working capital is effectively the same as increasing the cost of the transaction for the buyer.

However, sellers want to minimize the amount of working capital delivered with the company on the closing date, thus increasing their proceeds from the transaction. Prior to a sale, a seller could maximize his or her cash position by aggressively collecting receivables, reducing inventory levels, or pushing off vendor payables, thus short-changing the buyer.

To prevent this type of working capital manipulation (whether intentional or not) and to ensure a normal amount of working capital is transferred in the deal, most M&A transactions will include a provision to *peg* working capital and adjust for differences from the peg shortly after closing. Sometimes this is called a *working capital target*. The working capital peg or target is usually defined as a fixed negotiated amount (sometimes calculated using an average past month's balances). Typically, an estimated working capital balance is determined just before closing and a tentative adjustment is made to the purchase price. Then, actual working capital is calculated as of the closing date 30 to 90 days postclosing when actual financial data is available. The difference between the peg amount and the estimated closing working capital amount is then paid by the buyer to the seller or by the seller to the buyer based on the excess or deficit; this is often referred to as a *true-up*.

Seasonal Working Capital   In seasonal companies, using the past averages to peg working capital might not be appropriate, since seasonal companies can have large swings in inventory, receivables, payables, and so forth based on the time of year. In these situations it might be best to peg working capital based on a historical view of the same date in time over the past few years. For example, a Christmas tree company's working capital would look quite different in November compared to January. Pegged working capital couldn't be based on a 12-month average, since inventory would generally spike for a few months of the year. If closing were to occur on January 31, it might make sense to peg working capital based on the prior three years, at January 31, 20X1, 20X2, 20X3.

Negative Working Capital   Some companies actually carry a negative working capital balance (i.e., current liabilities being assumed actually exceed the current assets). This may be common in companies where there are large amounts of customer deposits or unearned revenues.

There are two schools of thought regarding this situation. Some believe it is acceptable to transfer a company with a negative working capital position and to actually peg working capital below zero. The theory behind this is that the company is a going concern and, as long as normal operations continue, the negative working capital position will never be "paid."

Others support the theory that working capital cannot be pegged below zero and that the business is just undercapitalized. In cases where normal or average working capital is a negative number, they believe it should be pegged at zero, but not below. The theory behind this is that the negative working capital position actually represents obligations to others (customers, vendors, etc.) that are in excess of the assets. At some point those obligations will need to be met or paid and therefore should not be assumed by the buyer.

Of course, which position is taken might depend on whom the advisor is representing. Sellers will generally support the negative working capital target while buyers will push for limiting working capital to zero.

Components of Working Capital   In addition to calculating the average working capital balance to establish a closing peg or target, the elements of working capital should also be evaluated in determining company valuation as well as creating initial diligence concerns.

Accounts Receivable One can learn a lot about a company's operations by analyzing the trends in accounts receivable balances. Reviewing monthly receivable balances could bring to light a number of questions or issues:

- Gradually increasing receivable balances (as a percentage of sales) could mean the company is allowing more lax trade credit policies, that certain customers are experiencing distress, or that the company is recording revenues that are not collectible.
- Deeper analysis of receivables through the review of account aging by customer can help to identify potential bad-debt issues. Perhaps the company has underestimated its bad-debt expense, which would affect historical EBITDA.
- Analysis and review of receivable aging detail can also help to identify customer concentration issues that might not have been disclosed. Large balances from a single customer might highlight a credit risk or concentration issue.

In an M&A transaction, actual collection of accounts receivable is a concern when receivables are included in transactional working capital. A well-structured M&A transaction can take advantage of hindsight by including postclosing measurements. These provisions can require that receivables included on the closing balance sheet but remaining uncollected within 90 to 120 days after closing can be excluded from the final working capital reconciliation.

Inventory For manufacturing and distribution companies, inventory can be the most significant part of working capital. However, unlike other elements of working capital (e.g., accounts receivable), inventory can be much more difficult to value and therefore reconcile as part of transactional working capital. Accounting methods for inventory may not necessarily identify slow-moving, obsolete, or spoiled stock. And, because even good inventory might take a while to turn over, postclosing reconciliations similar to those used in accounts receivable may not be practical. Therefore, inventory is generally evaluated more thoroughly during due diligence and prior to closing. Here are some common observations and tips regarding inventory:

- Watch for slow creeping of inventory values over time relative to sales volume; this might be indicative of accumulations of small parts or partial lots that might technically be valued correctly, but are practically difficult to sell.
- Inventory is generally tracked for accounting purposes at cost. Seek to validate current market prices and identify possible overpriced inventory

in industries where values fluctuate. For example, copper parts inventory purchased when copper prices were higher might now be worth much less.

- Preestablish or agree on valuation formulas for old or slow-moving inventory. Retail or distribution buyers and sellers might agree on discount percentages to apply for certain ages or classes of inventory.

Normalization

In addition to analyzing working capital, other components of the balance sheet should be reviewed in analyzing a company's financials. Many private company transactions are completed as asset transactions rather than stock transactions. In an asset transaction, each item of the balance sheet (assets and liabilities) will need to be identified and explicitly included or excluded. Therefore, it is generally a good idea to create a normalized balance sheet that projects estimated balances immediately after closing.

As discussed earlier, the pegged transactional working capital generally represents the current assets and current liabilities that are included in the normalized balance sheet. The remaining items are fixed assets, debt, and equity.

Fixed Assets Fixed assets are recorded at original cost less accumulated depreciation, which is generally an arbitrary cost recovery. The resulting net book value of assets rarely (if ever) represents fair market value of those assets. Therefore, in situations where fixed assets are a material component in the company's value, the book value generally cannot be relied on as a proxy for postclosing value; separate appraisal of these assets should be done. Of course, in cases where fixed assets are an immaterial part of the company, net book value is often used to estimate the value of these assets.

Sometimes private company owners will have accumulated personal assets within a business. These assets should be identified early in the process and listed as excluded items. As an example, it is not unusual for a transaction to be completed where the company owner assumed his personal vehicle was his to keep, only to find it was titled in the company's name and never listed as an excluded asset.

As mentioned earlier, CapEx requirements should also be evaluated. At a basic level, fixed asset cost increases from year to year can be used to approximate historical CapEx. From there, more complete evaluations of CapEx requirements may need to be done to determine future maintenance CapEx compared with CapEx to support growth and expansion.

Intangible Assets Intangible assets such as goodwill, patents, and capitalized research and development may be present on the balance sheet. The accounting rules that create these assets generally have little to do with their actual value. Rather, valuation of these assets is usually done by estimating the future cash flows that can be created from them. These cash-flow assumptions are likely already part of the overall company value; therefore, intangible assets rarely have separate value apart from the projected future cash-flow value of the business.

Debt In most M&A transactions, the seller's debt is paid in full and replaced with equity or debt of the buyer. In those cases, the buyer generally does not need to evaluate the seller's debt, other than to ensure it is satisfied at closing and any related liens are released. However, in the case where debt of the seller is transferred or assumed in a transaction, there are a few considerations:

- Interest from retained debt should not be included in the EBITDA calculation used for determining the enterprise value, if that enterprise value includes retained debt.
- Debt in privately held companies will usually include a personal guarantee from the owner. If the prior owner is no longer retaining ownership, or if his or her ownership is dramatically reduced, then the appropriateness of those personal guarantees should be evaluated.
- If personal guarantees are being removed from the debt, it will likely change the terms of that debt. Therefore, new debt terms should be considered when normalizing EBITDA.

Equity In addition to the basic common equity of the company, some privately held companies have other classes of stock or special member provisions. Companies often raise capital and issue equity that has debt-like provisions imbedded in their charter. These can include preferred return provisions, liquidity preferences, accrued dividends, ratchet provisions, antidilution provisions, first refusal rights, and so forth. These provisions need to be considered when evaluating the impact on new capital being raised, or during the distribution of selling proceeds.

Private Company Balance Sheets Here are a few specifically unique issues to watch for in evaluating the balance sheet of a privately held company:

- *Arbitrary cash balances.* Most private company owners do not manage cash balances in the same way as public companies. Rarely are there detailed analyses of minimum or maximum thresholds. Cash of a private company can generally be easily distributed and recontributed, especially in the case of a single owner.

- *Excess receivables.* Many small companies report their taxes on a cash basis. To prevent collecting receivables and creating taxable income, they delay billing just before year-end.
- *Personal assets.* Typical business owners will have personal-use vehicles on the balance sheet. Some will accumulate other unrelated assets inside their company, such as personal investment accounts, unrelated real estate properties, or personal equipment such as planes, boats, recreational vehicles, and so on.
- *Guaranteed debt.* In many cases the funded debt of a closely held company will be guaranteed by the owner and may have personal assets pledged as collateral. As a result, the terms of that debt will likely not compare to terms that will exist when those personal guarantees and assets are removed.
- *Shareholder debt/equity.* To manage the risk of their investment, shareholders of privately held companies may show their capital contribution as shareholder debt rather than as equity. In most cases, these debt balances should be viewed as equity for the purpose of analyzing an acquisition.

CHAPTER 11

Deal Structure and Legal Documentation

ATTORNEY'S ROLE

A fundamental principle of legal representation in a merger or acquisition transaction is that an attorney involved in the deal does not represent "the deal," but rather a party participating in the deal, generally the buyer or the seller. The interests of the buyer and the seller are adverse in a merger and acquisition transaction and any legal representation of the deal would result in a conflict of interest. An M&A attorney may not represent more than one party in a deal, specifically in a deal in which the recognized buyer or seller actually consists of multiple parties. In those transactions, a deal attorney may have conflicts of interest among those parties as those parties may have certain interests that are adverse to each other.

A transactional attorney adds value to the deal by identifying and understanding key legal, tax, and business issues early in the transaction in order to avoid surprises as the transaction proceeds. Understanding that no deal is risk free, an M&A attorney identifies the specific risks associated with each deal and attempts to place his or her client in a position such that the risks associated with that particular deal are reasonable given the economic terms of that transaction.

When representing the seller in a transaction, the attorney's role may vary based on the experience level of his or her client. For example, if the attorney is representing a first-time seller, the attorney's role may include preparing the client for the deal process, which is a role likely to be unnecessary with a more experienced client. Depending on the sophistication of other advisors in the deal, such as intermediaries and other M&A advisors, a deal attorney may assist the seller in certain up-front tasks that go beyond negotiation and documentation of the transaction, such as preparing the due diligence room (online or otherwise). In all transactions, a deal attorney prepares and/or reviews and negotiates the acquisition agreements and other transaction documents, and is commonly asked to review documents involved earlier in the negotiations, such as the confidentiality agreement(s), term sheet, or letter of intent. It is common practice for the buyer's attorney to prepare most of the acquisition documents in a transaction; accordingly, the seller's attorney generally reviews and then revises the acquisition documents proposed by the buyer's attorney. Ultimately, the goal of the seller's attorney is to allocate as much risk in the transactions as possible to the buyer by narrowing and qualifying representations and warranties and limiting indemnification. In all transactions, the goal of an experienced M&A attorney representing a seller is to be a valuable resource in finding solutions to issues that need to be resolved in order to close.

Representing the buyer in transactions generally presents similar concerns for a deal attorney as representing the seller. However, in representing the buyer, the attorney will usually play a significant role in the due diligence process. Like the seller's attorney, the buyer's attorney might participate in the review and negotiation of the confidentiality agreements, term sheet, or letter of intent. But, the buyer's attorney is customarily the first to draft the primary acquisition agreement, and other related documents, such as any promissory note, noncompete agreement, and so on. Ultimately, the buyer's attorney seeks to allocate as much risk to the seller as possible by broadening representations and warranties and expanding indemnification. As in representing the seller, an experienced deal attorney will be a valued partner

TABLE 11.1 Role of the Attorney

Role as Seller's Attorney	Role as Buyer's Attorney
Prepare client for the deal process	Prepare client for the deal process
Counsel client on deal points	Counsel client on deal points
Assist in preparing the due diligence data room and due diligence review	Conduct legal due diligence and coordinate other due diligence
Review, and negotiate transaction documents:	Prepare, review and negotiate transaction documents:
▪ Confidentiality agreement	▪ Confidentiality agreement
▪ Term sheet (if any)	▪ Term sheet (if any)
▪ Letter of intent	▪ Letter of intent
▪ Acquisition agreements	▪ Acquisition agreements
Allocate risk to buyer by:	Allocate risk to seller by:
▪ Narrowing and qualifying representations and warranties	▪ Widening representations and warranties
▪ Limiting Indemnification	▪ Expanding Indemnification
Find practical solutions to close deal	Find practical solutions to close deal

in the transaction by utilizing his or her experience to resolve issues that are impediments to closing.

Table 11.1 details some similarities and differences between legal representation of the seller and of the buyer in a transaction.

PRELIMINARY LEGAL DOCUMENTS

Most transactions have a pattern as to the type and timing of the acquisition documents, beginning with the confidentiality agreement through the final acquisition documents. In the early parts of any transaction, a confidentiality agreement and letter of intent or term sheet are generally executed.[1]

Confidentiality Agreement

Typically, a confidentiality agreement is the first document executed by the parties in a transaction.[2] In the early stages of a deal, the buyer seeks information regarding the target company to determine whether to move forward with the acquisition, and the target company seeks to protect the confidentiality of the trade secrets and other confidential information concerning its business that it discloses to the buyer.[3] A confidentiality agreement is often mutual in that it protects both parties in a deal (i.e., buyer and seller), since each may be disclosing information to the other. Confidentiality agreements are often mischaracterized as boilerplate documents; however, they do typically contain standard provisions requiring the recipient to keep the information confidential and not to disclose the information or use it for any purpose other than in connection with the proposed transaction.[4] A confidentiality agreement also contains certain standard exceptions from the definition of confidential information, such as information that is or becomes part of the public domain; information the recipient can prove it already knew before disclosure; or information the recipient subsequently acquires from a third party.[5]

Although most confidentiality agreements contain somewhat standard provisions, some agreements may contain unexpected, restrictive covenants, such as nonsolicitation provisions and noncompetition provisions. These provisions must be carefully negotiated and potentially deleted from the agreement.

Through the nonsolicitation provision, potential buyers who become familiar with the seller's employees as part of the due diligence process are precluded from soliciting those employees for employment if the deal does not close. Through the noncompetition provision, a buyer is prohibited from competing against the target company for a specified period of time if the deal does not close. These are critical provisions for a buyer to understand if included in the agreement.

Another provision in a confidentiality agreement often subject to negotiation is the termination provision. The agreement should include a clause providing that after a specified period of time, the confidentiality obligations no longer apply.[6]

It is prudent, for these reasons, to pay particular attention to the confidentiality agreement. It is also important to use the negotiations of the confidentiality agreement to set the tone for the negotiations that will ensue throughout the transaction. Especially for sellers in an auction mode, the tone established early on will set the stage and expectations going forward.

Letter of Intent

A buyer and seller involved in a transaction generally enter into a letter of intent or term sheet when they have reached an agreement in principle. The letter of intent sets forth the critical terms of the deal after those terms have been discussed by the buyer and the seller, either directly or through intermediaries.[7] Except for certain specific binding provisions, the letter of intent is generally nonbinding. Nonetheless, it is extremely important as it provides the framework of the deal and a road map for closing the transaction.

Generally, the letter of intent includes the following transaction terms:

- Purchase price
- Working capital adjustment, if applicable
- Payment terms
- Structure of the deal (asset or stock/merger)
- Assets being purchased and liabilities being assumed (in an asset purchase transaction)
- Other agreements relevant to the deal such as employment agreements, consulting agreements, covenants not to compete, financing agreements, and leases/licenses

A letter of intent may also detail specific conditions that must be satisfied prior to closing the deal, including satisfaction of due diligence, third-party consent to the assignment of critical contracts, third-party financing, agreements with key employees, and lack of a material adverse change in the business or prospects of the target company. It is important to note that, since a letter of intent is generally not binding on the parties, conditions to closing are not required in order for either party to not proceed with the transaction after signing the letter of intent. Those conditions, however, are useful in setting forth the expectations of the buyer as to the items that need to be satisfied in order for the buyer to close the transaction.

In addition to the nonbinding transaction terms, the letter of intent will include certain binding provisions for the benefit of the buyer, the most important of which is an *exclusivity* or "no-shop" provision. An exclusivity provision precludes a seller from negotiating, discussing, soliciting, or accepting other offers to purchase the target company for an agreed-on period of time. It is important to a buyer to include an exclusivity provision because the buyer is concerned that it will expend a significant amount of time and money to commence due diligence, retain professionals, negotiate transaction documents, and prepare for the transaction only to have the seller accept an offer from another party or attempt to renegotiate deal terms with the leverage of a new buyer. Thus, a buyer requires that an exclusivity provision be included in the letter of intent. This is a standard term for a letter of intent and typically is not dependent on any earnest deposit.

The other binding provisions of a letter of intent generally include a right of the buyer to conduct due diligence, inspect the seller's books and records, and meet with key employees; a limitation of the target company's conduct of the business prior to closing to ordinary course of business; the payment by each party of its transaction expenses; the restriction of public announcements regarding the deal; and, if applicable, the payment of breakup fees.

Table 11.2 contains examples of legally binding provisions in a letter of intent.

STRUCTURE OF THE DEAL

Two of the most common ways to structure an acquisition are a stock purchase/merger transaction and an asset purchase transaction.

Stock Sale/Merger

In a stock or merger transaction, as shown in Figure 11.1, the buyer acquires the equity interests of the target company, such as the capital stock in a corporation and the membership interests in a limited liability company, from the equity owners of the target company. Through this structure, the buyer obtains all the assets of the target company and, most concerning to the buyer, all the liabilities (known, unknown, and contingent) of the target company. The inability of the buyer to separate itself from the liabilities of the target company, namely unknown and contingent liabilities, generally makes a stock purchase or merger structure a less favorable structure to the buyer (though helpful to a buyer that wishes to negotiate a lower purchase price and is willing to accept some risk). Since this structure in essence includes all the assets and all the liabilities of the target company, it would

TABLE 11.2   Legally Binding Provisions Included in a Letter of Intent

Provision	Customary Language
Right to Inspect	At all times prior to the Closing, the Company shall provide Purchaser and its representatives with such information, materials, instruments, documents and agreements, and/or access to the Company's assets and such books and records of the Company, as Purchaser shall reasonably request in connection with its evaluation of the Company's assets, the Company and the Company's business. Each of the parties agrees to keep all information acquired as a result of these examinations, to the extent that such information is not in or shall not otherwise come into the public domain, confidential and will not disclose it to any person or use it for any other purpose than as required by law in order to enforce or exercise its rights hereunder. In the event that the contemplated Transaction does not close, each party will return to the other party all confidential information and materials relating to it.
Conduct of Business	Purchaser contemplates expenditures related to its pre-closing investigations and its legal and accounting work in connection with the proposed Transaction. Accordingly, from the date of this Letter of Intent until Closing or earlier termination of this Letter of Intent as provided herein, the Company will conduct its business only in the ordinary course with a view toward preserving the relationships of the Company's business with its suppliers, customers, employees and others.
Expenses	Each party will bear its own expenses and brokerage/finder's fees in negotiating and Closing the Transaction contemplated herein (it being understood that Purchaser will pay the fees of _____ and that Seller will pay the fees of _____).
Disclosure of Terms of Deal	Neither party will make any announcement concerning the transaction contemplated by this letter of intent prior to the execution of the purchase agreement without the prior written approval of the other, which approval will not be unreasonably withheld or delayed. The foregoing shall not restrict in any respect the Company's or Purchaser's ability to communicate information concerning this letter of intent and the transaction contemplated to our respective affiliates, officers, directors, employees, and professional advisors, and to the extent relevant, to third parties whose consent is required in connection with the proposed transaction.

(continued)

TABLE 11.2 *(Continued)*

Provision	Customary Language
No Shop/ Exclusivity	Each of the Company and the Selling Parties agrees that none of the Company or the Selling Parties, nor any of their respective officers, directors, employees, representatives, agents, advisors or affiliates (collectively, the "Company Parties"), will directly or indirectly initiate, solicit, negotiate or discuss with any third party any inquiry, proposal or offer relating to the acquisition of the Company's business, the stock of the Company or the Company's assets, or any portion thereof, whether by merger, by purchase of assets or stock or by any other transaction. In addition, none of the Company or the Selling Parties shall provide, and the Company and the Selling Parties shall cause any other Company Party to not provide, any information to any third party in connection with any third party's potential or anticipated inquiry, proposal or offer relating to the acquisition of the business of the Company, the stock of the Company or the Company's assets or any portion thereof, whether by merger, by purchase of assets or stock of by any other transaction. The Company further agrees that it will immediately disclose to Purchaser any offers or inquiries, including the material terms hereof, it receives regarding any such proposal or offer. The provisions of this Paragraph may be terminated by the Company by a written notice at any time from and after that date which is at least 90 days after the date this Letter of Intent is signed by all parties hereto.

not be the proper structure in a deal in which only certain assets of the target company are to be sold or in which the buyer is not willing to take on the risk of unknown or contingent liabilities of the target company. In a stock purchase structure, the transaction involves the equity owners of the target company and not the target company itself.

Typically a stock sale requires the approval of all shareholders. From a practical perspective, a merger enables the sale of the entire company with the consent of only a majority of the shareholders. Chapter 13 covers the details of the various types of mergers and their tax implications.

Asset Purchase

In an asset purchase transaction, as shown in Figure 11.2, the buyer purchases some, substantially all, or all of the assets (tangible and intangible, real or personal property) of the target entity and assumes certain identified

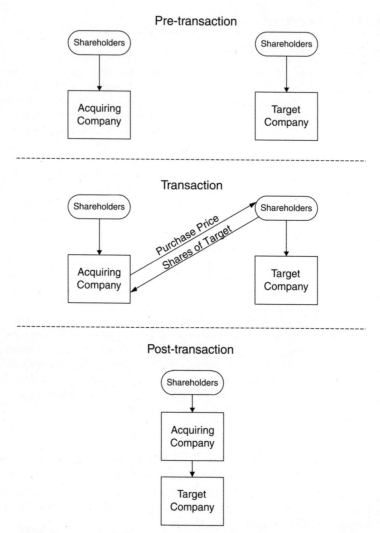

FIGURE 11.1   Stock Purchase

liabilities of the target entity.[8] In such a transaction, title to the assets is sold, transferred, and conveyed to the buyer. After the transaction has been completed, the target company may remain in existence and potentially may remain in business indefinitely.[9]

An asset sale does not require the target company to sell all its assets and, most importantly to the buyer, does not require the buyer to assume all the liabilities of the target company. Rather, the target company may

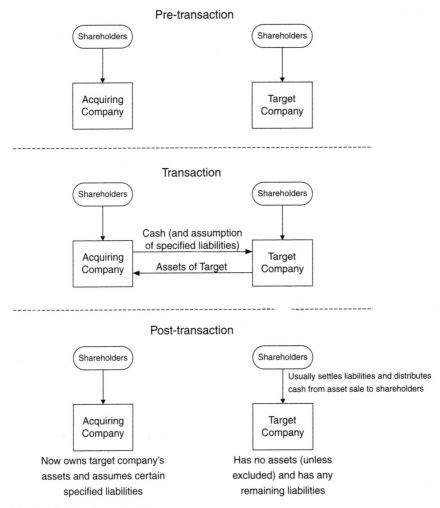

FIGURE 11.2 Asset Purchase

sell less than all its assets and the buyer may limit the assumed liabilities to certain identified liabilities of the target entity. The asset purchase structure will ordinarily require more closing documents than a stock purchase transaction in that documents of assignment and transfer must be prepared with respect to each type or class of asset that is being sold, and an assumption-of-liabilities document must be prepared with respect to the liabilities the buyer has agreed to assume.[10] It is important to note that an asset purchase structure does not ensure that the buyer has isolated itself from all liabilities of the target company other than those expressly assumed by the buyer as certain liabilities of the target company may as a matter of law follow the assets being sold, such as product liabilities, tax liabilities, and environmental liabilities.

An asset purchase transaction raises certain issues that do not arise in a stock purchase transaction. One important issue in an asset purchase transaction is determining whether the target company has entered into critical contracts that require third-party consent before an assignment of the contracts is effective. These contracts will generally contain clauses that prohibit their assignment to the buyer without the consent of the other party to the contract.[11] This is particularly important to discern in an acquisition of a regulated company (e.g., banking, energy, telecommunications, etc.) or a target company with government contracts. See Figure 11.2.

Section 338(h)(10) Election in a Stock Sale

Though the tax implications of the deal structure have not yet been addressed, there is some value in introducing what is referred to as a 338(h)(10) election.

Under Section 338(h)(10) of the Internal Revenue Code, a buyer and seller that have closed the sale of the stock of a corporation may elect to have the acquisition of the target company's stock treated as a purchase of assets rather than a purchase of stock solely for tax purposes.[12] In all other ways, the transaction will be treated as an acquisition of stock.

If a Section 338(h)(10) election is made in connection with a stock sale, the tax attributes of an asset sale apply to the stock purchase transaction. For example, the buyer may step up the basis in the assets, allowing the buyer to claim larger depreciation deductions following the election.

The tax considerations related to Section 338(h)(10) transactions are more fully explained in Chapter 13.

Purchase Price

There are various forms of acquisition consideration in a deal, such as cash, deferred purchase price (seller financing and earnouts), and equity. The type of consideration to be used in an acquisition depends on the resources of the buyer, the business objectives, the necessities of the parties, and the tax consequences applicable to the different forms of consideration.[13] The following are various forms of acquisition consideration:

- A buyer may finance an acquisition with cash.[14] The cash may come from the buyer's cash on hand, from loans to the buyer, or from the issuance of new equity by the buyer to third parties (i.e., not to the target company equity owners as consideration in the deal).[15]

- A buyer may finance an acquisition through a deferred purchase price mechanism, such as a promissory note or an earnout. A promissory note is an obligation to pay an agreed-on amount at an agreed-on time, and provides for the periodic payment of interest at an agreed-on interest rate.[16]
- An earnout is a payment to be made after the closing of the transaction based on the performance of the acquired business following the closing. In an earnout, the buyer agrees to pay a higher purchase price based on future performance.[17] However, the seller is paid the additional payments only if the future performance meets the agreed-on targets.[18]
- A buyer may finance an acquisition by using its own stock to acquire the stock or assets of a target company.[19]

Consulting and Employment Agreements

Consulting and employment agreements are often part of M&A transactions and represent the method by which current key employees or key consultants of the target company agree to remain in the employ of, or otherwise provide services to, the buyer following the closing of the transaction. A tax benefit of these agreements to the buyer is that the buyer can fully expense the payments made under these agreements in the year paid. If these additional amounts were included as additional purchase price, the buyer would, in an asset deal, allocate such amounts to goodwill and deduct the amounts over 15 years. In a stock deal, such additional amounts would be additional basis in the stock purchased.

DUE DILIGENCE

Chapter 16 addresses legal due diligence.

ACQUISITION AGREEMENTS

Generally prepared by the buyer's attorney, the acquisition agreement memorializes the transaction between the parties. The acquisition agreement sets forth the structure of the deal (stock purchase agreement, merger agreement, or asset purchase agreement); includes the key business terms of the deal; describes other agreements included in the deal, such as promissory notes, intercreditor/subordination agreements, employment agreements, or consulting agreements; and, most importantly, sets forth the applicable representations and warranties and indemnification obligations of the parties.

REPRESENTATIONS AND WARRANTIES

Representations and warranties are statements regarding the target company and its business made by the seller or other interested parties to the buyer. Representations and warranties have two purposes in a transaction: They smoke out or force disclosure, prior to closing, of issues that may be useful or concerning for a buyer, and they allocate risk between the seller and the buyer following the closing.[20]

Typical representations and warranties made by a seller in most transactions address the following topics:

- Taxes
- Accounts receivable
- Inventory
- Financial statements
- Books and records
- Title to assets being free of liens
- Compliance with laws
- Litigation and claims
- Intellectual property
- Liabilities
- Material contracts
- Employees
- No material adverse change

In a stock purchase transaction or merger, the seller will make additional representations and warranties concerning the target company's capital structure, as it is essential for the buyer to know the type of equity interests that exist and who owns the equity interests.[21] Additionally, in a stock purchase transaction, the sellers will represent and warrant that they own title to the equity interests free and clear and are legally entitled to sell their interests.[22]

Representations and warranties made by a buyer to a seller are fairly typical in most transactions, such as the buyer's authority to enter into the transaction, but far lesser in scope than the seller's representations. The seller may require the buyer to make additional representations and warranties in transactions in which the seller has an interest in the success of the buyer after the closing. Specifically, if the seller provides seller financing, agrees to an earnout, or receives an equity interest in the buyer as part of the transaction consideration, it would be fair to ask the buyer to make representations and warranties concerning its capital structure, its financial statements, and any litigation and claims.

Qualifications to Representations and Warranties

It would be highly unusual for a seller to be able to make all the representations and warranties that the buyer requests without any qualifications. A seller will generally prepare and deliver to the buyer a *disclosure schedule* that discloses exceptions to the representations and warranties requested by the buyer. The disclosure schedule in essence qualifies those representations and warranties and, to the extent of the disclosures made, shifts risk as to those disclosures to the buyer. In addition to qualifying representations and warranties through the delivery of the disclosure schedule, the seller will attempt to qualify representations and warranties by making them subject to the seller's "knowledge" (either actual or constructive). Without a knowledge qualifier, the seller is responsible for the representation and warranty regardless of whether the seller knew the representation and warranty was not true and correct at the time made. To the extent a buyer agrees to a knowledge qualifier, the buyer will combat the seller's attempt to limit its liability by defining *knowledge* as not only actual knowledge but also constructive knowledge.[23] Constructive knowledge incorporates into knowledge not just that which the seller actually knew but also that which the seller should have known, or should have known after reasonable investigation.

Indemnification

A breach of a representation and warranty will trigger indemnification by the breaching party in favor of the party for whose benefit the representation and warranty was made. An indemnification obligation requires the breaching party to indemnify conditionally or reimburse the other party for all damages, losses, costs, and expenses, including attorney's fees, incurred by the other party due to such breach. Indemnification is the contractual protection a buyer receives for breaches of representations and warranties made by the seller. To the extent the buyer incurs damages due to such a breach, it will be entitled to be indemnified for those damages by payment from the seller. Since indemnity requires the payment of funds by the indemnifying party to the indemnified party, the financial strength of the indemnifying party is critical. Strong representations and warranties without strong financial support of the associated indemnification obligations make those representations and warranties a "toothless tiger." The financial strength of the parties making or guaranteeing the indemnification obligations in a transaction is crucial to the party relying on the representations and warranties. To ensure indemnification in the event there is a breach of a representation and warranty, the buyer often seeks to create an escrow account, which will segregate funds from the purchase price and make those funds easily accessible if a breach of a representation and warranty occurs.[24] Establishing an escrow account is a common way to fund indemnification obligations.

Sellers generally negotiate limitations to their indemnification obligations, including finite survival periods of representations and warranties, thresholds before indemnification obligations are triggered, and caps on indemnification obligations. Survival periods for representations and warranties are generally included so that a seller knows that, after a certain period of time, its obligations for breaches of the representations and warranties will be extinguished. The survival periods of representations and warranties are generally not uniform across all representations and warranties, as certain fundamental representations and warranties (such as those relating to taxes, intellectual property, and compliance with laws) will have a longer survival period than other representations and warranties. Sellers often also include a *basket* or a *deductible* concept to limit indemnification, which prohibits the buyer from accessing indemnification funds until a certain dollar threshold of claims is reached.[25] Basket provisions are distinct from deductibles. When a basket is used, damages are reimbursed to the buyer back to the first dollar once the threshold is met; when a deductible is used, damages are reimbursed only above the threshold.[26]

Caps on the amount of the indemnification obligations are also typical in a deal. The caps are a product of negotiation and, like representations and warranties, are not uniform for all breaches and may differ depending on the specific representation and warranty breached.

EARNOUTS

Buyers and sellers often have differing expectations about the value of the target company.[27] An earnout is a common way to resolve differences of opinion as to the valuation of the target company and often bridges the gap between the buyer's determination of the value and the seller's determination of the value. An earnout allows buyers and sellers to disagree on valuation of the target company, but to nevertheless manage to agree on a transaction.[28]

In an earnout, a buyer agrees to increase the final purchase price to be paid to the seller based on the future performance of the acquired business, within a certain time frame following the closing of the transaction. These increases to the final purchase price may be fixed or determined through a formula based on economic milestones, such as revenue, gross profit, net income, or earnings before interest, taxes, depreciation, and amortization (EBITDA).[29] Typically, the earnout period is between one and three years following the closing of the transaction.

Parameters

Buyers generally seek to base earnouts on bottom-line earnings, determining purchase price increases based on net income or EBITDA, as buyers believe those financial standards are a better way to determine value. In contrast, sellers generally desire that earnouts based on above-the-line earning figures, specifically gross revenue, as gross revenue is easily measured and the seller is not at risk for increases in the expenses of the business, particularly overhead and general and administrative expenses that the buyers may add to the operations.

In an earnout situation, the seller's management team generally continues to operate the business after the closing. Because the seller has an economic incentive in operating the business to meet the earnout, the seller tends to have a short-term vision of the business, chasing numbers and revenue. With income as a priority, a seller tends to lose focus on the long-term goals of the business and long-term interest of the business, such as the credit of the customers and product quality.

Benefits of Earnouts

Earnouts tend to bridge the gap in differences of value between sellers and buyers. An earnout is often a viable option in obtaining an agreement as to the purchase price between parties in the transactions. Earnouts provide an efficient means of transferring some risk from a buyer to a seller.[30] A seller with high performance goals and expectations accepts a contingent payment while the buyer, likely less informed about the seller's future projections, is able to shift the valuation risk to the seller.[31]

Additionally, an earnout can act as an incentive for the seller and key employees to remain in place and commit to the business after the acquisition.[32] This allows a more seamless transition of the business from the seller to the buyer.

Shortcomings of Earnouts

Although earnouts provide several benefits, they also have several shortcomings. Earnouts may prevent post-acquisition integration of the target company into the buyer as the buyer needs to independently account for the financial performance of the target company during the earnout period. Additionally, an earnout can get extremely complicated and can create definitions and performance standards that may be difficult to administer. Measuring the results may pose serious difficulties.[33] Finally, earnouts may emphasize short-term profits over long-term growth if key management remains in the business with an incentive to maximize income at the expense of the long-term interest of the business.

REGULATORY COMPLIANCE

Chapter 14 addresses many of the regulatory and compliance topics for consideration in an M&A transaction.

CHAPTER 12

Tax Structure and Strategy

This chapter focuses primarily on federal income tax laws that impact how merger and acquisition (M&A) transactions for closely held or privately held companies are structured; however, fully understanding and evaluating the complete tax consequences of an M&A transaction is beyond the scope of this content.* It is not the goal of this chapter to educate one to become a tax expert, but rather to highlight the most common tax structural elements encountered by an M&A advisor in a typical middle market deal as illustrated in Figure 12.1. At the end of this chapter is a short "Tax Glossary" to provide additional clarification about some of the key concepts.

Understanding the tax attributes and the impact of taxes on an M&A transaction is important for a number of reasons:

- Federal and state income taxes resulting from a sale transaction can become as much as 50 percent of the transaction value. Selection of the transaction structure can result in significant differences in the tax liabilities of all of the parties of the deal. Think of the federal government as a silent partner in the deal.

- Often, sellers will not engage their tax accountant during the negotiation of a transaction, even though this is the time when these structural decisions are typically made. It becomes necessary for the M&A advisor to identify and understand the structural elements that impact taxes and to have an understanding of when to seek outside tax counsel.

- In negotiations, tax decisions tend to be a balancing act between buyers and sellers, each attempting to minimize the tax impact on itself for the purpose of maximizing the return on investment. Most tax

---

*The tax, accounting, and legal concepts herein are meant for educational purposes only and in no way should be used alone or without authoritative counsel from qualified tax and/or legal representation in providing advice or participating in a transaction.

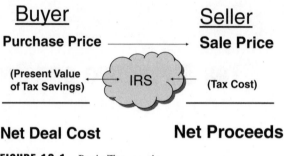

FIGURE 12.1 Basic Transaction

accountants are proficient at calculating and determining the consequences of a completed transaction. However, not all CPAs understand the balance between taxes and the other economic considerations in the deal. The M&A advisor is tasked with understanding all of the economics of the deal and the tax options that are available to both buyer and seller, as well as the impact those options may have on the overall economics of the transaction. By understanding how to minimize the income tax burden for his or her client, the M&A advisor gives the client a competitive bargaining advantage.

In this chapter, we will cover the following:

- Basic taxation terms and rates
- Stock versus asset transactions
- Asset transaction specifics
- Buyer's structural considerations

TAX FUNDAMENTALS

There are some basics of business taxation that an M&A advisor should be familiar with to begin to understand the implication of a transaction. The first question any tax advisor will ask of a closely held business owner is whether the business is structured as a C corporation or as a flow-through entity such as an S corporation, a partnership, or a limited liability corporation (LLC) taxed as either an S corporation or a partnership. Here are the basic tax characteristics of each entity structure:

C Corporation

- A C corporation is considered a separate taxable entity under the tax law. As such, it pays taxes on its earnings (including the sale of its assets).

TABLE 12.1 C Corporation Federal Tax Rates for 2010

Taxable Income Over	But Not Over	Tax Rate
—	$ 50,000	15%
$ 50,000	75,000	25%
75,000	100,000	34%
100,000	335,000	39%
335,000	10,000,000	34%
10,000,000	15,000,000	35%
15,000,000	18,333,333	38%
18,333,333	—	35%

- Federal tax rates for C corporations for 2010 are shown in Table 12.1, but most corporations with taxable income between $300,000 and $10 million are taxed at a flat 34 percent.
- C corporations do not have any preferential capital gains rates. All income is treated the same by a C corporation. Income from operations is taxed at the same rates as capital gain income from the sale of its assets.
- C corporations can deduct capital losses only to the extent they have capital gains and any unused capital losses may be carried forward five years. In contrast, an individual owner of a flow-through entity can use up to $3,000 of capital losses in excess of capital gains and may carry forward unused capital losses indefinitely.
- C corporation shareholders must pay tax on the receipt of assets from distribution or liquidation of the company following an asset sale. This is commonly referred to as *double taxation*. It occurs when a C corporation sells its assets and pays tax as described above, and then distributes the proceeds to its shareholders, who are taxed again for the dividend or capital gains distribution to the shareholders.

S Corporation

- An S corporation is legally the same as a C corporation, but makes a special election to be taxed differently by the IRS.
- S corporations do not pay tax on their earnings; rather the earnings of an S corporation flow through to the shareholders to be reported on their personal tax returns and added to other personal income. That income may be reduced by other personal deductions and losses.
- Because of the flow-through nature of an S corporation, taxes on earnings are assessed to the individual shareholders. A capital gain resulting from the sale of assets in a transaction will be taxed to the individual

TABLE 12.2 Entity Tax Attribute Comparison

	Corporation	Partnership	S Corporation
Flow-Through	No	Yes	Yes
Taxation of Profits	Double tax	Single tax + SE tax	Single tax—no SE tax
Utilizing Losses	Carry-forward	Partners (fewer limits)	Shareholders (more limits)
Type of Owners	Unrestricted	Unrestricted	Restricted

shareholders at favorable capital gain rates, while ordinary income from operations is taxed at ordinary individual rates.

- There is no double taxation from an S corporation. The tax to the shareholders is the only tax and there is generally no additional tax that results from the payment of a dividend or distribution.

Table 12.2 highlights and compares the attributes of the various taxable entities.

LLC/Partnership

- An LLC is a legal entity structure that is not specifically defined by the tax law and has the ability to elect to be taxed as a C corporation, an S corporation, a partnership, or a sole proprietorship; the default rule for a multimember LLC is to be taxed as a partnership and the default rule for a single-member LLC is to be taxed as a sole proprietorship. For purposes of this chapter, the terms *LLC* and *partnership* are used interchangeably given that most LLCs are taxed as partnerships.
- In general, LLCs follow tax laws very similar to S corporations. Earnings flow through to the members (or shareholders) and therefore are taxed at individual rates without concern for double taxation.
- There are a few differences between LLCs and S corporations. A primary difference between them is that earnings from LLC operations may be subject to additional self-employment taxes passed to members, whereas S corporation shareholders have much less of a risk as long as they are being paid reasonable compensation (as defined by the IRS) for their services to the corporation.

Most income of S corporations and LLCs is taxed at the individual rates (not corporate rates) of their owners. The 2010 individual ordinary income tax rates for married couples filing jointly are shown in Table 12.3 for reference.

TABLE 12.3 Individual Ordinary Income Tax Rates (Married, Filing Jointly)

Taxable Income				
Over	But Not Over	Tax	Tax %	On Amount Over
$ —	$ 16,750	$ —	10	$ —
16,750	68,000	1,675	15	16,750
68,000	137,300	9,362	25	68,000
137,300	209,250	26,687	28	137,300
209,250	373,650	46,833	33	209,250
373,650		101,085	35	373,650

While the individual and corporate ordinary tax rates differ, the top rates for higher levels of income are relatively similar (34 percent for corporations and 35 percent for individuals). It is important to understand the two material differences between flow-through entities and C corporations, specifically related to M&A transactions:

1. *Double taxation.* As noted, C corporations pay ordinary tax rates separate from the shareholders. This is especially significant in the event of a sale transaction, where the ultimate benefit of the sale is measured as the after-tax dollars in the hands of the individual owners or shareholders. In the case of a sale event, the gains from assets sold by the corporation are first taxed at the corporate entity level and then taxed again when the proceeds are distributed to its shareholders. In most cases this includes *both* federal and state income taxes at *both* levels. Therefore, the "all-in" tax rates that might be experienced in an asset sale such as this could be in the 45 to 60 percent range, depending on the state, size of transaction, and other factors.

2. *Capital gains rates.* While ordinary income tax rates for individuals can be similar to those for a C corporation, this is generally a moot point in most sale transactions taxed at individual rates. In many M&A transactions, the majority of the gain results from the sale of intangible assets (e.g., goodwill and customer lists), which are taxed as long-term capital gains to the individual shareholders in a flow-through entity. Current long-term capital gains rates for individuals are capped at 15 percent in 2011 and 2012, and at 20 percent in 2013. C corporations, however, have no special long-term capital gains rate. Therefore, the rate difference on the sale of capital gain assets is significant between C corporations and flow-through entities (e.g., individuals) even before the effects of double taxation.

TRANSACTION TAX BASICS

There are two primary structures in selling a private company in a taxable transaction: an asset sale and a stock sale. As discussed in Chapter 11, there are significant legal differences between these two approaches. Likewise, there are significant tax differences for both the buyer and seller.

Asset Transactions

In an asset transaction, the selling company sells the majority of its assets to the buyer, but ownership of the selling company itself does not change hands. The gain from this sale transaction is calculated at the company level, and either taxed to the company (in the case of a C corporation) or passed through and taxed to the individual selling owners or shareholders in the case of a flow-through entity.

In most asset purchases, the buyer will generally establish an *acquisition company*. This acquisition company becomes the new operating entity after the assets are purchased and transferred from the selling business.

To better understand the tax consequences of an asset transaction, we will look at the impact to the following parties:

- Buyer
- Seller as a flow-through entity
- Seller as a C corporation

Buyer Impact   In an asset transaction, the buyer and seller must agree on an allocation of the purchase price between the different classes and types of assets acquired. Using this allocation, the assets are *stepped up* in value or restated to a market value, equal in aggregate to the purchase price. The buyer may then begin depreciating or amortizing those assets postclosing (see additional discussion regarding allocation of purchase price under "Asset Transaction Details," later in this chapter).

The primary tax benefit of an asset transaction is the buyer's ability to obtain this stepped-up basis from assets acquired that in turn creates tax deductible depreciation, thus lowering the buyer's taxable income and reducing future tax costs. As will be discussed, the buyer does not generally get this stepped-up basis and depreciation benefit in a stock transaction.

In some cases, the selling company has tax attributes, the most common example being net operating losses (NOLs) that may be carried forward to offset future gains. However, because the selling company (shell) remains owned by the selling owners, there is no ability for the buyer to purchase or

TABLE 12.4   Asset Allocation Matrix

Tax Rates	Corporation	Shareholder
Ordinary income	35%	35%
Capital gains	35%	15%
Dividends	0%	15%

obtain these tax attributes of the selling company; these attributes remain with the selling company.

Seller Impact: Flow-Through Entity   The agreed-on asset allocation will also dictate the nature of the gains that result from an asset transaction for the flow-through seller. The sale of some assets, such as inventory, will result in ordinary income that will flow through to the individual owners or shareholders. The sale of other assets, such as goodwill or intangibles, will result in long-term capital gains that will also flow through to the owners. Because of this treatment, the seller is generally motivated to allocate more of the purchase price to these capital gain assets and less to those that generate ordinary income. See Table 12.4 for tax treatment of the various types of assets.

Because the flow-through entity does not pay its own tax on these gains, these gains are passed through to the individual owners and added to other income and losses on their personal tax returns. These gains increase the tax basis in the flow-through entity so when the company is liquidated, less gain results. This is where the double taxation is eliminated with a flow-through entity.

As noted, the selling company typically remains owned by the selling shareholders following the transaction. In some cases the selling owners may choose to keep the company shell alive or start a new enterprise with assets that were not acquired by the buyer, or to utilize tax attributes that remain in the selling company shell. In other cases the owners may choose to liquidate the company if there is no reason to keep it alive after the sale of its assets.

Seller Impact: C Corporation   An asset sale for a C corporation seller is generally the worst-case scenario for tax purposes because the seller is impacted with both of the material detriments of C corporations noted above. There is no favorable capital-gains rate for C corporations and the eventual distribution of the sale proceeds to the shareholders creates double taxation.

While the buyer and seller are still required to agree on an allocation of assets, it is essentially irrelevant to a C corporation seller because all gains are taxed at the same rates. Unlike the flow-through seller, there is no preferential tax rate for capital gains. Therefore, a favorable allocation to more capital gain assets in lieu of ordinary income assets does no good to the seller.

After the C corporation has paid its tax on the gains from the sale, the corporation must then liquidate the remaining assets to the shareholders/owners. This creates the double-tax scenario described earlier. Those liquidating distributions are generally taxed by the shareholders as long-term capital gains, but still become the second level of taxation of the sale proceeds.

Stock Transactions

In a stock transaction, the selling shareholders sell their shares to the buyer. In this case, the company's assets do not transfer, but rather the ownership of the company changes. The important distinction is that the *seller* is the shareholder—not the company. In comparison with an asset sale, there are different tax impacts to both buyer and seller in a stock transaction.

Buyer Impact   Because the assets of the company have not been sold, there is no event that can provide for a step-up in value of those assets for tax depreciation, as there is in an asset transaction. There is generally no allocation of purchase price for income tax purposes; however, if the company issues GAAP financial statements, FAS 141R may require the buyer to allocate the purchase price to the underlying assets. For income tax purposes, the buyer steps into the shoes of the seller and continues to depreciate the assets in the company from the seller's position. This is not as beneficial to the buyer when paying a premium over book value for the target. In the case of a stock purchase, the buyer gets no depreciation or amortization deduction for that premium.

The buyer's stock basis is usually equal to the purchase price. However, that basis cannot be depreciated or deducted in any way until such time as the stock is sold. Subject to some limitations, the company's tax attributes may be transferred and utilized by the buyer. In some situations the selling company's NOLs may provide value to the buyer and could contribute to the overall value of the deal to the buyer.

Seller's Treatment: Stock Sale   Stock sales are treated similarly for both S corporation and C corporation sellers. In both cases the individual shareholder reports the sale as a capital gain (assuming he or she held the stock for an adequate period of time). There is no gain transaction in the target company and therefore the stock transaction eliminates the negative tax impacts associated with an asset sale of a C corporation; the stock sale avoids the double-taxation concerns. Because of the potentially significant tax liability differences, many C corporation shareholders insist on a stock sale.

The stock sale of an S corporation is generally no worse, and possibly slightly better, than an asset sale. In the case of an asset sale, the typical assets that generate ordinary income are cash-basis receivables and depreciated/amortized assets. Sellers attempt to allocate the purchase price away from these ordinary assets where possible. However, some portion of the asset sale will invariably result in ordinary income. When the majority of assets being sold inside an S corporation are capital gain assets, the difference in taxes between an asset and a stock sale is most likely negligible.

LLC "Stock" Sale The sale of membership interests in an LLC creates an interesting discussion. As noted, the tax law does not separately define an LLC. Generally, most LLCs are taxed as partnerships under the tax law, so the sale of "stock" or membership interests in an LLC is actually treated as the sale of a partnership interest. In this case, the rules related to partnership sales prevail. They dictate that the buyer and seller effectively look inside the partnership and treat the "stock sale" as a sale of the underlying assets with respect to certain *hot assets*, as described below.

Accordingly, the sale of LLC membership interests is taxed similarly to, but not exactly like, an asset sale. The main difference between the stock sale and an asset sale in an LLC relates to the hot assets within the LLC. Hot assets are defined as unrealized receivables, substantially appreciated inventory, and depreciable assets. These assets are the only assets taxed as ordinary income when the equity interest, or membership interests, of the LLC are sold.

Stock versus Asset Sale Example

Following is an example illustrating how the structuring of a transaction as a stock sale, as opposed to an asset sale, can impact both the buyer and seller. Table 12.5 provides a reminder of the tax rates for the corporation and its shareholders.

Example Facts

- Seller is a C corporation.
- Seller has no debt.
- Shareholder has $0 stock basis.

TABLE 12.5 Tax Rate Comparison

Allocation Item	Buyer's Treatment	Seller's Treatment
Inventory	Deduct as sold	Typically sold at cost—no gain
Fixed Assets	3-, 5-, 7-, 15-year depreciation	Ordinary (up to original cost)
Noncompete	15-year amortization	Ordinary income
Training	Deduct as incurred	Ordinary income with payroll taxes
Goodwill	15-year amortization	Capital gain

Note: Fixed assets can include real properties that may have depreciable lives of 27.5 or 39 years.

- Seller lives in a state with no state income taxes.
- Sale takes place in 2011 or 2012.
- Seller's balance sheet is shown in Table 12.6.

Seller's Perspective Table 12.7 illustrates how the sale proceeds under both an asset deal and a stock sale would be calculated from the seller's perspective.

Assuming the sales price is constant at $10 million, the seller has $892,500 less in after-tax proceeds with an asset sale compared to a stock sale.

Buyer's Perspective In this same example, the basis in the tangible assets is equal to the fair market value. Therefore, the primary tax difference to the buyer in a stock versus an asset transaction is whether the buyer will be able to depreciate (amortize) the intangible assets. The buyer is allowed a 15-year amortization for goodwill and other intangibles purchased, resulting in annual ordinary income deductions of $200,000. The present value of these future deductions is approximately $600,000. See Table 12.8.

TABLE 12.6 Seller's Balance Sheet

Balance Sheet	Basis	FMV
Tangible	$7,000,000	$ 7,000,000
Goodwill	—	3,000,000
Total	$7,000,000	$10,000,000

TABLE 12.7 Stock versus Asset Sale

| | Asset Sale | | Stock Sale |
	Corporation	Shareholder	Shareholder
Sales price	$10,000,000		$10,000,000
Basis in assets	(7,000,000)		
Corporate gain	3,000,000		
Corporate tax	(1,050,000)		
Cash to shareholder	$ 8,950,000	$ 8,950,000	10,000,000
Basis in stock		—	—
Shareholder gain		8,950,000	10,000,000
Shareholder tax		(1,342,500)	(1,500,000)
Net cash to shareholder		7,607,500	8,500,000
Percent to shareholder		76%	85%
Difference			$ 892,500

The Net Effect The seller's tax differences between structuring the transaction as an asset sale versus a stock sale are summarized in Table 12.9.

The buyer's tax differences between structuring the transaction as an asset sale and a stock sale are summarized in Table 12.10.

In this example, if the seller accepts an asset sale transaction he is losing almost $900,000 in after-tax proceeds while the buyer is gaining $600,000 in tax savings. Even then, the buyer's tax savings in the first year is only $70,000 with the remaining tax savings spread equally over the next 14 years.

Negotiations Based on Structure

Understanding the tax impact of a stock versus an asset sale can be helpful in negotiating or renegotiating a transaction. This tax difference may be

TABLE 12.8 Impact of Deal Structure for the Buyer

	Net Asset Value	Amortization
Goodwill (15 years)	$3,000,000	$200,000
Tax rate		35%
Annual tax savings		70,000
Present value	15 years @ 8%	$600,000

TABLE 12.9 Tax Benefit to the Seller

	Asset Sale	Stock Sale
Net cash to shareholder	$7,607,500	$8,500,000
Percent to shareholder	76%	85%
Difference		$ 892,500

used by either party to possibly renegotiate a better deal or to create a more equitable transaction. Here are a few alternative structures, as presented by either party seeking a better solution.

What-If #1: Proposed by the Buyer

- Assume the buyer has already convinced the seller to accept the asset deal noted previously.
- What if the buyer proposed to change the deal to a stock purchase of $9 million?
- If the seller recalculates his taxes under this stock sale assumption, he would find he has $7.6 million of after-tax proceeds (same as a $10 million asset sale). Presumably the seller would be agreeable to this proposal if all other items are equal.
- The buyer has just reduced his purchase price by $1 million!
- While the buyer has lost his ability to deduct amortization of goodwill, this was only a $70,000 current year benefit. So, he is $930,000 better off in cash the first year.
- Even considering the present value of all 15 years of amortization, the buyer is still better off by $400,000 in total.
- The buyer still must accept the legal ramifications of a stock sale (see the related discussion in Chapter 11).

What-If #2: Proposed by the Seller

- Assume the buyer has already agreed to an asset deal as previously noted.

TABLE 12.10 Tax Benefit to the Buyer

Annual tax savings		$ 70,000
Present value	15 years @ 8%	$600,000

- What if the seller proposes to change the deal to a stock purchase for $9.4 million?
- The buyer will lose $600,000 in present value of tax deductions, but will pay $600,000 less for the company immediately. So, presumably the buyer will be okay with this proposal.
- The seller has just negotiated for $340,000 in additional after-tax cash proceeds.

Perhaps somewhere between $9 million and $9.4 million there is a solution.

Asset Transaction Details

As noted, an asset transaction requires the parties to allocate the purchase price to the various assets that are sold in the transaction. Understanding how to structure asset transactions requires a solid understanding of the concept of purchase price allocation.

Purchase Price Allocation   Congress enacted Internal Revenue Code (I.R.C.) Section 1060 to ensure that buyers and sellers of business assets agree on and follow a common allocation of purchase price. If not for this agreement, a buyer could allocate the purchase price to assets characterized as deductible over relatively short periods while the seller could then allocate the same sales price to assets characterized as capital assets (such as goodwill) to receive favorable capital gains treatment.

Under Section 1060, both the buyer and the seller must use the same *residual method* to allocate the purchase/sale price to the specific assets that change hands. The residual method essentially asks that the parties identify and agree on values for known assets (such as cash, inventory, equipment, etc.), and the "residual" is then allocated to "other intangibles."

Both sides must report this allocation on Form 8594, which is then filed with the buyer's and the seller's respective tax returns. This form follows the allocation classes referenced in Section 1060. Below are the asset classes that are to be allocated:

I. Cash
II. Securities
III. Mark-to-market financial assets (accounts receivable)
IV. Inventory
V. Depreciable assets (property, plant and equipment)
VI. Identifiable intangibles (patents, trademarks, etc.)
VII. Goodwill

In private company transactions, cash and securities are rarely included in the assets sold. Most private companies do not hold mark-to-market financial assets other than accounts receivable. There is little practical difference under the tax law between VI (Intangibles) and VII (Goodwill). In fact, these categories are combined for purposes of Form 8594. For practical purposes, most private-company middle market transactions negotiate the purchase price allocation among the following assets:

- Inventory
- Tangible personal property (property, plant and equipment)
- Intangibles/goodwill

Although these are the categories that the tax law requires be identified, there are other items that often get included in the allocation of purchase price. The most common additional allocated items include noncompete covenants and consulting agreements.

Noncompete Covenants While noncompete agreements are generally not considered intangibles, they are required to be amortized over 15 years by the buyer regardless of the duration of the contract. As a result, the IRS expects any allocation of noncompetes to be included as a Class VI asset for purposes of the 1060 allocation. However, unlike the rest of the Class VI assets, a noncompete is generally taxed as ordinary income to the seller. Noncompetes are often referred to as worst-of-both-worlds allocation items, because they are taxed at the highest rates by sellers and amortized over the longest period by buyers.

Consulting Agreements Unlike noncompete covenants, these agreements are *not* considered intangibles and therefore are *not* included in the 1060 allocation. However, knowing that buyers and sellers might use this to their advantage, the IRS has included a notes section to Form 8594 where these types of agreements are disclosed.

Although payments pursuant to consulting agreements are considered ordinary income to the recipient, consulting agreements can be used to avoid double taxation because the compensation can be paid directly to the individuals performing the "consulting." In addition, they are generally deducted in the year paid by buyers and reported on Form 1099-MISC. Consulting agreements can be a valuable part of the process of allocating the aggregate deal proceeds, as their use can avoid double taxation to the seller and create an immediate deduction to the buyer. Of course, care should be taken to determine that the payments made are reasonable in relation to the services actually rendered. Buyers should also keep employment law issues in mind when structuring these contracts. A lengthy consulting agreement, if not properly structured, may cause the consultants to be treated as employees of the buyer, with rights to benefits.

Asset Allocation Examples   Just as the stock-versus-asset decision can be used to negotiate purchase price for either party, so can the allocation of purchase price. Because the value of equipment, furniture, and other tangible assets in most private companies is rather subjective, opportunities may exist to negotiate and affect significant differences in taxes for both parties, depending on how the allocation is agreed on.

Asset Allocation Negotiation Favoring Seller   Assuming the seller is a flow-through entity (S corporation or LLC), the strategy for a seller in negotiating a favorable allocation is to shift value from tangible assets to goodwill. As a result of increases in I.R.C. Section 179 deduction and bonus depreciation rules since 2000, tangible assets are generally sold below original cost but above their income tax basis. Therefore, the gain on the sale of property, plant, and equipment (PP&E) is mostly recapture of depreciation and is taxed as ordinary income. Because of the residual method applied in the tax law, any reduction of value allocated to these tangible assets is automatically added to goodwill and is taxed as capital gain income.

Let's look at the tax difference to the seller for allocating $100,000 of value to goodwill (a capital gain asset) versus PP&E (an ordinary income asset), shown in Table 12.11.

Now look at the tax impact to the buyer from making this same shift between a capital asset, such as goodwill, and a PP&E asset. In this example calculation, we need to assume the transaction is taking place in a location with typical sales and use tax laws. In most cases, these laws require that the buyer pay use tax (similar to sales tax) on the purchase of tangible assets. However, most of these use-tax laws do not apply to intangible assets, such as goodwill. See Table 12.12.

TABLE 12.11   Asset Allocation for the Seller

	Ordinary	Capital
Price allocation	$100,000	$100,000
Marginal tax rate	35%	15%
Tax	35,000	15,000
Difference	$ 20,000	

TABLE 12.12 Asset Allocation for the Buyer

	5-Year	15-Year
Price allocation	$100,000	$100,000
Use-tax rate	6%	0%
Additional use tax	6,000	—
Total cost	106,000	100,000
Present value of depreciation	30,850	21,252
Less use tax	(6,000)	—
Present value of savings	24,850	21,252
Difference	$ 3,598	

As seen in these two examples, the tax savings created by a seller from shifting $100,000 of value is $20,000, whereas the present value of tax deductions to the buyer is only $3,600. That is approximately a 6:1 ratio of seller tax benefit to buyer tax benefit. As a result, it is generally in the seller's best interest to negotiate an allocation of purchase price that minimizes the values assigned to tangible assets, which generate ordinary income, in exchange for intangible assets, which generate capital gain income.

Asset Allocation Negotiation Favoring Buyer   Just because the seller's taxes are positively affected by this allocation shift does not mean the seller is the only one who can benefit. A savvy buyer can use these facts to her advantage and possibly propose a reduction in purchase price if she can show the seller how his willingness to accept a new allocation will yield similar after-tax results. Note in the example shown in Table 12.13 how the buyer can provide the seller the same after-tax proceeds and reduce the purchase price.

C Corporation Asset Allocation Issues   As noted, asset sales by a C corporation can result in significant tax liabilities for the seller. When possible, sellers will try to convince the buyer to move to a stock transaction providing for more favorable tax treatment. However, in many cases the buyer is unwilling to do this (see legal discussions related to asset versus stock transactions in Chapter 11). In this case the seller might want to consider tactics in negotiating the transaction that might help to mitigate the impact, including:

- Favorable allocation to buyer
- Personal compensation/consulting
- Noncompete allocations
- Personal goodwill allocation

TABLE 12.13 Asset Allocation Scenario Favoring the Buyer

Original Allocation		Amounts
Equipment	@ 35% tax	$2,000,000
Goodwill	@ 15% tax	5,000,000
Total purchase price		7,000,000
Tax (assuming no basis)		1,450,000
After-tax cash to seller		$5,550,000
Revised Allocation		
Equipment	@ 35% tax	$1,000,000
Goodwill	@ 15% tax	5,764,706
Total purchase price		6,764,706
Tax (assuming no basis)		1,214,706
After-tax cash to seller		$5,550,000
Impact		
Reduction in buyer's price paid		235,294
Present value difference of buyer's tax savings		(145,990)
Total savings to buyer		$ 89,304

Favorable Allocation to Buyer   As mentioned earlier in this section, C corporations do not have favorable capital gains rates, so the allocation between ordinary income assets and capital gain assets is irrelevant for most purposes. A C corporation seller has the ability to offer an allocation to the buyer that completely favors that buyer. Doing so creates the negotiating opportunity for the seller to seek other deal terms in his favor. The allocation should still be reasonable in order to satisfy IRS scrutiny.

Consulting and Noncompete Allocations   To avoid the double taxation that takes effect when corporate assets are sold, a seller might want to have a significant portion of the purchase price paid to him as personal compensation. There are a few strategies that the seller might use to justify larger amounts paid in this manner:

- *Consulting/training.* In most private company transactions the selling shareholder(s) need to provide some transition consulting or training to the buyer's management team. If this is negotiated as "contracted services," perhaps the seller can justify an amount that is two to three times the normal salary rate for that individual.

- *Deferred compensation.* In some cases private business owners have had periods in their company's history when the business was unable to pay them an adequate or market salary. Many times these owners have merely deferred their compensation. With some level of supporting documentation (e.g., board minutes, etc.) they may be able to justify funding payment of those deferred compensation amounts with the proceeds of the transaction. This tactic should be evaluated with caution, given compensation laws under I.R.C. Section 409A.
- *Severance.* If the buyer is replacing the owner with new management, the seller might negotiate that a portion of the price be allocated to a reasonable severance payout to the individual owner/operator.

Noncompete Allocations Similar to compensation for services, noncompete agreements may help the C corporation seller legitimately avoid the double taxation issue. In some private company transactions the value of the noncompete applies at the level of the individual owner, not his company. In this case the value of the noncompete should be appropriate to the situation and the buyer and seller may consider the following facts-and-circumstances tests:

- Would the seller want to compete with the buyer?
- Would the seller effectively be able to compete with the buyer in that market?
- Would the seller be able to compete in the market at that specific time and area?

Without the ability to compete, the IRS may not accept an allocation of the purchase price to the noncompete. As noted, an allocation to noncompete will be treated as ordinary income to the seller and must be amortized by the buyer over 15 years.

Personal Goodwill An allocation to personal goodwill might be the only best-of-both-worlds solution for a C corporation seller to avoid double taxation and actually allocate to the shareholder a capital gain asset while still allowing the buyer to purchase an amortizable asset. If the facts support the case, a C corporation seller might have some of the goodwill or intangible value of the transaction paid directly to the owner as consideration for his personal goodwill. This part of the price would be recognized by the individual seller personally, and as a capital gain transaction.

The concept of personal goodwill was first established with professional corporations, such as dental practices and accounting firms, where the intangible goodwill value (customer relationships, knowhow, etc.) was really deemed to be owned by the individual owner and not the corporation. However, the 1998 Tax Court case *Martin Ice Cream v. Commissioner* demonstrated how a nonprofessional company could use the same concept. Since *Martin Ice Cream*, many tax practitioners have created valuation and structuring techniques to value personal goodwill and to follow the examples given in the case law to substantiate its use.

The concept of personal goodwill can be used in more than the minimization of double-taxation scenarios. Personal goodwill may be used in an entity to allocate more funds to a particular shareholder or partner. The viability of utilizing personal goodwill should be considered in transactions where there are a few key individuals/owners who make the entity valuable.

FAS 141R   FAS 141R became part of GAAP in 2009 and is used to account for certain business combinations. FAS 141R requires the purchase price allocation to adjust the carrying cost of all assets acquired in a stock or asset deal to their fair value for accounting purposes. The fair value standard is slightly different from the IRS's fair market value standard. As such, there may be differences in the GAAP and tax purchase price allocation. Although there may be differences, in some cases the IRS will use a GAAP value for a particular asset instead of the value used on the tax return. Caution should be exercised when preparing a tax purchase price allocation if GAAP financial statements will be issued so that the two allocations are reasonable in relation to each other.

Buyer Tax Issues

Tax consequences for a buyer are usually focused on maximizing the ability to reduce taxes from operations. The tax benefits sought by buyers typically are in one of two categories:

1. Capturing tax basis in their purchase price (discussed in the asset-versus-stock analysis for buyers), or
2. Accelerating the depreciation or deduction of the basis in the assets acquired

The following are a few issues that impact the buyer's ability to accomplish these goals:

- Capitalization of transactions costs
- Depreciation/amortization lives
- Special rules for intangibles
- Amortization recapture
- Cost segregation studies on real estate

Capitalization of Acquisition Costs   During an acquisition a buyer may incur a large number of expenses—specifically legal fees, buy-side investment banking fees, accounting fees, and so on. The buyer will want to deduct those expenses as they are incurred. However, in the case of *Indopco v. Commissioner*, the Supreme Court ruled that costs related to the acquisition of assets must be added to the costs of those assets, and may be depreciated or amortized only as allowed in the law. To be related to the acquisition of the assets, the costs must be facilitative to the transaction. Generally, costs incurred after the letter of intent (or similar nondisclosure and exclusivity document) and before the sale closing are deemed to be facilitative.

In April 2011, the IRS issued Revenue Procedure 2011-29 allowing a buyer a current deduction equal to 70 percent of the amount paid for success fees with the remaining 30 percent being capitalized. This safe harbor does not replace the facilitative-versus-nonfacilitative rules currently in place, but instead allows a default deduction without the effort needed to support which costs were facilitative or nonfacilitative.

Depreciation and Amortization   When a buyer purchases a company in an asset transaction, he is generally permitted to begin depreciating the assets at the allocated purchase price. Depreciation lives are the same regardless of whether the assets being purchased are new or used. The following are common depreciation lives:

Software	3 years
FFE	5 to 7 years
Land	No depreciation
Land improvements	15 years
Goodwill, intangibles	15 years
Noncompete (regardless of life)	15 years
Residential real estate	27 years
Nonresidential real estate	39 years

Special Rules for Intangibles   Purchased intangibles may be depreciated by buyers over 180 months (15 years). Although GAAP financial statement reporting may require different treatment of certain intangibles, the tax law merely groups them together into a 15-year amortization pool.

Just as the depreciation lives of used equipment are no different from those of new equipment, the amortization life of an expiring intangible (such as a patent or trademark) is also 15 years. For example, if a patent is

TABLE 12.14 Recapture: No Specific Intangibles Identified

Purchased intangibles	$ 4,500,000
Less amortization (5 years)	(1,500,000)
Remaining basis at sale	3,000,000
Sale price	6,000,000
Amortization recapture	1,500,000
Ordinary tax rate	35%
Ordinary tax	525,000
Capital gain	1,500,000
Capital gain tax rate	15%
Capital gain tax	225,000
Total taxes paid	$ 750,000

acquired for $1.5 million and has only 5 years remaining before it expires, it is amortized over 15 years. The buyer cannot write off the remaining $1 million after the patent expires unless it was the only asset purchased on that particular day by the buyer. Any remaining basis from an intangible that was acquired as part of a bulk asset purchase is deemed to be part of the goodwill acquired in that purchase.

Amortization Recapture Similar to depreciation of tangible assets, the amortization of intangibles is subject to recapture when it is sold, at ordinary tax rates as opposed to capital gains rates. Because of this, buyers may want to specifically identify certain intangible assets and amortize them separately (even though there is no annual amortization advantage). This may be beneficial for the buyer in a future sale of the company or when specific assets are subsequently sold.

As an example, assume an acquisition includes $3 million that could be allocated to patents and $1.5 million allocated to goodwill for a total of $4.5 million of intangibles. Then assume the same company is sold 5 years later with an allocation of $2 million to the patents (since they are 5 years older) and $5 million of goodwill for a total $6 million of the sale price for the intangibles. Tables 12.14 and 12.15 illustrate the benefits of separately amortizing the patent from the goodwill, even though they both have 15-year amortization lives.

There is no difference in annual amortization since both the patents and goodwill would be amortized over 15 years. However, as can be seen in this example, by specifically identifying the intangibles the company saves $200,000 in taxes when it sells.

TABLE 12.15 Recapture: Specific Intangibles Identified

	Patent	Goodwill	Total
Purchased intangibles	$ 3,000,000	$1,500,000	$ 4,500,000
Less amortization (5 years)	(1,000,000)	(500,000)	(1,500,000)
Remaining basis at sale	2,000,000	1,000,000	3,000,000
Sale price	2,000,000	4,000,000	6,000,000
Amortization recapture	—	500,000	500,000
Ordinary tax rate	35%	35%	35%
Ordinary tax	—	175,000	175,000
Capital gain	—	2,500,000	2,500,000
Capital gain tax rate	15%	15%	15%
Capital gain tax	—	375,000	375,000
Total taxes paid	—	$ 550,000	$ 550,000

Cost Segregation Studies on Real Estate   In the event the purchase transaction involves commercial real estate, the buyer may want to consider a *cost segregation study*. These studies are performed with the intent of identifying components of a commercial building that can be depreciated over shorter lives than the traditional 39-year life provided by the tax law. This is purely a timing advantage, but can reduce taxes in the early years following a purchase. Cost segregation studies should be performed following rules recognized by the IRS (and subsequently established through the court case *Hospital Corporation of America v. Commissioner*). These rules generally require that an independent engineering study be conducted to identify the components. There are a number of engineering companies and CPA firms that now offer these studies as a service to their clients.

TAX GLOSSARY AND REFERENCE

The following discussions are to support the core text of this chapter. Code Sections refer to the I.R.C., and Reg. sections refer to the Treasury Regulations that interpret and supplement the I.R.C. and are binding on taxpayers.

Asset allocation. In the case of any applicable asset acquisition, for purposes of determining both (1) the transferee's basis in such assets and (2) the gain or loss of the transferor with respect to such acquisition, the consideration received for such assets shall be allocated among such assets acquired in such acquisition in the same manner as amounts are allocated to assets under Section 338(b)(5). Code Section 1060(a).

Capitalization of assets. In general, capital expenditures are amounts paid for the acquisition of property or for a permanent improvement or betterment of the property extending beyond the tax year. Code Section 263. However, this doesn't mean that *only* expenditures that create or enhance separate and distinct assets are to be capitalized. Accordingly, the creation of a separate and distinct asset may be a sufficient, but isn't a necessary, condition to classification as a capital expenditure. Where expenditures produce significant benefits to the taxpayer extending beyond the tax year in question, the expenditures had to be capitalized. *Indopco Inc. v. Commissioner* (1992, S. Ct.) 69 AFTR 2d. 92-694.

Corporate capital gains tax rate. The alternative tax for capital gains under Section 1202 isn't imposed unless the top regular corporate tax rate imposed for the year is higher than 35 percent (determined without regard to the additional tax equal to the lesser of 5 percent or $11,750 on taxable income over $100,000 or the additional tax equal to the lesser of 3 percent or $100,000 on taxable income over $15,000,000). Code Sections 1201(a) and 11(b).

Cost segregation studies. Cost segregation studies generally produce listings or groups of assets, based on asset classes under ACRS (Accelerated Cost Recovery System) or MACRS (Modified Accelerated Cost Recovery System). The IRS has written audit procedure manuals that define acceptable methods for performing these studies, following the tax court ruling in *Hospital Corporation of America, Inc. v. Commissioner*, 109 T.C. 21 (1997).

Depreciation and amortization. Property used in a trade or business or held for the production of income is said to depreciate as it gradually wears out over the period of its use because of wear and tear, exhaustion, or obsolescence. Code Section 167(a)(1). Under Code Section 197, many intangibles, including most intangibles acquired in connection with the purchase of a business, must be ratably amortized over a 15-year period.

Depreciation and amortization recapture. Upon disposition of most property on which depreciation or cost recovery deductions were taken, taxpayers must recognize ordinary income in an amount equal to all or a portion of the gain realized as a result of the disposition. There are two types of property that are subject to depreciation recapture: Section 1245 property and Section 1250 property. Section 1245 property is property that is or has been property of a character subject to the depreciation allowance. Amortizable Section 197 intangibles, such as purchased goodwill, are considered Section 1245 property. Reg. Section 1.197-2(g)(8).

Generally Accepted Accounting Principles (GAAP). This term is used to refer to the standard framework of guidelines for financial accounting used in any given jurisdiction; generally known as *accounting standards*. GAAP includes the standards, conventions, and rules accountants follow in recording and summarizing transactions and in the preparation of financial statements.

Individual capital gains rates. If a noncorporate taxpayer has a net capital gain (excess of net long-term capital gains over net short-term losses, subject to certain netting rules, and increased by qualified dividend income) for a tax year, a maximum tax of 15 percent is imposed on the adjusted net capital gain. Code Sections 1(h)(1) and 1(h)(1)(C).

LLC/partnership basics. Partnerships are not subject to income tax. A partnership's income, gains, losses, deductions, and credits are attributed to its partners and taken into account only for purposes of determining the partners' individual income tax liabilities. Code Section 701.

Noncompete allocation. For purposes of the residual allocation rules, any covenant (including a covenant not to compete) made between a seller and purchaser in connection with an applicable asset acquisition is treated as an asset transferred as part of a trade or business. Reg. Section 1.1060-1(b)(7).

Personal goodwill. The notion of personal goodwill has been identified and used in a number of tax court cases: *Martin Ice Cream Company* (110 T.C. 189, 1998); *William Norwalk* (T.C. Memo 1998-279); *George J. Staab* (20 T.C. 834, 1953). Recently, a taxpayer failed to provide strong proof that the parties to an acquisition of the taxpayer's meat-producing company intended payments under a noncompetition agreement to be for the taxpayer's personal goodwill and not compensation. *Muskat, Irwin* (101 AFTR 2d. 2008-1606).

S corporation basics. An S corporation's items of income, loss, deduction, and credit are passed through to, and taken into account by, the corporation's shareholders in computing their own tax liability for the shareholder's tax year in which the S corporation's tax year ends. Subject to certain conditions regarding the recognition of losses, each shareholder takes a pro rata part of the items passed through into account. Code Section 1366(a)(1).

CHAPTER 13

Tax Provisions Used in M&A

T his chapter is somewhat of a continuation of Chapter 12 and provides more in-depth discussion of the tax rules applied in many merger and acquisition (M&A) transactions for closely held companies.* As in Chapter 12, at the end of this chapter is a short "Tax Glossary" to provide additional clarification about some of the key concepts used. This chapter addresses the following:

- Installment sales
- Section 1031 (like-kind) exchanges
- Partnership M&A
- Corporate M&A

INSTALLMENT SALES

When a company sells its assets, but the receipt of the consideration is deferred, the tax law allows for the seller to defer the recognition of tax gain along with it. The basic installment method requires that a *gross profit percentage* be determined for the asset being sold, using the total sale price less the seller's basis in the assets sold. Then, as payments are received, the payments are multiplied by the gross profit percentage to arrive at the recognized gain for that year. Table 13.1 illustrates this concept.

---

*The tax, accounting, and legal concepts herein are meant for educational purposes only and in no way should be used alone or without authoritative counsel from qualified tax and/or legal representation in providing advice or participating in a transaction.

TABLE 13.1 Installment Sale Calculation

Maximum sales price	$1,000,000
Cost basis in assets	(300,000)
Gross profit	700,000
Gross profit %	70%
Yearly principal payments	100,000
Gross profit %	70%
Gain recognized (plus interest)	$ 70,000

That is the basic rule. But, of course, with any tax law, there are exceptions and rules that must be followed. The deferral can take place in many different forms:

- Promissory note
- Holdback
- Escrow
- Earnout
- Other staged payments

Risk of Forfeiture

Any of these deferred payment structures can generally qualify for installment treatment, as long as the seller has a "substantial risk of forfeiture" with regard to the pending payments. For example, a promissory note from the buyer is generally assumed to have a risk of forfeiture, since the payments are dependent on the buyer's creditworthiness. However, merely deferring the payment by establishing a third-party escrow (that has no risk of being reclaimed by the buyer) would likely not meet the "risk of forfeiture" test.

Assets that Qualify for Installment Treatment

Not all assets sold by the company will necessarily qualify for installment treatment. In general, capital gains can be deferred while ordinary income cannot. Therefore, in most company sale transactions the portion of the sale price that is allocated to inventory or equipment (creating depreciation recapture) cannot qualify for installment treatment.

Generally, the cash and installment components of the sale are allocated over all the assets being sold. Therefore, in a company sale when both capital gains and ordinary income are being triggered, the full value of the installment note cannot be used for deferral (i.e., the ordinary income is recognized regardless of whether paid in cash or note). In addition, because some assets have a larger basis (and thus a lower gross profit percentage), deferring the gain on certain assets is more valuable than deferring gain on others. This creates a potential planning opportunity for deal structuring.

Installment Planning Opportunity

Rather than just allocating the installment note equally across all assets being sold, the transaction could be structured such that certain assets (capital assets with low basis) are sold for the note, while ordinary assets with high basis are sold for cash. To accomplish this transaction structure, the documents should reflect this same strategy. If possible, separate contracts should be drawn for cash and for installment assets being sold. Table 13.2 illustrates this concept.

Below is a partial list of installment rules to keep in mind when contemplating their use:

- Installment agreements are required to have interest calculated. In the case of earnouts, holdbacks, or escrow arrangements where there is no interest paid, the IRS requires interest to be imputed.
- Distribution of an installment note from a corporation can trigger the full gain to be recognized (except in the case of S corporation liquidation).
- Pledging an installment note or escrow as collateral can trigger gain as well.
- There are limitations on the use of installment reporting for related-party transactions.

TABLE 13.2 Installment Sale Structure

Asset	Sales Price	Basis	Note	Cash
Equipment	$1,000,000	$600,000	$ —	$1,000,000
Noncompete	500,000	—	500,000	—
Goodwill	3,000,000	—	1,500,000	1,500,000
Total	$4,500,000	$600,000	$2,000,000	$2,500,000

Contract 1: Sell equipment for $1,000,000 in cash, resulting in gain of $400,000 in first year.
Contract 2: Sell all other assets for $1,500,000 in cash and a $2,000,000 note. Gain is 100% capital and taxed when cash is received.

- Detailed rules exist for calculating installment gains when a contingent sale price exists, as in the case of earnouts.

SECTION 1031 (LIKE-KIND) EXCHANGES

A *1031 exchange*, also known as a *like-kind exchange*, is a transaction where a replacement property is acquired after the sale of "like-kind" property, and the gain can be deferred. The *1031* refers to the code section within the Internal Revenue Code (I.R.C.) where this rule is listed.

Section 1031 exchanges are most commonly used in real estate transactions; however, these rules can also be used for other business and investment assets. In the case of real estate, generally any type of real estate can be exchanged for another piece of real estate (i.e., apartments exchanged for office building, or raw land exchanged for apartments). For business and investment assets (other than real estate), the replacement property must be nearly exact to the asset sold. The tax law specifically rules out generic goodwill as an asset eligible for 1031 exchanges.

Third-Party Exchanges

In its simplest form, a 1031 exchange is completed when an asset is exchanged directly for another similar asset (as in an auto trade-in). However, in most real estate 1031 exchanges a third-party intermediary is employed to facilitate the transaction. The intermediary holds the proceeds from the sale and then reinvests the proceeds in the replacement property. The seller must identify a replacement property within 45 days and close on the replacement purchase within 180 days following the initial sale.

PARTNERSHIP M&A

In practical terms, LLCs and LLPs have replaced the old general and limited partnerships that were once used. Most states recognize and provide statutory formation and protections for LLCs and LLPs, which now gives the closely held business owner the legal benefits of a corporate structure while retaining the tax flexibility of partnership law. There are no separate tax laws defining taxation of an LLC. Rather the tax law requires LLCs to choose whether they are to be taxed as partnerships or corporations. In many cases, LLCs will choose to be taxed as partnerships.

Specific to M&A transactions, partnership tax law does provide some interesting challenges and some opportunities that are different than those available to corporate structures. Below is a discussion of the main partnership tax topics related to M&A transactions:

- General partnership doctrine
- Partnership versus S corporation differences
- Gain tracking rules
- Purchase price allocation for buyers (Section 754)

General Partnership Doctrine

One of the most significant differences between a partnership and a corporation is that a corporation is considered a "separate person" under the tax law, while a partnership is considered to be a mere collection of its partners. This concept is the basis for many of the partnership tax laws discussed below.

Partnership versus S Corporation

Many tax advisors and business owners will simplify the tax laws, implying that LLCs and S corporations are essentially the same. While this is true in many respects, there are some significant differences, and many of these differences are highlighted in an M&A transaction. Both S corporations and partnerships are treated as *flow-through* entities for tax purposes, where the company itself is not taxed on transactions, but rather the income is reported and taxed by the owners. However, the partnership doctrine does not apply to an S corporation. As a result, the two differ in the following areas:

- Self-employment tax
- Mark-to-market distribution of assets
- Stock versus asset transactions
- Special profit allocations
- Ownership flexibility

Self-Employment Tax   Ordinary income generated in an S corporation is never subject to self-employment tax when it flows through to an owner as a result of his or her ownership interest (assuming that any owner performing services for the company is paid reasonable compensation for such services); this is not necessarily the case for a partnership. The partners in a partnership must determine whether they are active participants in the activity. If so, then the income may be subject to self-employment tax. Even if the owner is already past the FICA tax limit due to other income, the Medicare rate of 2.9 percent will apply indefinitely to any income subject to self-employment.

While this difference can impact taxes on an annual basis for an operating company, it can dramatically impact an M&A transaction if a substantial portion of the sale creates ordinary income (such as from the sale of inventory, depreciation recapture, consulting allocations, etc.).

Mark-to-Market Distribution of Assets   When a corporation (S or C) distributes an asset, the tax law requires that the corporation first recognize any imputed gain (i.e., it must mark-to-market). In the case of an S corporation this will trigger taxable income at the company level, which then flows through to the owners proportionately. A partnership, however, does not have to recognize this mark-to-market gain and can distribute assets to a selected partner without triggering this gain.

This issue is most commonly encountered during an M&A transaction when a seller wishes to retain certain assets (such as real estate) that the buyer does not want. An LLC or partnership can allow for the distribution of these assets before the M&A transaction without any tax impact on the seller in most cases.

Stock versus Asset Transactions   Because of the partnership doctrine, all company sale transactions are essentially treated as asset transactions because the tax law does not recognize stock in a partnership. Of course, legally, an LLC can and often does engage in transactions where the members sell their membership interest (the LLC's equivalent to stock). But the tax law interpretation of that transaction can be viewed as a distribution of a percentage of the underlying assets followed by the partner then selling those assets.

Here is an example, illustrated in Table 13.3. Assume an LLC member wishes to sell a 25 percent membership interest for $2,000. He has an underlying basis in his membership interest of $1,000. Legally, this appears

TABLE 13.3   Sale of an LLC Membership Interest

Partnership Assets	Total Assets	25% Partner	Sales Price
Cash	$ 500	$ 125	$ 125
Inventory	1,500	375	375
Equipment	3,000	750	1,000
Intangibles	1,000	250	1,000
Total assets	6,000	1,500	2,500
Liabilities	2,000	500	500
Partners' equity	$4,000	$1,000	$2,000

to be a simple transaction and the LLC member may view this as similar to an S corporation sale of stock, which would result in a transaction with a $1,000 capital gain. However, for tax purposes the LLC must treat this as a distribution of a percentage of the underlying assets (and share of underlying debt). We have made a number of simplifying assumptions in order for this scenario to work in practice; nonetheless, it serves to illustrate the concept.

As can be seen in this example, an otherwise-stock transaction is essentially converted into an asset transaction for tax purposes. This requires the member to report the transaction on his personal tax return as if he had sold each of these individual assets (some creating ordinary gains and some creating capital gains). It also requires the seller and buyer to allocate the purchase price (or somehow agree on an allocation of purchase price).

Special Profit Allocations   Another benefit of the LLC/partnership structure is the ability to specially allocate profits and losses between partners. C corporations are permitted to create these special equity allocations in the form of preferred stock. However, when a corporation makes an S election, it gives up the ability to issue preferred stock and as a result it may not have different economic classes of equity. LLCs, however, will commonly have multiple levels and classes of membership interests. The partnership tax laws allow for each partner's income allocations to be specially determined as long as they follow "substantial economic effect" provisions of the I.R.C.

Ownership Flexibility   The following criteria apply to S corporation shareholders:

- Each shareholder must be a U.S. citizen or resident alien.
- Each shareholder must be an individual (not a corporate, LLC or partnership entity).
- There can be more than 100 shareholders.
- Only common stock can be issued.

Partnerships do not have any of these ownership restrictions. This provides a great deal of flexibility in structuring joint ventures or recapitalization transactions between parties like private equity groups, foreign corporations, or multiple-owner organizations. As a result, an LLC structure is common when a buyer is seeking the benefits of a flow-through entity yet does not meet the restrictions of an S corporation.

Partnership Gain Tracking Rules

Because partnerships allow for contribution and distribution of property without any tax consequences, additional rules were enacted to prevent deemed sale transactions between partners. Without these gain tracking rules, partner A could contribute cash and partner B could contribute assets he wished to sell. Then, the partnership could distribute the assets to partner A and the cash to partner B. Without gain tracking rules, this would have effectively accomplished a tax-free exchange of property.

That was not the intent of the partnership rules. The gain tracking rules prevent this type of structure by requiring that any *built-in gain* associated with property at the time of contribution must be tracked and allocated back to the partner who contributed it. This built-in gain tracking is triggered if the property is sold to a third party or distributed to another partner within certain time periods defined in the I.R.C.

While these rules were put in place to prevent blatant tax avoidance as described, the same rules can create complications in legitimate recapitalization and joint venture agreements. M&A advisors should be aware of situations where LLCs or partnerships are formed with contributions of depreciated assets, business assets, or other appreciated property, so that possible unintended tax consequences do not impact the economics of the deal.

Purchase Price Allocation for Partnership Buyers

As noted, the purchase or sale of a partnership (membership) interest is effectively treated as an asset transaction by the seller. Even in situations where the transaction is legally structured as a "stock" sale of an LLC membership interest, the seller must determine the pro rata fair market value of the underlying assets within the partnership and treat the sale ultimately as the sale of multiple assets.

Likewise, the buyer may treat the purchase of a partnership interest as an asset purchase and obtain a step-up in basis and subsequent depreciation or amortization of the underlying assets she has acquired. Of course, practically, these assets are still located within the partnership and no "transaction" has occurred that would cause their increase in basis. The tax law provides an election that can be made by the partnership and partner whereby this additional basis is booked by the partnership and can be depreciated. This is known as a *754 election* and is treated as if this new basis is contributed by the buying partner.

In addition to obtaining the basis increase, the gain tracking and special allocation rules noted previously will allow for the contributing partner to obtain all the benefit of this additional basis (since he is the one who paid for it). This will cause the additional basis to be specifically allocated to the contributing partner in the event the assets are sold. And, any depreciation or amortization of that additional basis can be specifically allocated to the contributing partner.

CORPORATE M&A ISSUES

Most M&A transactions will involve the sale of a corporation. In addition to the decision to sell assets versus stock (as noted in the beginning of this chapter) there are a number of specific tax laws that govern the sale and reorganization of corporate entities. This section will cover the following specific tax issues that relate to corporations:

- Contributions to corporations
- Mergers and reorganizations
- Net operating loss limits
- Stock/asset sale election (338 election)
- Issues specific to S corporations

Contributions to Corporations

To form a corporation, shareholders are permitted to exchange any variety of tangible assets, and most forms of intangible assets for the stock of the corporation and not pay tax on the transaction. This principle seems obvious when a corporation is formed with a cash contribution. But, without some limitations this rule could be abused to disguise traditional sale transactions. Therefore Section 351 of the I.R.C. provides rules where contributions of property can be made without gain recognized:

- The contribution must be made solely in exchange for stock in the corporation. Any nonstock contribution (referred to as *boot*) will trigger tax.
- The parties to the contribution must have 80 percent or more control of the corporation following the transaction.

In addition to formation of a new corporation, these contribution rules can be used to structure a type of merger transaction known as a *contributing merger*, shown in Figure 13.1. This type of transaction is often used when two or more partnerships or sole proprietorships wish to merge.

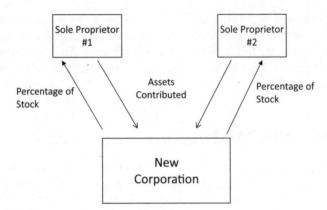

FIGURE 13.1 Contributing Merger Diagram

The contributing parties are each individually valued and shares are issued proportionate to the value being contributed.

Mergers and Reorganizations

The tax law provides for specific transactions where corporate buyers can issue shares of stock in exchange for either assets or stock of the seller, and the gain from the sale can be deferred by the sellers. These types of transactions are individually described in I.R.C. Section 368(a)(1), and have become known by their subsection letter designations:

> A = Merger
> B = Stock-for-Stock
> C = Stock-for-Assets
> D = Divisive Breakups
> E = Recapitalization
> F = Name Change
> G = Bankruptcy

General Tax-Free Deal Structures   The general goals and rules associated with these transactions are as follows:

- Seller does not pay any tax on the sale transaction until the stock that was received is sold (i.e., the gain is deferred into the buyer's stock).

TABLE 13.4 Type A Merger

Sales price	$1,000,000
Stock basis	(700,000)
Gain	300,000
Buyer stock issued	600,000
Cash paid	400,000
Gain recognized	300,000
Gain deferred	—

- Any boot (something other than stock) received in the transaction will trigger gain to be recognized by the seller.
- Boot is taxed on a first-in first-out (FIFO) basis as explained below.
- Buyer does not get any step-up in basis of the assets acquired.

Type A Mergers The first type of merger is referred to as *Type A*, also known as a *statutory merger* because the transaction must be structured under state law in the state in which the parties are incorporated. To safely qualify as Type A under the tax law, the compensation received by the seller must be at least 40 percent of the total compensation (i.e., boot received must be no more than 60 percent). However, because the gain is taxed on a FIFO basis as boot is received, the tax deferral works only if the gain is bigger than the boot received. Table 13.4 illustrates the basic concept.

Type A Triangular Mergers In practice, most corporate buyers (known as *P* for *parent*) will establish an acquisition corporation (known as *Newco*) for the sole purpose of acquiring the target company (known as *T* for *target*). This creates a *triangular* merger. One of the parties must dissolve as a result of the transaction with one of the corporations being the survivor. Depending on which party survives, the transaction will be described as a *reverse triangular* or *forward triangular* merger. Figure 13.2 is a diagram of a forward triangular merger and Figure 13.3 illustrates the reverse version.

Type B Mergers Whereas Type A mergers may be completed only in conjunction with state law and therefore are referred to as *statutory* mergers, the remaining B, C, D, E, F, and G mergers are found only in the tax code. Specifically, Type B mergers are defined in the tax law as purely a stock-for-stock exchange. No cash or other nonstock assets may be paid by the buyer for the seller's stock. However, because the Type B merger does not

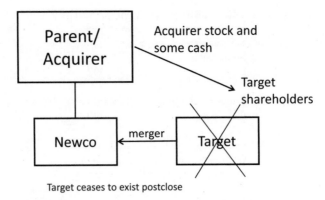

FIGURE 13.2   Type A Forward Triangular Merger

need to be registered under state law, some transactions qualifying as Type B mergers can be done quickly and without filing any articles of merger with the secretary of state.

Type C Mergers   In essence, a Type C merger is an asset transaction (i.e., the seller is selling assets), whereas a Type A merger is a stock transaction. The buyer is still using its stock as purchase consideration, but the selling corporation is selling its assets. The goal is still the same, which is to allow the selling shareholders to defer the gain from the transaction into the stock received from the buyer.

To qualify as a Type C merger under the tax law, the buyer's stock must make up at least 80 percent of the deal consideration (i.e., there can only be 20 percent or less cash or other boot, including the assumption of liabilities).

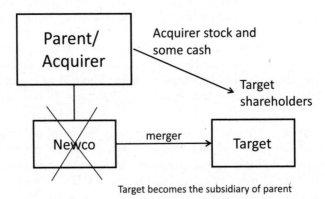

FIGURE 13.3   Type A Reverse Triangular Merger

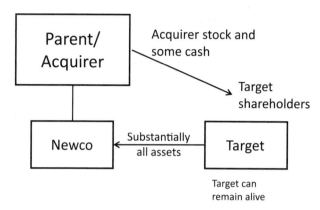

FIGURE 13.4 Type C Forward Triangular Merger

Because C transactions are asset deals, the buyer and seller must agree on an allocation of purchase price, as well as determine which liabilities are going to be assumed along with the acquired assets. This can create difficulties when large amounts of debt are being assumed in the transaction, as debt assumed is considered boot.

Type C mergers are also generally done in a triangular structure, as illustrated in Figure 13.4.

Divisive D Reorganizations Unlike mergers referred to in A, B, or C transactions, the D subsection of the reorganization tax laws is used to divide or separate out a portion of a company. Hence these are referred to as *divisive D* reorganizations, and are typically referred to as *spinoffs* or *spinouts*, where a group of existing shareholders wishes to take a division or group of assets from the company in exchange for their shares in the parent corporation. The corporation may do so without recognizing taxable gains that would otherwise result from the sale of the same division or assets. There are limitations to these D reorganizations, including:

- The assets used to form the new spinoff company must constitute an active business with a significant operating history—not just investment activities.
- There must be prior shareholder control of the new company immediately after the transaction.
- There are limitations for subsequent sale or change in control of post–D reorganization companies.

Type E Recapitalizations　Recapitalizations defined in Section E of the tax law allow some shareholders to turn in their stock in a corporation and receive other stock or securities in the same corporation. This is sometimes a tool used in closely held businesses to transition stock from the older generation to the younger generation—where the older generation accepts nonvoting shares or preferred shares in exchange for common ownership retained by the children.

Type F Reorganizations　Type F transactions allow mere changes in identity, form, or place of organization of one corporation. This is typically used to change state of incorporation, without any tax impact.

Type G Bankruptcies　Subsection G allows for the tax-free transfer of assets from one corporation to another in a Chapter 11 or similar bankruptcy proceeding.

Net Operating Loss Limitations

Net operating losses (NOLs) are operating losses generated by a corporation that may be carried forward up to 20 years. They belong to the corporation and can be transferred to a buyer in a stock purchase. However, to prevent buyers from specifically buying corporate shells just for the NOLs, certain limitations were put in place to limit the use of NOLs upon the sale of a corporation.

The limitation is triggered whenever there is an ownership change of greater than 50 percent. The NOL is not reduced, but rather the amount of the NOL that can be recognized in any year is limited to the value of the corporation's stock multiplied by the long-term tax-exempt rate for the month in which the ownership changes. This limitation effectively neuters any attempt to purchase the shares of a corporation solely for the NOL benefits.

Stock/Asset Sale Election: Section 338

There are situations where the choice of whether to treat a particular transaction as a stock sale or asset sale can have conflicting legal and tax implications. In situations where both the buyer and seller wish to treat the transaction as a stock sale for legal purposes, but treat the sale as an asset sale for tax purposes, the tax law provides for an election known as a *338 election.*

The 338 election is often misquoted or misunderstood, and is sometimes referred to as a best-of-both-worlds solution to the age-old dilemma that arises when the seller wants a stock sale and the buyer wants an asset purchase. But do not be confused. A 338 election does *not* provide that magical solution. Rather, the 338 election is treated as follows:

Legal Treatment	Tax Treatment
Buyer is buying stock	Buyer is treated as though it bought assets
Seller is selling stock	Seller treats sale as an asset sale

The 338 election allows *both* parties to treat the transaction as a stock sale for legal purposes. And, it requires *both* parties to treat the transaction as an asset sale for tax purposes. There are two types of 338 elections:

1. Section 338(h)(10) election—where the seller recognizes the taxable income resulting from the sale of the assets
2. Section 338(g) election—where the buyer recognizes the taxable income resulting from the sale of the assets

Section 338 elections can be made by both S corporations and C corporations, depending on the circumstances and the type of election, although each type of election is only available in certain circumstances. In all cases more than 80 percent of the stock must be acquired in the transaction, and the buyer must be a corporation (S or C).

Common 338(h)(10) Transaction Scenario

- The entity being sold is an S corporation.
- The corporation holds certain licenses or contracts that would be difficult or impossible to transfer in an asset sale.
- There is likely a large imputed intangible (goodwill) value.
- An asset sale would result in mostly capital gain (mostly intangibles, little depreciation recapture or ordinary income items).

In this example, the buyer would prefer (and maybe demand) a stock sale transaction, as the buyer does not want to lose the licenses or contracts owned by the corporation. However, the buyer also does not want to forgo the amortization of goodwill and desires a step-up in basis for the intangible assets. Legally, the buyer wants a stock transaction, but prefers an asset transaction for tax purposes. Since the seller is an S corporation and since either an asset sale or stock sale would result in mostly capital gains for the seller, an asset sale for tax purposes is likely acceptable.

The 338(h)(10) transaction can also work well in situations where the seller is a C corporation with significant NOLs, provided the C corporation target is qualified to make a 338(h)(10) election (i.e., is a member of a consolidated or affiliated group). Similar to the S corporation situation, if the gain from the sale of assets is offset by NOLs, then the tax results of an asset sale and a stock sale are nearly identical to the seller.

Common 338(g) Transaction Scenario

- The seller is an S or C corporation.
- The buyer is a C corporation with large or expiring NOLs

In these circumstances, the buyer can enhance his value to the seller by offering a 338(g) transaction conveying much of the tax impact of the sale to the buyer. In addition, the buyer is utilizing NOLs that are unlikely to be used or may be expiring and converting the NOL into depreciable or amortizable assets, thus extending their deduction life.

S Corporation Issues

An S corporation is legally the same as a C corporation, but makes a special election to be taxed differently by the IRS. This election converts the company into a flow-through entity and allows the shareholders to pay tax on the company's earnings (including gains resulting from the sale of the company), similar to a partnership. However, all of the corporate merger and reorganization tax laws still apply to S corporations. To become an S corporation, the corporation must meet and maintain certain ownership requirements:

- Only individuals—no corporations, LLCs, or partnerships—may own shares.
- There must be fewer than 100 shareholders.
- No preferred stock may be issued, only common stock.
- Only U.S. citizens or resident aliens may own shares.

Built-in Gains Tax   When a former C corporation makes an election to become an S corporation, any asset that has a built-in gain can become subject to C corporation tax if it is sold within 5 to 10 years following the election (the applicable time period has been subject to change over the last few years). The *built-in gain* is defined as the *fair market value* of the asset less its adjusted basis at the time of the election. However, the built-in gain subject to C corporation tax cannot exceed the total gain from the actual sale. Likewise, any gain greater than the original built-in gain is just reported

TABLE 13.5 Built-in Gains Tax Example

C Corp Makes S-Election in 2005	
Fair market value at S election	$5,000
Basis at S election	3,000
Built-in gain	2,000

Asset Sold in 2012	
Sale price	4,000
Basis at time of sale	3,000
Total gain from sale	1,000
Gain subject to built-in gain tax	1,000
C corporation tax rate	34%
Built-in gain tax paid by S corporation	$ 340

as S corporation gain and flows through to the shareholders. Finally, the total of all built-in gains cannot exceed the net built-in gains less built-in losses existing at the time of S election. Built-in losses may exist from loss assets that have not been recognized, or from deductible expense items that have not been recognized due to tax laws prohibiting their deduction (such as deferred compensation, bad-debt expenses, certain accrued expenses, etc.). Table 13.5 provides an example.

Specific assets to be concerned with when evaluating built-in gains include:

- Real estate assets
- Unrealized receivables (cash-basis taxpayers)
- Goodwill and other intangibles

There are a few planning opportunities to help alleviate or eliminate built-in gains tax:

- *Properly defining fair market value at the time of the S election.* Specifically, valuations should be completed by those who are experienced in defining fair market value and are not swayed by possible strategic sale events that have taken place in the market.
- *Taking personal goodwill into consideration.* As noted, personal goodwill and corporate goodwill should not be confused, and have been recognized by the tax courts. Therefore, when obtaining a valuation for

purposes of identifying built-in gains, the appraiser should be asked to separately value personal goodwill from corporate goodwill.

- *Offsetting with built-in losses.* Because built-in gains cannot exceed the net amount of gains and built-in losses, it is important to capture as many accrued expenses or pending losses as possible when the S election is made.

TAX GLOSSARY AND REFERENCE

The following discussions are to support the core text of this chapter. Code Sections refer to the I.R.C., and Reg. sections refer to the Treasury Regulations that interpret and supplement the I.R.C. and are binding on taxpayers.

Contributions to corporation. A person or persons recognize no gain or loss on a transfer to a corporation if all the following requirements are met: (1) Property is transferred to the corporation; (2) transfer of property is solely in exchange for stock of the transferee corporation; and (3) the person or persons making the transfer are in control (80 percent or more) of the transferee corporation immediately after the exchange. Code Section 351(a).

Divisive D reorganizations. In order for a distribution of stock of a controlled corporation to qualify as a Code Section 355 tax-free corporate division, so that it is not taxable to the distributing corporation and to the shareholders who receive the distribution, the requirements found in Code Section 355(a)(1) must be met.

Installment risk of forfeiture. If an escrow agreement incident to an installment note imposes a substantial restriction, in addition to the payment schedule, upon the seller's right to receive the sales proceeds, the amounts deposited in the escrow agreement aren't considered to be payments in the year of the sale. An example of a substantial restriction would be a requirement that the seller refrain from entering a competing business until paid in full. But if no substantial restriction exists, the substitution of an escrow deposit for a deed of trust as collateral for the installment sale would represent a payment of the unpaid balance of the installment obligation. Revenue Ruling 77-294, 1977-2 CB 173.

Installment sales. "Installment method" means a method under which the income recognized for any taxable year from a disposition is that proportion of the payments received in that year that the gross profit (realized or to be realized when payment is completed) bears to the total contract price. Code Section 453(c).

Net operating loss limitations. If an ownership change occurs, a loss corporation's taxable income for a postchange tax year that may be offset by certain losses arising before the ownership change is limited by the Section 382 limitation. The section 382 limitation for any post-change year is an amount equal to the value of the old loss corporation multiplied by the long-term tax-exempt rate. Code Section 382.

Partnership allocations. A partner's distributive share of the partnership's income, gains, losses, deductions, and credits is determined by the partnership agreement (Code Section 704(a)), unless: the agreement doesn't provide for the allocation of an item or items (Code Section 704(b)(1)), or the allocation provided for in the agreement doesn't have substantial economic effect (Code Section 704(b)(2)).

Partnership basis adjustment upon sale. Upon transfer of a partnership interest or the death of a partner, if there is a Code Section 754 basis adjustment election in effect or there is a substantial built-in loss immediately after the transfer, the partnership's basis in its property with respect to the transferee partner is *increased* by any excess of the adjusted basis to the transferee partner of his partnership interest over his share of the adjusted basis of the partnership property (Code Section 743(b)(1); Reg. Section 1.743-1(b)(1)), or *decreased* by any excess of the transferee partner's proportionate share of the adjusted basis of the partnership property over the basis of his interest in the partnership (Code Section 743(b)(2); Reg. Section 1.743-1(b)(2)).

Partnership doctrine. For federal tax purposes, the Code defines the term *partnership* to include a syndicate, group, pool, joint venture, or other unincorporated organization through or by means of which any business, financial operation, or venture is carried on, and which is *not,* within the meaning of the Code, a corporation, trust, or estate. Code Sections 761(a) and 7701(a)(2).

Partnership gain tracking. A partnership's income, gain, loss, and deduction with respect to property contributed by a partner to a partnership must be specially allocated so as to take account of the difference between the fair market value of the property and its basis in the partnership's hands at the time of the contribution. Code Section 704(c)(1)(A). The purpose of these rules is to prevent partners from shifting the tax consequences with respect to unrealized gain on property to other partners by contributing the property to the partnership. Reg. Section 1.704-3(a)(1).

Qualifying assets for installment method. The installment method may not be used to report income from the following dispositions: dispositions resulting in losses; stock sales where the sale is treated as a contribution to capital followed by a redemption; dealer dispositions, including (with some exceptions) any disposition of personal property by a person who regularly sells personal property of the same type in the ordinary course of business, and dispositions of real property held for sale in the ordinary course of the seller's trade or business; income that is recapturable under Code Sections 1245 or 1250; certain sales of depreciable property to a controlled entity; sales of publicly traded property; and dispositions of property under a revolving credit plan. Code Section 453.

S corporation built-in gains tax. An S corporation is subject to a corporate-level tax (built-in gains tax) in any tax year beginning in the recognition period (10 years) in which it has a net recognized built-in gain. Code Section 1374(a). Net recognized built-in gain means, with respect to any tax year in the recognition period, the lesser of: (1) the amount that would be the taxable income of the S corporation for that tax year if only recognized built-in gains and recognized built-in losses are taken into account, or (2) the corporation's taxable income for that tax year. Code Sections 1374(d)(2)(A)(i) and 1374(d)(2)(A)(ii).

Section 338 election. If a purchasing corporation makes an election under Section 338, then in the case of any qualified stock purchase, the target corporation shall be treated as having sold all of its assets at the close of the acquisition date at fair market value in a single transaction, and shall be treated as a new corporation that purchased all of the assets as of the beginning of the day after the acquisition date. Code Section 338(a).

Section 1031 like-kind exchanges. No gain or loss is recognized on the exchange of property held for productive use in a trade or business or for investment if that property is exchanged solely for property of a like kind that is to be held either for productive use in a trade or business or for investment. Code Section 1031(a)(1).

Type A reorganizations. For purposes of Code Section 368(a)(1)(A), a statutory merger or consolidation is a transaction effected under the statute or statutes necessary to effect the merger or consolidation (in which, as a result of the operation of the statute or statutes) the following events occur simultaneously at the effective time of the transaction: (1) All of the assets (other than those distributed in the transaction) and liabilities (except to the extent such liabilities are satisfied or discharged in the transaction or are nonrecourse liabilities to which assets distributed in the transaction are subject) of each member of one or more combining units (each a transferor unit) become the assets and liabilities of one or more members of one other combining unit (the transferee unit; Reg. Section 1.368-2(b)(1)(ii)(A)); and (2) the combining entity of each transferor unit ceases its separate legal existence for all purposes (Reg. Section 1.368-2(b)(1)(ii)(B)).

Type B reorganizations. The acquiring corporation must acquire the stock of the target corporation solely, in exchange for all or a part of its (acquiring corporation's) voting stock and the acquiring corporation must have control of the target immediately after the acquisition. Code Section 368(a)(1)(B).

Type C reorganizations. In a Type C reorganization, the acquiring corporation must acquire substantially all the assets of the target corporation solely in exchange for all or a part of the acquiring corporation's voting stock. Code Section 368(a)(1)(C).

CHAPTER 14

Regulation and Compliance

This chapter discusses securities laws that may be encountered in the deal process. The federal securities laws (and to a lesser extent state securities laws, also known as blue-sky laws) frequently influence the decisions and behaviors of parties to a corporate transaction. A basic familiarity with these laws will help advisors understand the framework within which their clients often must operate, and help them avoid legal exposure for their own actions.

PROTECTING INVESTORS: SECURITIES ACT OF 1933

The Securities Act of 1933 (33 Act), sometimes referred to as the "truth in securities" law, was the first substantial attempt at federal regulation of the offer and sale of securities. Congress enacted the 33 Act during the Great Depression for two principal purposes: (1) to prohibit deceit, misrepresentations, and fraud in the sale of new issuances of securities, and (2) to ensure that investors receive financial and other significant information concerning securities being offered for public sale. The aim was for an investor to have sufficient information to make a reasonable decision about the purchase of a security.

The 33 Act generally requires registration with the Securities and Exchange Commission (SEC) of any security being offered to the public for the first time and, in connection with the registration, disclosure of information about the offering and the issuer. Don't be deceived by the word *first*. The law applies to secondary offerings as well, meaning offerings by someone other than the company that issued the securities, such as individuals or institutions who may have acquired the securities that have not been previously registered and wish to sell them to someone else.

The 33 Act has implications not only for strategic financing transactions, but also for mergers and acquisitions in which stock represents a portion of the transaction's consideration. Any time a security may be making its way into public hands for the first time, it is important to remember the 33 Act's basic mandate: Register—or find an exemption.

One of the most frequent conceptual applications of the 33 Act is to a well-known corporate financing method: issuing equity to investors. Whether it's going public or simply raising a discrete amount of additional capital, selling stock is one of the most traditional means for a company to raise money.

Section 5 of the 33 Act prohibits the direct or indirect use of interstate commerce to offer or sell a security before a registration statement has been filed and is effective. Section 5 also makes it unlawful to send a security through the mails unless preceded or accompanied by an informational document, called a *prospectus*, that meets certain requirements. Thus, when a company is raising capital by issuing new securities to the public, it will generally need to comply with the registration and prospectus requirements of the 33 Act, unless there is an exemption available.

The requirements of the 33 Act also apply to nontraditional issuances of new equity in a capital-raising venture. Rule 145 makes the 33 Act applicable to a plan or agreement submitted for the vote of shareholders in a stock-for-stock business combination. The rule's rationale is that the decision to accept a new or different security in exchange for an existing security constitutes a new investment decision for the shareholders, requiring the information and protection that the 33 Act is intended to afford. Rule 145 also covers reclassifications of securities—other than standard stock splits, reverse stock splits, or changes in par value—in which one security is substituted for another and certain transfers of assets in exchange for the issuance of securities. Thus, if you are working on a deal that involves stock as the currency, be sure to consider the need for a registration of the shares being exchanged, or the availability of an exemption from registration.

Exemptions under the 33 Act

The focus of the 33 Act is the protection of the public investor. In some corporate transactions, the nature of the investors or the transaction removes the need for that protection. Take, for example, a traditional private placement. A limited number of sophisticated investors with abundant access to the resources necessary to evaluate the investment probably do not need the same protections as someone who lacks investment sophistication.

Sometimes known as the *private placement exemption*, Section 4(2) of the 33 Act removes transactions by an issuer not involving any public offering from the scope of the Section 5 requirements. What constitutes a public offering is determined by an analysis of the investors: Do they need the protections afforded by the 33 Act? Several factors may help answer that question, such as the number of potential investors and their relationship to the offeror, the investors' sophistication, the availability of information to the investors, the size of the offering, and the manner in which the offer was communicated to potential investors. Once securities are issued pursuant to this exemption, they become *restricted securities*, meaning they have certain conditions attached to their resale.

In a transaction involving the issuance of new securities, advisors need to consider not only the initial offering, but also what may happen to those securities down the road. Once unregistered securities have been placed into an investor's hands via a private placement, that investor may very well wish to sell those securities to another investor in order to liquidate the investment. It is best to remember the basic mandate: Register the security or find an exemption. It applies at every sale of unregistered securities. Rule 144 under the 33 Act provides a safe harbor for the resale of restricted securities, such as those received in a private placement, and outlines conditions under which a later transaction will also be exempt from the Section 5 requirements. Generally, the determination depends on the seller's relationship with the issuer, the availability of public information regarding the issuer, how long the seller has held the securities, and, in some cases, the manner in which the shares will be resold.

Other 33 Act exemptions focus on the type of securities issued in the transaction rather than the investors who will receive them. For example, Section 3(a)(11) of the 33 Act provides that any security offered and sold only to residents of a single state (where the issuer is resident and doing business) need not be registered with the SEC. Remember, however, that the securities may still be required to be registered at the state level.

Commonly Used Private Placement Exemptions

The SEC, recognizing that the registration requirements may be an excessive burden that hinders the ability to raise capital, has adopted rules to ease this burden in an attempt to balance risks.

Regulation D is one of these rules. It is, in effect, a series of mini-exemptions from the registration requirements. Several of the exemptions may be relevant to strategic transactions in middle market companies, and each has its own list of conditions that must be met in order to qualify for the safe-harbor protection. Generally, factors to consider will include the size of the offering, the manner of the offering, and to whom the offer is made.

A Rule 504 transaction allows companies to offer up to $1 million of securities without complying with registration and prospectus requirements, so long as certain conditions are met. Since transactions qualifying for the Rule 504 exemption are relatively small and often take place in a limited geographic area, the SEC generally defers to the states for their regulation.

Rule 505 provides an exemption for a transaction in which a company that meets certain conditions offers up to $5 million of securities, and no more than 35 purchasers are involved. In determining the number of purchasers in a transaction, the regulation considers each purchaser's characteristics. *Accredited investors* are investors who fall into designated categories under the rules, such as banks, directors and executive officers of the issuer, and high-net-worth individuals. Accredited investors are presumed to have greater resources and/or investment sophistication than nonaccredited investors and do not count toward the 35-purchaser limit.

Unlike 504 and 505, Rule 506 has no maximum offering price. Much like Rule 505, the principal requirements are that a company meet certain conditions and that there be no more than 35 nonaccredited purchasers involved. The catch is that all nonaccredited investors must meet a certain sophistication requirement. General business or legal experience is typically insufficient; the rule contemplates those investors who have the knowledge and experience necessary to evaluate the merits and risks of a particular investment.

Be wary of multiple issuances in close proximity. If a company engages in multiple issuances of securities, they may all be aggregated when evaluating whether the company's offering will qualify for an exemption. The integration doctrine is the SEC's way of ensuring that an issuer cannot evade the registration requirements of the 33 Act by simply dividing a single offering into several parts. This can be problematic where, for example, there are fewer than 35 nonaccredited investors in each issuance, but more than 35 when aggregated. Typically, five factors determine whether a series of offerings will be integrated into one:

1. Whether the separate transactions are part of a single plan of financing
2. Whether the offerings involve the same class of securities
3. Whether the offerings were made at or about the same time
4. Whether the same type of consideration was received for the offerings
5. Whether the offerings were made for the same general purpose

However, offers and sales made more than six months before or six months after a Regulation D offering will not be integrated, regardless of the five-factor test.

KEEPING THE MARKETS HONEST: SECURITIES EXCHANGE ACT OF 1934

The Securities Exchange Act of 1934 (34 Act) regulates the public trading of securities. It is the birthplace of the SEC and the source of the SEC's broad authority to (1) register, regulate, and oversee brokerage firms, transfer agents, clearing agents, and the nation's stock exchanges and (2) require periodic reporting of information by companies with publicly traded securities. The 34 Act regulates not only securities and parties in securities transactions, but also conduct in the marketplace.

Requirements and Rules

One of the principal requirements of the 34 Act piggybacks on the 33 Act's mandate to register the security issued in a transaction unless the security or transaction is exempt. Under the 34 Act, it is unlawful for any broker-dealer to effect any transaction in a nonexempt security on a national securities exchange unless a proper registration for that security is effective. Issuers register a class of their securities for trading on a national securities exchange by filing a registration statement with the SEC and a listing application with the exchange, which contains, among other things, information about the issuer and its securities, organizational documents, and material contracts.

For those involved with strategic corporate transactions, one of the most important parts of the 34 Act is its general antifraud provisions. Rule 10b-5 requires certain disclosure for strategic corporate transactions and also prohibits trading in a company's securities based on information not yet disclosed to the public. The rule makes it unlawful for any person to:

1. Employ any device, scheme, or artifice to defraud
2. Make any untrue statement of material fact or omit to state any material fact necessary to make a statement made, in light of the circumstances under which it was made, not misleading
3. Engage in any act that would operate as a fraud or deceit upon any person in connection with the purchase or sale of any security

Failure to disclose material facts about the issuer, such as pending merger transactions, may operate as a fraud on the issuer's securities. There is some uncertainty surrounding at what point preliminary merger discussions become material depending on the probability of the merger's consummation and the magnitude of the transaction. Those involved in the proposed transaction also must be careful not to trade in the securities based on material nonpublic information (often the existence of discussions will be deemed material information). There are two important enforcement aspects to note: (1) *Any* person who fraudulently induces the purchase or sale of a security may be found liable under the rule; and (2) in addition to the SEC, private citizens may bring lawsuits under the rule.

Williams Act

In 1968, Congress passed the Williams Act, amending the 34 Act to regulate tender offers and other takeover actions. To further the federal securities laws' aim of investor protection, the Williams Act requires that any person making a tender offer for a public company or any person acquiring more than 5 percent of a class of a company's registered securities disclose a variety of information through an SEC filing, including the source of funds being used in the offer, the purpose of the offer, the prospective purchaser's plans if successful, and any contracts or arrangements concerning the target company. Additionally, if any material change occurs in the facts disclosed, the acquirer must amend the disclosure.

Since the disclosure requirements are triggered when an individual acquires more than 5 percent of a class of the company's registered securities, the company and investors effectively get an early warning of takeover plans and are afforded greater time to analyze their options. In addition to this early warning mechanism, the regulation alleviates the pressures of quick decision making for investors by requiring that a tender offer remain open for a minimum of 20 business days. If the offeror increases or decreases the percentage of the class of security being sought, the offer must also remain open for at least 10 business days from the date that the first notice is published or sent to the shareholders. The offeror may extend the required period, as it may desire to do if a longer offer period would increase the likelihood of obtaining more shares. Investors have the opportunity to withdraw their shares at any time during the entire period that the offer remains open.

In addition to requiring the provision of information in tender offers, the Williams Act amended the 34 Act to prohibit fraudulent communications with respect to the offer. It made it unlawful for any person undertaking a tender offer to make any untrue statement of a material fact or omit to state any material fact necessary to make statements not misleading, or to engage in any fraudulent, deceptive, or manipulative acts or practices. Additionally, it endowed the SEC with the power to define, and prescribe means reasonably designed to prevent, those acts and practices that are fraudulent, deceptive, or manipulative.

ANTITRUST ISSUES AND LAWS YOU MAY ENCOUNTER IN THE DEAL

Antitrust laws aim to prohibit anticompetitive behavior and unfair business practices in the United States. In the late 1800s, growing concern that "big business" was destroying the competitive roots of capitalist America prompted federal regulation of large business enterprises. In 1890, Congress enacted the Sherman Antitrust Act to limit cartels and monopolies and protect consumers from price inflation due to artificial trade or supply restriction. The Clayton Antitrust Act followed in 1914 to tie up some loose ends of the Sherman Antitrust Act by specifying particular prohibited conduct, such as mergers and acquisitions whose effect may substantially limit competition, and outlining an enforcement scheme and exemptions.

Antitrust laws are principally governed by two regulatory bodies that have overlapping enforcement authority: the Department of Justice and the Federal Trade Commission. The Federal Trade Commission is entirely dedicated to enforcing the antitrust laws of the United States, and the Department of Justice has a separate division dedicated to promoting economic competition through enforcing those same laws.

Hart-Scott-Rodino Act

The Hart-Scott-Rodino Act (HSR) is an antitrust law that requires parties to mergers and acquisitions transactions of a certain size to (1) report the proposed transaction to the Federal Trade Commission and Department of Justice and (2) wait a statutorily prescribed period (typically 30 days) before consummating the transaction. Parties can request early termination of the waiting period, which may be granted within two to three weeks if the regulatory agencies agree there are no substantive anticompetitive issues with the transaction. The law examines both the size of the merging entities (in terms of total assets or annual net sales) and the size of the transaction (in terms of the dollar value of the buyer's interest in the surviving entity) to determine whether the parties need to report the transaction. The threshold levels for reporting are indexed every year to reflect changes in gross national product from the prior year.

As of February 24, 2011, a transaction is generally reportable under the HSR if all of the following conditions are met:

- One party has sales or assets of $131.9 million.
- The other party has sales or assets of $13.2 million.

- As a result of the transaction, the acquiring party will hold an aggregate amount of stock and/or assets of the acquired party valued at more than $66.0 million.

A transaction is reportable regardless of the size of the parties if, as a result of the transaction, the acquiring party will hold an aggregate amount of stock and/or assets of the acquired party valued at more than $263.8 million.

Premerger notification for transactions that meet the applicable thresholds involves submitting a Notification and Report Form for Certain Mergers and Acquisitions with information about each company's business and paying a filing fee determined by the size of the transaction, which is measured by the aggregate total amount of voting securities, assets, or noncorporate interests being acquired. Generally, in 2011, transactions valued between $66.0 million and $131.9 million have a filing fee of $45,000; transactions valued between $131.9 million and $659.5 million have a filing fee of $125,000; and transactions valued at or above $659.5 million have a filing fee of $280,000. After filing, the Federal Trade Commission and Department of Justice review the filing to determine whether a preliminary investigation is warranted. If an investigation ensues, only one agency will conduct it.

HSR contains many exemptions, under which transactions that would typically meet the reporting thresholds do not need to report. Known as the "investment purposes only" exemption, the law provides that any person may acquire up to 10 percent of an issuer's securities, irrespective of their value, without filing the premerger form if the acquisition is solely for investment purposes, as opposed to other purposes, such as gaining control of the issuer. Another well-known exemption is the "ordinary course of business" exemption, under which acquisitions of goods or realty transferred in the ordinary course of business, not including those that are part of an acquisition of all or substantially all of the assets of an operating unit of a company, need not make a premerger filing.

Specific Industries

Some industries receive additional antitrust scrutiny. Like those of many transportation industries, the operational structure of the airline industry lends itself to higher competitive scrutiny by the federal government. In the 1970s, the airline industry underwent a wave of deregulation, substantially altering its competitive landscape and leading to a hub-and-spoke operational system. This increased governmental concern over market power and competitive conditions on the spoke routes, especially with respect to monopolization of routes and price-fixing opportunities. The government also takes heightened interest in mergers and acquisitions in the airline industry and frequently examines how a proposed merger will affect market concentration in a particular area.

Similarly, deregulation and technological advancement in the telecommunications industry led to increased governmental scrutiny. Particularly in the late 1990s, after the passage of the Telecommunications Act of 1996, the federal government was concerned with merger activity leading to overly concentrated market power, increased prices, and reduced choices for consumers and reduced innovation. Similar to its scrutiny of the airline industry, the government's scrutiny of proposed telecommunications mergers looked at factors such as market concentration, potentially adverse effects on competition, ease of entry into the market, and efficiencies likely to be created by the proposed merger. Other governmental agencies are often involved in these reviews, particularly the Federal Communications Commission.

Exon-Florio

The Exon-Florio provision of the Defense Production Act gives the president of the United States the authority to block proposed or pending foreign acquisitions that threaten national security. Under the provision, the president may take "appropriate" action to suspend or prohibit the questionable transaction. Before the president can exercise that authority, however, he must believe that other U.S. laws are inadequate to protect national security and have "credible evidence" that the foreign transaction will impair national security.

OTHER REGULATORY ISSUES AND LAWS YOU MAY ENCOUNTER IN THE DEAL

In addition to securities and antitrust regulations, some transactions may fall within the purview of certain state or federal laws, such as the Bulk Sale Laws and Worker Adjustment and Retraining Notification Act (WARN Act). Following is an overview of each.

Bulk Sales Laws

Historically, many jurisdictions had procedural laws that applied when a business sold all or substantially all of its assets. Bulk sales laws would apply when a business sold goods that constituted all or substantially all of its inventory to a single purchaser, unless the sale was in the ordinary course of business. Today, most states have repealed their bulk sales laws, as fraudulent transfers are handled in other legal ways. For those bulk sales laws still existing, such laws generally require registration of the sale, which includes the business filing an affidavit with the appropriate government office that outlines its secured and unsecured creditors and includes information about the business selling the goods and the purchaser. If there is doubt that the debts of the business transferring the assets will be paid as they become due, the notice must also include certain other information about the sale, such as a description of the property to be transferred and a schedule of amount of debts owed and to whom. The affidavit providing notice to the creditors is generally required 12 days in advance of the sale. If the creditors have no objections, the sale may proceed as normal. If, however, creditors object to the sale, additional laws may come into play. If a business does not properly register the sale, then its creditors may obtain a declaration that the sale was invalid against them and proceed with ordinary recourses for default, such as possession of the goods or obtaining a judgment for proceeds from the sale.

The WARN Act

The WARN Act generally provides that most employers with more than 100 workers (not counting workers who have worked fewer than 6 of the last 12 months or who work less than 20 hours per week) must give 60 days' advanced notice before any mass layoff or plant closing. A mass layoff is a reduction in the workforce not due to a plant closing that affects either at least one-third of the employees at a particular site, equaling at least 50 people, or at least 500 employees. A plant closing is a permanent or temporary shutdown of all or part of a single site of employment that results in employment loss of 50 or more employees during any 30-day period.

These definitions have important implications for mergers and acquisitions transactions. If, for example, the transaction constitutes a sale of the business, then it likely will not trigger the WARN Act. Regardless of whether the employer sells all or part of its business, there will be no plant closing so long as there are continuing operations. Similarly, if enough of the workforce is immediately hired by the purchaser, there also won't be any mass layoff under the statute.

THE INVESTMENT BANKER'S PERSPECTIVE

As presented in Chapter 5, the securities laws may affect the types of transactions that M&A advisors participate in and how they conduct business. Below is an overview of the 34 Act as it relates to the advisor, a review of the Investment Advisors Act of 1940, and notes on the recent creation of a Series 79 license by the Financial Industry Regulatory Authority (FINRA).

SEC Provisions for Broker-Dealers

The 34 Act governs the registration process required for broker-dealers. Since federal laws extensively regulate the actions of broker-dealers, it is important for advisors to consider whether they fall within the definition of a broker or dealer and to properly register with the SEC if they do. Although there are exceptions, a broker typically includes any person, other than a bank, who is engaged in the business of buying and selling securities for others, and a dealer typically includes any person, other than a bank, who is engaged in the business of purchasing securities for his or her own account. The key to these broad definitions is the phrase "engaged in the business." The SEC examines the regularity of participation in the securities transactions to determine whether someone is engaged in the business. For example, if someone participates at key points in the chain of distribution of the securities, there is a much greater likelihood that such person will be considered a broker-dealer under the rules. The factors considered when determining whether a person is engaged in the business focus on evidence that will indicate whether the person is effecting transactions in securities or soliciting securities transactions. Among other things, those factors include:

- Does the person receive transaction-related compensation, such as commissions, success fees, or referral fees?
- Does the person hold himself out as a broker, such as by executing trades or assisting others in completing securities transactions?
- Is the person involved in negotiations between an issuer of securities and potential or current investors?
- Does the person make valuations as to the merits of the investment or give advice with respect to the investment?
- Is the person active or passive in locating investors?
- Does the person participate in the securities business with some degree of regularity?

Remember, even if a person is engaged in the business, that business must be either effecting transactions in securities for the accounts of others or buying and selling securities for the person's own account.

Advisors often seek exemption from registration as a broker-dealer. If they do *any* of the following, then registration is necessary:

- Execute transactions for their clients.
- Charge fees based on the amount of securities transactions effected by their clients.
- Take possession of their clients' funds or securities.

By comparison, registration is typically not required if the advisor merely provides the issuer with advice and assistance in preparing the securities offering, such as recommending financing methods, interpreting applicable laws, suggesting administrative procedures, and the like.

If a person classifies as a broker-dealer under the rules, that person must properly register with the SEC before conducting business by filing a Form BD, which requires information relating to the broker-dealer's financial condition and assets. Broker-dealers must also be members of a national exchange or FINRA.

There are also several regulatory provisions applicable to the practice of registered broker-dealers engaged in securities transactions, the most important of which relate to fraud. Broker-dealers are subject to the general antifraud provisions of Sections 10(b) and 15(c) of the 34 Act. The securities laws that govern fraud cover not only deliberate false statements or misrepresentations, but also omissions of material facts, even if inadvertent.

Investment Advisers Act and Investment Company Act of 1940

The Investment Advisers Act of 1940 regulates persons who, with certain exceptions, for compensation, engage in advising others as to the value of securities or as to the advisability of investing in, purchasing, or selling securities, or who, for compensation and as part of a regular business, issue or promulgate analyses or reports concerning securities. It outlines the manner by which such investment advisors must register with the SEC, and the laws and regulations under which an investment advisor must operate, and prohibits fraudulent action by investment advisors toward any potential investor. Congress amended this law in 1996 and determined that investment advisors must generally register with the SEC if they manage at least $25 million in assets or advise an investment company that is registered with the SEC. In the wake of the Dodd-Frank Act, which made sweeping regulatory changes following the financial crisis, the law governing registration of investment advisors has changed. The law generally eliminated the private advisor exemption from registration and replaced it with exemptions for foreign private advisors, advisors to venture capital funds, and advisors to private funds that manage less than $150 million in assets in the United States. The SEC has proposed rules that further define these exemptions. The law also now recognizes a middle-level class of advisors, those who manage between $25 million and $100 million in assets, and provides that the states (rather than the SEC) will have primary responsibility for such advisors. Advisors in this middle range will have to transfer their registrations from the SEC to the states sometime in 2011 or 2012.

The Investment Company Act, also passed in 1940, defines and regulates investment companies, which generally include those companies, including mutual funds, that engage primarily in investing, reinvesting, and trading in securities, and whose securities are offered to the investing public. This regulation requires such investment companies to disclose certain information to potential public investors, such as information about the company's financial condition, investment policies, structure, and operations, as well as information about a particular fund and its investment objectives.

FINRA Provisions for Broker-Dealers

The FINRA issued a new limited registration category in 2009 known as a Series 79 registration. Broker-dealers registered to effect certain transactions, such as advising on or facilitating debt or equity offerings through private placements or public offerings, or advising or facilitating mergers, acquisitions, tender offers, financial restructurings, asset sales, divestitures, or other business combinations or reorganizations, can now hold a Series 79 registration and depending on their actual activities may also be required to hold a Series 7 registration. Please note that a Series 7 alone is not enough to conduct the above activities; the advisor would be required to hold a Series 79 in addition to the Series 7 registration. In certain cases, obtaining a Series 62 instead of the Series 7 or Series 79 will achieve the required registration.

THE COMPANY'S PERSPECTIVE

When contemplating certain M&A transactions, management and its advisors should be generally aware of the implications that the securities laws may have. Following is an overview of major topics for consideration.

Process of Issuing and Selling Securities in the Deal

The 33 Act generally requires the registration of securities to be offered for sale to the public. The registration typically occurs by the company preparing a specified form and filing it with the SEC. The registration form contains information about the company's business and property, a description of the securities to be offered, information about the company's management, and financial statements of the company that have been certified by an independent accountant. The information that companies file on a registration statement becomes publicly available upon filing. Additionally, the SEC may examine and comment on the registration statements as part of its efforts to protect investors and ensure appropriate disclosure.

There are various forms for different types of issuances contemplated. For example, a company will use a Form S-1 (or short-form S-3, if applicable) if it intends to engage in a public offering (where securities are issued to the general public) but a Form S-4 if it is engaging in a business combination transaction (where securities are issued to the equity owners of the acquired business).

Remember that not every issuance requires registration. Several exemptions exist in the securities laws that allow companies to engage in financing transactions without engaging in the registration process. One of the most commonly used exemptions, Rule 506 of the 33 Act permits companies to raise unlimited funds through private placements without registering the securities with the SEC, so long as the transaction satisfies the rule's requirements. Generally, these offerings are to accredited investors, including institutional buyers and high-net-worth individuals, and the securities, which are acquired for investment purposes, may not be resold for an indefinite period of time. Any company that intends to avoid the registration process by taking advantage of such an exemption should be mindful of the limitations that come along with it. For example, in addition to the restrictions on the investor's purpose and length of time the investor must hold the securities, a company making a Rule 506 offering cannot utilize general solicitation or advertising with respect to the offering, meaning that it cannot advertise, engage in a mass mailing, or issue a press release that discusses the existence of the private placement until after the offering and all sales have been finalized.

When considering a securities offering, a company should also be mindful of the consequences of violating the registration or antifraud provisions of the securities laws. The penalty for violation, at a minimum, is that investors can rescind their purchase and receive a refund of their investment. Additionally, states and/or federal agencies with enforcement authority may, in appropriate circumstances, impose fines or pursue criminal penalties.

State Blue-Sky Laws

Blue-sky laws govern securities regulation at the state level. Each state has its own statutory law governing securities, and today these blue-sky laws are most important with respect to regulating fraudulent transactions, broker-dealers, and investment advisors.

Blue-sky laws have traditionally operated concurrently with federal regulation of securities, but federal legislation now preempts many significant areas of regulation. For example, public offerings that are registered federally generally cannot be governed by states beyond limited administrative regulation, such as coordination of filings. States are also preempted from requiring registration of a significant number of transactions and securities that are governed by the federal securities laws, but exempted transactions involving sales of securities to unsophisticated purchasers generally remain open to state regulation. Always check your particular state's laws to see whether they require state registration (or notice filings and the payment of nominal fees).

Federal regulation also preempts a significant amount of state regulation of broker-dealers. Any investment company registered under the Investment Company Act of 1940 is exclusively governed by federal law. Additionally, the SEC has exclusive regulatory authority over investment advisors who manage more than $100 million in assets. Investment advisors who do not fall within the federal government's exclusive regulatory authority are governed by the regulation of the state of their principal place of business.

CONSIDERATIONS FOR PUBLIC COMPANIES

Once a company has registered its securities with the SEC, it becomes a *reporting company* under the 34 Act. Such reporting company status subjects the company to substantial, continuous disclosure obligations. The SEC requires reporting companies to file annual reports, quarterly reports, and current reports when certain material events occur. These reports are designed to help investors make decisions about the company's securities and include information relating to the company's business, financial statements, and management. In addition to issuing periodic reports, public companies must file reports at certain key times for their investors, so that the investors may make a fully informed decision about how to exercise their ownership rights. Before an annual shareholders' meeting, for example, a reporting company must file with the SEC and distribute a proxy statement containing information with respect to the proposals to be voted on. The proxy statement includes information about directors who stand for election at the meeting, executive compensation, and the voting procedures that will apply for the meeting. It is important to note that these requirements can also apply to private companies in certain circumstances. Generally, once an issuer has total assets exceeding $10,000,000 and a class of shares held of record by 500 or more persons, it must register that class of securities with the SEC and become a reporting company.

Public companies must always consider their reporting obligations when engaging in strategic transactions. For example, a letter of intent may constitute a material definitive agreement that will trigger a reporting obligation to the extent it is binding upon the company, even if its provisions are subject to customary closing conditions. However, if the company has something more akin to a memorandum of understanding that contains a mixture of nonbinding provisions and limited, binding provisions, such as a confidentiality agreement or no-shop provision, the memorandum would not need to be filed since the binding provisions are considered immaterial. Additionally, the company will need to be mindful as to whether the transaction is one that will require shareholder approval, and if it is, be mindful of its corresponding reporting obligations.

Public companies also have special obligations with respect to going private transactions. Generally, it is unlawful for such companies to engage in any fraudulent, deceptive, or manipulative act or practice with respect to the transaction, and the SEC has created certain rules for going private transactions to help prevent such fraud. The company must file a Schedule 13E-3 for the transaction, amendments promptly for any material changes, and a final amendment promptly reporting the results of the transaction. The company must also report certain information about the class of securities going private to its shareholders, with additional requirements pertaining to the dissemination of such information if the transaction implicates shareholder authorization.

CHAPTER 15

Financing Sources
and Structures

As we have attempted to illustrate throughout this handbook, mergers and acquisitions (M&A) transactions—acquiring, recapitalizing, or divesting (exiting)—can be viable alternatives for accomplishing a number of strategic objectives in the context of building and realizing value for the investors and owners of emerging-growth and middle market companies (those from start-up to about $500 million in revenue), for corporate acquirers and corporate development teams, and for private equity investors.

This chapter takes a high-level view of financing transactions and presents a framework for thinking about the various alternatives, and then provides a financing primer and overview of various funding sources and types.

PERSPECTIVE

In many instances the distinction between selling a company (i.e., an *exit*) and raising capital is measured by the amount of equity sold and the contractual rights obtained by the buyer or investor. Financing growth and acquisitions raises the issue of long-term shareholder objectives, which most of the time involves eventual liquidity.

As the wave of business transitions driven by Baby Boomers planning their legacy and succession continues, some shareholders are confronted with a multifaceted decision of how to finance the continued growth of their business, create liquidity for their owners, and lay the foundation for operations independent of the owner/founder.

Others see the opportunity to buy out partners or create some liquidity while staying in the game for what may be deemed a "second bite at the apple." This is the concept of selling a controlling interest in a company to a financial buyer (i.e., a private equity group, or PEG) and *rolling over* or keeping a minority interest until a subsequent sale or liquidity event happens, when the company is expected to have grown in value (under the watch of the new owners with their capital). There are numerous examples where the sale of the minority interest in the follow-on transaction (three to five years from the first transaction) resulted in as much economic gain as the original sale to the financial buyer.

Shareholders and partners may find a full or partial exit attractive for many reasons, including:

- Diversifying away the risk of having too much personal net worth in a single asset
- Minimizing the risk of growth by obtaining a financial or strategic partner
- Buying out passive partners and making room in the capital structure for management and employees without dilution to existing active shareholders

Several potential solutions and structures exist, including recapitalization, sale to a financial buyer while keeping a minority stake, or an outright sale to a strategic or financial buyer with contractual rights for some level of future performance, and there are many variations.

Growth alternatives usually include various external initiatives like acquisitions or strategic partnerships. Although somewhat dependent on how they are structured, these initiatives usually require capital or investment by the sponsor. To address this span of topics and how to finance them, this chapter weaves the concepts together, beginning with buyouts and finishing with acquisitions.

BUYOUTS[1]

Buyouts (or leveraged buyouts) are generally change-of-control transactions whereby a financial sponsor (i.e., a private equity fund called a *buyout fund*) purchases the majority of a company using its capital plus debt that has recourse only to the target company (and not to the buyout fund). Depending on the size and complexity of the deal, there may be more than one level of debt employed. A typical middle market transaction will have only one buyout investor (as opposed to the syndicated financing that may be done in larger deals). The same concepts employed for a financial sponsor can also be used by a strategic buyer seeking to finance an acquisition.

Whereas every buyout is unique with respect to its specific capital structure, the one common element of all buyouts is the use of financial leverage to complete the acquisition of a target company. In a buyout, the private equity firm acquiring the target company will finance the acquisition with a combination of debt and equity, much like an individual buying a house with a mortgage. Just as a mortgage is secured by the value of the house being purchased, some portion of the debt incurred in a *leveraged buyout* is secured by the assets of the acquired business. Unlike a house, however, the bought-out business generates cash flows that are used to service the debt incurred in its purchase. In essence, the acquired company helps pay for itself.

The amount of leverage used in a particular buyout varies, but is generally a function of the absolute amount of earnings before interest, taxes, depreciation, and amortization (EBITDA) and the size of the deal. According to Pitchbook Data, Inc., in their summer 2011 PE Presentation Deck, transactions of less than $250 million used on average 43 percent leverage to fund the deal. That average increased to 62 percent for transactions between $250 million and $1 billion.

The use of significant amounts of debt to finance the acquisition of a company has a number of advantages as well as risks. The most obvious risk associated with a buyout is that of financial distress. Unforeseen events such as recession, litigation, or changes in the regulatory environment can lead to difficulties meeting scheduled interest and principal payments, technical default (the violation of the terms of a debt covenant), or outright liquidation. Weak management of the target company or misalignment of incentives between management and shareholders can also pose threats to the ultimate success of the deal.

There are a number of advantages to the use of leverage in acquisitions. Interest payments are a tax shield. Further, large interest and principal payments can force management to improve performance and operating efficiency. This "discipline of debt" can encourage management to focus on certain initiatives such as divesting noncore businesses, downsizing, cost cutting, or investing in technological upgrades that might otherwise be postponed or rejected outright. In this manner, the use of debt serves not just as a financing technique, but also as a management tool and catalyst to change leadership behavior.

Another characteristic of the leverage in buyout financing is that, as the debt ratio increases, the equity portion of the acquisition financing shrinks to a level at which a private equity firm can acquire a company by investing only 25 to 60 percent of the total purchase price with its own capital and leveraging the rest.

Using debt to fund a significant portion of the purchase price turbocharges the financial buyer's rate of return. Again, using the homebuyer as an example, assume the purchase price of the home the buyer wants is $500,000 and the buyer sells the home for $1 million five years later. If the homebuyer funds the entire purchase, the homebuyer will end up doubling her investment. However, if the homebuyer invests $100,000 and borrows $400,000 from the bank, then the homeowner will make six times her initial investment ($1 million less $400,000 mortgage repayment equals $600,000 in excess proceeds to the homeowner). This same dynamic is present in a buyout when the PEG funds the purchase price with a disproportionate level of debt (typically a combination of senior and mezzanine/subordinated debt) to equity.

In middle market buyout transactions, it is typical to see the selling shareholders, who are active in leadership of the business, roll over or reinvest a portion of their proceeds in the go-forward company. In a buyout led by management (i.e., management buyout) who are not currently equity holders (or who own a very minor portion of the company), the buyout fund will encourage (if not require) top executives who are leading the buyout to commit a significant portion of their personal net worth to the deal. By requiring the target's management team to invest in the acquisition, the private equity firm guarantees that management's incentives will be aligned with its own.

Buyout Deal Structure

In recent years, the leveraged buyout in the middle market has taken on several forms. For shareholders desiring a clean exit from their investment, the purchase of their company by a buyout fund can provide a transition path with speed and certainty of close. Alternatively, buyouts have an advantage for those owner/operators desiring to stay engaged and continue to grow their business while at the same time diversifying their investment away from their business. As mentioned before, there are many examples of entrepreneurs getting what investors have called a second bite at the apple. These are buyout transactions where the owners retain or roll over a minority percentage of their existing company holdings while partnering with and using the capital of the private equity investors to accelerate the growth of the business. Then they eventually sell their minority holdings in a future transaction. The result is two payouts: the first being at the initial closing when they sell a controlling interest in their business to the buyout fund, and the second when the company is sold in its entirety three to five years later. In some instances, the amount of the second exit is more than that of the first. Here are a few factors that affect the structure of the buyout:

- Role of existing owners and managers in the go-forward business
- Absolute value of the company's cash flow

- Predictability and cycle of cash flow
- Amount and timing of investments to achieve the growth plans
- Liquidity in the capital markets

The strategy behind structuring the buyout is to layer debt by priority to efficiently use the underlying assets and cash flow of the business to obtain a weighted cost of capital balanced against the cash flow (and expected variability) of the business coupled with the required investments in working capital and CapEx (capital expenditures). In smaller deals, much of the senior debt is based on collateral. As the deal size and free cash flow of the target company increase, debt can be obtained as a multiple of the cash flow. For example, the buyout of a company with EBITDA of $2.0 million is likely to obtain its senior debt as a function of its accounts receivable and inventory values, as opposed to a company with $10 million of EBITDA, which may very well qualify for senior debt of several times its EBITDA.

Figure 15.1 demonstrates the structure of a buyout in which the owners are selling to a private equity fund. They have negotiated to sell their products company, which has reasonably stable growth and earnings, for $25.2 million based on the trailing 12-months EBITDA of $4 million. This implies an EBITDA multiple of 6.3. The owners operate the business and desire to continue to grow the company for several more years. They have negotiated to keep approximately 15 percent of the business (i.e., roll over approximately 15 percent of their equity*). Given the industry benchmark information shown in the figure, the PEG will layer debt using as much of the cheapest capital and as little of the most expensive as possible. In this case, the senior-term debt is the least expensive. The bank has agreed to lend $8.4 million. A mezzanine lender has agreed to provide $4 million. The owners keep $3.8 million of their equity at risk, which typically is in the form of common stock in a newly formed entity (Newco) and structurally subordinated to the PEG's equity investment, thereby guaranteeing that at exit, the PEG will be able to get all of its original equity investment in Newco back before the sellers receive any of their rollover equity. The buyer funds $1.2 million in buyer-related transaction costs at closing, leaving the sellers with $20.2 million in gross proceeds. To accomplish this transaction, the PEG invested just over $9.0 million. This example makes the assumption

---

*Negotiation of the rollover ownership can be a tricky issue depending on the perspective of the buyer or seller, and whether the denominator in the calculation is the amount of invested capital or the valuation of the entity. One solution to address the potential conflict in approach is the use of preferred stock to protect the institutional investor.

($000s)	Amount
Revenue	$33,333
EBITDA	4,000
Purchase Price	$25,200

	Transaction ($000s)				Benchmark	
	Multiple	%	Amount	Mix	Multiple	%
TEV/EBITDA	×6.30		$25,200	100%		
EBITDA			4,000			
Senior Debt	×2.10	33%	8,400		×1.8–2.3	
Mezzanine	×1.00	16%	4,000			
Total Debt	×3.10	49%	12,400	49%	×2.5–3.5	42%–60%
Equity		51%	$12,800	51%		40%–55%

Sources of Funds

Revolver	$ —
Senior Term Loan	8,400
Subordinated Debt (Mezzanine)	4,000
Seller Note	—
Rollover Equity	3,780
PEG Equity	9,020
Total	$25,200

Uses of Funds

Purchase of Equity	$20,220
Rollover Equity	3,780
Fees and Expenses	1,200
Total	$25,200

FIGURE 15.1 Buyout Transaction

that there is not any existing debt to be repaid or assumed at closing; if there were, it would be a deduction from the seller's takeaway proceeds.

Note that the line of credit was not used. Although there is not a balance sheet shown in this example, the company had adequate cash flow and underlying assets to entice the bank to provide a revolver postclosing for working capital purposes. As long as the revolver has an adequate level of unused availability, many PEGs run their companies with zero cash balances and strictly rely on the revolver to fund ongoing operations.

The previous example shows gross proceeds to the seller of $20.2 million. However, there are three circumstances that could lead to the seller receiving less than that at closing:

- If there is a sell-side fee payable to an M&A advisor representing the seller, that fee is typically the seller's obligation and deducted from the seller's proceeds.
- If there is funded debt on the books that is either repaid or assumed by the buyer, the amount of that debt is deducted from the seller's proceeds.
- It is common to hold a portion of the seller's proceeds in escrow as security for the buyer for some period of time after the transaction closes (typically 12 to 18 months) to protect the buyer.

Buyout investors will likely favor an asset purchase versus a stock deal. Purchasing assets allows them to limit liability and write up the value of the assets for tax purposes. See Chapter 11 for additional information about deal structure alternatives.

Bridging the Valuation Gap

Frequently there is a gap in valuation between what the buyer is willing to pay and the price that the seller is willing to accept to close the transaction. As discussed in Chapter 11, earnouts are one type of contingent consideration that, in effect, provides seller financing that is paid based on postclosing performance or events of the business.

RECAPITALIZATION

Generally, a recapitalization will involve a lower cash-out (as a partial exit or staged exit) for the active owners than a buyout (which involves a change of control). A recapitalization will most likely be focused on increasing the debt of the company to generate growth capital, fund shareholder dividends, and/or repurchase equity (i.e., one partner buying out another).

ACQUISITIONS

The financing strategy to support the acquisition should initially be thought of in the context of the overall acquisition process and be defined as part of the acquisition strategy, understanding that the process will evolve and is somewhat iterative as knowledge is gained from the marketplace. If the acquiring company is cash flush or the acquisition target is immaterial in value, the financing strategy may be as simple as funding the transaction from operational cash flow or cash reserves. However, if the deal requires external funding, management must consider a financing strategy, which typically begins with understanding the acquiring or buying company. This involves:

- Determining its valuation and financial strength
- Establishing financial objectives and benchmarks for vetting possible acquisitions
- Determining parameters around how much the buyer can afford
- Conducting internal discussions around an ideal or preferred deal structure
- Establishing relationships with financing sources and obtaining buy-in regarding the acquirer's plans
- Obtaining evidence for potential sellers of the buyer's ability to finance and close a deal

From these parameters, management can then think about financing a specific target company, which is a function of the value of the target, the likely cash flow of the target, the deal structure, and the integration strategy.

Start by assessing the value of the target acquisition as a stand-alone business using traditional valuation approaches; then value the acquisition in the context of your business, giving consideration to the cost savings and lift (improved performance) that may be obtained on a combined basis. Another metric that may be useful in the process is to determine the *financeable value*. This is the amount that can be paid using external financing based on the assets and cash flow of the target, including pro forma adjustments resulting from new ownership.

The deal structure and financing strategy are developed by weighing a number of factors to find the optimum solution to meet the objectives of the parties involved. Among other things, these factors include the integration strategy and the *valuation gap*, which is the value that a company is willing to pay and what is required to get the deal done.

Management should keep in mind some core concepts as they take an objective view and embark on the acquisition process:

- Begin with the end in mind; set clear objectives and benchmarks to gauge attractiveness of potential target companies and particular deals.
- Develop the financing strategy up front and establish relationships with likely sources of financing.
- Terms are likely more important than absolute valuation.

- Align the financing strategy with the operating/integration plan and deal structure.
- Focus on value creation.

Figure 15.2 uses the same niche company being sold as in the prior example (see Figure 15.1); however, the buyer is a middle market industry player with $50 million in revenue and $5 million of EBITDA. On a consolidated basis, and without synergies, the two businesses will have $9.0 million of EBITDA. In an actual transaction, another analysis would be done illustrating the pro forma financials with synergies applied. In most deals, synergies are realized over time, not on the first day after closing.

The purchase price remains the same as in the prior example, at 6.3 times EBITDA, or $25.2 million. In this case, the seller agrees to personally finance $2.7 million to bridge the funding gap between the limit that the mezzanine lender will provide and the purchase price. The senior credit facility and borrowing base is being reserved for working and growth capital to fund expansion post-closing.

FINANCING PRIMER

This section provides a brief overview of the core concepts used in financing private companies and sets the stage for a deeper discussion of financing deals and funding strategic initiatives.

Capital Structure[2]

Proactive management of the capital structure of the company usually provides the greatest chance of obtaining the financing required to execute on management's plans. Establishing a financing plan and addressing the capital structure is done after management has clearly articulated the company's business plan and can delineate how much funding is required, how it will be deployed, and when it is needed. The overall financing strategy will result in a target capital structure and plans to obtain financing from various sources. There are internal sources (i.e., better asset utilization and profits), related-party sources (i.e., financing from customers, suppliers, and industry players), and external sources (i.e., financing from commercial banks, private equity investors, etc.). Most of the financing content in this handbook is focused on external and related-party sources as they relate to mergers and acquisitions.

Defining the capital structure is a critical decision for any business organization to make. The capital structure of a company refers to the amount of its debt and equity and the types of debt and equity used to fund the

($000s)				Seller	Buyer	Combined
Revenue				$33,333	$50,000	$83,333
EBITDA	×6.30			4,000	5,000	9,000
Purchase Price				$25,200		

	Transaction ($000s)		
	Multiple	**%**	**Amount**
EBITDA (combined)			9,000
Senior Debt			—
Mezzanine	×2.50	100%	22,500
Total Debt	×2.50	100%	22,500

Sources of Funds	
Revolver	$ —
Senior Term Loan	—
Subordinated Debt (Mezzanine)	22,500
Seller Note	2,700
Rollover Equity	—
Total	$25,200

Uses of Funds	
Purchase of Equity	$24,000
Rollover Equity	—
Fees and expenses	1,200
Total	$25,200

FIGURE 15.2 Strategic Acquisition

operations and growth of the company. The selection of capitalization alternatives is important not only because of the drive to maximize returns to various organizational constituencies, but also because of the impact such a decision has on an organization's ability to deal with its competitive environment.

The prevailing argument,* originally developed by Franco Modigliani and Merton Miller ("The Cost of Capital, Corporate Finance, and the

---

*As mentioned in Chapter 1, these concepts are being challenged for application in the private capital markets by the work of one the authors of this handbook, Rob Slee, and his research being conducted with Pepperdine University.

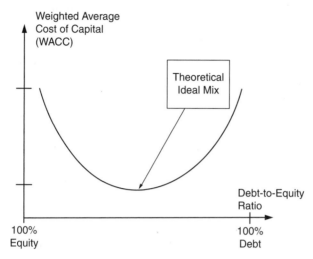

FIGURE 15.3 Capital Structure and the Weighted Average Cost of Capital

Theory of Investment," *American Economic Review*, June 1958), is that an optimal capital structure exists that balances the risk of bankruptcy with the tax savings of debt. In other words, a company should use both equity and debt to fund its operations. Once established, a capital structure comprised of debt and equity should provide greater returns to stockholders than they would receive from an all-equity firm. This strategy is accomplished by reducing the amount of equity and increasing the amount of debt, thereby, in theory, reducing the overall cost of capital. Illustrated in Figure 15.3 is the concept that the cost of capital for a company capitalized entirely with equity is high, and that the cost of capital for a company completely leveraged with debt is also high. In between these two extremes, at the point designated as the *theoretical ideal mix*, or the low point on the cost of capital curve, a theoretical company has maximized its use of debt and equity to achieve the lowest possible cost of capital.

In deciding on the right capital structure for a company, shareholders and management must balance the risk of default in repaying debt with the availability of equity capital to pursue growth opportunities. Some emerging-growth and middle market companies may find it easier to obtain debt than equity, making this decision more difficult (when what they really need is equity). If a growth company is too conservative and does not leverage its equity to provide increased capital to invest, it may miss market opportunities and actually erode the overall value of the business by becoming a smaller player in the market—market position and share weigh into company valuation. However, being too aggressive and overleveraging the company may lead to missed financial performance and business failure when things do not go exactly according to plan. There is also the issue (which is sometimes more a matter of perception than reality) of relinquishing control when issuing new equity.

Despite extensive study and some theoretical appeal, researchers in financial management have not found the optimal capital structure. The best that academics and practitioners have been able to achieve are prescriptions that satisfy short-term goals. In some publications, readers are left with the impression that the use of leverage is one way to improve the performance of an organization. While this can be true in some circumstances, it fails to consider the complexities of the competitive environment, the long-term survival needs of the organization, the discipline of the management of a specific company, or the risk tolerance of the shareholders (particularly as it relates to privately held companies). *Agency costs* are the costs incurred or opportunities lost by the shareholders of a company when the interest of management is placed before the interest of the shareholders. The shareholders want managers to operate the firm in ways that maximize the value of their shares, whereas the managers' priority may be, say, to build a business empire through rapid expansion, mergers, or acquisitions, which may not increase their firm's share price or value. There is an inherent conflict between management and shareholders in a corporation where management does not have the incentive to optimize performance. There are also situations where a major shareholder in a privately held company settles for a suboptimal capital structure so the shareholder can extract greater and disproportionate wealth as a manager through operational actions or other means.

An approach to addressing agency costs is to provide increased incentives for management to perform and to weight the capital structure of the company more heavily with debt so that cash flow is significantly tight due to debt service obligations. This debt structure causes the company to operate in a manner designed to meet certain principal and interest payments, in effect focusing management on the return of capital to shareholders disguised as creditors. There is the argument that this use of leverage either to discipline managers or to achieve economic gain is the easy way out, and, in many instances, can lead to the demise of the organization.

There are several ways to view the logic behind the capital structure decision based on how one frames the issue. Rather than "What is an optimal mix of debt and equity that will maximize shareholder wealth?" consider "Under what circumstances should leverage be used to maximize shareholder wealth, and why?" And for many start-up, emerging-growth, and middle market companies the question is often, "What type of capital can we obtain—either debt or equity?" From another perspective, and arguably more appropriate for the readers of this handbook, the capital structure is most likely defined by the stage (and industry) of the company. In general, equity may be the only alternative capital available to early stage companies, but the pool of financing alternatives grows as the critical mass of the company grows. Small-, medium-, and large-cap publicly traded companies have a broader range of financing alternatives than do smaller, privately held businesses. Public company capital structures are studied and tracked by analysts based on industry.

Our desire is that management and advisors of emerging-growth and middle market companies proactively shape the capital structure of their businesses instead of reacting to the need for cash based on a sequence of events in the corporate life cycle. In reality, there is no one ideal structure for a specific company; there are a range of alternative structures that suffice, some more preferable than others. For the intended readers of this handbook, the desired capital structure will change as the company moves from one business stage to another, and will be influenced by the available sources at the time funding is required.

Factors Shaping the Capital Structure

Shareholder objectives, preferences, and motives are common themes among the factors influencing deals in the private capital market. As shown in Figure 15.4, they are a key driver in determining the capital structure and selection of financing alternatives. Following is a brief discussion of the main factors.

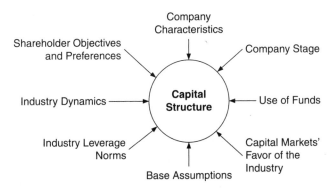

FIGURE 15.4 Factors Influencing Capital Structure

Shareholder Objectives   The shareholder objective for small-cap through large-cap publicly traded companies is generally accepted as increasing shareholder value. This cannot be generalized for privately held or lifestyle businesses, where in many cases the shareholder objective is to maximize cash distributions to the shareholders. Whatever the objective, it directly affects the capital structure. For example, the capital structures would be significantly different for companies with divergent objectives designed to advance social missions such as creation of employment and meeting certain religious objectives, establishing a legacy for successive generations, or creating cash flow for current shareholder consumption. Along with these objectives come limits and constraints, all of which need to be articulated and understood.

As mentioned earlier, the objectives and preferences of the shareholder(s) of the company influence and shape a company's capital structure. For example, if the shareholder of a middle market company views the business as a personal legacy and desires that it remain in the family for future generations, this begins to limit and define what types of new equity issuance can be appropriate and the deal terms. In another situation, the company may operate as a minority- or woman-owned business enterprise and the owner(s) may desire to maintain that status. This imposes limits on the types and terms of equity financings to ensure certain regulatory requirements are met.

Whereas it might not seem appropriate for personal preferences to sway the company decision regarding capital structure, it is the reality. In weaker companies and those whose success is closely linked to the participation of shareholders in the business, the willingness to guarantee company liabilities directly affects the types of financing that can be obtained. The following is a list of example shareholder preferences or shareholder-specific factors:

- Company importance in the shareholders' overall investment portfolio
- Shareholders' past experiences with debt and their philosophical preferences—in effect, the shareholders' risk profile
- Tax preferences of the shareholders
- Shareholders' confidence and outlook for the company

Company Characteristics   We have assembled a list of drivers that are company specific and that affect the capital structure. These weigh heavily in the process of determining the right mix of debt and equity. The single most influential determinant in raising capital is the quality of management. Although it is not the only determinant, a stronger management team will have greater flexibility in choosing the type and sources of capital than will a weaker team, which may be forced to take what it can get or get none at all. The drivers are:

- Management strength
- Stage and progress of the company
- Ability to generate cash flow
- Predictability and variability of cash flow
- Risk profile
- Competitive strength
- Lead time/runway (adequate time to complete a task) to shape the balance sheet
- Outlook for business performance
- Current capital structure and ownership
- Need for financial flexibility to seize unplanned opportunities
- Strategic initiatives and plans (i.e., acquisitions, alliances, new product lines, etc.)

In addition to these characteristics, the ability of a company to obtain third-party credit enhancements will impact the overall capital structure of a company. For example, many early-stage companies have no ability to obtain debt financing; however, the company obtains a credit facility based on the strength of a bank guaranty of a shareholder or strategic partner.

Company Stage   The stage of a business directly influences investors' or lenders' interest based on the mission of their firm aligned with your company's progress. For example, if your company is experiencing significant growth in a solid market and yet is not cash-flow positive, it may be able to attract a growth equity investor to fund an acquisition while not being very attractive to a buyout fund.

Each of these stages has specific financial characteristics coupled with it that begin to define its relative importance. An expansion-stage company may have a history of predictable earnings and positive cash flow that enable it to attract certain levels and types of debt. A turnaround will most likely have a period of losses and negative cash flow and will have recently made a change for the better, allowing it to attract a different type of debt that is willing to take certain risks.

Use of Funds   The use of funds is a determinant in the capital structure of a company. Use of funds is an output of the financial planning process and allows the company to establish not only the amount of capital required, but also a detailed list of what assets and resources will be acquired and when. A core financing concept in this process is to match the maturity of the debt with the life of the asset being funded.

In the context of acquisitions we would want to determine whether the funds are staying within the target company or whether the company is going to cash out (in whole or in part) its shareholders.

Impact of the Industry   There are three drivers that relate to the industry in which a company operates: (1) the economic and regulatory dynamics within the industry, (2) the favor with which the capital markets view the industry, and (3) the historical leverage norms of the industry (i.e., debt-to-equity ratio). The combination of these three determinants will influence the type of investors and lenders interested in funding transactions in a given space.

The discussion about the impact of the specific industry includes the level of competition and expected rates of growth and profitability in the future. We find that industry attractiveness persuades or dissuades lenders and investors in waves. Think about the run-up (and sometimes bust) of investments in many sectors over the past decades in areas like the Internet, real estate, biotechnology, and clean technologies. When the wave or herd is traveling in a positive direction, it is relatively easier to access capital and do deals than when those same influences are trending backward or downward. With this said, knowing the direction of the industry momentum and the position on the curve can be important in deciding whether and how to finance a transaction.

Base Assumptions   The final set of influences on the capital structure relate to the environmental factors that are not under the control of the company. These include:

- Interest rates
- Availability of debt (i.e., tightness of credit)
- Regulatory environment
- Availability and cost of raw materials and labor
- Timing within the overall economic business cycle

SOURCES AND TYPES OF FUNDING

This section presents a high-level overview of some of the potential funding sources that might be involved in financing an acquisition. For a deep-dive analysis of these and other potential sources, consider reading *Private*

Capital Markets and the *Handbook of Financing Growth: Capital Structure, Strategies, and M&A Transactions* (both published by John Wiley & Sons).

The final subsection of the chapter is on personal guarantees, primarily written for those owners in the lower-middle market who will be required to personally sign for some portion of the financing in a deal.

Debt

There are a wide variety of lenders available to private companies, depending on a number of factors—primarily cash flow, collateral base, company leverage, and the outlook for the business until maturity of the funding.

Commercial Banks   Commercial banks are widely known as a source of debt financing for businesses. They generally provide lines of credit, term loans, and revolving loans. Traditionally, commercial banks are cash-flow lenders first and view collateral as a secondary source of repayment.

In negotiating the terms and conditions in regard to an acquisition, financial covenants are likely more important to a company than the interest rate or up-front fees charged in establishing a credit facility with a bank. The financial covenants need to be structured in a manner that will provide the least constraint given a company's business and operations, particularly during the integration period and any predictable seasonality.

In some cases, the U.S. Small Business Administration (SBA) will provide the bank with a loan guarantee that enables it to finance a portion of the deal with senior debt for a period of time much longer and in a greater amount than the bank would otherwise lend without the guarantee. The current maximum amount under the SBA 504 loan program is $5 million.

Asset-Based Lenders   Unlike commercial banks, asset-based lenders (ABLs) make their lending decisions based primarily on the quality of the underlying assets and secondarily on cash flow. There are many specialty lenders and commercial finance companies that provide various forms of debt; these lenders tend to understand a specific form of debt exceptionally well and have the business processes in place to manage their risk, or they have expertise in a specific industry and have adjusted their lending program and structure to accommodate the nuances of that business. Many larger regional and national banks have asset-based lending divisions.

Asset-based lenders can be an excellent source of financing for acquisition or bridge financing based on the specifics of the transaction and the outlook of the go-forward company.

While asset-based credit facilities can be expensive (based on the overall risk or situation of the borrower and the deal), there are a number of benefits when compared to employing equity capital:

- The entire cost of an asset-based loan is paid with pretax dollars, unlike most equity costs.
- ABLs do not seek a seat on the board or any control of the company, just a risk-adjusted and fair return on their money.
- ABL relationships usually can be terminated by paying off the balance of outstanding debt to the ABL and any accrued interest and fees. Equity and other sources can be much more difficult to exit.
- Asset-based loans are evergreen in nature, with no set amortization or payment schedule. Unlike many other forms of financing, they can grow as the business grows.

Leases   Leasing companies provide a layer of capital independent of the bank and other senior lenders, thus potentially expanding the available credit to fund a transaction, particularly for companies that have significant fixed assets. Some leasing companies focus on specific industries and have special programs tailored for certain types of equipment, while others are broad-based in scope. Those with industry specialization sometimes have the ability to be more aggressive in pricing given their understanding of the equipment values and paths to liquidation or resale. In some cases and depending on the amount of the lease, leases are easier to obtain and less sensitive to the customer's creditworthiness, particularly when the equipment being leased is ordinary.

When a company utilizes lease financing, the lease will be categorized as either an operating lease or a capitalized lease. Operating lease payments are fully expensed and the asset is not reflected on the balance sheet. Capital lease payments are segmented into two components, principal and interest, and both the asset and the lease liability are reflected on the balance sheet (in addition, depreciation expense is incurred). GAAP guidelines determine which approach should be utilized. To the extent the company has flexibility negotiating the lease terms, it can realize potential benefits from the way the lease is recognized. If the company wants to limit reported debt levels, it is better to enter into operating leases rather than capital leases because none of the lease obligations are reported as debt on the balance sheet. However, if the company wants to report higher EBITDA levels (for example, an owner that is positioning the company for exit may be able to get a higher valuation if the purchase price multiple times the operating lease expense savings is less than the lease obligation on the balance sheet), it is better to structure the lease as a capital lease rather than an operating lease because the payments do not reduce EBITDA (where interest expense is excluded from EBITDA and principal payments are recognized as a reduction in the lease liability).

Subordinated Debt   See "Mezzanine Funds," later in this chapter.

Seller Financing   Seller financing is debt funding provided by the seller of a company in an M&A transaction. It can be a balloon note or term loan, and it usually carries a nominal interest rate. In the middle market, seller financing is typically used to:

- Bridge a price gap between what institutional lenders and investors will finance and the amount for which the sellers are willing to trade the business.
- Preserve the senior credit capacity of the business for working capital.

In both cases, seller financing is typically unsecured and subordinated.

Private Equity

Private equity groups are used to broadly group funds and investment companies that provide capital on a negotiated basis, generally to private businesses and primarily in the form of equity (i.e., stock). This category of firms is a superset that includes venture capital, (leveraged) buyout, special situation (i.e., turnaround), mezzanine, and growth equity or expansion funds.

PEGs are usually managed by general partners with well-established corporate finance backgrounds and successful investment track records. Their limited partners are high-net-worth individuals, endowments, and pension funds. The industry expertise, amount invested, transaction structure preference, and return expectations vary according to the mission of each.

Growth Equity Funds   For initiatives requiring permanent capital, growth equity may be an appropriate alternative for your company. Growth equity funds make up a minor percentage of the total population of private equity investors. You can think of growth equity investors as being at the intersection of venture capital and noncontrol private equity funds in their appetite for risk balanced with cash flow and control. Unlike venture capitalists, whose interests extend to start-up or early-stage opportunities, growth equity investors do not make investments expecting many to fail, so their risk tolerance is lower. These investors are looking for operating companies that have revenues, a proven technology or service, and proven market demand. As Ed McCarthy of River Cities Capital Funds says, "They look to avoid concept risk, preferring to invest in execution." Growth equity investors will fund operating losses if the company is in a growth or expansion mode and where the losses are an investment in capturing market share or long-term customers. In some cases, growth equity investors may be willing to fund a partial recapitalization or minority shareholder buyout.

Buyout Funds   See the "Buyouts" section, earlier in this chapter.

Mezzanine Funds   Mezzanine funds are similar in their positioning in the world of private equity relative to growth equity. However, their investments are primarily in the form of subordinated debt with double digit interest rates and an equity kicker (warrants to purchase stock) that allows them to participate in the value growth of the business. Many mezzanine funds are partially capitalized using debt provided by the Small Business Administration's small business investment company program.

As debt, mezzanine funds have a defined repayment period to recapture their initial investment (usually four to seven years). In some cases you will find that mezzanine funds will make a portion of their investment in the form of pure equity. Mezzanine is thought of as a hybrid type of financing, providing a lower cost of capital while having some characteristics of equity, given that it is subordinated to any bank or senior debt and that most banks will exclude subordinated debt in the total debt calculation for testing leverage ratios. Repayment is typically interest only with the principal due at maturity. Keep in mind that mezzanine capital works only if a company is generating positive cash flow, which will likely need to be at least $1 million in EBITDA. Typical uses of funds include an acquisition, major new initiatives like product launches or business unit startups, and partner buyouts or recapitalization.

Mezzanine funds can be segmented into two broad groups: those that invest by themselves as growth capital and those that will invest only side-by-side with a buyout fund as part of the buyout capital structure.

Venture Capital   On a stand-alone basis, venture capital financing is not usually a source of funding for acquisitions. However, there are many venture-funded companies that make acquisitions as part of their growth strategy.

Special Situation Funds   Special situation funds (sometimes called *turnaround funds*) specialize in investing in troubled or undermanaged companies. This type of investor has significant experience buying companies out of bankruptcy, restructuring debt in companies that are overleveraged, and negotiating with creditors and through workouts.

PERSONAL GUARANTEES

Significant shareholders or owners of small to midsized businesses securing bank debt or lease credit facilities will likely be required to sign a personal guarantee as part of the loan documentation (though typically not when an institutional buyer is involved). For several years prior to the recent recession, credit was easy and it was possible to obtain a line of credit or lease new equipment without having to personally backstop the liability. With rare exceptions for those businesses with extraordinary financial strength, obtaining credit of almost any type for emerging-growth or middle market businesses will require guarantees by the owners with 20 percent or more of the equity in a company. This means that the owners need to be prepared to pay out of their own pocket if their company no longer can make the scheduled debt payments.

Developing an effective strategy for structuring and managing the personal guarantee begins with understanding the lender's objectives and perspective. Start by asking the lenders or lessors why they want the guarantee. Some may say it is to ensure that the principals are tied to the business to increase their likelihood of being repaid (especially if things do not go as planned). In the case of a financially weak business, they may be requiring additional collateral or assets to make the loan or lease.

Next determine the maximum out-of-pocket amount that the principals are willing (or able) to actually pay if everything goes wrong and they must personally write a check. Knowing this amount will play into the terms and the amount that is guaranteed. As an example, some owners do not mind guaranteeing their company's debt as long as they are never really at risk of loss—in other words, their worst-case out-of-pocket amount is zero. This can be accomplished by ensuring that the amount of debt guaranteed never exceeds the liquidation value of the assets of the business, taking into account the priority of liens and repayment if the business went bankrupt. If taking some financial risk is acceptable, then calculate the same liquidation value and add the acceptable amount. Once the limit is established, have a monthly or quarterly estimate generated of the liquidation value based on actual financial statements. This will provide visibility to track and manage the risk being taken.

If the borrower is in a position to shape the deal, he can use the information gained by understanding the lender's objectives and by setting personal limits to negotiate the terms of the guarantee to fit the situation. Here are some of the key points to consider:

- *Guarantee of payment versus guarantee of collection.* The most common guarantee is that of payment. This means that if the company does not meet the agreed payments, the lender (or lessor) can demand payment directly from you as the guarantor without pursuing further action against the company. As the guarantor, you would rather be a guarantor of *collection*. This arrangement typically requires the lender (or lessor) to first exhaust its options against the company before it can demand payment from the principals. If the company is never allowed to borrow more than the liquidation amount of its assets and the principals made a guarantee of collection, they can avoid ever having to write a check from their personal assets. Alternatively, they might seek to completely limit any risk except for fraud in managing the business; this type of guarantee is sometimes referred to as a *fiduciary* guarantee.

- *Limiting scope and collateral.* Limit the scope of the guarantee to exclude recourse against personal residences or other specific property. In addition, do not agree up front to liens against personal property or a pledge of the stock in the business.

- *No spouse signature.* Avoid having a spouse sign the guarantee, so that the guarantee is based solely on the principal's assets. Be prepared to provide financial statements showing only the principal's individually owned assets and liabilities. In most states, this limits the risk to assets held solely in the principal's name, as opposed to joint assets or those held with the spouse.

- *Setting limits.* Quantify the limits on the amount of the guarantee in either relative terms or absolute terms. For example, the company may have a line of credit with $2 million total availability. Seek to limit personal exposure to 20 percent of the outstanding balance or a maximum of $400,000. This is particularly appropriate with multiple owners who may desire to limit their exposure based on their percentage ownership. Additionally, negotiate to reduce the guarantee as the performance of the company improves. For example: A company has a debt-to-equity ratio of 3:1 after financing. Seek agreement to reduce or limit the personal guarantee when the company's debt-to-equity ratio falls below 2:1. Also consider having the guarantee become less onerous over time, based on the bank's continued relationship with the company. For example, a guarantee of payment could convert to a guarantee of collection after a couple years of a spotless repayment record, or the guarantee could burn off gradually.

- *Adequate insurance.* Insure the supporting collateral for the loan or lease on a replacement cost with limits commensurate with the cost to replace the property. The principals do not want to find themselves caught off guard in the event of theft or hazard and then obligated to personally pay for lost inventory or property that is part of the deal. Also, take the time to make sure the business interruption (business income and extra expense coverages) limits are in sync with the amount of time and additional expense it would take to restore normal operations after a disaster. In addition, consider fraud insurance to protect against an officer or employee stealing from the company and incurring debt on a line of credit. Broad-form property insurance usually covers only a small amount unless specifically added to the policy; increase this policy limit to match the credit facility limit. Finally, consider personal guarantee indemnity insurance.

From a practical perspective, guarantees are difficult to negotiate or change from standard forms unless the lender (or lessor) wants the company's business and unless there is competitive pressure giving the company and the guarantor the ability to haggle for improved terms. Negotiating these terms is done in the context of the overall credit facility or lease agreement at a time of change.

Get good, independent advice from experienced legal counsel and financial experts. If there are partners or other shareholders, each may want separate counsel representing them in regard to the company. The nuances of the guarantee are specific to each and their circumstances. Get qualified legal advice to ensure the terms and concepts fit each guarantor's situation.

CHAPTER 16

Due Diligence

This chapter provides an overview of some of the basic aspects of traditional or technical due diligence as applied to mergers and acquisitions, including background, process, and participants. There is a brief discussion in Chapter 3 about strategic due diligence and how it differs.

Regardless of whether an acquisition is being undertaken by a financial (i.e., private equity) or strategic buyer, or an investor or lender, the ultimate goal behind every acquisition is to create or enhance value. However, before they can truly achieve the value proposition of a deal, an acquirer and financier will face numerous pitfalls that must be considered throughout each aspect of the transaction lifecycle. Figure 16.1 provides a perspective on how to think about interconnections of the various aspects of the deal and how due diligence may play into them and the transaction.

Because each transaction has different goals and objectives, these matters greatly impact the focus and extent of due diligence to be undertaken. The due diligence process is often the acquirer's first opportunity to conduct an in-depth (or *deep-dive*) analysis and investigation of the financial, tax, legal, and operational aspects of a target's business. When properly executed, these efforts may reduce the overall transaction risks faced by the acquirer.

TRADITIONAL DUE DILIGENCE

Due diligence is the process used to investigate key aspects of a target's business, in an attempt to both better understand the risk of the deal and allow the parties to structure the transaction to appropriately allocate such risks based on the relative bargaining power of each. The typical areas of focus in the due diligence process include:

- Financial matters
- Income tax structuring and compliance

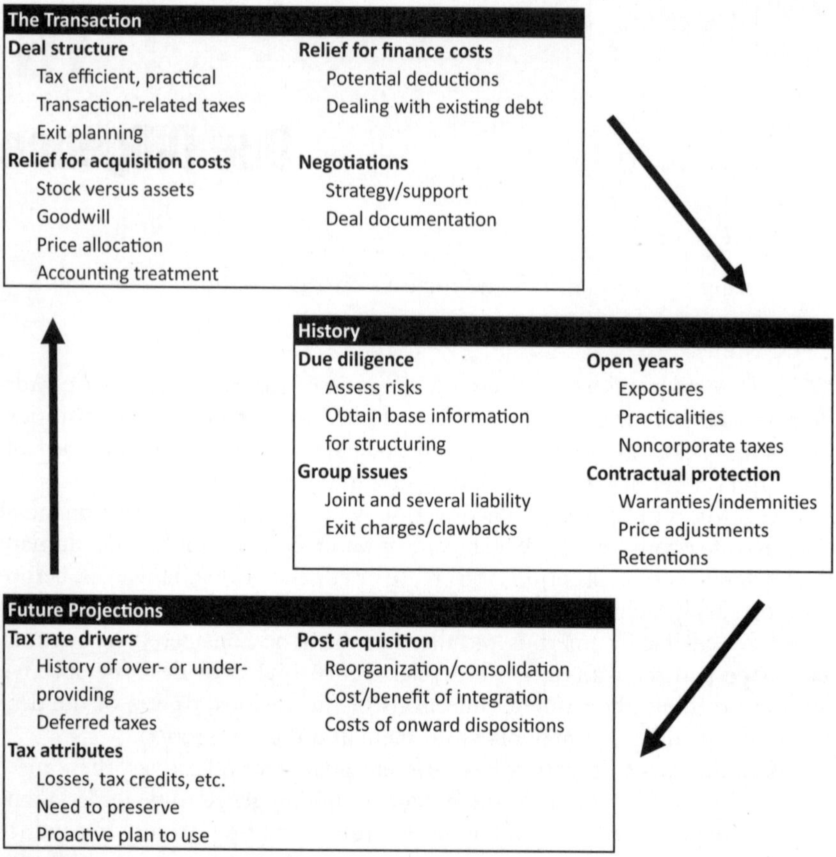

The Transaction

Deal structure	**Relief for finance costs**
Tax efficient, practical	Potential deductions
Transaction-related taxes	Dealing with existing debt
Exit planning	
Relief for acquisition costs	**Negotiations**
Stock versus assets	Strategy/support
Goodwill	Deal documentation
Price allocation	
Accounting treatment	

History

Due diligence	**Open years**
Assess risks	Exposures
Obtain base information	Practicalities
for structuring	Noncorporate taxes
Group issues	**Contractual protection**
Joint and several liability	Warranties/indemnities
Exit charges/clawbacks	Price adjustments
	Retentions

Future Projections

Tax rate drivers	**Post acquisition**
History of over- or under-	Reorganization/consolidation
providing	Cost/benefit of integration
Deferred taxes	Costs of onward dispositions
Tax attributes	
Losses, tax credits, etc.	
Need to preserve	
Proactive plan to use	

FIGURE 16.1 Transaction Life Cycle for Due Diligence

- Compensation and benefits
- Legal compliance
- Information technology

Companies operating in certain industries, such as healthcare, energy, telecommunications, or financial services, also typically face significant regulatory issues and their financial statements present many items unique to their particular industry. A target's compliance with these specialized reporting requirements also needs to be fully understood and investigated as part of the diligence process.

Financial Matters

The financial statement analysis is often the single most important aspect of due diligence because the numbers significantly drive the transaction. Financial due diligence is routinely delegated to accounting firms or others with specialized knowledge of the financial statement process. The focus of financial due diligence is to obtain an understanding of the story behind the numbers. For example, in situations where target companies have consistently produced better financial results than their competition, much of the diligence process will be focused on the sustainability of these results. Conversely, in situations where companies have produced less-than-optimal financial performance, much of the due diligence process will focus on whether these negative trends can be reversed and ultimately elevate the profitability of the target. The financial due diligence process focuses on both the balance sheet and the income statement.

The balance sheet presents the assets owned by a company and the nature of its liabilities. Key assets reflected in the balance sheet usually consist of cash and cash equivalents, accounts receivable, inventories, property and equipment, and prepaid expenses. Depending on the nature of the business, certain intangible assets may not be reflected on the balance sheet. These intangible assets might consist of customer relationships, patents, trademarks, or specialized formulas and processes that are critical in the day-to-day operations of the business. The liabilities of the company represent its obligations to vendors and creditors. Typical liability accounts include accounts payable, accrued expenses, debt, and deferred revenue. While it is important to understand the nature of recorded assets and liabilities, it is also important to consider any off-balance-sheet assets or liabilities (i.e., pending lawsuits, patents, trademarks, etc.) that could impact the assessment of both the balance sheet and the income statement.

Although the balance sheet of a company is always important, the due diligence process typically places a greater focus on the target's income statement. This statement serves as the ultimate measure of profitability, earnings power, and, ultimately, cash flow of operations.

In addition, consideration of the working capital needs of a business is also critical to understanding the story. Typically, separate working capital statements are not included within the financial statements themselves. However, working capital is derived from the balance sheet and is defined as the difference between current assets and current liabilities. In assessing the working capital levels of a company, consideration should be given to trends in working capital requirements. For example, is the business experiencing rapid growth that requires additional levels of working capital above those historically encountered, or does the company operate in a seasonal environment that requires higher levels of working capital at certain periods of the year? Both of these situations would require a detailed assessment of both historical and anticipated working capital requirements. In addition, to the extent any adjustments are made to balance sheet or income statement amounts as a result of the due diligence process, the impact of these adjustments on the working capital requirements after closing should be considered.

Typically, the financial due diligence process begins with reading and analyzing both the year-end and monthly financial statements. The goal of this process is to obtain an understanding of the business as a whole, to identify any unusual financial trends that might be present in the financial results, and to understand whether the annual financial statements are subject to an audit or any other level of service by a certified public accounting firm. The year-end financial statements can be subject to various levels of service by independent, certified accounting firms. The annual audit is the highest degree of verification that can be applied to financial statements. However, most companies are not required to have their financial statements audited, and companies often opt for financial statement reviews and compilations, which are less expensive than audits and generally offer negative assurance on the financial statements rather than the positive assurance provided in the audit process. In designing the due diligence process, it is important to understand the level of service provided by the public accountant, as this will typically impact the extent of due diligence procedures that need to be undertaken.

It is also important to understand any differences between the monthly and year-end financial statement closing process. In this regard, it is not uncommon for nonpublic companies to adjust certain accounts only at or near the year-end. These annual adjustments are typically associated with accounts that are established based on subjective estimates. For example, allowances for doubtful accounts receivable, allowances for excess and obsolete inventory, and bonus accruals may be evaluated by management only on an annual basis. Differences in the month-end and year-end closing process often provide a road map of key areas to be considered in formulating the approach to the financial due diligence process and assessing potential inaccuracies that are inherent in the monthly financial statements.

In assessing unusual trends in the business, there is typically a focus on understanding the drivers that are producing increases or decreases in revenue and why these trends are taking place. The results of any changes in revenue trends will also impact the company's gross profit trends, and as part of the diligence process it will be critical to understand what is truly impacting the overall gross profit of a business. In obtaining an understanding of the key drivers impacting these line items, diligence teams often uncover details that would not be readily apparent from merely reading the financial statements. For instance, in analyzing the reason for increases or decreases in revenue the diligence team could uncover certain changes in sales product mix or products lines that are considered mature and subject to higher-than-average degrees of price sensitivity from competitors. These facts could explain declines in both overall sales and gross profit margins and would be key information a potential buyer might use in assessing the sustainability of the company's earnings and overall profitability. In analyzing these aspects of the financial statements it is important to understand certain key financial ratios or financial measures of the business and how these might compare to industry averages. Some key ratios and measures that are typically analyzed include:

- Accounts receivable turnover
- Inventory turnover
- Gross profit percentage
- Revenue and profit per employee
- Revenue per unit sold
- Gross profit per unit sold
- Current ratio: current assets divided by current liabilities
- Earnings per share
- Earnings before interest, taxes, depreciation, and amortization (EBITDA) as a percent of revenue

GAAP Compliance

As part of the financial due diligence process, there is also a focus on understanding any potential departures from Generally Accepted Accounting Principles (GAAP). This is an important assessment because GAAP serves as the underlying basis for financial statement comparability between different companies and any deviation from this standard could impact the previously reported financial results. Understanding the nature of these differences will also enable a potential buyer to better assess key drivers behind the financial results. Certain GAAP requirements are more complex than others and often companies may deviate from GAAP in these more complex areas. Revenue recognition has become one of the most complex areas under GAAP; because of these complexities this is an area that is typically subject to a great deal of focus during the diligence process. If there is a potential for a change in application of GAAP after closing of the transaction, the buyer will want to fully understand the financial implications associated with these proposed changes as early in the diligence process as possible. Other financial statement risk indicators that would require additional investigation can include items such as:

- Shipping a large portion of product at or near month-end
- Companies that have made prior acquisitions
- Transactions in the books and records that are complex or difficult to understand
- Routine changes in audit firms or professional service providers
- Large differences between actual and projected financial results as well as close or exact matches between actual and projected financial results
- Improper cutoff of expenses between periods
- Bill-and-hold transactions
- Premature revenue recognition
- Inability to establish accruals for certain expenses
- Accounting principles that deviate from industry standards
- Numerous or recurring adjustments posted by the auditor

As part of the audit process, it is also common for auditors to identify proposed adjustments that are not considered material to the financial statements and are not posted to the books and records. These unposted adjustments are frequently referred to as *waived* or *passed* adjustments but are items that should be analyzed by the due diligence team.

Tax Impact and Compliance

Figure 16.1 also illustrates the interrelated aspects of taxes and the areas of potential impact on a transaction. The tax due diligence process is generally focused on tax structuring and tax compliance. Structure is more about how to best formulate the proposed transaction to produce the most beneficial tax consequences to both buyer and seller. As discussed earlier in this handbook, one of the most critical initial transaction steps is the design of the acquisition structure. The chosen structure can impact the resulting approach to every other aspect of the due diligence process. Specifically, the key item that has to be considered is whether the acquisition will be completed through the purchase of the target company's stock or by purchasing assets of the target.

There are pros and cons associated with each structure and often the tax implications for buyer and seller can put these parties at odds in the initial design of the transaction structure. For example, a seller strives to minimize the tax liability created by the sale of the company, often seeking a stock sale to obtain capital gains treatment of the resulting income. However, a stock acquisition affords a buyer little or no opportunity to receive a step-up in basis, which can produce valuable future tax deductions in the form of depreciation and/or amortization of the excess purchase price. In addition, a stock transaction will result in the buyer inheriting all liabilities (known or unknown/contingent or otherwise) of the target. Because of this, a stock transaction typically results in more extensive diligence activities related to both known and contingent liabilities of the target company.

Conversely, an asset acquisition will generally result in more ordinary income recognition by the seller than a stock transaction, and ordinary income is typically taxed at rates higher than capital gain rates currently in effect. However, the buyer will typically be able to deduct the excess purchase price in the form of future amortization and depreciation. Furthermore, in an asset acquisition the buyer can more effectively manage its exposure to acquisition-related liabilities.

Because the transaction structure can impact the focus and extent of diligence activities, it is often beneficial to address this matter as early in the transaction life cycle as possible.

The compliance aspect of tax due diligence is focused on the quality and accuracy of tax filings, which might include federal and state income tax returns, sales and use tax filings, payroll tax filings, and business personal property tax filings. The nature of the entity (corporation, subchapter S corporation, partnership, limited liability company, or other business entity) will also impact the nature and scope of the tax due diligence process. Companies that operate in multiple states or foreign jurisdictions will typically have greater tax risks associated with their operations than single location businesses, and the tax due diligence process should address these risk factors accordingly. In assessing tax compliance matters, it is also helpful to understand the results of any tax notices or tax examinations impacting the business, as these typically indicate higher-than-average areas of risk that will need to be fully understood and investigated as part of the tax due diligence process. Another part of the tax diligence process focuses on missed tax opportunities where companies may not have taken full advantage of tax deductions or credits (like research and development credits) that can reduce a company's overall tax liability. Many privately owned companies place a great deal of focus on minimization of taxes. This desire can often result in aggressive deductions being claimed in the income tax returns. Depending on the structure of the transaction, aggressive deductions that are later overturned by tax authorities can create unanticipated liabilities after the close of the transaction. The overall complexity of a business combined with understanding the tax motivations of the seller will impact the ultimate level of tax diligence to be undertaken in a transaction. The tax matters often impact other areas of the diligence process.

Compensation and Benefits

In many businesses, compensation and benefits is one of the largest single groups of expenses in the company. In addition, the level of compensation and benefits varies a great deal from company to company. To further complicate matters, many aspects of company-sponsored benefit plans are subject to regulation by the Department of Labor or other oversight agencies. Due diligence around the compensation and benefits aspect of a company often requires the efforts of team members from different disciplines working together. In assessing the aspects of compensation and benefits, the diligence focus will not only include compliance with regulatory and tax matters and understanding the levels of benefits provided, but will also include obtaining an understanding of matters such as:

- Employee bonus plans
- Compensation levels of key employees
- The nature of retirement plans in place
- Vacation and sick time
- Deferred compensation agreements
- Stock option plans
- Any employment agreements in place
- Any self-insured arrangements used by the company
- Any noncompete agreements with employees
- Policies used to produce annual employee evaluations
- Trends in merit increases that have been awarded to employees
- Severance packages offered to employees
- Litigation involving the company and former employees

While these items are critical to any buyer in allowing it to understand the details behind the operations of a target company, strategic buyers will often have a higher degree of interest in assessing the compensation and benefits aspects of a proposed transaction. As you might expect, there are complexities and material risks when two companies merge compensation philosophies and benefit plans. Because of this, there is often a great deal of analysis that is undertaken with regard to existing benefit plans and how they will be merged or combined with plans currently offered by the acquirer. Because of the complexities associated with the assessment of compensation and benefit plans, this area often requires buyers to utilize the resources not only of their internal human resource teams but also of external parties such as accountants, specialized consultants, and legal advisors.

Legal

Legal due diligence is a critical component of the overall due diligence process and one that complements, and at times overlaps with, the financial and operational due diligence in a transaction. The focus of legal due diligence is centered on the key components of the specific target company. For example, legal due diligence of a service or technology company may focus heavily on intellectual property, major contracts, and key employee agreements. Legal due diligence of a heavy-manufacturing company may focus on those items and, in addition, environmental and real estate issues. The focal points of legal due diligence in any deal depend on the attributes of the specific target company and its industry, type of business, and particular risks.

On a more generic level, across most transactions legal due diligence will focus on at least the following items: company equity structure, major contracts, intellectual property, litigation, liens, and key employee issues.

Equity Structure   Legal due diligence regarding the equity structure of the target company generally involves a review of the company's charter documents and corporate governance documents (e.g., articles of incorporation, articles of organization, bylaws, operating agreement, and shareholders' agreement). The goal of this review is to ensure that the target company has the required authority to consummate the transaction, to understand the equity structure of the target company (particularly in a stock transaction), and to determine whether the corporate governance documents require that any specific actions be undertaken to consummate the transaction.

Major Contracts   Legal due diligence regarding the major contracts of the target company generally involves a review of key contracts to determine the following:

- The material business terms, including the economics of the contract and its term
- Restrictions on assignment of these contracts (particularly in an asset deal)
- Change of control provisions (particularly in a stock deal)
- Default provisions

Intellectual Property   Legal due diligence involving intellectual property generally focuses on trademarks, trade names, patents, copyrights, ownership of intellectual property, licenses of intellectual property, and infringement claims. This aspect of due diligence is critical in a transaction involving a target company that is intellectual property intensive, such as technology companies. The goal of this due diligence is to confirm the ownership of the intellectual properties, understand the license arrangements for licensed intellectual property, and deal with any potential infringement issues.

Litigation   Legal due diligence involving litigation generally focuses on current litigation and on claims and litigation that occurred within a prior period of time, such as within five years of the closing. In the event that litigation or claims are disclosed, due diligence would involve a review of the litigation and claims, the facts surrounding such litigation and claims, and the result, if any, of any concluded or settled litigation.

Liens   Legal due diligence involving liens generally involves two areas: (1) Uniform Commercial Code judgment and tax lien searches on the assets of the target company and (2) if real estate is involved, a title search of the real estate, which will disclose mortgages, covenants, restrictions, and easements.

Key Employees   Legal due diligence of key employees in service businesses, particularly intellectual property–intensive and knowledge-based businesses such as technology companies, is critically important. The focus of the legal due diligence is centered on noncompete agreements, nonsolicitation agreements, nondisclosure agreements, employment agreements, work-for-hire agreements, stock option agreements and other equity compensation, and independent contractor agreements. The goal is to determine the ability to keep key employees and consultants engaged after the closing, to confirm ownership of developed intellectual property, and to understand all employee benefits.

Information Technology

Information technology (IT) applications are changing rapidly and companies have become much more reliant on IT in every aspect of their business. In spite of this reliance, information technology due diligence is often an afterthought if even considered at all. Too frequently, IT matters are relegated to the postmerger integration team, at which point it may be too late to avoid problems. Just like the other areas of due diligence, effective planning and review can reduce the transaction risks associated with information technology.

Understanding the IT systems in place and utilized by the business is a critical aspect in assessing a company's ability to accumulate and process information necessary to produce accurate financial statements as well as assessing future capital expenditure needs. These systems are frequently integrated into not only the financial aspects of a company but also its operational aspects. In some companies, it is not uncommon to learn that many of their IT applications have not undergone routine updates and that because of this the systems may be unable to advance to the most current version of applications without undergoing numerous changes in the overall IT environment. In more progressive companies, it is common to encounter software that has been specifically tailored to meet the needs of the business. Highly tailored software programs pose a certain degree of additional risk if adequate documentation of the modifications has not been maintained. Another key area of IT diligence is focused on making sure the hardware and software utilized by the target company is properly licensed by the users. Improperly licensed software can subject users to significant fines and penalties. Understanding and assessing the degree of IT sophistication is critical to designing an effective due diligence strategy that will enable the acquirer to realize the overall values and merits of a transaction.

THE DILIGENCE TEAM

Because the diligence process covers so many different areas and frequently includes the execution of very complex strategies, it is often impossible for one group to possess all of the resources necessary to successfully undertake a complete due diligence process. For this reason, most due diligence teams consist of cross-functional specialists and utilize both internal and external resources. The internal resources to an acquisition typically include:

- The C suite: CEO, CFO, COO, CIO
- In-house legal counsel
- Key members of management

The internal team is frequently charged with the development of post-merger integration strategies, including establishment of the time frame and prioritization of these activities. Although the internal team possesses certain skills, these resources are typically supplemented by the use of outside service providers, including:

- Accountants
- Consultants
- Attorneys
- Environmental engineers
- Lenders
- Investment bankers

Effective due diligence requires all members of the team to work together to address the risks associated with the transaction and integration. In selecting outside service providers consideration should be given to their overall M&A experience, their track record in completing transactions, and whether they possess the necessary industry experience to fully advise the parties. Utilization of outside service providers essentially extends the reach of the management team and it can increase the speed with which a transaction can be completed.

DUE DILIGENCE PROCESS

Experienced dealmakers know that it is difficult to predict the timing of a transaction; numerous factors impact how long it will take to successfully complete a deal. Transaction life cycles can range from just a few months to several years—and due diligence is informally and formally taking place throughout that period. Larger and more complex transactions will require longer periods of time to complete the necessary investigation and analysis. However, long due diligence periods are not confined to just large transactions. Some of the most difficult and time-consuming transactions involve acquisitions of small, privately owned companies. In these settings it is often difficult for the seller's management team to provide all of the necessary information to complete the due diligence process. This may arise from a general lack of information or may be attributable to a lack of resources or sophistication that inhibits the seller from devoting the necessary time and staff to complete the diligence process in an expeditious manner while continuing to focus on the day-to-day aspects of running the business.

PUBLIC VERSUS PRIVATE

There is a difference between conducting due diligence in a public company environment and in a private deal. Generally, private companies do not have the level of financial reporting sophistication and resources found in a public company. Some of the most successful entrepreneurs continue to run their businesses based on gut instinct and have intentionally forgone the investment in financial reporting processes and systems because of a perceived lack of payback on the investment that would be required.

Because of this, the ability to obtain detailed and accurate financial information needed to complete the due diligence process may be more challenging than what would be found in a public company due diligence setting or in an administratively progressive private company. The inclusion of representations and warranties in the purchase agreement is typically more extensive in transactions involving privately held companies than in their public company counterparts. Many privately owned businesses are also family owned. In these situations, the family dynamic component of the business cannot be underestimated.

Management of a public company is charged with the goal of enhancing shareholder value. Private companies are typically focused on opportunities to minimize income taxes and to meet other motives of the owners. Accordingly, most privately held companies have higher levels of non–business-related expenses, or owner expenses, running through the income statement. Understanding and anticipating these differences is critical to not only the design of the diligence process but its overall execution as well.

IMPACT OF GLOBALIZATION

Globalization has had a dramatic impact not only on the ways companies operate but also on conducting due diligence in cross-border transactions or ones that involve companies with global operations. In undertaking transactions that involve international operations it is critical to assess compliance with local laws and regulations, many of which are very different from those in the United States. International operations can be as basic as having a sales representative located in a foreign county. Even this relatively simple situation can create numerous pitfalls and risks that will have to be fully investigated during due diligence. Inherent in cross-border transactions are elevated degrees of tax risks and opportunities. These risks can be confined to domestic matters, local country matters, or a combination of both. Cultural and language differences also present unique challenges in undertaking international due diligence assignments. In order to fully identify all potential transaction risks, international aspects cannot be ignored.

WHO RELIES ON DUE DILIGENCE?

The consideration paid in many transactions is comprised of both equity and debt. As such, both acquirers and their lenders rely on the result of due diligence to evaluate the merits and potential risks of the transaction. Because each transaction is different and each industry may have its own unique financial reporting or regulatory requirements, due diligence is often considered as much an art as a science. A well-executed due diligence process allows a buyer to better quantify the overall expected benefits of a transaction while managing key risks related to the acquisition.

QUALITY OF EARNINGS

Once the initial structure of a deal is established, and a basic understanding of the company and its financial results have been achieved, the diligence focus generally turns to obtaining an in-depth understanding of the target's historical operating performance. As part of this analysis, buyers will typically undertake a quality of earnings analysis or assessment. This process attempts to quantify and normalize the impact of certain revenue and expenses contained in the target's historical income statements that are considered either nonroutine or non–business related. The due diligence process attempts to normalize the impact of these items on the historical operating results.

Most transactions are structured as a multiple of EBITDA, which is further adjusted for the impact of any nonrecurring or nonbusiness items reported in the historical operating results of the target. Adjusted EBITDA typically serves as the foundation for buyers in building their overall valuation model and this model drives the determination of the ultimate purchase price. When transactions are based on adjusted EBITDA it is critical to assess the true baseline earnings power of the acquisition target or acquirers will quickly find themselves overpaying for an acquisition and thus diminishing the opportunity to achieve the value proposition so critical to each transaction.

For example, if a target company recently won a lawsuit and received a $1 million settlement, a buyer would not consider this to represent an ongoing source of revenue or earnings and would therefore exclude this nonrecurring item from the adjusted EBITDA of the target.

Chapter 7 contains some additional insight into the quality of earnings assessment and the impact on the buy-side process.

FINANCIAL STATEMENT AUDITS

Financial statement audits are based on the concept of materiality and typically auditors may identify misstatements that are individually or in the aggregate not considered material to the financial statements taken as a whole. While these items that may not be material to the audit process, they could easily become material to a transaction when a multiple is applied to the unposted audit adjustments. For example, an auditor may determine a $100,000 understatement of historical warranty expense is not material to the financial statements; however, if the transaction is based on an EBITDA multiple of ×7, this could result in adjusted EBITDA being overstated by $700,000.

Financial statement audits also focus on internal controls that allow the company to accurately capture financial transactions and report them in the form of financial statements. In most acquisition situations, buyers are less concerned about historical operating practices and they typically seek to identify opportunities to enhance controls and operating efficiencies as part of their postclosing implementation process.

While the financial statement audit process has changed dramatically over the years, auditors still tend to focus a large extent of their testing on balance sheet accounts. The due diligence process typically focuses much more extensively on the income statement as this is the ultimate measure of a company's ability to produce a profit, which in turn drives the value in a transaction.

Even in situations where a target company has been subject to a financial statement audit, it is not uncommon to find due diligence adjustments. The most common adjustments relate to revenue and expenses that are not reflected in the proper period. Employee bonuses are an area that typically requires a more detailed analysis to ensure the expense is reported in the proper period. Many companies may expense employee bonuses when they are paid instead of accruing for them throughout the year in which they are earned. This type of adjustment could impact both the reported earnings as well as working capital of a target.

CHAPTER 17

Market Valuation

This chapter presents a practical approach to valuation as applied to middle market mergers and acquisitions (M&A).* In this context, market value is the highest value of a business in the marketplace. If an owner says his business is worth a certain price, he is generally referring to this value world (see Chapter 2 for a refresher on value worlds). These valuations determine possible open market selling prices for a business interest. An alternative method being used in middle market M&A is referred to as *Transaction Valuation*; an overview is provided in the appendix.

Every company simultaneously has at least three market values. This explains why market value, much like all of business valuation, is a *range* concept. Each market value level is called a *subworld*. A subworld represents the most likely selling price based on the most likely investor type. The subworlds are: *asset, financial,* and *synergy.* The asset subworld reflects what the company is worth if the most likely selling price is based on net asset value. This is because the most likely buyer bases his or her purchase on the company's assets—not on its earnings stream. The financial subworld reflects what an individual or nonstrategic buyer would pay for the business. With either buyer type, the appraisal relies on the company's financial statements as the main source of information. The synergy subworld is the market value of the company when unintended benefits from a possible acquisition are considered.

In the construct of value worlds, the appraisal process focuses on an owner's wish to derive the highest value obtainable in the marketplace. The financial subworld reflects the market reality that the highest value

---

*Market valuation and the approach discussed in this chapter are based on the work and research of Robert T. Slee. Some of the terms and concepts are consistent with those used in traditional business valuation. However, others have been broadened and their application presented based on empirical data and evidence in consummating actual M&A transactions in the middle market.

for many businesses is found by selling to an individual or nonstrategic buyer. Financial intermediaries are the authorities governing the financial subworld, as opposed to IRS regulations, court precedents, or insurance company rules. Substantial market knowledge is required to determine value in this subworld.

REASONS FOR APPRAISAL

As with other value worlds, the world of market value employs a unique process for determining value, as shown in Figure 17.1.

The reason (also called *purpose*) for the appraisal selects the appropriate subworld. If the subject is underperforming financially, the asset subworld is in control. If the likely buyer is an individual or nonstrategic company (financial buyer), the financial subworld is in control. Finally, if the buyer is likely to be synergistic with the subject, then the synergy subworld is used.

DETERMINE THE VALUE SUBWORLD

The next step is to decide if the financial subworld is appropriate. Figure 17.2 shows this step within the market valuation process.

Table 17.1 lists information that helps determine which subworld should be used for the valuation. The facts and circumstances of the situation help determine in which subworld the subject will be viewed.

If the asset subworld is chosen, the subject's net asset value is calculated. With this process the company's assets and liabilities are adjusted to fair market values, which then derives an adjusted equity. In this subworld, the most likely buyer doesn't base the purchase on the company's earnings

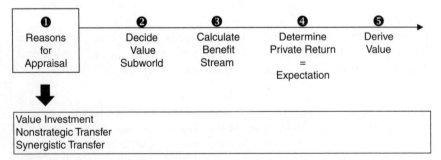

FIGURE 17.1   Market Value Process: Select Appraisal Reason

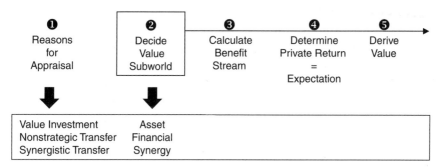

FIGURE 17.2 Market Value Process: Determine Subworld

stream. The buyer in this subworld does not give credit to the seller for goodwill beyond the possible write-up of the assets. Goodwill is the intangible asset that arises as a result of name, reputation, customer patronage, and similar factors and results in some economic benefit a buyer is willing to pay beyond the company's asset value.

Within the financial subworld, the buyer brings no synergies to the deal. Because of this, the target must supply the earnings and the collateral for the transaction's finances itself. This effectively creates a boundary around the valuation in the form of a definable limit as to how much a financial buyer can pay for a business, with the target providing most of this answer.

The synergy subworld is the market value of the company when synergies from a possible acquisition are considered. Because of this, it is accessed only when a strategic or synergistic buyer or group of buyers is identified.

CALCULATE THE BENEFIT STREAM

Once it is determined that either the financial or synergy subworld is appropriate to use, the next step is to calculate the company's benefit stream, shown in Figure 17.3.

Each value world employs a different *benefit stream* to value a business interest. The benefit stream is pertinent to the value world in question. It is comprised of earnings, cash flow, and distributions.

These benefit streams are *economic* since they are not conventionally reported on the company's financial statement or tax returns. They are either recast for a particular valuation, or derived on a pro forma basis. Benefit streams often vary by industry based on dealmaking conventions. For instance, throughout the years sellers and buyers of accounting practices have agreed to use net revenues as the stream, whereas many segments of the

TABLE 17.1 How to Tell When Each Subworld Is Appropriate to Use

Asset Subworld

1. The company has no earnings history, and future earnings expectations cannot be reliably estimated. In this context, *earnings* are defined as *recast* earnings before interest, taxes, depreciation, and amortization (EBITDA). EBITDA is recast for one-time expenses and discretionary expenses of the owner. This lack of an earnings base prohibits the buyer from using the company's earnings as the basis for the valuation.
2. The company depends heavily on competitive contract bids and there is no consistent, predictable customer base.
3. The company has little or no added value from labor or intangible assets.

Financial Subworld

1. Earnings are used as the basis for the valuation by the acquirer. No synergies are valued in the financial subworld.
2. The company is unlikely to attract a synergistic buyer, because the likely acquirer is either an individual, who brings no synergies to a deal, or a nonstrategic institution.
3. The company's owner/manager will not entertain a synergistic sale since it might result in staff reductions and other expense consolidations. Many owners are paternalistic regarding the people within their organizations and will not sell to a consolidator, even if it means receiving a higher selling price.

Synergy Subworld

1. The company participates in an industry that is being vertically or horizontally integrated, or it can be determined that a buyer can synergistically leverage the company's capabilities.
2. Synergies can be quantified with some level of certainty prior to a transaction.
3. Some of the following strategic motivations exist between the company and prospective acquirers:
   a. The company possesses technology or patents difficult or impossible to duplicate.
   b. The company employs a management team that is considered exceptional.
   c. The company has a strong market position that enjoys monopolistic attributes.
   d. The company uses business practices or processes dramatically more efficiently than its counterparts.
   e. The company has developed a unique business model that is transferable to an acquirer.
   f. The company has access to worldwide markets that enable it to purchase and sell more effectively than the competition.

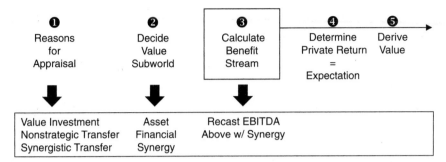

FIGURE 17.3 Calculate the Benefit Stream

software industry use subscription revenues as the stream. Some industries use gross margin dollars as the stream. The key here is that the appraiser needs to understand how stream is defined in the subject industry before a proper market valuation can be completed. For the purposes of this handbook, the stream by subworld is:

Financial subworld benefit stream: Recast EBITDA

Synergy subworld benefit stream: Synergized recast EBITDA

Recast EBITDA has been chosen here mainly for descriptive reasons. Once again, no single benefit stream metric is usable across all industries.

Recast EBITDA includes adjustments for one-time expenses and various discretionary expenses of the seller, with these earnings measured before interest since valuation assumes a debt-free basis. Recast EBITDA is also stated on a pretax basis since the market value world typically does not consider the tax status of either party. Private companies are non–tax-paying flow-through entities, such as S corporations or limited liability companies. Valuators cannot determine tax rates for various parties with certainty as there are significant differences in individual tax rates. A pretax orientation enables the parties to view the business on a similar basis. Table 17.2 lists some of the numerous recast adjustments.

The process for adjusting, or *normalizing*, the income statement is as follows (also see Chapter 10):

- *Determine the company's pretax earnings for the appropriate period.* Generally, pretax earnings in the most recent period are the starting place for this determination. Depending on the circumstances, earnings over several periods may be weighted to best reflect likely earnings in the future. Most buyers are less concerned with financial results from

TABLE 17.2 Recast Earnings Adjustments

Owner Related
- Excess compensation—compensation beyond what the owner is willing to receive postsale or the amount required to hire competent professional management
- Personal travel and entertainment
- Vehicle expense beyond what is considered normal
- Unearned family compensation, including wages, vehicles, trips, insurances
- Directors' fees
- Insurances beyond what is considered normal
- Management fees
- Excessive rent

Employee Related
- Excessive bonuses or compensation beyond industry norms, if they can be eliminated
- Business practices that will be discontinued after a sale (extravagant automobiles, trips, etc.)

One-Time Expenses
- Bad-debt expense that is unusual compared to past averages
- Uninsured accident or casualty loss
- Trial advertising
- Legal (one-time lawsuit, audits, etc.)
- Loss incurred in opening a new branch or launching a new product line
- Some R&D expenses

Discretionary Business Practices
- Donations
- Accounting audits, if compilations or review will occur going forward
- All above-market close transactions
- Customer incentives that will be discontinued going forward

Accounting/Finance
- Add depreciation; subtract normalized capital expenditures
- Discretionary overpaid expenses to reduce taxes

two or three years ago unless there is a negative trend. Some level of projections is used for the current year. For example, six months of projections can generally be used to supplement six months of actual results. Weighting is discretionary and sometimes controversial.

- *Adjust for owner-related discretionary items.* There are a variety of owner-related discretionary items, most of which are adopted to limit taxation. Not all owner's compensation is recast—it is only excess compensation that is added back to pretax earnings. This is compensation beyond what the owner is willing to receive postsale or the amount of the difference required to hire competent professional management. For example, if an owner who did not plan to continue working after the sale of her business had been receiving $300,000 per year in compensation, and it would cost $200,000 per year to hire two managers to replace her, only $100,000 is added back to pretax earnings.

- *Adjust for employee-related items.* Certain employee-related items may be changed postsale, and they are added back to pretax earnings. However, it is important to recast only those items that would not alter the company's postsale morale or prospects.

- *Adjust for one-time expenses.* As with the other adjustments, one-time expenses must be made judiciously. The items listed in Table 17.2 are not encompassing, since these kinds of adjustments are unique to the circumstances of the company.

- *Adjust for discretionary business practices.* These adjustments are difficult to quantify as judgment is required regarding the business practices of the prospective buyer. The deciding factor should be: Is it reasonable for the business practice to continue beyond the sale?

- *Add interest expense and any noncash charges, such as depreciation and amortization.* The valuation assumes the company is debt-free at the valuation date, so interest expense is added to pretax earnings. Only interest expense associated with debt that will not survive the transaction should be considered. For example, if the buyer as part of the transaction will assume a credit line, the interest on this line should not be recast. Noncash charges like depreciation and amortization are typically added back as they reduce earnings but do not affect the cash position of the company.

- *Deduct interest income and normalized capital expenditures.* Generally the cash of the company is not part of the transaction, and therefore interest income generated by cash and marketable securities is excluded from recast EBITDA. Once EBITDA is determined, normalized capital expenditures are deducted to then arrive at a realistic adjusted EBITDA. In practice, most sellers are reluctant to show capital expenditures as an offset to EBITDA while buyers tend to be quite insistent on doing so.

Table 17.3 provides an example of how these adjustments are used to recast PrivateCo's income statement.

The recast EBITDA is substantially higher than the reported pretax profits. However, this is not unusual. The key here is to add back only those expenses that are specific to the current ownership and that will not be incurred by a new owner.

TABLE 17.3   PrivateCo Recast EBITDA ($000)

Item	Y/E 20X3	Y/E 20X2	Y/E 20X1
Pretax Profits	$1,500.0	$1,068.0	$1,650.0
Adjustments			
Depreciation	356.0	360.0	358.0
Excess Owner Comp[a]	250.0	250.0	250.0
Management Fees[b]	200.0	189.0	304.0
Interest[c]	95.0	99.0	97.0
Officer Insurances[d]	5.0	4.5	4.6
Excess Accounting[e]	6.5	10.5	8.5
Excess Legal[f]	9.9	9.6	12.0
Excess Rent[g]	8.7	—	—
Excess Health Insurance	8.2	14.0	14.0
Casualty Loss: Fire[h]	35.0	—	—
One-Time Consulting[i]	—	55.0	—
Donations[j]	74.0	69.0	72.0
Employee Incentives[k]	125.0	115.0	117.0
Total Adjustments	1,173.0	1,176.0	1,237.0
Recast EBITDA	$2,673.0	$2,244.0	$2,887.0

[a] Since the majority owner is passive, all his compensation will be added back.
[b] Management fees are charged each year by another company that the majority owner also controls.
[c] Interest expense is added back to accurately depict cash flow.
[d] Officer insurances are added back since the majority shareholder will not be on the payroll after the sale.
[e] Some accounting services are performed mainly for another company the majority owner controls, but are billed to PrivateCo.
[f] One-time expense. Former employee illegally took blueprints and PrivateCo successfully sued against this person.
[g] Assumes current rent will not continue under new ownership.
[h] The uninsured part of a fire (one-time expense).
[i] A consultant was hired to perform design studies for a new product, which was not produced
[j] The company gives donations each year to a charity the majority owner supports.
[k] Employee incentives includes bonuses that only a passive shareholder would institute.

Table 17.4 shows the weighted recast EBITDA calculation for PrivateCo (our example company). The goal is to choose a recast EBITDA that is reasonable and reflects the company's likely earnings capacity in the future. The appraising party chooses how to weight the numbers, if at all. There will probably be a difference of opinion between the seller and buyer here. The

TABLE 17.4 PrivateCo Weighted Recast EBITDA

Period	Recast EBITDA	Weighted Factor	Weighted Value
Y/E 20X3 (current year)	$2,673,000	3	$ 8,019,000
Y/E 20X2	2,244,000	2	4,488,000
Y/E 20X1	2,887,000	1	2,887,000
Weighted Recast EBITDA	$2,500,000 (as rounded)		$15,394,000

seller wants the numbers weighted to show the highest possible value. The buyer, meanwhile, typically uses a scheme that shows the lowest number, even if it means going back into the history of the company. Many market valuations use the trailing 12-months recast EBITDA as the basis for the appraisal. This approach often places more weight on recent years, since they may be more indicative of the future prospects of the company. For presentation purposes, PrivateCo's recast EBITDA is weighted on a 3-2-1 basis, which means that the current year's EBITDA has a weight of 3, the previous year has a weight of 2, and the earliest year has a weight of 1.

PrivateCo's weighted-average recast EBITDA using a 3-2-1 weighting is $2,500,000. This is achieved by taking the total weighted value of $15.4 million and dividing by the sum of the weighted factors, 6. Thus, the financial subworld stream is $2.5 million.

To determine the synergy subworld stream we start first with the financial subworld stream ($2.5 million) and then add synergies credited to the seller. This process requires additional discussion.

Synergies

The synergy subworld stream includes adjusted EBIT plus the amount of synergies enjoyed by the company. The amounts of *enjoyed synergies* are the estimated synergies credited to, or kept by, a party in a deal. First, the total expected synergies in a deal are forecast. Then, an estimate of the enjoyed synergies credited to each party is made. Usually, the buyer is responsible for creating synergies, but buyers do not readily give the value of synergies away as the realization of the synergies happens only while they own the business. A high level of realism and significant experience are necessary when quantifying enjoyed synergies. The following quantifiable synergy types may be available to the parties in a deal:

- Cost savings
- Revenue enhancements

- Gross margin enhancements
- Strategic combinations

Cost Savings   Often referred to as *hard synergies* because they emanate from hard numbers, cost savings are generally the easiest synergies to estimate with certainty. Several examples of cost savings are elimination of jobs, facilities, and related expenses no longer needed due to consolidation. There are three primary types of cost savings grouped by the type of expected acquisition: horizontal integration, vertical integration, and financial structure.

Revenue Enhancements   Occasionally, an acquirer and its target together can achieve a higher level of sales growth than either company could separately. Revenue enhancements are difficult to quantify, but they can dramatically add synergy. The most quantifiable revenue enhancement occurs when the distribution channel of the company or acquirer can be used to increase sales of the other party. For example, if a large government supplier acquires a manufacturer of products that are not currently sold to the government, the acquirer may be able to enhance its revenues.

Gross Margin Enhancements   Occasionally, gross margins can be enhanced when business leaders combine companies. This occurs when the buying power of the acquirer is far superior to the company. For example, if PrivateCo considers an acquisition by a company that purchases a shared raw material 10 percent cheaper than PrivateCo, some part of this enhancement should be credited to PrivateCo as an enjoyed synergy.

Gross margin enhancements through market pricing power are more difficult to rationalize. This happens when the acquirer increases market share to the point where sustainable price increases may be possible. Although gross margins are increased, the company cannot enjoy these synergies as the realization of the price increase comes only after the transaction. It may not be sustainable, and it may be realized in stages to test the market.

Strategic Combinations   Sometimes deals are negotiated and valued under the belief that *strategic* reasons exist for a combination. A preemptive purchase is an example of a strategic acquisition that occurs when the transaction must be accomplished before competitors have an opportunity to move. Strategic synergies are nearly always difficult to quantify. Therefore, they are at the bottom of the certainty list.

For instance, assume that the buyer agrees to share $500,000 of synergies with the seller. Why would a buyer agree to give credit for synergies that will not be realized until after a deal is closed? There is only one reason: The buyer must agree to share in order to achieve her goal of acquiring the business. In addition, the buyer will still meet her return on investment goals as the buyer rarely will share more than 50 percent of the total expected synergies.

Thus, for demonstration purposes, the synergized recast stream is $3 million.

DETERMINE PRIVATE RETURN EXPECTATION

The next step, shown in Figure 17.4, determines the return a prospective investor, or group of buyers, requires when undertaking an acquisition. Private return expectation (PRE, or *expectation*) converts a benefit stream into a market value. The PRE introduces the concept of market risk and return into the valuation process. As explained in Chapter 2, private investor expectations drive private valuation. The private return expectation is the quantification of these return expectations in the private capital markets:

> *Private return expectation:* The expected rate of return private capital markets require in order to attract funds to a particular investment

The private return expectation converts an economic benefit stream to a present value. Therefore, the PRE can be stated as a discount rate, capitalization rate, acquisition multiple, or any other metric that converts the benefit stream to a present value. There are four different ways to calculate the private return expectation in the financial and synergy subworlds:

1. Specific investor return
2. Specific industry return
3. General return
4. General acquisition selling multiples

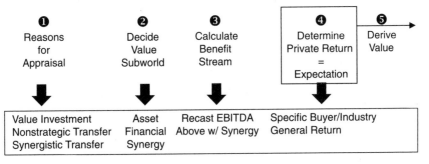

FIGURE 17.4 Determine Private Return Expectation

It should be noted that the private return expectation (i.e., acquisition multiple) is typically the same in the financial and synergy subworlds. This is because the acquisition multiple is an assessment by the buyer of how likely the benefit stream will be realized. For example, a multiple of 5 means that the buyer thinks that the current benefit stream will continue for 5 years. This assessment is usually the same for both subworlds.

Specific Investor Return

The returns required by individual investors differ from those required by corporate investors. Multiple studies show that regardless of interest-rate levels or the general economic environment, individual financial buyers require about 30 percent returns on their investment, corresponding to roughly a 3.3 selling multiple.[1] As the corporate investor has already raised capital for its business, return expectations are driven by its capital structure.

If only one corporate prospective buyer is contemplated, the minimum expectation can be determined by calculating the weighted average cost of capital for that investor. The actual return expectation depends on the capital's use. A company should not use a company return expectation to evaluate a potential investment if the investment differs from the risk profile. From a valuation/acquisition viewpoint, it is generally not possible to know how a potential acquirer views the risk of achieving expected returns. This means that the acquirer's weighted average cost of capital must be used to determine the specific investor return.

Weighted average cost of capital (WACC) is an opportunity cost equivalent to a rate of return investors could expect to earn by investing in stock of other companies of comparable risk. Essentially, WACC is the sum of the weighted cost of debt and the weighted cost of equity. Typically, the weighted cost of debt is the after-tax interest rate on loans and bonds. The cost of equity, however, is more difficult to calculate. For public companies, it involves analyzing shareholders' expected return implicit in the price they have paid to buy or hold their shares. Investors have the choice of buying risk-free Treasury bonds or investing in other, riskier securities. They obviously expect a higher return for their higher risk.

Private companies do not have access to the public securities market by which to calculate cost of equity. One approach for these companies has been to use a modified or adjusted version of the capital asset pricing model. In recent years, two studies have been conducted to generate cost of capital data for privately held companies: the formal Pepperdine private cost of capital (PCOC) survey project begun in 2007 resulting in the Private Capital Market Line, and the cost of capital survey originally conducted in 2004 (and subsequently in 2009) in the base research for publishing the

TABLE 17.5 PrivateCo Private Cost of Capital Calculation

Capital Type	Market Value	Percent of Total	Return Expectation	Tax Effect	Rate Factor
Term loan	$ 500,000	4%	5.7%	0%	0.2%
Equity	$13,700,000	96%	25.0%	0%	24.0%
Weighted average cost of capital					24.2%

Handbook of Financing Growth: Strategies, Capital Structure and M&A Transactions (second edition, John Wiley & Sons, 2009). Both show the effective cost of private debt and equity capital. The data from the most recent Private Capital Market Line report shows that private equity returns range from 30 percent to about 40 percent. If equity is the only component in the capital structure, equity holders must receive returns of 30 to 40 percent to adequately compensate them for the risk of ownership.

The WACC for PrivateCo is determined in Table 17.5.

To calculate a company's WACC, first weigh the various elements of capital structure based on their proportion of the whole. If the benefit stream for market value was stated on an after-tax basis, then the debt portion of the capital would be tax-effected at the marginal tax rates. As the stream in this case is stated on a pretax basis (recast EBITDA), therefore the debt is not tax-effected. For presentation purposes, an expected equity return of 30 percent is used. In this example, PrivateCo has a WACC of 24 percent (as rounded). This means that Joe Main Street of PrivateCo creates shareholder value by investing in projects returning more than 24 percent.

An additional way of considering expected investor returns is to calculate the reciprocal of the capitalization rate, which then becomes a selling multiple. For example, a 24 percent WACC corresponds to an acquisition multiple of approximately 4.2 (1/0.24). In general terms, a prospective buyer could pay 4 times the stream for an acquisition candidate and still meet his or her return expectation. In this case, the buyer bets the benefit stream will continue for a minimum of 4 years. Increases in the benefit stream beyond 4 years add to the buyer's overall return.

Due to lack of information, it is difficult to directly calculate a potential buyer's WACC. Typically, WACC can be calculated only for public companies. In situations where more than one buyer is present, or if the single buyer's WACC cannot be determined, the next step is to calculate an industry-specific selling multiple.

Industry-Specific Return

A private guideline acquisition search can be used to determine a private return expectation profile for the likely investor group. This method locates comparable acquisitions, using the resulting information to draw a value conclusion. The following steps are used for this method:[2]

1. *Set criteria for collection of acquisition multiples, including time frames.* There is latitude here to decide how many years back to consider. Criteria include:
   - *Line of business.* Transactions from companies may be useable if they are similar to the company from an investment perspective. Normally, this is determined on a Standard Industrial Code (SIC) basis.
   - *Relative asset size and revenues* comparable to the company.
   - *Financial information* relative to the company must be available.
   - *Guideline transactions* probably should have occurred in the past five years.
2. *Identify the sources from which the data is gathered.* A number of databases contain acquisition multiples, the most useful including recast EBITDA multiples. The key here is to develop search criteria that match the valuation requirements. In other words, a company with a $1 million recast EBITDA should be compared with data from a company of a similar size. Information about data sources is referenced in the appendix.

General Investor Returns

If no industry-specific selling multiples are available or the sample size is not large enough, the next step is to calculate a general investor return. This is accomplished either through the use of databases with general acquisition selling multiples or through a general investor return matrix.

General Acquisition Selling Multiples

To determine a general acquisition selling multiple, first start with general databases of private acquisition transactions. These databases provide summarized results rather than specific deal transactions. That information is useful when the private guideline industry return method does not yield comparable transactions. Alternatively, it can serve to supplement those results.

Figure 17.5 shows acquisition multiples over a period of years by transaction size (indicated as total enterprise value, or TEV). The information in

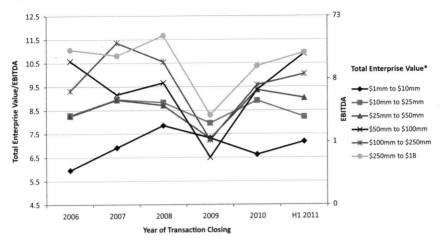

*North American M&A targets of strategics and private equity investors.

FIGURE 17.5   Historical Acquisition Multiples: Strategics and PEGs
Data source: Copyright © Capital IQ, Inc., a Standard & Poor's business. Standard & Poor's, including its subsidiary corporations, is a division of The McGraw-Hill Companies, Inc. Reproduction of this chart in any form is prohibited without Capital IQ, Inc.'s prior written consent.

this chart is a blend of strategic and private equity transactions in North America.

There are several noteworthy items regarding Figure 17.5. First, larger transactions typically realize larger acquisition multiples, meaning that the market perceives lower risk of achieving the benefit streams of larger transactions and thus pays a higher multiple for them. Also, acquisition multiples vary with the amount of senior debt available in the marketplace. For instance, credit was tight in 2009 and multiples were lower as a result.

Figure 17.6 shows the valuation multiples for private equity deals only. Comparing the broad market valuations with those of private equity helps illustrate, though not fully explain, the difference in financial and strategic valuations.

DERIVE VALUE

As shown in Figure 17.7, the final step is to calculate the value. After the appropriate economic benefit stream and private return expectations are determined, a final value can be derived. The stream is either capitalized or

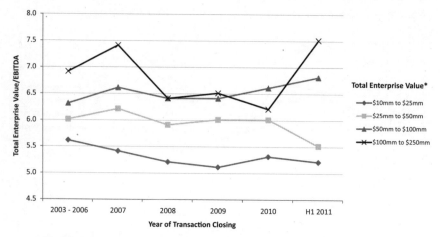

*North American transactions—private equity investors only.

FIGURE 17.6   Historical Acquisition Multiples: Private Equity Only
Data source: GF Data Resources, 2011

discounted by the private return expectation to create a present value. A review of capitalization versus discounting benefits follows.

The end result of either capitalizing or discounting a benefit stream is the same: Both convert the benefit stream to a present value. *Present value* is a financial term that describes what something received tomorrow is worth today. To calculate present value, a benefit stream of earnings or cash is discounted or *reverse compounded*, requiring a discount rate. Thus, $100 received a year from now is worth something less today. This is the present value. For instance, assume money is invested at 5 percent a year right now with 5 percent chosen as the discount rate. The *present value*, then,

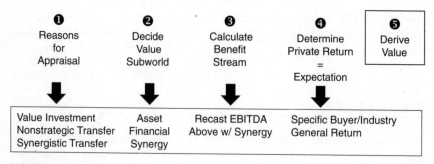

FIGURE 17.7   Derive Value

of \$100 promised a year from now using 5 percent as the discount rate is 95.24 percent or

$$(\$100 \div 105\%) \times 100\%$$

To summarize, \$95.24 invested today at 5 percent interest yields \$100 next year.

The following shows the contrast between capitalization and discounting:

Capitalization: A method used to convert a single year's benefit stream to a value, such as:

$$\text{Capitalized value} = \frac{\text{Benefit stream}}{\text{Capitalization rate}}$$

Using the example above:

$$\frac{\$5 \text{ (Interest received per year; i.e., benefit stream)}}{5\% \text{ (Capitalization rate)}} = \$100$$

In the market value world, another way of saying *capitalization rate* is the expected investment return of the buyer, expressed as a percentage.

Discounting: A method used to convert the expected future benefit streams to a present value, such as:

$$\text{Discounted Value} = \frac{\text{Cash}_1}{(1+i)^1} + \frac{\text{Cash}_2}{(1+i)^2} + \frac{\text{Cash}_3}{(1+i)^3} + \dots$$

$$\text{Or} = \frac{\$5_1}{(1+5\%)^1} + \frac{\$5_2}{(1+5\%)^2} + \frac{\$5_3}{(1+5\%)^3} + \dots$$

$$= \$100$$

Given the same benefit stream, capitalization/discount rate, and growth rate, both capitalizing and discounting yield the same answer. The two rates are the same when the expected economic benefits into the future are the same as in the first period. The two rates are different when the economic benefits vary in the future. For an investment with infinite life, the difference between the discount rate and the capitalization rate is the annually compounded percentage rate of growth or decline in perpetuity

TABLE 17.6 Financial Metrics for PrivateCo

PrivateCo Recast EBITDA	$2,500,000
Synergies Credited to Seller	$500,000
Synergized Recast EBITDA	$3,000,000
PrivateCo Long-Term Debt	$500,000
Likely Acquisition Multiple	6×

in the benefit stream being discounted or capitalized. In other words, in the open market where economic benefits change in unstable ways in the future, the capitalization rate is equal to the discount rate minus the annual compounded rate of growth of the benefit stream.

Capitalizing a benefit stream is done for the following reasons:

- *It is simple to use.* With only one calculation, it is easy to perform.
- *It is accurate.* If the benefit stream is stable or growing at a fairly even rate, the capitalization of benefit stream method determines a value as accurate as the discounted benefit stream method.
- *It is accepted.* The use of selling multiples (the reciprocal of the capitalization rate) has been employed for many years and has wide acceptance among sellers and buyers.
- *It relies on what is known.* This method is not based on pie-in-the-sky futuristic estimates; rather, it uses historical or current numbers.

Now it is possible to determine the financial and synergy market values for PrivateCo. Table 17.6 summarizes the financial metrics developed throughout this chapter.

$$\text{Financial market value} = (\text{Recast EBITDA} \times \text{Acquisition multiple})$$
$$- \text{Long-term debt}$$
$$= (\$2,500,000 \times 6) - \$500,000$$
$$= \$14,500,000$$

The financial market value of PrivateCo is $14.5 million. Since the long-term debt (LTD) was deducted from the enterprise value, it is important to note that this figure is a 100 percent equity value for the company:

$$\text{Synergy market value} = (\text{Synergized recast EBITDA}$$
$$\times \text{Acquisition multiple}) - \text{LTD}$$
$$= (\$3,000,000 \times 6) - \$500,000$$
$$= \$17,500,000$$

In this example, there is a substantial difference between the financial and synergy market values. Only companies that are highly attractive to strategic acquirers can achieve the higher synergy market valuation.

GLOBAL PERSPECTIVE

The application of valuation approaches varies from country to country. In Germany, for example, valuation has traditionally taken an asset-based approach. The reason for this is the strong role of banks as providers of financing for companies. In Germany, banks have focused on the asset values of businesses as the basis for lending because these are frequently pledged as collateral for bank loans.

With the emergence of capital markets and private equity as a source of refinancing for companies, the use of financial-based approaches to valuation has taken on greater importance in recent years. Banks no longer rely exclusively on the asset values of companies but now increasingly consider the cash flows and earnings potentials of businesses as the basis for lending decisions. This is also the approach taken by purveyors of equity capital. In fact, a study by the Institute of CPAs (IdW) in Germany indicates that the financial-based discounted cash flow (DCF) approach is the most widely used valuation method followed by the market-based comparable companies approach.

Synergy-based approaches are seldom used in Germany because there is a feeling that these lead to inflated values, which are not financeable under the lending restrictions of most German banks.

Epilogue for Business Owners

Congratulations! The American dream is yours—financial independence at last. You are the owner of a business worth a fortune. Now what?

As the Chinese proverb reads, "If you don't know where you're going, you won't know when you get there."

If you are the owner of a privately held company, the information provided in this book will be of significant help to you as you consider the value of your business and determine how to obtain the most from it as you consider a transition.

Just a short while ago, the idea that you might wish to sell all or part of your business might have been unthinkable. Now that you have begun to think seriously about it, there is uncertainty, some doubt, and a kind of lonely uneasiness. This is very understandable. Your leadership has required enormous energy and more than a little emotional attachment, so the changed role you are now considering—that of a seller—is quite unfamiliar. You are not alone. No owner has ever been trained for this, and most business leaders do it no more than once in an entire career.

Selling your business will be one of the most important decisions in your life. It will have not only a direct impact on your business life but also a profound effect on your personal well-being and financial status. With all of the effort and personal sacrifice required to build a business, it is wise to take extra time to carefully consider your transition plan.

> *More gold has been mined from the thoughts of men than has ever been taken from the earth.*
> —Napoleon Hill, *Think and Grow Rich*

In starting the process, you may want to think about the following:

- What important changes are you now considering that would impact the long-term market value of your company?

291

- Are you committed to increasing your knowledge of the global marketplace as a business leader of the twenty-first century?
- How can you identify the most critical issues impacting value?
- How can you learn about best practices to increase value being implemented at other companies of your size and industry?
- Is there a gap between what you think your company is worth and what the market considers the value of your company?

In today's economic environment the lines between formerly distinct disciplines are fading, and experienced technical experts require business advisory and transaction skills to better understand and collaborate with all the many other experts essential to the completion of successful transitions, transfers and corporate financial transactions.

"The biggest mistake that consultants make is to overspecialize.... Clients start out, saying, 'I do need an expert in this area.' But, ultimately, they stick with the professionals who provide synthesis, a big picture view, more than just expertise," says consultant Andrew Sobel in his book, *Clients for Life: Evolving from an Expert-for-Hire to an Extraordinary Adviser* (Free Press, 2002).

Successfully carrying out such responsibility is more important now than ever before, due to today's dynamic forces of technology, innovation, high expectations, and hard-driven international competition. These advisory skills are interdisciplinary, requiring that professionals integrate knowledge from a wide variety of business disciplines and cultures.

The best M&A advisors identify and think through issues, problems, and opportunities. They tenaciously apply focused, talented effort of appropriate temperament and drive to get deals done. And, ideally, these advisors act in close cooperation as a special temporary extension of the corporate leadership team.

The "buy-side" M&A advisor earns the cost of his services by helping to accomplish the external aspects of his client's corporate development program more quickly, effectively, economically, and at better transaction terms than one could expect from an insiders-only effort. Few executives ever get to repeatedly practice and perfect this essential corporate development function, particularly at companies in the middle market.

Experienced professionals create value in organizations by (1) supporting and participating in management decision-making roles in governance, strategy, and performance management, and (2) overseeing the allocation of resources to ensure long-term sustainable value creation.

The best-in-class strategy and transition plan begins with a careful review of what is most important to you, the business owner. Do you wish to exit the business now or stay on in some capacity after the sale? There are many transaction alternatives to accomplish the desired objectives once they are clearly identified, including:

- Hold and grow organically
- Grow externally by acquiring another company
- Sell only a portion while keeping operating control
- Recapitalize the business by adding an equity partner for growth
- Improve internally by reorganizing existing management or operations
- Evaluate any and all other options that may satisfy your personal needs and obligations

If you need more time to prepare, there are many ways to increase business profitability and generate additional market value, including the few below:

- Increase/expand sales and marketing efforts
- Expand geographically
- Add new (related) products/services
- Penetrate new markets
- Open new outlets/branches
- Concentrate on high-growth areas of business
- Capitalize on market/industry trends
- Revise pricing policies/credit terms
- Add personnel/equipment to relieve production constraints
- License technology or patented products to other firms

Taking sure-footed steps and making strategic decisions is not always intuitive in new areas. So, selecting experienced and certified professionals to support and assist you in the process is key. Your attorney and accountant play important roles in the sale of your business. They have the special skills and knowledge of your business to provide invaluable assistance, and should be involved in the process at the right time. Here are examples of items that will likely be required of your attorney:

- Provide corporate information needed by the investor and your M&A advisor
- Review and approve the letter of intent (nonbinding offer to purchase)
- Assist in negotiating, reviewing, and approving the final contract (definitive agreement)
- Provide and review numerous documents required for the closing
- Make certain all documents connected with the sale ensure the agreed-upon performance
- Attend and assist with the closing of the sale as your legal advocate

Your accountant will likely be asked to:

- Provide financial information needed for the M&A advisor's analysis and valuation of your business
- Provide financial information needed by the investor during due diligence
- Advise on the income tax consequences of alternative deal structures
- Advise on unique balance sheet and income statement items that may affect contract provisions
- Support your attorney in drafting appropriate representations and warranties

However, in most transitions, you need more expertise and experience than provided by your attorney and accountant. There is a need to understand the market and connect the dots in the entire transition process, from understanding the transition alternatives; to preparing yourself, your team and your company for a change; to leading the transaction process and closing the deal. This is the role of the ultimate M&A advisor, and the reason the Certified Merger & Acquisition Advisor credential was created.

In writing this handbook, we have endeavored to make this a nonbiased, noncommercial work. Yet in reflecting on the number of authors, contributors, and reviewers that hold the Certified Merger & Acquisition Advisor (CM&AA) credential, we felt remiss in not mentioning why so many invested their time and money to become certified. It was done to enable them to add more value for their clients and lead the transition process with a holistic perspective.

You will find a broad cross-section of advisors with the CM&AA credential:

Accountants/CPAs and others who are engaged to render front-end financial advice to existing clients will find this training extremely useful. This is a very diverse constituency, and can include employees, consultants, and self-employed owner-managers or advisers in commerce, industry, financial services, the public sector, education, and the not-for-profit sector.

Attorneys engaged in M&A planning will find this training a useful source for understanding the pros and cons of their legal advice. Its structure makes it easy to assess the tax implications of recommended legal courses of action and to help ensure that intended tax results are actually achieved.

M&A consultants/advisors who counsel clients on M&A transactions will get the greatest benefit from this training. Because it gives an

overall template for deal making, the training is a road map for
running an M&A practice.

Corporate employees. The view from the inside is always different.
While outside gurus can get away with chanting, "Don't sweat the
small stuff," in-house employees don't have this luxury. To them,
details always count. Accordingly, industry professionals such as
chief financial officers, controllers, and in-house attorneys will find
this credential a valuable resource.

Board members and owners. Board members bear the ultimate responsibility for the success or failure of a deal. In many cases, unfortunately, they are the least prepared to make this call. For them,
this training can provide independent perspective for evaluating the
pros and cons of a proposed transaction.

Personal financial planners. Those who offer financial planning advice to
business owners can use this training to understand the options available to the business owner when he decides to dispose of his business. In addition, the discussions of funding alternatives and income
and estate tax planning will be helpful for the financial planner.

Private investors. Based on our years of experience in the market, we
know that individuals and private equity groups are seeking this
type of hands-on practical know-how.

In bringing closure to the main body of this handbook, we advocate that
you seek out and engage a team of trusted advisors with the relationships,
skills, and experiences to assist in what is likely a significant and critical step
for you and your stakeholders. The same concepts of getting the right players
and team in place to build your business should be applied to formulating
and executing on the transition of your company.

www.MiddleMarketMA.com

Appendix

TRANSACTION EXAMPLES

As an extension of this handbook, you have access to example transactions to illustrate the concepts and provide real-world applications of the techniques discussed herein. Each example deal is provided by an actual investor or lender based on a real situation and includes the following:

- Case company
- Case industry
- Case description
- Case country
- Type of transaction
- Situation and shareholder objectives
- Transaction value
- Investor/lender's solution and deal structure
- Notes/comments
- Firm profile and category
- Investment/lending criteria for publication
- Status as a cross-border deal
- Firm contact information

To access the online database of examples, go to www.Middle MarketMA.com and register using reader code **MMMA2012**.

www.MiddleMarketMA.com

TRANSACTION VALUATION

Transaction Valuation* is an alternative method for valuing businesses in the context of a merger or acquisition. In concept, the transaction value is the optimized value that simultaneously meets the multiple objectives of the buyer and seller. It uses the discounted cash flow (DCF) technique, often known as the *income approach*, but its execution and implementation include additional value drivers.

The Transaction Valuation method uses the DCF technique, but, unlike current methods, it does so in compliance with the basic principle of discounting, which is the *time value of money*. Discounting should be applied to cash outflows and inflows, not to available cash flows. To compute distributed cash flows, one has to consider debt amortization and debt priority. These variables are absent in most other techniques utilized today. Further, Transaction Valuation recognizes that a buyer and seller will not exchange a property unless capital is available and debt can be serviced. Specifically, in Transaction Valuation:

- DCF is applied to *distributed* cash flow, not to *available* cash flow.
- DCF is applied to buyer's cash flow, not seller's cash flow.
- Seller's capital structure, or industry average capital structure, is not used, because such use is a violation of the M&M-1[†] theory of finance.
- WACC (weighted average cost of capital) is not used as a discount rate because WACC discounting ignores debt repayments and the changing capital structure.
- *Terminal value* is not calculated using the Gordon Growth Model or the capitalization method, or by assuming an exit price multiple. Instead, terminal value is calculated through an iterative process by recognizing that *price multiples are constant in perpetuity*.

---

*Mike Adhikari developed the Transaction Valuation method. Mike has been an M&A advisor and investment banker since 1986. He is a guest speaker in the Entrepreneurial Finance class at the Kellogg Business School of Northwestern University, and president of the Alliance of Merger & Acquisition Advisors (AM&AA), a national association of M&A advisors. He teaches Transaction Valuation as part of the Certified Merger & Acquisition Advisor (CM&AA) credentialing program. He developed Business ValueXpress™ valuation software (www.BusinessValue Xpress.com), which incorporates the Transaction Valuation method.

[†]Referring to the first corporate finance theory of Franco Modigliani and Merton Miller ("The Cost of Capital, Corporate Finance, and the Theory of Investment," *American Economic Review*, June 1958).

- DCF is necessary but not sufficient to determine value. Value is impacted by additional market-driven variables like debt availability, debt service, equity availability, transaction structure, organization structure, and tax policy. These variables are an integral part of the Transaction Valuation method.
- The Transaction Valuation method satisfies the seller's objective of maximum value while simultaneously satisfying the buyer's objectives of minimum equity infusion, achieving targeted return on equity, ability to fund the total transaction, ability to service the debt, and meeting lender requirements.
- The Transaction Valuation method determines the enterprise value, required buyer equity, amount of debt that can be supported, and optimal capital structure.

The Transaction Valuation method is implemented using optimization algorithms and iterations to satisfy the business seller's objective of maximum value subject to satisfying the buyer's multiple requirements.

A commercial software package that uses the Transaction Valuation method is Business ValueXpress^{TM} (BVX). BVX prepares the buyer's pro forma financial statements using standard accounting methods. It calculates actual equity return on a cash-in/cash-out basis using the cash flow statement. BVX then tests the financial statements for the multiple requirements of buyer, seller, and lender. If all requirements are not satisfied, BVX prepares a new set of pro forma statements by changing equity and enterprise value, and continues doing so until it finds a combination of value and equity that satisfies all requirements. The result is the maximum enterprise value for the seller that the buyer can afford, while at the same time minimizing equity, achieving targeted return, and satisfying other conditions.

TOOLS, MODELS, RESOURCES, AND TEMPLATES

The M&A business involves the collection, management, and analysis of a significant volume of information. As an extension of this handbook, the authors have established a database of resources that include information about the following:

- Virtual data rooms
- Valuation databases and sources
- Transaction databases
- Financial models
- Transactions tools

- Industry surveys
- Industry information

To access the online database of tools, models, resources, and templates, go to www.MiddleMarketMA.com and register using reader code **MMMA2012.**

www.MiddleMarketMA.com

Glossary

H erein is a glossary of terms and deal slang used in the M&A business of the private capital markets and middle market transactions.[1] We have attempted to provide a comprehensive listing of terms generally used, as well as those referenced within this handbook.

10b-5   Rule 10b-5 is an SEC rule that prohibits any act or omission resulting in fraud or intentional deceit (scienter) and relied on by the injured party in connection with the purchase or sale of a security. A *10b-5 representation* is a catchall representation in the merger agreement modeled from the SEC rule but without the scienter or reliance requirement, expanding buyer's ability to claim breach of the agreement.[2]

accelerated depreciation   A depreciation method that yields higher depreciation in the early years and less in the later years.

accounts payable   See **payables.**

accounts receivable   See **receivables.**

accredited investor   A person or legal entity, such as a company or trust fund, that meets certain net-worth and income qualifications and is considered to be sufficiently sophisticated to make investment decisions in complex situations. Regulation D of the Securities Act of 1933 exempts accredited investors from protection under the Securities Act. Typical qualifications for a person are: $1 million net worth and the two most recent years of annual income equal to or exceeding $200,000 individually or $300,000 with a spouse, and the expectation of the same level of income for the current year; $5 million in assets for an entity.

advisory board   See **board of advisors.**

affiliated person   An individual in a position to exert direct influence on the future activities of a corporation. Usually these persons include directors, senior corporate officers, members of the immediate family, and owners of 10 percent or more of the voting shares of stock.

alternative asset class   A class of investments that includes private equity, real estate, and oil and gas, but excludes publicly traded securities. Pension plans, college endowments, and other relatively large institutional investors typically allocate a certain percentage of their investments to alternative assets with an objective to diversify their portfolios.

antidilution A contract clause that protects an investor from issuances of securities at a price below that paid by the investor; upon a sale at a lower price, the clause applies a formula to the investor's investment that increases the number of shares issuable to the investor. There are two basic antidilution provisions—weighted average and ratchet.

appraisal report A written report designed to arrive at a valuation of a property, equipment, or a business.

appraisal rights The statutory right available in most states to a corporation's minority shareholders who object to a merger to have a fair price of their stock determined in a judicial proceeding and to require the corporation to repurchase their stock at that price. Appraisal rights are usually not available unless the shareholder meets certain requirements, such as voting against the merger or abstaining from voting.[3]

asset-based lending (ABL) The traditional definition of asset-based financing refers to a loan extended to a borrower in the form of a revolving credit facility or term loan. An asset-based loan in the form of a revolving credit facility focuses on the level of current assets of a company. A loan amount is negotiated up front, and the amount of the loan that a lender funds will be a function of the levels of assets generated or held by the borrower. Typical revolving credit facilities apply a negotiated percentage to the level of accounts receivable and the level of inventory in order to determine the variable levels of borrowing capacity available to a borrower during the life of a loan.

bankruptcy Bankruptcy law provides for the development of a plan that allows a debtor who is unable to pay his or her creditors to resolve the debts through the division of his or her assets among creditors. This supervised division also allows the interests of all creditors to be treated with some measure of equality. Certain bankruptcy proceedings allow a debtor to stay in business and use revenue generated to resolve his or her debts. An additional purpose of bankruptcy law is to allow certain debtors to free themselves (to be discharged) of the financial obligations they have accumulated, after their assets are distributed, even if their debts have not been paid in full. There are two basic types of bankruptcy proceedings. A filing under chapter 7 is called *liquidation*. It is the most common type of bankruptcy proceeding. Liquidation involves the appointment of a trustee who collects the nonexempt property of the debtor, sells it, and distributes the proceeds to the creditors. Bankruptcy proceedings under chapters 11, 12, and 13 involve the rehabilitation of the debtor to allow him or her to use future earnings to pay off creditors.

basket The basket is the threshold claim amount that must be reached before the seller becomes liable for the buyer's losses. Typically, baskets function in one of two ways. Under a "deductible" basket, the seller is liable only for damages in excess of the threshold amount. If the agreement includes a "first dollar" basket, the seller is liable for all damages once the threshold amount has been reached.[4]

basis point   The measure used for quoting yields on bonds and notes. A basis point is 0.01 percent of yield.

beta   A product that is being tested by potential customers prior to being formally launched into the marketplace.

blue-sky laws   State regulations governing the sale of securities. These regulations provide investors with full and complete disclosures regarding contemplated investment opportunities.

board of advisors   A group of individuals, typically composed of technical and industry experts, who provide guidance and feedback to the company's managers and board of directors. The board of advisors does not have a fiduciary responsibility and is usually established by the senior management and the board of directors.

board of directors   A group of individuals, typically composed of managers, investors, and experts, who have a fiduciary responsibility for the well-being and proper guidance of a corporation. The board is elected by the shareholders.

boat anchor   In business, a person, project, or activity that hinders the growth of a company.

book   See **private placement memorandum (PPM)**.

boot   Nonstock contribution in a merger or reorganization.

breakeven   The level of revenue in a business in which sales minus variable costs minus fixed costs equals zero.

breakup fee   Amount paid by a selling company to a potential buyer when the seller terminates an agreement in favor of a higher bid for the selling company.

bridge financing   Temporary funding that will eventually be replaced by permanent capital from equity investors or debt lenders. In venture capital, a bridge is usually a short-term note (6 to 12 months) that converts to preferred stock; in addition to receiving interest, a bridge lender receives warrant coverage to compensate the investor for taking an early risk in the company. Typically, the bridge lender has the right to convert the note to preferred stock at a price equal to the price of the preferred stock in the next financing round that meets minimum specified levels of funding. See **Hamburger Helper bridge; wipeout bridge**.

broad-based weighted average ratchet   A type of antidilution mechanism. A weighted average ratchet adjusts downward the price per share of the preferred stock of investor A due to the issuance of options, warrants, convertible securities, or shares to new investor B at a price lower than the price investor A originally paid. Investor A's preferred stock is repriced to a weighted average of investor A's price and investor B's price. A broad-based weighted average antidilution formula uses all common stock outstanding on a fully diluted basis (including all convertible securities, warrants, and options) in the denominator of the formula for determining the new weighted average price. See **narrow-based weighted average antidilution.**

burn rate The rate at which a company with little or no revenue uses cash to cover expenses, usually expressed on a monthly or weekly basis. The term is typically used in reference to start-ups.

business structures Legal alternatives of business ownership.

- **Corporation:** An ownership structure that allows a number of individuals or companies to own shares of the capital investment in a business. A corporation is a stand-alone legal entity, so it offers risk protection to its owners, managers, and investors from liability resulting from its actions, including bankruptcy. The invested moneys are at risk.

- **C corporation:** A designation for tax purposes but not relevant for structural purposes; with respect to taxation, there is no limit to the number of shareholders. Profit and loss remains on the C corporation books. Ownership is represented by the possession of common or preferred stock. The C corporation pays income taxes. Earnings are distributed to shareholders in the form of dividends. Dividends are taxable to the recipients when received. Income taxes on profits are paid twice: once by the corporation each fiscal year and a second time by the shareholders receiving distributions from the corporation.

- **Partnership:** Relationship between two or more persons who join to carry on a trade or business, with each person contributing money, property, labor, or skill and each expecting to share in the profits and losses of the business as reported in Form K-1 for each partnership fiscal year. Earnings are taxed only once. Related glossary terms follow:
  - **General partner (GP):** A class of partner in a partnership. Each general partner retains liability for the actions of the partnership and is personally liable for partnership debts. In the private equity world, the GP is the fund manager while the limited partners (LPs) are the institutional and high-net-worth investors in the partnership. The GP earns a management fee and, after limited partners receive a return of their capital, a percentage of profits (see **carried interest**) typically based on an 80/20 split, where 80 percent is distributed to the limited partners.
  - **Limited liability company (LLC):** An ownership entity formed under state law and designed to limit the founders' and investors'

losses to the amount of their investment. An LLC does not pay taxes; rather its owners pay taxes on their proportion of the LLC profits at their individual tax rates. An LLC may be classified for federal income tax purposes as either a partnership or an entity disregarded as an entity separate from its owner by applying the IRS regulations, and as determined on IRS Form 8832, Entity Classification Election. LLCs may elect to be taxed as corporations.

- **Limited liability partnership (LLP):** A legal entity formed under a state limited partnership law for professionals. Generally, a partner in an LLP is responsible for the partner's own actions, but not personally liable for the debts of the LLP or any other partner, nor is a partner liable for the acts or omissions of any other partner, solely by reason of being a partner.

- **Limited partner (LP):** An investor in a limited partnership. The general partner is liable for the actions of the partnership while the limited partners are generally protected from legal actions and any losses beyond their original investment.

- **Limited partnership:** A legal entity formed under a state limited partnership law and composed of at least one general partner and one or more limited partners. The general partner manages the business or trade and is liable for the actions of the partnership while the limited partners are generally protected from legal actions and any losses beyond their investment. The general partner receives a management fee and a percentage of profits (see **carried interest**), while the limited partners receive income, capital gains, and tax benefits.

- **S corporation:** A tax designation that is not relevant for structural purposes; with respect to taxation, an ownership structure that limits its number of shareholders to 75. An S corporation does not pay income taxes; rather its owners pay income taxes on their proportion of the corporation's profits allocated to them on their K-1 tax form for each fiscal year. Taxes are paid on income allocated to shareholders whether or not the income is actually distributed to them. Losses are also passed to shareholders as reported on Form K-1. Losses can be deducted from shareholder taxable income under certain IRS rules. S corporation earnings are taxed only one time because earnings pass through to the investors.

- **Sole proprietorship (SP):** An unincorporated business owned and controlled by one person under his or her name, or doing business as (DBA) a name other than the owner's. Many successful SPs start as garage operations and are subsequently converted into entities such as corporations or LLCs.

buyout firm   An entity in the private equity industry that purchases a controlling interest in a company (as in a leveraged buyout), in many cases accompanied by a management team (as in a management buyout).

buy-sell agreement   A contract that sets forth the conditions under which a shareholder must first offer his or her shares for sale to the other shareholders before being allowed to sell to entities outside the company.

C corporation   See **business structures**.

cap   The maximum recovery a buyer may obtain for indemnification claims. Many agreements include separate caps for different types of breaches.[5]

CapEx   See **capital expenditure**.

capital asset pricing model (CAPM)   Used to determine the required rate of return for stocks.

capital call   When a general partner requests that an investor in a partnership or LLC provide additional capital. Usually an investor will agree to a maximum investment amount and the general partner will make a series of capital calls over time to the investor as opportunities arise to finance the capital requirements of targeted companies.

capital charge   The product of the cost of capital times the amount of capital used by a particular company or business unit. Typically referred to in the calculation of economic profits versus operating profits.

capital efficiency (leverage alliances)   Refers to the concept of efficient deployment of capital by venture capitalists. Best practices include offshore development and understanding the sales and distribution model for a start-up business before ramping operations; hire two to four people to experiment and test the market, then ramp.

capital expenditure   Also referred to as *CapEx*. This is the investment of funds in fixed or capital assets of a company. Among other things, this can include software, office equipment, buildings, land, factory, and equipment.

capital gains (losses)   A tax classification of investment earnings (losses) resulting from the purchase and sale of assets. Typically, an investor prefers that investment earnings be classified as long-term capital gains (held for a year or longer), which are taxed at a lower rate than ordinary income.

capitalization table   A table showing the owners of a company's shares and their ownership percentages. It also lists the forms of ownership, such as common stock, preferred stock, warrants, and options.

capital stock   Stock authorized by a company's charter and having par value, stated value, or no par value. Capital stock includes common stock and preferred stock.

capped participating preferred   Preferred stock whose participating feature is limited so that an investor cannot receive more than a specified amount without converting to common stock. See **participating preferred stock.**

carried interest A share in the profits of a private equity fund. Typically, a fund must return the capital given to it by limited partners before the general partner can share in the profits of the fund. The general partner will then receive a 20 percent carried interest, although some successful firms receive 25 percent to 30 percent. Also known as *carry* or *promote*.

cash cow One of the four categories (quadrants) in the Boston Consulting Group's growth-share matrix. The cash cows fund their own growth, pay the corporate dividend, pay the corporate overhead, pay the corporate interest charges, supply the funds for R&D, and supply the investment resources for other products. They justify the debt capacity for the whole company, so protect them. By definition, a cash cow has a return on assets that exceeds the growth rate. Only if that is true will it generate more cash than it uses. This requires high return and slow growth if the cash generation is to be high. Almost invariably the cash cow has a high market share relative to the next two or three competitors.

cash flow The amount of cash generated from operations. This amount may be negative. Generally considered the amount of cash available to stockholders and long-term lenders of the corporation. There are several calculations that serve as a proxy for cash flow: net operating profit less adjusted taxes (NOPLAT), earnings before interest and taxes (EBIT), or earnings before interest, taxes, depreciation, and amortization (EBITDA).

catch-up A clause in the agreement between the general partner and the limited partners of a private equity fund. Once the limited partners have received a certain portion of their expected return, the general partner can then receive a majority of profits until the previously agreed-on profit split is reached.

change of control bonus A bonus of cash or stock given to members of a management group upon successful completion of the sale of a company.

clawback A clause in an agreement between the buyer and seller or an investor and a company. The clawback gives one party the right to reclaim a portion of the investment or purchase price from the other in the case of certain negative events or failure to perform.

closing The conclusion of a transaction whereby all necessary legal documents are signed.

CM&AA The Certified Merger & Acquisition Advisor (CM&AA) designation is awarded by the Alliance of Merger & Acquisition Advisors and their academic partners Loyola University Chicago, DePaul University, or Pepperdine University to professionals that evidence mastery of the M&A body of knowledge and a commitment to staying abreast of new developments in the field of investment banking and mergers and acquisitions. It also recognizes professional achievement and competence, serves as a tool to both attract and serve new clients, provides identification with other professionals in the field, and potentially stimulates career advancement.

CM&AA professionals are accredited experts in one or more professional fields (e.g., CPA, accountant, lawyer, corporate finance, valuation expert, CFA, or MBA with Wall Street–type investment banking experience) and understand the overall investment banking process for selling and buying middle market companies.

collateral   Assets of the borrower, such as real estate, accounts receivable, or equipment, for which a lender has an equitable interest until a loan obligation is fully paid.

comfort letter   A nonbinding indication of interest by an investor or lender in a potential transaction.

commercial bank   Widely known as a source of debt financing for businesses. Commercial banks generally provide lines of credit, term loans, and revolving loans. Traditionally, commercial banks are cash-flow lenders and view collateral as a secondary source of repayment; from experience, bankers' actions do not always evidence this thinking. Focus is placed on lending to borrowers that have durability and predictability of cash flows. To assure liquidity and stability for the public, banks are highly regulated by states, by the Federal Deposit Insurance Corporation (FDIC), and by the operating cash cycle (OCC).

commitment   An obligation, typically the maximum amount that an investor or lender agrees to invest in a fund or to loan to a company.

common stock   A type of security representing ownership rights in a company. Usually, company founders, management, and employees own common stock while investors own preferred stock. In the event of a liquidation of the company, the claims of secured and unsecured creditors, bondholders, and preferred stockholders take precedence over common stockholders. See **preferred stock**.

comparable   A publicly traded company with similar characteristics to a private company that is being valued. For example, a telecommunications equipment manufacturer whose market value is two times revenues can be used to estimate the value of a similar and relatively new company with a new product in the same industry. See **liquidity discount**.

consequential damages   Damages that are not a direct result of an act, but a consequence of the initial act. To be awarded consequential damages, it typically must be shown that the damages were a foreseeable result of the initial act.[6]

consolidation   See **rollup**.

contingent value rights (CVR) Provides the holder with the right to sell a share of stock in the underlying company at a fixed price during the life of the right.

contribution margin Selling price minus variable cost. For a business operating above breakeven, the contribution margin from incremental sales becomes operating profit.

control The authority of an individual or entity that owns more than 50 percent of equity in a company or owns the largest block of shares compared to other shareholders.

convergence The Financial Accounting Standards Board (FASB) is working with the International Accounting Standards Board (IASB) to converge their respective accounting standards into a set of rules that will meet the needs of preparers and users of financial statements and other accounting information in all global constituencies.

conversion The right of an investor or lender to force a company to replace the investor's preferred shares or the lender's debt with common shares at a preset conversion ratio. A conversion feature was first used in railroad bonds in the 1800s.

convertible debt A loan that allows the lender to exchange the debt for common shares in a company at a preset conversion ratio.

convertible preferred stock A type of stock that gives an owner the right to convert to common shares of stock. Preferred stock is granted certain rights not normally granted to the holders of common stock, such as decision-making management control, a guaranteed return on investment, or senior priority in receiving proceeds from a sale or liquidation of the company. Convertible preferred is the most common tool for private equity funds to invest in companies.

convertible security A security that gives its owner the right to exchange the security for common shares in a company at a preset conversion ratio. The security is typically preferred stock or debt.

corporate charter The document prepared when a corporation is formed. The charter sets forth the objectives and goals of the corporation, as well as a general statement of what the corporation can and cannot do while pursuing these goals.

corporate resolution A document stating that the corporation's board of directors has taken a specified action, such as authorizing management to act on behalf of the corporation.

corporate venturing Venture capital provided by in-house investment funds of large corporations to further their own strategic interests.

corporation See **business structures**.

cost of capital Actual or implied interest rate for the use of money or assets of a company.

cost of goods sold (COGS)   Same as **cost of sales.**

cost of revenue   Same as cost of goods sold, though the term usually refers to costs incurred to generate service revenues versus those of product revenues. Cost of revenue and cost of goods sold are usually comprised of direct and indirect costs. Direct costs are those that are attributed directly and proportionally to creating the product or service (i.e., materials and labor). Indirect costs are those expenses that are attributed to creating the product or service but are general in nature and not easily allocated on a per-unit basis (i.e., engineering support costs and facilities costs related to producing the product or service).

cost of sales (COS)   The burdened expenses incurred to generate the revenue of a company; includes direct and indirect costs.

covenant   A legal promise to do or not do a certain thing. For example, in a financing arrangement, company management may agree to a negative covenant whereby it promises not to incur additional debt. The penalties for violation of a covenant may vary from repairing the mistake to losing control of the company. In a merger agreement, covenants may require the parties to take actions both before and after the closing.[7]

cumulative dividends   The owner of preferred stock with cumulative dividends has the right to receive accrued (previously unpaid) dividends in full before dividends are paid to any other classes of stock.

current ratio   The ratio of current assets to current liabilities. Less than 1 indicates negative working capital. The current ratio is used to measure liquidity.

data room   Central location for due diligence materials provided by a company to all potential purchasers or investors in connection with an acquisition or investment. Most data rooms are now electronic storage locations, also referred to as *virtual* data rooms.

days sales outstanding (DSO)   The average period in days in which a company's accounts receivable remain due from the customer.

deal flow   A measure of the number of potential investments or transactions that a fund, lender, advisor or buyer reviews in any given period.

debt-for-equity swaps   A voluntary exchange of outstanding debt for equity of equal market value.

debt service   The ratio of a loan payment amount to available cash flow earned during a specific period. Typically, lenders insist that a company maintain a certain debt service ratio or else risk penalties such as having to pay off the loan immediately.

debt-to-equity (D/E) ratio   Total liabilities divided by total equity of the entity as shown in its balance sheet. The D/E measures the entity's leverage level. A debt-to-equity ratio of 1 indicates that the entity's total liabilities equal the equity dollar amount.

default   A company's failure to comply with the terms and conditions of a financing arrangement.

definitive agreement   The final, fully negotiated agreement between parties, containing all material terms, conditions, and agreements relating to the subject matter of the transaction in question.

deficiency guaranty   A guarantee limited in amount to the deficiency suffered by the creditor in event of default on a loan or debt, usually covering the first loss by the lender. A limited deficiency guaranty will contain a maximum or limit of exposure for the guarantor.

demand right   A type of registration right. Demand rights give an investor the right to force a company to register its shares with the SEC.

dilution   The reduction in the ownership percentage of current investors, founders, and employees caused by the issuance of new shares to new investors.

dilution protection   See **antidilution; ratchet.**

direct costs   See **cost of revenue.**

disbursement   An investment by a fund in a company.

discounted cash flow (DCF)   Calculation of the present value of a stream of forecasted cash flow discounted using an interest rate appropriate to the risk of the venture creating the cash flow.

discounted free cash flow (DFCF)   Equity valuation method in which a discount percentage is applied to a stream of forecasted free cash flows, where free cash flow is defined as net operating cash flow increased by net debt issuances and decreased by net investment.

discount rate   The interest rate used to determine the present value of a series of future cash flows.

distribution   The transfer of cash or securities to a limited partner resulting from the sale, liquidation, or IPO of one or more portfolio companies in which a general partner chose to invest.

dividends   Payments made by a company to the owners of its securities out of earnings of the company based solely on the amount of securities owned.

dividend yield   The dollar dividend per share divided by the current price per share.

domain expertise   Intelligence of an investor, partner, or potential employee in the specific business or industry occupied by a company.

double taxation   Refers to the same income being taxed twice, once at the entity level and once at the individual level. Thus, dividends, which are paid out of after-tax corporate profits, are double taxed when individuals have to pay taxes on them as well.

down round   A round of financing whereby the valuation of the company is lower than the value determined by investors in an earlier round.

drag-along rights The contractual right of an investor in a company to force all other investors to agree to a specific action, such as the sale of the company.

due diligence The investigatory process performed when considering a transaction with a third party to evaluate the business and finances of a company. In M&A, traditional or technical due diligence focuses on financial information, taxes, legal and regulatory compliance, environmental compliance, human resources, contracts, information technology, and so on. Strategic due diligence explores whether the potential of the deal is realistic by testing the rationale.

earnout An agreement in the sale of a company where the buyer agrees to pay the seller consideration in the future (typically cash or stock) based on certain future events or performance of the business post-close.

earnings before interest and taxes (EBIT) A measurement of the operating profit of a company. One possible valuation methodology is based on a comparison of private and public companies' value as a multiple of EBIT.

earnings before interest, taxes, depreciation, and amortization (EBITDA) A measurement of the cash flow of a company. One possible valuation methodology is based on a comparison of private and public companies' value as a multiple of EBITDA less funded debt.

economic profit The difference between the amount received in connection with the sale of a good or service and the cost of goods or services sold analyzed on the basis of their opportunity cost. Also defined as EBIT minus a charge for the cost of capital deployed to generate the EBIT.

elevator pitch A concise presentation, lasting only a few minutes (an elevator ride), by an entrepreneur to a potential investor about an investment opportunity.

emerging growth company A growth company with revenues from $1 million to $10 million.

employee stock ownership program (ESOP) An equity plan established by a company that permits the grant of options on stock of the company for long-term incentive compensation for employees.

equity The ownership structure of a company represented by common shares, preferred shares, or unit interests: Equity = Assets – Liabilities.

escrow A portion of the consideration that is deposited with a neutral third party (in the case of an escrow) or withheld by the buyer (in the case of a holdback) to be applied toward potential future indemnification claims by the buyer. After a specified period of time (the survival period) any consideration remaining in the escrow or holdback account is released to the selling shareholders.[8]

evergreen fund   A fund that reinvests its profits in order to ensure the availability of capital for future investments.

exit alternative   The options or alternatives that the owners of a business may have to create liquidity (or monetize) from their investment in the business. See **exit strategy.**

exit strategy   The plan for generating profits for owners and investors of a company. Typically, exit strategies include mergers and acquisitions, recapitalizations, ESOP, and initial public offerings (IPOs).

expansion stage   The stage of a company characterized by a complete management team and a substantial increase in revenues.

factoring   The selling of a company's accounts receivable, at a discount, to a third party who either then assumes the credit risk of the account debtors, known as nonrecourse factoring, or assumes no credit risk, known as recourse factoring, and receives cash as the company's customers pay their accounts.

fairness hearing   The hearing conducted by a state agency in connection with a proposed business combination, merger, or acquisition that results in the issuer of securities receiving a transactional exemption from registration of the securities, and the target shareholders, other than affiliates of the resulting company, receiving freely tradable shares.

fairness opinion   A letter issued by an investment bank to assess the fairness of a transaction such as the negotiated price for a merger or an acquisition.

Financial Accounting Standards Board (FASB)   The private-sector organization empowered to establish financial accounting and reporting standards. Although this function legally resides with the Securities and Exchange Commission for public companies, the SEC has traditionally provided the private sector with the opportunity for self-regulation. Since 1973, the SEC has relied on the FASB for standard setting. The FASB operates under the oversight of the Financial Accounting Foundation, which is responsible for funding the activities of both the FASB and its counterpart for state and local government, the Governmental Accounting Standards Board. The Financial Accounting Foundation also is responsible for selecting the members of both accounting standards boards and their respective advisory councils. Eleven members of the board of trustees of the Financial Accounting Foundation are nominated by eight organizations and approved by the trustees. The nominating organizations are:

1. American Accounting Association
2. American Institute of Certified Public Accountants

3. Association for Investment Management and Research
4. Financial Executives International
5. Government Finance Officers Association
6. Institute of Management Accountants
7. National Association of State Auditors, Comptrollers and Treasurers
8. Securities Industry Association

Five additional trustees serve as at-large members and are selected by the board of trustees. The Foundation is incorporated to operate exclusively for charitable, educational, scientific, and literary purposes within the meaning of Section 501(c)(3) of the Internal Revenue Code.

financial engineering Refers to the financial structuring of a company or particular transaction.

financial intermediaries Institutions that provide the market function of matching borrowers and lenders or traders.

financial investor An investor interested solely in achieving a financial return from an investment, rather than a return coupled with a strategic benefit associated with the investment.

financing slack The difference between the debt that a firm chooses to carry and the optimal debt that it could carry, when the former is less than the latter.

financing statement Document filed with a lender detailing personal property taken as collateral from a borrower. The financing statement, a standard document under the Uniform Commercial Code, is filed with the secretary of state or other designated public official. The document is time stamped, the filing date is noted, and a file number is assigned, placing the public on notice to the lender's claim to the specified collateral.

fire sale The sale of merchandise and other assets after a fire at very low prices. It is also used figuratively when merchandise and other assets of companies are sold at very low prices to ensure a fast disposal of surplus items.

firm commitment A commitment by a syndicate of investment banks to purchase all the shares available for sale in a public offering of a company. The shares will then be resold to investors by the syndicate.

fixed charge coverage ratio This ratio is used by lenders to compare committed fixed payments to available cash flow. Listed here are two actual formulas used by asset-based lenders to illustrate the concept:

1. The ratio calculated on a rolling four-quarter basis of (i) EBITDA to (ii) the sum of (a) cash interest expense, plus (b) cash tax expense, plus (c) current maturities of long-term debt, subordinated debt, and

capital leases of the borrower, plus (d) the sum of dividends or distributions paid by the borrower during this period, plus (e) nonfinanced capital expenditures.

2. The ratio of (i) EBITDA plus cash equity minus unfinanced capitalized expenditures made during such period minus cash taxes, dividends and distributions, if any, made during such period to (ii) all senior debt payments plus, without duplication, all subordinated debt payments during such period. In this case, senior debt payments include all cash actually expended by borrower to make (a) interest payments on any advances hereunder, plus (b) payments for all fees, commissions, and charges set forth herein and with respect to any advances, plus (c) capitalized lease payments, plus (d) payments with respect to any other indebtedness for borrowed money.

flipping The act of selling shares immediately after an initial public offering. Investment banks that underwrite new stock issues attempt to allocate shares to new investors who indicate they will retain the shares for several months.

Form S-1 Registration statement under the Securities Act of 1933. This form is typically used in conjunction with a company's initial public offering of securities.

forward contract An agreement to buy or sell the underlying asset at a fixed price at a future point in time.

founder A person who participates in the creation of a company. Typically, founders manage the company until it has enough capital to hire professional managers.

free cash flow The amount of cash a company has after expenses, debt service, capital expenditures, and dividends. Free cash flow measures the financial comfort level of the company as a going concern.

friends and family financing Capital provided by the friends and family of founders of an early stage company. Founders should be careful not to create an ownership structure that may hinder the participation of professional investors once the company begins to achieve success.

full ratchet An antidilution protection mechanism whereby the price per share of the preferred stock of investor A is adjusted downward due to the issuance of options, warrants, or securities to new investor B at a price lower than the price investor A originally received. Investor A's preferred stock is repriced to match the price of investor B's option, warrant, or securities. See **broad-based weighted average ratchet; narrow-based weighted average antidilution.**

fully diluted basis A methodology for calculating any per-share ratios whereby the denominator is the total number of shares issued by the company on the assumption that all warrants and options are exercised and that all convertible securities have been converted.

funded debt　A liability resulting from a financing transaction where cash was loaned to the business, as opposed to a liability created as a result of company operations. Examples include a bank credit facility, subordinated note from a lender, or a note payable to an investor. Examples that are not funded liabilities include accounts payable or accrued payroll.

fund of funds　A fund created to invest in private equity funds to minimize portfolio management efforts.

GAAP　See **Generally Accepted Accounting Principles (GAAP)**.

Generally Accepted Accounting Principles (GAAP)　A voluminous set of standards, interpretations, opinions, and bulletins developed by the Financial Accounting Standards Board.

general partner (GP)　See **business structures**.

going-concern value　The value of a company to another company or individual in terms of an operating business. The difference between a company's going-concern value and its asset or liquidation value is deemed goodwill and plays a major role in mergers and acquisitions.

golden parachute　A contractual clause in a management contract that allows the manager to be paid a specified sum of money in the event the control of the firm changes.

GP　See **business structures**.

greenmail　The purchase of a potential hostile acquirer's stake in a business at a premium over the current fair market value of the stock.

grossing up　An adjustment of an option pool for management and employees of a company that increases the number of shares available over time. This usually occurs after a financing round whereby one or more investors receive a relatively large percentage of the company.

gross margin　Revenue associated with the sale of a product or service less the direct costs of providing the product or service.

growth stage　The stage of a company when it has received one or more rounds of financing and is generating revenue from its product or service. Same as **middle stage**.

haircut　Reduction in value taken by one party in order to compensate another party or facilitate a transaction.

hair on the deal　Refers to certain negative or less-than-desirable attributes, situations, events, or characteristics of a transaction (or the target of an investment or acquisition), particularly those that create additional risk for the buyer or investor.

Hamburger Helper bridge　A colorful label for a traditional bridge loan that includes the right of the bridge lender to convert the note to preferred stock at a price that is a 20 percent discount from the price of the preferred stock in the next financing round.

Hart-Scott-Rodino Act A law permitting the Federal Trade Commission and the U.S. Department of Justice to examine potential investments and acquisitions and to deny permission to the companies to consummate the proposed transaction where the transaction has the potential for reducing competition in an industry or business segment.

harvest To generate cash or stock from the sale or IPO of companies in a private equity portfolio of investments.

hedge A transaction that reduces the risk of an investment.

hockey stick The general shape and form of a chart showing revenue, customers, cash, or some other financial or operational measure that increases dramatically at some point in the future. Entrepreneurs often develop business plans with hockey stick charts to impress potential investors.

holdback See **escrow.**

holding period Length of time an asset (property) is held by its owner. The holding period for short-term capital gains and losses is one year or less. The holding period for long-term capital gains and losses is more than one year. To figure the holding period, begin counting on the day after you receive the property and include the day you disposed of it.

hot assets The term *hot assets* is not found in the tax code but is used to define assets that have an ordinary income taint when a partnership interest (a capital asset) is sold. Since 1997, hot assets in the sale of a partnership interest are unrealized receivables and inventory items of the partnership. When gain is recognized with certain partnership distributions, the hot asset definition is modified to include unrealized receivables and substantially appreciated inventory.

hot issue Stock in an initial public offering that is in high demand.

hurdle rate A minimum rate of return required before an investor will make an investment.

incidental damages Damages that are awarded as compensation for the buyer's commercially reasonable expenses resulting from a breach by the seller. Examples include the costs of handling, shipping, and replacing faulty inventory, costs associated with restatement of the seller's financials, and the costs associated with bringing the seller into compliance with applicable regulations.[9]

indemnification Where one party (typically the seller) to an agreement reimburses the other (typically the buyer) for any losses they incur as a result of the transaction.[10]

indicative offer   Short-form term sheet in which a potential investor, partner, or acquirer provides a target with an informal description of the material terms and conditions of an offer.

information asymmetry   Imbalance that arises any time one party to a transaction or agreement has more or better information than others.

initial public offering (IPO)   The first offering of stock by a company to the public. New public offerings must be registered with the Securities and Exchange Commission.

insider information   Material information about a company that has not yet been made public. It is illegal for holders of this information to make trades based on it, however received.

inside round   A round of financing in which the investors are the same investors as the previous round.

insiders   Directors and senior officers of a corporation—in effect, those who have access to inside information about a company. An insider also is someone who owns more than 10 percent of the voting shares of a company.

insolvency risk   The risk that a firm will be unable to satisfy its debts. Also known as *bankruptcy risk*.

insolvent   Unable to pay debts (i.e., a firm's liabilities exceed its assets).

institutional investors   Organizations that invest, including insurance companies, depository institutions, pension funds, investment companies, mutual funds, and endowment funds.

interest   The price paid for borrowing money. It is expressed as a percentage rate over a period of time and reflects the rate of exchange of present consumption for future consumption. Also, a share or title in property.

interest coverage ratio   Earnings before interest and taxes divided by the interest expense. The interest coverage ratio is a measure of the firm's capacity to service its interest payments, with higher coverage ratios representing more safety.

interest coverage test   A debt limitation that prohibits the issuance of additional long-term debt if the issuer's interest coverage would, as a result of the issue, fall below some specified minimum.

interest deduction   An interest expense, such as interest on a margin account, that is allowed as a deduction for tax purposes.

interest expense   The money the corporation or individual pays out in interest on loans.

interest in arrears   Interest that is due only at the maturity date rather than periodically over the life of the loan.

interest-only loan   A loan in which payment of principal is deferred and interest payments are the only current obligation.

interest tax shield   The reduction in income taxes that results from the tax-deductibility of interest payments.

interim statement   A financial statement that reflects only a limited period of a company's financial statement, not the entire fiscal year.

internal finance   Finance generated within a firm by retained earnings and depreciation.

internal growth rate   Maximum rate a firm can expand without outside sources of funding. Growth generated by cash flows retained by the company.

internal rate of return (IRR)   Interest rate that is applied to a stream of cash outflows and inflows that causes the sum of the outflows and inflows to equal zero.

International Accounting Standards Board (IASB)   In March 2001, the International Accounting Standards Committee (IASC) Foundation was formed as a not-for-profit corporation incorporated in the state of Delaware. The IASC Foundation is the parent entity of the International Accounting Standards Board, an independent accounting standard-setter based in London, UK. On April 1, 2001, the International Accounting Standards Board (IASB) assumed accounting standard-setting responsibilities from its predecessor body, the International Accounting Standards Committee.

International Financial Reporting Standards (IFRS)   A set of accounting standards, developed by the International Accounting Standards Board (IASB), that is becoming the global standard for the preparation of public company financial statements.

intrinsic value of a firm   The present value of a firm's expected future net cash flows discounted by the required rate of return.

inventory turnover   A measure of how often the company sells and replaces its inventory. It is the ratio of annual cost of sales to the latest inventory. One can also interpret the ratio as the time for which inventory is held. For example, a ratio of 26 implies that inventory is held, on average, for two weeks. It is best to use this ratio to compare companies within an industry (high turnover is a good sign) because there are huge differences in this ratio across industries.

invested capital   Total assets minus non-interest-bearing liabilities. This term is used in the calculation of return on invested capital (ROIC).

investment banking   Financial intermediaries who perform a variety of services, including aiding in the sale of securities, facilitating mergers and other corporate reorganizations, acting as brokers to both individual and institutional clients, and trading for their own accounts.

investment tax credit   Tax credit provided by some states for investments made into qualified investments.

investment thesis/investment philosophy   The fundamental ideas that determine the types of investments that an investment fund will choose in order to achieve its financial goals.

IPO   See **initial public offering (IPO)**.

IRR   See **internal rate of return (IRR)**.

issuer   A company that sells its debt or equity securities.

joint and several   When several persons sign a note, loan or obligation where each person is legally obligated to become liable for the payment of the entire note (versus their prorate share).

junior debt   A loan that has a lower priority than a senior loan in case of a liquidation of the assets of the borrowing company. Also referred to as *second lien, last-out participation*, or *tranche B* debt. While subordinated debt is technically junior to the senior debt in a company, it typically sits below junior debt and is unsecured.

junk bond   A bond with a speculative credit rating of BB (S&P) or BA (Moody's) or lower. Junk or high-yield bonds offer investors higher yields than bonds of financially sound companies. Two agencies, Standard & Poor's and Moody's Investors Service, provide the rating systems for companies' credit.

Keogh plan   A type of pension account in which taxes are deferred. Available to those who are self-employed.

kicker   An additional feature of a debt obligation that increases its marketability and attractiveness to investors.

last-out participation   See **junior debt**.

later stage   The stage of a company that has proven its concept, achieved significant revenues compared to its competition, and is approaching cash-flow breakeven or positive net income. The rate of return for venture capitalists who invest in later-stage, less risky ventures is lower than in earlier stage ventures.

LBO   See **leveraged buyout (LBO)**.

lead investor   The investor that makes the largest investment in a financing round and manages the documentation and closing of that round. The lead investor sets the price per share of the financing round, thereby determining the valuation of the company.

letter of intent   A document confirming the intent of a party to enter into a transaction under certain broadly agreed to terms and conditions subject to verification. By signing this document, the subject company agrees to begin the legal and due diligence process prior to the closing of the transaction. See **term sheet**.

leverage   The use of debt to acquire assets, build operations, and increase revenues. By using debt, a company is attempting to achieve results faster than if it used only its cash available from preleverage operations.

leveraged buyout (LBO)   The purchase of a company or a business unit of a company by an outside investor using mostly borrowed capital.

leveraged recapitalization   Transaction in which a firm borrows money and either buys back stock or pays a dividend, thus increasing its debt ratio substantially.

LIBOR   See **London Interbank Offered Rate (LIBOR)**.

limited deficiency guaranty   See **deficiency guarantee**.

limited liability company (LLC)   See **business structures**.

limited liability partnership (LLP)   See **business structures**.

limited partner (LP)   See **business structures**.

limited partnership   See **business structures**.

line of credit   An informal loan arrangement between a bank and a customer allowing the customer to borrow up to a prespecified amount. Also called *credit line*.

liquidation   The selling off of all assets of a company prior to the complete cessation of operations. Corporations electing formal insolvency proceedings to liquidate declare Chapter 7 bankruptcy. In a liquidation, the claims of secured and unsecured creditors, bondholders, and preferred stockholders take precedence over common stockholders.

liquidation analysis   Consideration of the market factors that influence the values of assets to be liquidated in connection with the cessation of a going concern's operations.

liquidation balance sheet   A company's balance sheet adjusted to reflect reductions in the value of assets that are normally experienced when the assets of a going concern are sold off after the entity stops conducting business. See **liquidation value**.

liquidation preference   The contractual right of an investor to priority in receiving the proceeds from the liquidation of a company. For example, a venture capital investor with a "2x liquidation preference" has the right to receive two times its original investment upon liquidation.

liquidation value   The estimated amount of money that an asset or company could quickly be sold for, such as if it were to go out of business.

liquidity discount   A decrease in the value of a private company compared to the value of a similar but publicly traded company. Since an investor in a private company cannot readily sell his or her investment, the shares in the private company are normally valued less than a comparable public company.

liquidity event   A transaction whereby owners of a significant portion of the shares of a private company sell their shares in exchange for cash or shares in another, usually larger company. For example, an IPO is a liquidity event.

lockup agreement   Investors, management, and employees often agree not to sell their shares for a specific time period after an IPO, usually 6 to 12 months.

London Interbank Offered Rate (LIBOR)   A short-term interest rate often quoted as a one-, three-, or six-month rate for U.S. dollars.

LP   See **business structures.**

M&A   Acronym for *mergers and acquisitions.* Used in the middle market to mean the buying and selling of companies.

management buyout (MBO)   A leveraged buyout controlled by the members of the management team of a company or a division.

management fee   A fee charged to the limited partners in a fund by the general partner. Management fees in a private equity fund typically range from 0.75 percent to 3 percent of capital under management, depending on the type and size of fund.

management presentation   A program presented by the officers, directors, or management of a company in connection with a potential equity or debt transaction, strategic or collaborative partnering agreement, or sale of a business or product line.

management rights   The rights often required by a venture capitalist as part of the agreement to invest in a company. The venture capitalist has the right to consult with management on key operational issues, attend board meetings, and review information about the company's financial situation.

marginal cost   An increase or a decrease in the total costs of a business firm as the result of one more or one less unit of output. Also called *incremental cost* or *differential cost.* A firm is operating at optimum output when marginal cost coincides with average total unit cost. Thus, at less-than-optimum output, an increase in the rate of production will result in a marginal unit cost lower than average total unit cost; production in excess of the optimum point will result in marginal cost higher than average total unit cost.

market capitalization   The value of a publicly traded company as determined by multiplying the number of shares outstanding by the current price per share.

MBO   See **management buyout (MBO).**

merchant banking   A merchant bank invests its own capital in leveraged buyouts, corporate acquisitions, and other structured finance transactions. Merchant banking is a fee-based business, where the bank assumes market risk but no long-term credit risk. The Gramm-Leach-Bliley Act allows financial holding companies, a type of bank holding company created by the Act, to engage in merchant banking activities.

mezzanine A layer of financing that has intermediate priority (seniority) in the capital structure of a company. For example, mezzanine debt has lower priority than senior debt but higher priority than equity. Mezzanine debt usually has a higher interest rate than senior debt and often includes warrants. In venture capital, a mezzanine round is generally the round of financing that is designed to fund the operations of a company to a liquidity event such as an IPO.

middle market The term generally refers to companies with revenues from $5 million to $500 million, but has recently been expanded to $1 billion. The core of the middle market (or the middle-middle market) is about $50 million to $500 million and the lower-middle market is $5 million to $150 million. There is obviously some crossover in the ranges in the definitions given the evolution of the term in the industry. Also see **emerging growth companies.**

middle-middle market See **middle market.**

middle stage The stage of a company when it has received one or more rounds of financing and is generating revenue from its product or service. Same as **growth stage.**

monetary assets and liabilities Assets and liabilities in which the amounts are fixed in currency units. If the value of the currency unit changes, it is still settled with the same number of units.

multiple A valuation methodology that compares public and private companies in terms of a ratio of value to an operations figure such as revenue or net income. For example, if several publicly traded computer hardware companies are valued at approximately 2 times revenues, then it is reasonable to assume that a start-up computer hardware company that is growing fast has the potential to achieve a valuation of 2 times its revenues. Before the start-up issues its IPO, it will likely be valued at less than 2 times revenue because of the lack of liquidity of its shares. See **liquidity discount.**

narrow-based weighted average antidilution A type of antidilution mechanism that adjusts downward the price per share of the preferred stock of investor A due to the issuance of options, warrants, or securities to new investor B at a price lower than the price investor A originally paid. Investor A's preferred stock is repriced to a weighted average of investor A's price and investor B's price. A narrow-based weighted average antidilution formula uses only common stock outstanding in the denominator for determining the new weighted average price.

Nasdaq Formerly an acronym for the National Association of Securities Dealers Automated Quotation system. An electronic quotation system that provides price quotations to market participants about the more actively traded common stock issues in the over-the-counter market. About 4,000 common stock issues are included in the Nasdaq system.

NDA See **nondisclosure agreement (NDA)**.

net capital expenditure The difference between capital expenditures and depreciation. It is a measure of the financing needed, from internal or external sources, to meet investment needs.

net operating income (or loss) See **operating profit (or loss)**.

net operating profit less adjusted taxes (NOPLAT) Represents the after-tax operating profits of a company after adjusting the taxes to a cash basis.

net present value (NPV) The sum of the discounted present values of the expected cash flows of the investment.

noncompete An agreement often signed by employees and management whereby they agree not to work for competitor companies or form a new competitor company for a certain time period after termination of employment.

noncumulative dividends Dividends that are payable to owners of preferred stock at a specific point in time only if there is sufficient cash flow available after all company expenses have been paid.

nondisclosure agreement (NDA) An agreement issued by entrepreneurs to protect the privacy of their ideas when disclosing those ideas to third parties.

noninterference An agreement often signed by employees and management whereby they agree not to interfere with the company's relationships with employees, clients, suppliers, and subcontractors for a certain time period after termination of employment.

nonrecourse Term referring to the absence of any legal claim against a seller or prior endorser. The seller (or the endorser of a check or other negotiable document) is not liable or otherwise responsible for payment to the holder.

nonsolicitation An agreement often signed by employees and management whereby they agree not to solicit other employees of the company regarding job opportunities.

NOPLAT See **net operating profit less adjusted taxes (NOPLAT)**.

normalized EBITDA EBITDA adjusted with add-backs and other adjustments so that the operating EBITDA of the business fairly represents the financial performance of the business independent of the specific costs related to the owners (in a privately held company). A mental framework from which to view this concept is to consider what costs the business would incur as a stand-alone entity of a larger company. For example, what is market rate compensation for the individual(s) that will replace the current owners; what perks are beyond market expectations that would go away when the current owner no longer works there (cars, planes, country club, excess insurance premiums, compensation for other family members, etc.).

NYSE   See **New York Stock Exchange (NYSE)**.

offering memorandum   A legal document that provides details of an investment to potential investors. Sometimes called the *book*. See **private placement memorandum (PPM)**.

OID   See **original issue discount (OID)**.

operating profit (or loss)   Earnings before interest and taxes or operating income.

opportunity cost   The cost assigned to a project resource that is already owned by the firm. It is based on the next best alternative use.

optics   The way a concept is presented. Sometimes entrepreneurs' presentations are strong on optics but weak in content.

option pool   A group of options set aside for long-term, phased compensation to management and employees.

options   See **stock option**.

original issue discount (OID)   A discount from par value of a bond or debt-like instrument. In structuring a private equity transaction, the use of a preferred stock with liquidation preference or other clauses that guarantee a fixed payment in the future can potentially create adverse tax consequences. The IRS views this cash-flow stream as, in essence, a zero-coupon bond upon which tax payments are due yearly based on so-called phantom income imputed from the difference between the original investment and guaranteed eventual payout.

origination fee   A fee charged by a lender or investor to formally process a loan or conduct due diligence. Generally expressed as a percentage of the amount to be lent or invested.

orphan   A start-up company that does not have a venture capitalist as an investor.

outstanding shares   The total amount of common shares of a company, not including treasury stock, convertible preferred stock, warrants, and options.

oversubscription   When demand exceeds supply for shares of an IPO or a private placement.

owner motives   What the owner/seller of a business cares about for the current and future of his or her business. It is their ambitions, value, desires and expected outcomes. In the public markets, the owners' motives are to increase shareholder value. In the private capital markets, owner motives vary broadly from financial returns, to protecting employees, to family ambitions, to societal objectives, to career or retirement goals.

par   Equal to the nominal or face value of a security.

pari passu A legal term referring to the equal treatment of two or more parties in an agreement. For example, an investor may agree to have registration rights that are pari passu with the other investors in a financing round.

participating dividends The right of holders of certain preferred stock to receive dividends and participate in additional distributions of cash, stock, or other assets.

participating preferred stock A unit of ownership that repays an investor the face amount of the original investment, plus an amount equal to the investor's pro rata ownership of a company.

partnership See **business structures**.

payables Accounts payable resulting from purchases of materials and services from vendors and other creditors on credit terms.

payback The length of time it will take for nominal cash flows from a project to cover the initial investment.

pay to play A clause in a financing agreement whereby any investor that does not participate in a future round agrees to suffer significant dilution compared to other investors. The most onerous version of pay to play is automatic conversion to common shares, which in essence ends any preferential rights of an investor, such as the right to influence key management decisions.

PEG Abbreviation for *private equity group*.

piggyback rights Rights of an investor to have shares included in a registration filed with the SEC.

PIK Abbreviation for *payment in kind*.

pink sheets Refers to over-the-counter trading. Daily publication of the National Quotation Bureau that reports the bid and ask prices of thousands of OTC (over the counter) stocks, as well as the market makers who trade each stock.

PIPE See **private investment in public equities (PIPE)**.

placement agent A company that specializes in finding institutional investors that are willing and able to invest in a transaction. Management typically hires a placement agent so the managers can focus on operating their company rather than on raising capital.

poison pill A security or a provision that is triggered by the hostile acquisition of a company, resulting in a large cost to the acquirer.

portfolio company A company that has received an investment from an investment fund.

PPM See **private placement memorandum (PPM)**.

preference Seniority, usually with respect to dividends and proceeds from a sale or dissolution of a company.

preferred stock   A type of stock that has certain rights that common stock does not have. These special rights may include dividends, participation, liquidity preference, antidilution protection, and veto provisions, among others. Private equity investors usually purchase preferred stock when they make investments in companies.

private equity   Equity investments in nonpublic companies.

private investment in public equities (PIPE)   A PIPE is a transaction in which accredited investors are allowed to purchase stock in a public company, usually below the listed market price. The stock is registered with the SEC so that it may later be resold to the public.

private placement   The sale of a security directly to a limited number of institutional and qualified individual investors. If structured correctly, a private placement avoids registration with the Securities and Exchange Commission.

private placement memorandum (PPM)   A document explaining the details of an investment to potential investors. For example, a private equity fund will issue a PPM when it is raising capital from institutional investors. Also, a start-up may issue a PPM when it needs growth capital. Same as an **offering memorandum**.

private securities   Securities that are not registered with the Securities and Exchange Commission and do not trade on any exchanges. The price per share is negotiated between the buyer and the seller (the issuer).

pro rata   Shared or divided according to a ratio or in proportion to participation.

prospectus   Formal written document to sell securities that describes the plan for a proposed business enterprise, or the facts concerning an existing one, that an investor needs to make an informed decision. Prospectuses are used by mutual funds to describe fund objectives, risks, and other essential information. Also called *offering circular* or *circular*.

Prudent man rule   A fundamental principle for professional money management, which serves as a basis for the Prudent Investor Act. The principle is based on a statement by Judge Samuel Putnam in 1830: "Those with the responsibility to invest money for others should act with prudence, discretion, intelligence and regard for the safety of capital as well as income."

public and private information   Public information refers to any information that is available to the investing public, whereas private information is information that is restricted to only insiders or a few investors in the firm.

purchase order (PO) financing   Credit obtained from a third party based on advancing a portion of the proceeds of the company's potential sale in connection with the promise by a customer that products or services will be purchased in specific quantities.

puts The right to sell an underlying asset at a price that is fixed at the time the right is issued and during a specified time period.

qualified opinion An auditor's opinion expressing certain limitations of an audit. Opposite of unqualified opinion.

quartile One-fourth of the data points in a data set. Often, private equity investors are measured by the results of their investments during a particular period of time. Institutional investors often prefer to invest in private equity funds that demonstrate consistent results over time, placing in the upper quartile of the investment results for all funds.

quiet period Refers to the period of time during which a company makes no public comments, and approximates the period of time during which a company has a registration statement filed with the SEC. Same as **waiting period.**

raider Individual or corporate investor who intends to take control of a company (often ostensibly for greenmail) by buying a controlling interest in its stock and installing new management. Raiders who accumulate 5 percent or more of the outstanding shares in the target company must report their purchases to the SEC, the exchange of listing, and the target itself.

ratchet A mechanism to prevent dilution. An antidilution clause is a contract clause that protects an investor from a reduction in percentage ownership in a company due to the future issuance by the company of additional shares to other entities. A ratchet protects an investor by reducing the effective purchase price paid by the investor to the lowest price paid by a subsequent investor for options, warrants, or securities.

realization ratio The ratio of cumulative distributions to paid-in capital. The realization ratio is used as a measure of the distributions from investment results of a private equity partnership compared to the capital under management.

recapitalization The reorganization of a company's capital structure.

receivables Accounts receivable resulting from sales of products or services to customers on credit terms.

recourse Term describing a type of loan. If a loan is with recourse, the lender has the ability to fall back to the guarantor of the loan if the borrower fails to pay. For example, Bank A has a loan with Company X. Bank A sells the loan to Bank B with recourse. If Company X defaults, Bank B can demand Bank A fulfill the loan obligation.

redeemable preferred Preferred stock that can be purchased by a company in exchange for a specific sum of money, or preferred stock that an investor can force a company to repurchase.

redemption or call Right of the issuer to force holders on a certain date to redeem their convertibles for cash. The objective usually is to force holders to convert into common prior to the redemption deadline. Typically, an issue is not called away unless the conversion price is 15 to 25 percent below the current level of the common. An exception might occur when an issuer's tax rate is high, and the issuer could replace it with debt securities at a lower after-tax cost.

redemption rights The right of an investor to force a company to buy back the shares issued as a result of the investment. In effect, the investor has the right to take back his or her investment.

registration The process whereby shares of a company are registered with the Securities and Exchange Commission under the Securities Act of 1933 in preparation for a sale of the shares to the public.

registration rights The rights of investors to have their shares included in a registration. Demand rights are granted to investors to permit the investors to force management to register the investors' shares for a public offering. Piggyback rights are granted to investors to permit the investors to add their shares to a registration statement filed by the company on behalf of the company or on behalf of other investors.

Regulation D (Reg D) An SEC regulation that provides a safe harbor from the registration requirements of the Securities Act of 1933. An unlimited number of accredited investors may participate, but only 35 nonaccredited investors can participate.

Regulation S (Reg S) An SEC regulation that governs offers and sales of securities made outside the United States without registration under the Securities Act of 1933.

REIT See **real estate investment trust (REIT)**.

reps & warranties See **representations and warranties**.

representations and warranties Representations are statements of fact by the seller regarding the condition of its business, covering virtually all aspects of the company. Warranties are the seller's assurances to the buyer that the representations are true, and that if they are not, the buyer will be entitled to seek legal remedies.[11]

reserve

1. In asset-based lending, the difference between the value of the collateral and the amount lent. From the point of view of financial statements, reserves are provided as an estimate of liabilities that have a good probability of arising; bad-debt reserve attempts to estimate what percentage of the firm's debtors will not pay (based on previous records and practical experience). Reserves are always a subjective estimate (since they reflect contingent liabilities).

2. An accounting entry that properly reflects contingent liabilities.

restricted stock   Shares that cannot be traded in the public markets. In some instances these shares are subject to transfer restrictions in the private market.

restructure   Transaction or series of transactions associated with rearranging the debt or equity structure of a company, and typically associated with poor financial performance of the company.

return on assets (ROA)   Indicator of profitability. Determined by dividing net income for the past 12 months by total average assets. Result is shown as a percentage. ROA can be decomposed into return on sales (net income/sales) multiplied by asset utilization (sales/assets).

return on equity (ROE)   Indicator of profitability. Determined by dividing net income for the past 12 months by common stockholder equity (adjusted for stock splits). Result is shown as a percentage. Investors use ROE as a measure of how a company is using its money. ROE may be decomposed into return on assets (ROA) multiplied by financial leverage (total assets/total equity).

return on invested capital (ROIC)   NOPLAT divided by invested capital. Invested capital is calculated by subtracting non-interest-bearing liabilities from total assets.

return on investment (ROI)   The proceeds from an investment, during a specific time period, calculated as a percentage of the original investment.

return on sales (ROS)   A measurement of operational efficiency equaling net pretax profits divided by net sales expressed as a percentage.

reverse split   A proportionate decrease in the number of shares, but not the total value of shares of stock held by shareholders. Shareholders maintain the same percentage of equity as before the split. For example, a 1-for-3 split would result in stockholders owning one share for every three shares owned before the split. After the reverse split, the firm's stock price is, in this example, three times the prereverse split price. A firm generally institutes a reverse split to boost its stock's market price. Some think this supposedly attracts investors.

revolving loan   Loan with a stated maximum loan amount, but variable amounts that can actually be drawn down by a borrower that are determined periodically by reference to certain levels of borrower assets. Assets used to determine a borrower's available loan amount normally include accounts receivable and inventory. Also called *revolver* or *revolving credit facility*.

right of co-sale with founders   A clause in venture capital investment agreements that allows the VC fund to sell shares at the same time that the founders of a start-up choose to sell.

right of first refusal   A contractual right to participate in a transaction. For example, a venture capitalist may participate in a first round of investment in a start-up and request a right of first refusal in any following rounds of investment.

rights offering   An offering of stock to current shareholders that entitles them to purchase the new issue.

road show   Presentations made in several cities to potential investors and other interested parties. For example, a company will often conduct a road show to generate interest among institutional investors prior to its IPO.

ROI   See **return on investment (ROI)**.

rollup   The purchase of relatively smaller companies in a sector by a rapidly growing company in the same sector. The strategy is to create economies of scale.

round   A financing event usually involving several private equity investors.

Rule 144   A rule of the Securities and Exchange Commission that specifies the conditions under which the holder of shares acquired in a private transaction may sell those shares without registration.

salvage value   The estimated liquidation value of the assets invested in the project at the end of the project's life.

Sarbanes-Oxley   Corporate regulations resulting from the Sarbanes-Oxley Act of 2002. The Act creates a set of disclosure obligations intended to restore confidence in the financial information provided by publicly traded companies to the investing public. The Act creates a five-member Public Company Accounting Oversight Board (PCAOB), which has the authority to set and enforce auditing, attestation, quality control, and ethics (including independence) standards for auditors of public companies. It also is empowered to inspect the auditing operations of public accounting firms that audit public companies as well as impose disciplinary and remedial sanctions for violations of the board's rules, securities laws, and professional auditing and accounting standards.

scalability   A characteristic of a new business concept that entails the growth of sales and revenues with a much slower growth of organizational complexity and expenses. Venture capitalists look for scalability in the start-ups they select to finance.

scale-up   The process of a company growing quickly while maintaining operational and financial controls in place.

Schedule K-1   IRS form sent by legal entities that pay no income taxes to each owner of the entity, indicating the recipient's share of income or loss for the fiscal year.

S corporation   See **business structures**.

SEC See **Securities and Exchange Commission (SEC)**.

secondary market A market for the sale of partnership interests in private equity funds. Sometimes limited partners choose to sell their interest in a partnership, typically to raise cash or because they cannot meet their obligation to invest more capital according to the takedown schedule. Certain investment companies specialize in buying these partnership interests at a discount.

second lien debt See **junior debt**.

Securities and Exchange Commission (SEC) The regulatory body that enforces federal securities laws such as the Securities Act of 1933 and the Securities Exchange Act of 1934, as amended over the years.

security A document that represents an interest in a company. Shares of stock, notes, and bonds are examples of securities.

seed capital Investment provided by angels, friends, and family to the founders of a start-up in its seed stage.

seed stage The stage of a company when it has just been incorporated and its founders are developing their product or service.

seller financing A note payable or loan to the shareholder(s) or owner(s) of a business provided in the sale or transition of a company by the buyer. Seller financing is typically used to bridge a valuation gap either where other forms of financing are not available or where a buyer desires to preserve the borrowing ability of the selling company for secured financing. Seller financing is typically unsecured and subordinated below all other debt.

seller note See **seller financing**.

senior debt A loan that has a higher priority in case of liquidation of the assets of a company.

seniority Higher priority.

series A preferred stock Preferred stock issued by a company in exchange for capital from investors in the A round of financing. The preferred stock has priority over common stock for dividends and the proceeds of any liquidation or sale of a company.

shell Usually refers to a company with little or no assets with more than 300 shareholders that is formed for the purpose of becoming a de facto public entity. This shell company is used to acquire or merge with a privately held company as a vehicle for the private company to become public without an initial public offering.

SIC A four-digit industry code used by most services in the United States to classify firms. For a broader aggregation, the classification is often done using the first two digits of the code.

Small Business Administration (SBA) An agency of the United States government that focuses on aiding, counseling, assisting, and protecting the interests of small businesses. As it relates to financing growth companies, the SBA sometimes provides loans directly and through commercial banks for small businesses.

Small Business Investment Company (SBIC) A company licensed by the Small Business Administration to receive government loans in order to raise capital to use in venture investing.

sole proprietor (SP) See **business structures.**

spinoff A company can create an independent company from an existing part of the company by selling or distributing new shares in the so-called spinoff.

spinout A division of an established company that becomes an independent entity.

stalking horse Third-party bidder in the investment or acquisition process that is used by a company to obtain a higher share or acquisition price.

stock A share of ownership in a corporation.

stock grant Determination by the board of directors of a company to issue stock to an employee or third party in connection with the provision of services to a company or the extension of debt or equity to a company.

stock option A right to purchase or sell a share of stock at a specific price within a specific period of time. Stock purchase options are commonly used as long-term incentive compensation for employees and management of fast-growth companies.

strategic due diligence See **due diligence.**

strategic investor A third party that agrees to invest in a company in order to have access to a proprietary technology, product, or service. By having this access, the third party can potentially achieve its strategic goals.

structured overadvance A loan in excess of the agreed-on borrowing base. Repayment is typically scheduled within 12 to 24 months.

subordinated debt A loan that has a lower priority than a senior loan in case of a liquidation of the asset or company. See **junior debt.**

survival The time period after closing in which the buyer may make a claim against the seller or selling shareholders for breach of their representations, warranties, and covenants. The time period is usually shorter than the applicable statute of limitations.[12]

sweat equity Ownership of shares in a company resulting from work rather than investment of capital.

sweetener A feature of a security that makes it more attractive to potential purchasers. An example is a warrant.

synergy The additional value created by bringing together two entities and pooling their strengths. In the context of a merger, synergy is the difference between the values of the merged firm and the sum of the values of the firms operating independently.

tag-along rights The right of an investor to receive the same rights as owners of a majority of the shares of a company. For example, if a majority shareholder wants to sell his or her interest in a company, an investor with minority ownership and tag-along rights would be able to sell his or her interest as well.

takedown A schedule of the transfer of capital in phases in order to complete a commitment of funds. Typically, a takedown is used by a general partner to secure capital from an entity's limited partners to fund the entity's investments.

takeover The transfer of control of a company.

TED spread The difference between LIBOR and the three-month U.S. Treasury bill rate.

ten bagger An investment that returns 10 times the initial capital.

term loan A fixed amount of money advanced by a lender to a borrower where the borrower is expected to repay the loan amount plus interest over a specified period of time. The repayment terms are negotiated based on the ability of the borrower to repay the loan based on financial projections provided by the borrower and agreed to by the lender. A term loan may be repaid in a lump sum at the end of a fixed period or amortized and paid in specified periodic payments during the term of the loan.

term sheet A document confirming the intent of an investor to participate in a round of financing or for one party to purchase or sell a company to the other party. More broadly, a term sheet refers to a summary of the most important terms and conditions that the parties are agreeing to for a transaction. By signing this document, the subject company agrees to begin the legal and due diligence process prior to the closing of the transaction. Very similar to a **letter of intent**.

tranche The piece, portion, or slice of a deal or structured financing. The so-called A-to-Z securities of a collateralized mortgage obligation (CMO) offering of a partitioned mortgage-backed securities (MBS) portfolio. It can also refer to segments that are offered domestically and internationally. Tranches have distinctive features that for economic or legal purposes must be financially engineered or structured in order to conform to prevailing requirements.

tranche B See **junior debt**.

transition In the context of M&A, to transfer the management, control, and ownership of a business over time.

treasury stock Common stock that has been repurchased by the company and held in the company's treasury.

turnaround   A process resulting in a substantial increase in a company's revenues, profits, and reputation. Typically used to describe a poorly performing or distressed situation.

underwriter   An investment bank that chooses to be responsible for the process of selling new securities to the public. An underwriter usually chooses to work with a syndicate of investment banks in order to maximize the distribution of the securities.

unitranche financing   A hybrid senior loan product that blends first and second lien debt, and in some instances mezzanine, into a single tranche.

unrestricted stock   Freely tradable shares.

venture capital   A segment of the private equity industry that focuses on investing in companies with high growth rates and the potential of very high returns.

venture capital method   A valuation method whereby an estimate of the future value of a company is discounted by a certain interest rate and adjusted for future anticipated dilution in order to determine the current value. Usually, discount rates for the venture capital method are considerably higher than public stock return rates, representing the fact that venture capitalists must achieve significant returns on investment in order to compensate for the risks they take in funding unproven companies.

vintage   The year that a private equity fund stops accepting new investors and begins to make investments on behalf of those investors.

virtual data room   See **data room.**

voting rights   The rights of holders of preferred and common stock in a company to vote on certain acts affecting the company. These matters may include payment of dividends, issuance of a new class of stock, merger, or liquidation.

waiting period   See **quiet period.**

walk-away point   A predetermined amount at which either the buyer will not pay a higher price or the seller will not accept a lower price.

warrant   A security that gives the holder the right to purchase shares in a company at a predetermined price. A warrant is a long-term option, usually valid for several years. Typically, warrants are issued concurrently with debt instruments in order to increase the appeal of the debt instrument to potential investors.

washout round   A financing round whereby previous investors, the founders, and management suffer significant dilution. Usually as a result of a washout round, the new investor gains majority ownership and control of the company.

weighted average antidilution   An antidilution protection mechanism whereby the conversion rate of preferred stock is adjusted in order to reflect the issuance of options, warrants, or securities at a price less than the conversion rate of the existing preferred stock.

weighted average cost of capital (WACC) A calculation of the cost of capital by adding the products of relative amounts of equity, debt, and preferred stock investments multiplied by their respective rates of return:

$$r_{WACC} = r_E[E/(E + D + P)] + r_D[D/(E + D + P)]$$
$$+ r_P[P/(E + D + P)]$$

white space Refers to market opportunities not being pursued within a company's plan; new opportunity areas.

wipeout bridge A short-term financing that has onerous features whereby if the company does not secure additional long-term financing within a certain time frame, the bridge investor gains ownership control of the company. See **bridge financing**.

wipeout round See **washout round**.

write-down A decrease in the reported value of an asset or a company.

write-off A decrease in the reported value of an asset or a company to zero.

write-up An increase in the reported value of an asset or a company.

yield The percentage return paid on a stock in the form of dividends, or the effective rate of interest paid on a bond or note.

zombie A company that has received capital from investors but has generated only sufficient revenues and cash flow to maintain its operations without significant growth. Typically, a venture capitalist has to make a difficult decision as to whether to kill off a zombie or continue to invest funds in the hopes that the zombie will become a winner.

Notes

Chapter 1

1. Unless otherwise stated, *public companies* are defined herein as those entities that trade on a public exchange and have a float of more than $500 million.
2. Robert T. Slee, "Public and Private Capital Markets Are Not Substitutes," *Business Appraisal Practice*, Spring 2005.
3. Richard M. Trottier, *Middle Market Strategies* (Hoboken: John Wiley & Sons, 2009), Chapter 1.
4. John K. Paglia, Pepperdine Private Capital Markets Project Survey Report, http://bschool.pepperdine.edu/privatecapital, April 2010.
5. Robert T. Slee and Richard M. Trottier, "Capital Market Segmentation Matters," *Business Appraisal Practice*, Summer 2006.
6. Paglia, Pepperdine Private Capital Markets Project Survey Report.

Chapter 3

1. Deloitte & Touche LLP, "Corporate Development 2010: Refining the M&A Playbook."
2. Robert T. Uhlaner and Andrew S. Wes, "Running a Winning M&A Shop," *McKinsey Quarterly*, www.mckinseyquarterly.com, March 2008.
3. Allen Burchett, SR VP Strategic Initiatives, ABB North America, "Corporate Development," presentation, Fall 2010.
4. *Id.*
5. *Id.*
6. Gerald Adolph, Simon Gillies, and Joerg Krings, "Strategic Due Diligence: A Foundation for M&A Success," in *The Whole Deal: Fulfilling the Promise of Acquisitions and Mergers*, ed. Michael Sisk and Andrew Sambrook (New York: strategy+business Books, 2006).
7. *Id.*
8. Allen Burchett, "Corporate Development."
9. Consolidated Communication, 7/2/2007 8-K SEC Filing.
10. David A. Cohen, managing director of Diamond Capital Partners and a leading member of the AM&AA. Personal correspondence.
11. Gerald Adolph et al., "Strategic Due Diligence."
12. Allen Burchett, "Corporate Development."

Chapter 4

1. Information regarding the Fellowes case was retrieved from Fellowes, Inc., "Fellowes Shredders Shipments Blocked by Joint Venture Partner," press release, n.d. www.fellowes.com/fellowes/site/aboutus/about_releases_48.aspx.
2. Caroline Firstbrook, "Cross-Border M&A: Handle with Care," *Accenture Outlook* (September 2008), www.accenture.com/us-en/outlook/pages/outlook-journal-2008-transnational-mergers-acquisitions.aspx.
3. *Id.*
4. *Id.*
5. *Id.*
6. *Id.*
7. Interview with Robert Lowere, general counsel and director of finance, National Railway Equipment Co., 2011, Dixmoor, Il.

Chapter 5

1. David H. Maister, "Managing the Professional Services Firm," 1st ed. (New York: Free Press, 1997).
2. An excerpt from "AM&AA Campaign for Clarity Update 2011."
3. www.sec.gov/divisions/marketreg/mr-noaction/cbi110806.htm.

Chapter 9

1. U.S. Census Bureau, "Employers and Nonemployers," 2007. About three quarters of all U.S. business firms have no payroll. Most are self-employed persons operating unincorporated businesses, and may or may not be the owners' principal source of income. Because nonemployers account for only about 3.4 percent of business receipts, they are not included in most business statistics, such as most reports from the Economic Census, for example.
2. J. H. Astrachan and M. C. Shanker, "Family Businesses' Contribution to the U.S. Economy: A Closer Look," *Family Business Review* 16, no. 3: 211–220.
3. The Family Firm Institute, "Global data points." Retrieved May 30, 2010 from http://ffi.org/default.asp?id=398.
4. Robert B. Avery, "The Ten Trillion Dollar Question: A Philanthropic Gameplan," Cornell University (February 2006).

Chapter 11

1. Dale A. Oesterle, *Mergers and Acquisitions in a Nutshell* (Thompson/West, 2006), 41. Oesterle maintains that a good confidentiality agreement creates and delineates expansive categories of confidential information and obligates the buyer to keep information received in confidence.
2. *Id.*
3. The 15th Annual National Institute on Negotiating Business Acquisitions (American Bar Association Business Law Section Committee on Mergers and Acquisitions 2010), 4.

4. Edwin L. Miller, *Mergers and Acquisitions: A Step-By-Step Legal and Practical Guide*, (Hoboken: John Wiley & Sons, 2008), 41. *See also*, William J. Carney, *Mergers and Acquisitions* (Aspen, 2009), 81 (declaring that a typical confidentiality agreement presumes that all information disclosed is confidential. In return, the buyer promises not to disclose any information to third parties).

5. Edwin L. Miller, *Mergers and Acquisitions: A Step-By-Step Legal and Practical Guide*, 41.

6. *Id.*, 43.

7. Steven M. Bainbridge, *Mergers and Acquisitions,* 2nd ed. (Thompson Reuters/Foundation Press, 2009), 70.

8. See Dale A. Oesterle, *Mergers and Acquisitions in a Nutshell*, 11–12 (describing an example of an asset sale). According to Oesterle, in the first step of an acquisition by asset sale, Corporation A pays Corporation B consideration for Corporation B's assets. Corporation A may accept some or all of Corporation B's liabilities, but does not have to do so. After the asset acquisition, Corporation B must then either reinvest the cash received in operating assets or pass the cash in a liquidation distribution back to its shareholders. The result of the transaction is that the shareholders of Corporation B have cash consideration (no shares) and Corporation A holds title to Corporation B's assets (and possibly obligations of Corporation B's liabilities). After the sale of assets, the constitutional documents of each company do not change, nor is there any change in the shares outstanding of either corporation

9. Steven M. Bainbridge, *Mergers and Acquisitions*, 18.

10. *Id.*

11. William J. Carney, *Mergers and Acquisitions*, 19.

12. Monty W. Walker, *Deal Structuring: The Magic of IRC Section 338* (M&A Source Webinar, March 19, 2009), 3, www.masource.org/portals/0/Presentation%20Slides%20IRS%20338.pdf.

13. Edwin L. Miller, *Mergers and Acquisitions: A Step-By-Step Legal and Practical Guide*, 90.

14. William J. Carney, *Mergers and Acquisitions*, 39 (declaring that it is frequently the case where a larger company acquiring a smaller company has large accumulations of cash available for acquisitions).

15. Edwin L. Miller, *Mergers and Acquisitions: A Step-By-Step Legal and Practical Guide*, 110.

16. Dale A. Oesterle, *Mergers and Acquisitions in a Nutshell*, 41.

17. William J. Carney, *Mergers and Acquisitions*, 100.

18. *Id.*

19. *Id.*, 41.

20. See also Edwin L. Miller, *Mergers and Acquisitions: A Step-By-Step Legal and Practical Guide*, 214 (asserting that representations and warranties (1) create a basis for due diligence by confirming that elements of the business are financially sound, without hidden or unknown contingent liabilities; (2) give the buyer additional opportunity to review the business in transactions that involve a delay between signing and closing; and (3) serve as the basis for buyer's indemnification rights).

21. *Id.*, 218.
22. *Id.*, 225.
23. See also Edwin L. Miller, *Mergers and Acquisitions: A Step-by-Step Legal and Practical Guide*, 217 (opining that another way that a buyer may limit the seller's ability to disclaim knowledge is with a provision containing the language that: "where any representation or warranty contained in the agreement is expressly qualified by reference to the knowledge or best knowledge of the target, the target confirms that (i) the target has in effect procedures that are reasonably designed to inform the target fully as to the matters that are the subject of such representation and warranty and that that target has observed such procedures, and (ii) the target has made due and diligent inquiry as to the matters that are the subject of such representation and warranty").
24. *Id.*, 233. According to Miller, additional questions arise, including what percentage of the purchase price the escrow account should contain, as well as how long it should last.
25. *Id.*, 235. The rationale underlying a seller's desire to include a provision for "baskets" is the idea that small mistakes are likely. Therefore, the parties should agree in advance that neither side should be bothered with the time or expense of small claims.
26. *Id.*
27. Ninon Kohers and James Ang, "Earnouts in Mergers: Agreeing to Disagree and Agreeing to Stay," *Journal of Business* 73, no. 3 (July 2000): 445.
28. *Id.*
29. Edwin L. Miller, *Mergers and Acquisitions: A Step-By-Step Legal and Practical Guide*, 113.
30. Jeffrey J. Reuer, "Mitigating Risks in International Mergers and Acquisitions: The Role of Contingent Payouts," *Journal of International Business Studies* 35, no. 1 (January 2004): 20.
31. Ninon Kohers and James Ang, "Earnouts in Mergers: Agreeing to Disagree and Agreeing to Stay," 445.
32. *Id.*
33. *Id.*, 450.

Chapter 15

1. The base content of this section is derived from the "Buyout Funds" section of Chapter 5 of the *Handbook of Financing Growth: Strategies, Capital Structure, and M&A Transactions*, 2nd ed., by Kenneth H. Marks et al. (Hoboken: John Wiley & Sons, 2009).
2. The base content of this section is derived from *id.*, Chapter 4.

Chapter 17

1. Robert T. Slee, "Different Buyers Pay Different Multiples," Data Link, May 1997.

2. Shannon P. Pratt, Robert F. Reilly, and Robert R. Schweihs, *Valuing a Business: The Analysis and Appraisal of Closely Held Companies*, 4th ed. (New York: McGraw-Hill), 268.

Glossary

1. The base content of this glossary is derived from *Handbook of Financing Growth: Strategies, Capital Structure, and M&A Transactions*, 2nd ed. (Hoboken: John Wiley & Sons, 2009).
2. Shareholder Representative Services LLC, "2010 SRS M&A Deal Terms Study."
3. *Id.*
4. *Id.*
5. *Id.*
6. *Id.*
7. *Id.*
8. *Id.*
9. *Id.*
10. *Id.*
11. *Id.*
12. *Id.*

About the Authors

Kenneth H. Marks, CM&AA, is founder and managing partner of High Rock Partners and also the lead author of the *Handbook of Financing Growth: Strategy, Capital Structure, and M&A Transactions*. His firm creates value by working with the leaders of emerging-growth and middle market companies through transitions of ownership and transitions to the next level, to reposition the company using a unique and proven blend of experiences and tools in strategic management, mergers and acquisitions, finance and deals, organizational alignment, technology launches, globalization, and lean operating systems—coupled with a been-there-done-that confidence.

Kenneth's past positions include president of JPS Communications, Inc., a fast-growth technology subsidiary of the Raytheon Company, and president/CEO of an electronics manufacturer that he founded and grew to $22 million. He was a director for a Research Triangle–area investment bank focused on raising capital during the late 1990s.

He was a member of the Young Presidents Organization (YPO) and is the founding YPO Sponsor of the Entrepreneurs Organization (EO, formerly YEO) in the Research Triangle Park, North Carolina, chapter; a member of ACG; a member of the board of the North Carolina Technology Association; and the founding president of the Research Triangle chapter of the National Funding Association.

Kenneth teaches MBA electives in financing and M&A at North Carolina State University. He lectures at DePaul University, Loyola University Chicago, and Pepperdine University as part of the Alliance of M&A Advisors certification program. He obtained an MBA from the Kenan-Flagler Business School at UNC Chapel Hill, and his undergraduate studies were in electrical engineering at NCSU. He attended executive programs at the Wharton School and MIT.

Kenneth can be reached at khmarks@HighRockPartners.com.

Robert T. Slee, CM&AA, is founder of MidasNation, a community dedicated to helping business owners dramatically increase the value of their firms. He has authored more than 250 articles on private finance topics in a variety of legal and business journals. Rob's book *Private Capital Markets* was published in mid-2004 by John Wiley & Sons and is now considered the seminal work in finance for private companies. Law schools and MBA programs around the world use this book in a new course of the same name. A second edition of this book was released in May 2011. Rob's second book, *Midas Managers*, was released in 2007 and describes how super-successful private business owners create substantial wealth in a global economy. *Midas Marketing: How Midas Managers Make Markets*, was released in March 2009 and *Midas Metrics* (Burn the Boats Press) was released in 2011.

He is an adjunct faculty member at DePaul University and Pepperdine University, and coteaches a course at both schools on mergers and acquisitions. He speaks more than 60 times each year to trade associations, family and entrepreneurial programs, and legal, CPA, and valuation conferences.

Rob is also president of Robertson & Foley, a middle market private investment bank. Robertson & Foley raises substantial amounts of private capital each year, provides certified business valuations, and advises on the transfer of middle market businesses.

Rob co-architected the Pepperdine Cost of Capital Surveys in 2009 and co-created the Private Cost of Capital discount rate model. He has been a Certified Business Appraiser for more than 15 years.

He is a board member of numerous professional associations and private companies. He has owned equity positions in a variety of midsized private businesses. He is a Phi Beta Kappa graduate of Miami University, and received a Master's degree from the University of Chicago and an MBA from Case Western Reserve University.

Rob can be reached at r.slee@midasnation.com.

Christian T. Blees, CPA/ABV, CM&AA, currently serves as president and CEO of BiggsKofford Certified Public Accountants and BiggsKofford Capital Investment Bank, both located in Colorado Springs, Colorado.

BiggsKofford has been the premier CPA firm in Colorado Springs for over 25 years, with approximately 30 professionals working in tax, audit, and consulting. Chris began his career with BiggsKofford in 1994 after graduating from Western State College of Colorado, and quickly became a partner in the CPA firm in 1999, at the age of 28.

In 2003, Chris expanded the firm beyond traditional CPA services and launched the firm's M&A and Investment Banking practice, now operating as BiggsKofford Capital. Since 2003, the firm has become a leader in this sector throughout the western United States, as demonstrated by the firm's involvement in over 200 merger, acquisition, or sale transactions in California, Washington, Arizona, New Mexico, and Colorado. Chris's commitment to the acquisition and sale industry is personified by earning the Certified

Merger & Acquisition Advisor (CM&AA) designation, and by obtaining his Series 7 and Series 79 securities licenses in 2004.

Chris contributes to the national M&A community through his service on the Board of Advisors for the Alliance of M&A Advisors (AMAA), where he chairs the Certification Committee. As chair of the Certification Committee, Chris currently serves as the lead instructor for the Certified Merger & Acquisition Advisor (CM&AA) designation, taught through Loyola, DePaul, and Pepperdine Universities' Executive MBA programs, where he coordinates the curriculum, instructors, and testing for the program.

Locally in Colorado, Chris remains active in many professional organizations, including serving as treasurer for the Colorado Springs Chamber of Commerce, and sitting on the boards of Colorado Springs Technology Incubator, CU Chancellor's Leadership Council, and is cofounder of High Altitude Angel Investors Club. He is a member of the Alliance of M&A Advisors (AMAA), Association of Corporate Growth (ACG), Colorado Association of Business Intermediaries (CABI), AICPA, and the Colorado Society of CPAs.

Chris can be reached at blees@biggskofford.com.

Michael R. Nall, CPA, CM&AA, is the founder of the Alliance of Merger & Acquisition Advisors® (www.amaaonline.org). The AM&AA is the leading association and credentialing body for 760+ middle market M&A professionals in 19 countries, providing connections, best practices, and education.

An experienced corporate financial advisor with a proven track record as a transaction advisor for privately held companies, Mike is a published author and recognized speaker on the valuation, growth, and sale of middle market companies. With the benefit of over 25 years of experience in the industry, he led the AM&AA development and launch of a first-of-its-kind professional training and credential designation for the independent corporate financial advisory community: Certified Merger & Acquisition Advisor (CM&AA).

A licensed and retired CPA, having sold his business over 25 years ago, Mike holds a Bachelor of Science degree in Business Administration and Accounting, graduating with honors from Eastern Illinois University.

Mike can be reached at mnall@amaaonline.org.

About the Contributors and Reviewers

Darrell V. Arne, ASA, CBI, CM&AA has been a CPA since 1974, which included 11 years with the public accounting firms of McGladrey & Pullen and KPMG. He holds designations as an Accredited Senior Appraiser (ASA) in business valuation with the American Society of Appraisers, a Certified Business Intermediary (CBI) with the International Business Brokers Association, and a Certified Merger & Acquisition Advisor (CM&AA) with the Alliance of M&A Advisors. Darrell is also licensed through FINRA as an Investment Banking Representative (Series 79) and State Securities Agent (Series 63).

Austin Buckett, ACA, CM&AA, serves as manager of BiggsKofford Capital, LLC, the investment banking subsidiary of BiggsKofford Certified Public Accountants, located in Colorado Springs. Since 2003, the firm has become a leader in middle market mergers and acquisitions throughout the western United States, as demonstrated by the firm's involvement in over 200 merger, acquisition, or sale transactions in California, Washington, Arizona, New Mexico, and Colorado.

Austin, originally from England, has over 14 years of public accounting experience, in both the United States and the United Kingdom, with a focus on small to middle market companies. For the past nine years, he has been assisting and advising clients in the process of buying and selling businesses.

Combining an audit and management accounting background with substantial transaction experience enables him to help clients look beyond the numbers of a transaction. Austin also acts in an outsourced CFO capacity for a number of clients, providing consulting in financial performance as well as developing growth and exit strategies and succession plans. Austin is a chartered accountant and a Certified Merger & Acquisition Advisor, and holds Series 7 and 79 securities licenses.

Allen Burchett, CM&AA, is the senior vice president for Business Development for ABB in North America. In this role, he is focused on organic and inorganic strategic initiatives to enable ABB to achieve its future growth

347

plans in North America. These initiatives span several market segments including Smart Grid, Wind, Solar, Electric Vehicles, Energy Efficiency, Water, Rail, Datacenters, and Semiconductors. The leaders of these efforts along with the Power Strategic Marketing Team report to Allen.

Since joining ABB in 1995 from PepsiCo, he has led several of the company's operations as general manager and manager of Marketing and Sales for Medium Voltage Products in North America. In his most recent role, Allen was the head of M&A in North America.

Allen is a graduate of North Carolina State University, where he earned his Bachelor of Science in Engineering and a minor in Industrial Engineering. Allen completed executive leadership courses at Duke University and an international business management course with ABB. He is on the advisory board for Advanced Energy for West Virginia University. He is a Certified Merger & Acquisition Advisor through Alliance of M&A Advisors and a member of the Association for Corporate Growth. Allen is based in Cary, North Carolina at ABB's headquarters and reports to the CEO of North America.

Stephen Cazalet is co-owner and a managing director of Double Eagle Advisory, LLC, a boutique firm specializing in financial due diligence and advising on M&A transactions. Steve has a successful track record of leading transaction due diligence teams in evaluating acquisition targets, including identifying target company value drivers, core earnings adjustments, items of balance sheet exposure, and working capital issues, and advising on sale and purchase agreement provisions.

From 1999 to 2010, Steve was a partner in Ernst&Young's Transaction Advisory Practice, where he led both buy- and sell-side due diligence projects on over 200 transactions in numerous industries, including business services, manufacturing, retail, healthcare, and technology. In addition, Steve led Ernst&Young's Transaction Support Practice in Beijing, China, from 2005 to 2007, successfully growing that practice from zero to 25 professionals during that time. Prior to joining Ernst&Young, Steve spent 14 years with KPMG Peat Marwick, initially spending 10 years in that firm's audit practice, and then 3 years in the Corporate Finance Group performing buy- and sell-side advisory services, and one year in KPMG's Mergers & Acquisitions Group, focused on performing financial due diligence.

Steve has a Master of Business Administration degree from Emory University and a Bachelor of Science degree in Mathematical Economics from Wake Forest University.

Brandon Clewett is an associate vice president with McGladrey Capital Markets and possesses more than nine years of investment banking experience.

Prior to joining McGladrey and focusing solely on capital markets transactions, he served in a corporate finance role as a senior financial planning analyst for The Capital Group (The American Funds), where he completed asset acquisitions, financing agreements, and new product modeling. Prior to joining The Capital Group, Brandon worked as a senior associate for Morgan Stanley Equity Research, covering public companies in the wireless telecom and technology industries. He received a bachelor's degree in business administration from the University of California at Berkeley from the Walter A. Haas School of Business. He holds FINRA Series 7 and 63 securities licenses.

David A. Cohn, CM&AA, is a managing director of Diamond Capital Partners. After 40 years as a business owner and an investment banker, it is easy for David to step into a client's shoes. David has co-founded two previous investment banking firms, along with operating an investment banking division for City National Bank, based in Beverly Hills, in the late 1990s.

David started his career in manufacturing, eventually owning and operating two firms. The first firm, which was engaged in the fabrication and distribution of plumbing and bath products, he later sold to Beatrice Foods Co. The other firm was engaged in the manufacturing of HVAC components for home and industrial use, which he acquired out of bankruptcy, restructured, and later sold successfully to a strategic buyer. He acquired nine years of corporate M&A experience with Beatrice, as a group manager of their Home Products Group, as well as facilitating further acquisitions for the parent firm. David brings to Diamond Capital Partners a concentration of completed deals in manufacturing, aerospace, distribution, and engineered plastics over many years in the M&A business. His hands-on experience in the entire transaction process allows him to thoroughly prepare clients for raising capital or selling all or part of their business, which could be their major source of future liquidity

David has served on several corporate boards, including that of a Midwestern regional bank; a 600-bed hospital; and two major professional organizations, the Association for Corporate Growth (ACG) and the Association of Merger & Acquisition Advisors (AMAA), where he currently serves. He is a graduate of Washington University School of Business. He currently serves on the CM&AA faculty, which delivers M&A certification classes at DePaul University in Chicago, and Pepperdine University, and is on the speaking roster for the California CPA Education Foundation. He is certified by FINRA as General Securities Principal and Representative.

Daniel A. Cotter is a member of Korey Cotter Heather & Richardson, LLC, a law firm of trusted business advisors. Dan focuses on providing broad outside general counsel and commercial transactional support for start-up, small, and midsized businesses. He is the treasurer of the Chicago Bar Association and is a CPA. Daniel graduated summa cum laude from the John Marshall Law School, and graduated magma cum laude with a BA in Accounting from Monmouth College.

Champ W. Davis III, CM&AA, has significant experience providing investment banking services to clients in a wide variety of manufacturing, distribution, and service industries. His clients have ranged from closely held private companies to large-cap publicly traded corporations. Champ has advised clients on mergers and acquisitions, financial restructurings, and private placements of debt and equity. In addition, he has advised clients on structuring and financing ESOPs, recapitalizations, leveraged buyouts, management buyouts, and going-private transactions, and has provided complex financial analysis for the rendering of fairness and solvency opinions.

Champ has authored and co-authored numerous investment banking presentations to both professional and industry associations. Recent presentations include "Accurately Valuing the Target Company's Worth," presented to the Second Annual Metals Industry Mergers & Acquisitions Forum, "Doing the Right Deal at the Right Time: Understanding Transactions from a Seller's Perspective," presented to the Fifth Auto Parts Industry Mergers & Acquisitions Institute, and "Selling a Troubled Company: Issues and Techniques," presented to the Executive Institute.

In addition, Champ has delivered presentations to numerous educational institutions, including the University of Chicago's Graduate School of Business and the Massachusetts Institute of Technology (MIT) Sloan School of Management, and has provided classroom and case study material for MBA courses at the University of Chicago. He also recently served as an investment banking instructor and panelist for the Turnaround Management Association's (TMA) 13-week cash-flow workshop presented in the Gleacher Center at the University of Chicago's Graduate School of Business.

Champ was most recently a managing director of Stout Risius Ross (SRR) and a founding member of the firm's Chicago office, where he played an integral role in the firm's growth. Prior to joining SRR, Champ was with Houlihan, Lokey, Howard & Zukin, where he specialized in mergers and acquisitions, corporate finance, and financial restructurings. Preceding his experience at Houlihan Lokey, Champ served in the investment banking group of the Chicago Corporation (subsequently ABN AMRO), where he provided mergers and acquisitions and corporate finance advisory services to both public and private investment banking clients. Champ earned a Master's degree from Indiana University's Graduate School and a Bachelor's degree from the university honors division at Indiana University's School of Business and has completed a variety of continuing education and postgraduate coursework, including the Program on Negotiation at Harvard University and the AMAA's certification program for Merger & Acquisition Advisors at Northwestern University.

Champ is currently on the board of directors for the Alliance for Merger & Acquisition Advisors, and is a member of the Association for Corporate Growth, the National Funding Association, the Business Valuation Association, the TMA, and the Illinois CPA Society. He also currently serves on the Finance Committee for the National ESOP Association and is a past board member of the Entrepreneurship Institute (Chicago chapter).

Mark Devine, CM&AA is a part-time independent consultant serving middle market and large clients developing customized templates and processes covering business development, strategic planning and M&A to ready themselves for sale. He also provides market intelligence and reverse due-diligence advice. He is a full-time business developer for a company serving defense, intelligence community, cyber, research and law enforcement market clients.

He is experienced in developing M&A processes to include candidate acquisition gate reviews, preliminary/detailed target identification reporting templates, and has supported integration and strategic planning efforts. Mark has also developed templates for program management and business opportunity reviews, and has conducted market and competitive analysis. Prior to engaging in business, he served 21 years in the United States Air Force.

Willis E. Eayrs, CVA, CM&AA, CMAP, is an independent corporate financial advisor based in Stuttgart, Germany. In this role, he advises management and shareholders with respect to the purchase and sale of corporate assets and shares of middle-market companies. His work includes valuing and financing business enterprises and negotiating business exchanges. Previously, he was senior vice president and head of M&A at Landesbank Baden-Wuerttemberg and an assistant director of J. Henry Schroder & Co. Ltd. in London.

Willis lectures in banking and finance at City University of Seattle and at the Hochschule (University of Applied Science) in Esslingen, Germany. He has authored or co-authored several books and articles on the topic of Corporate Finance and M&A, including Corporate Finance Training. His academic and research interests focus on corporate valuation.

Willis is a graduate of the University of Maryland (B.S. in Business Management) and Boston University (M.S. in Business Administration). He is a Certified Valuation Analyst (CVA) and a Certified Merger & Acquisition Advisor (CM&AA). Willis is deputy chairman of the International Association of Consultants, Valuators and Analysts (IACVA) in Germany.

Mike Ertel, BSEE, MSIA, CBI, MM&AI, CM&AA, is managing director of Legacy M&A Advisors, LLC, a boutique M&A advisory firm specializing in representation of sellers and buyers in lower middle market mergers, acquisitions and sales.

Prior to opening Legacy in 2009, Mike managed the Tampa Bay office of The Bradway Group, a business brokerage and M&A advisory firm, from October 2000 until December 2008. Following his graduation with honors from Purdue University in 1969 with a B.S. in Electrical Engineering and an M.S. in Industrial Administration, Mike spent the next 30 years in progressive marketing, strategic planning and senior management roles with 3M Company; Bemis Packaging; General Electric; and Batesville Casket, a division of Hillenbrand Industries. Mike moved to Tampa in early 1999 to serve as President and COO of Premier Bedding Group before it was acquired by Sealy in mid-2000.

Mike holds Real Estate Broker licenses in Florida and Indiana, and has recently become a registered representative with StillPoint Capital LLC. Mike has earned the following professional designations: Certified Merger & Acquisition Advisor (CM&AA), Master Merger & Acquisition Intermediary (MM&AI), and Certified Business Intermediary (CBI).

Since mid-2006, Mike has served as co-chair of AM&AA's Licensure Taskforce, which is actively working to clarify—and hopefully simplify—the various securities regulations that affect M&A Advisors.

B. Graeme Frazier, IV, is the founder and president of Private Capital Research LLC, a consulting firm that sources, originates, and invests in buyout and recapitalization transactions for middle market private equity firms and corporate clients (www.pcrllc.com). He is also a partner in GF Data Resources LLC, a searchable proprietary database of transaction data on private equity–sponsored M&A transactions with $10 million to $250 million in total enterprise value (www.gfdataresources.com). Graeme is also a non-executive founder of Private Equity Co-Investment (PECO) fund group (www.rbprice.com/PECO.html).

Prior to PCR, Graeme was director of research for the Private Capital Group of Berwind Financial Group LP, (a subsidiary of the Berwind Corporation) where he was responsible for industry research and company research relating to the private capital activities at Berwind. Graeme has a B.A. in Economics from Trinity College in Hartford, CT, and an M.B.A.

from Temple University (Executive Program), where he received the Dean's Certificate of Excellence and was elected to the Beta Gamma Sigma honor society.

John A. ("Buddy") Howard, CFA, ASA, has more than 30 years of experience as a valuation and financial analyst. In addition to his work with High Rock Partners, Inc., he owns Equity Research Services, Inc. (www.equityresearchservices.com), a contract equity research, investor relations, and business valuation firm that was started in 1989, and currently publishes financial reports on approximately 25 publicly traded companies.

He has completed more than 200 valuations assignments, covering a wide variety of industries, and has served as an expert witness in the area of business valuation approximately 30 times. Buddy has also been a financial advisor to many community banks and has, on multiple occasions, been listed in *U.S. Banker* as one of the 50 largest mergers and acquisitions advisors in the nation, based on transaction volume.

He has achieved his Chartered Financial Analyst (CFA) designation and his Accredited Senior Appraiser (ASA) designation and is a member of the Association for Investment Management and Research. He has attained his Series 7 (General Securities), Series 24 (General Securities Principal), and Series 86/87 (Research Analyst) licenses from the NASD.

Amanda L. Keister is an associate of Smith, Anderson, Blount, Dorsett, Mitchell & Jernigan, LLP, in Raleigh, North Carolina, concentrating her practice on corporate and securities law. Smith Anderson is the largest law firm based in Research Triangle Park and one of the largest in the State of North Carolina.

Amanda graduated from the Olin School of Business and Washington University School of Law, where she served as primary editor on the *Washington University Journal of Law and Policy*. While in law school, Amanda interned with the U.S. Securities and Exchange Commission's Division of Enforcement and the General Counsel of Nokia Corp.

David G. Kostmayer, CPA, CM&AA, is a partner of Barrett & Kostmayer, located in Charlotte, North Carolina. He is dedicated to helping clients make intelligent financial decisions and minimizing their income tax liability. David has a successful history in the public accounting arena, providing traditional accounting, tax, and business consulting services to privately held companies throughout the past 16 years. The scope of his experience also includes expertise in corporate finance, strategic consulting, mergers and acquisitions, valuations services, and multistate taxation.

In addition to being a certified public accountant, David received his credentials as a Certified Valuations Analyst (CVA) from the National Association of Certified Valuation Analysts (NACVA) and as a Certified Merger & Acquisition Advisor (CMA&A) from the Alliance of Merger & Acquisition Advisors. His additional training and accreditations enhance the close working relationships he develops with business owners and managers.

David's expertise is also recognized by the academic community. In association with Loyola University in Chicago and the Alliance of Merger & Acquisition Advisors, David is an adjunct professor responsible for lecturing and maintaining course content for the tax section of the Certified Merger & Acquisition Advisor Credentialing Program.

David received his Bachelor of Business Administration, magna cum laude, from the University of Southern Mississippi, and his Master of Tax Accounting from the University of Alabama. He supports both the academic and athletic programs of both universities.

Bruce N. Lipian is a founding principal of StoneCreek Capital, a private equity firm that invests in growth-oriented middle market companies with unique and defensible market positions in a wide range of industries. Targeting investments in companies with $2 million to $20 million in EBITDA, the principals of StoneCreek have sponsored the acquisition or recapitalization of more than 35 companies totaling over $1.4 billion in enterprise value. StoneCreek was originally founded in 1992 as The Gordon + Morris Group after the founding principals left Kelso & Company.

Bruce's previous experience includes four years as an associate/vice president at Kelso & Company and three years as an assistant vice president in the High Technology Division of the Bank of Boston. Bruce received his BA (Economics) from the University of Washington and his MBA (Finance) from the Wharton School, University of Pennsylvania. Bruce is a founding member of the Orange County Private Equity Connection, is on the Organizing Committee for the Southern California ACG MBA Cup, is an Adjunct Professor in the Mihaylo College of Business and Economics at California State University, Fullerton and serves as Vice Chairman on the Board of Kids Konnected.

Annette Mason, CM&AA has two decades of corporate development experience spanning strategic planning, merger integration, acquisition execution, business development, program management and finance. She has led multidisciplinary teams in the due diligence and acquisition of firms from the size of $10 million to $1 billion.

Previously, Annette was integration general manager, AIT, leading an integration effort of merging AIT within a multibillion-dollar operating group.

Her focus was to develop a balance of small company entrepreneurialism while establishing a working rapport to enable collaborative business pursuits across very diverse cultures.

Annette has lived in various places both in the United States and Asia. Her deep appreciation of her citizenship stems from her early high school years while living under martial law in Seoul, Korea. She holds a bachelor's degree in Business Administration with an emphasis in Computer Science from Stephens College, Columbia, Missouri and a Masters of Science in Systems Management from the University of Southern California, Los Angeles. She has attended executive management programs in mergers and acquisitions, strategic planning, solving complex business problems, and managing technical professionals and organizations at UCLA Anderson School, University of Michigan, and the MIT Sloan School of Management respectively.

Scott Moss, CPA, is the managing partner of Cherry, Bekaert & Holland, LLP's (CB&H) Transaction Advisory Services practice. Over his career of more than 20 years, he has advised numerous domestic and multinational companies and private equity funds in all areas of mergers, acquisitions, and due diligence. Scott is a frequent speaker and author on all aspects of mergers and acquisitions activities.

While working closely with both strategic and financial organizations, Scott has successfully advised clients undertaking acquisitions and divestitures with transaction values ranging from less than $10 million to over $700 million. These transactions have covered industry segments such as manufacturing and distribution, governmental contracting, technology, sports and entertainment, consumer products, business services, health care, life sciences, and transportation. Scott also specializes in accounting for business combinations.

Scott has previously served as a member of the CB&H Executive Board and is also an active participant in CB&H's membership with Baker Tilly International.

He received a Bachelor of Business Administration with a concentration in Accounting from the College of William & Mary and completed the Merger & Acquisition Program at the Wharton School of the University of Pennsylvania. He is a member of the American Institute of Certified Public Accountants (AICPA), the North Carolina Association of Certified Public Accountants (NCACPA), and the Virginia Society of Certified Public Accountants (VSCPA).

Deirdre Patten started her career in 1983, specializing in training and compliance for the financial services industry. Over the past 27 years, she has worked with thousands of financial services professionals to help them successfully obtain their securities qualification exams. Deirdre also serves as the education chair on the Board of Directors for the Securities and Insurance Licensing Association (SILA). She currently teaches all FINRA, NYSE, MSRB, NFA, and NASAA series exams, in addition to providing regulatory compliance solutions.

Patten Training & Review, LLC, has access to the top instructors around the country to provide the best training possible. The firm additionally provides expert industry talent to support all of a company's compliance needs. Deirdre has operated as the financial and operations principal as well as general securities principal, options principal, and municipal principal for several regional firms throughout the country. For almost 17 years, she instructed classes while overseeing the quality of classroom content and classroom instructors for Dearborn Financial Institute and for Kaplan Financial Education. Patten Training & Review, LLC, provides complete training and compliance solutions.

Other services offered include mergers and acquisitions, custom content development, editorial review, product rollouts, in-house custom corporate training programs, and executive training programs, and Deirdre and the staff are also available for public speaking engagements.

Mona Pearl's experience in international strategic development and global entrepreneurship has been vital in helping companies design and execute their global strategies. Mona is known for her out-of-the-box thinking and developing creative solutions to tough challenges that produce bottom-line results.

Mona founded and operated three successful businesses and sits on boards of several organizations. From operations to organization to top-line growth strategies, Mona initiates and executes cost-effective and creative opportunities for companies to make money across borders. From actionable due diligence to integration processes, she helps companies increase global market share, enhance leadership, and engage the stakeholders along the value chain. These activities lead companies to grow their business across borders, leverage their global competitiveness, and address operational and strategic growth trends in international markets.

Projects across industries and across borders include Deutsche Telekom, GM, Rover, Jaguar, Marriott, Hyatt Corp., IMF, Fermilab, the Export Institute, SES GmbH, A. B. Dick, Navistar, Accenture, Michelin, State of Illinois—DCEO, Philip Morris, Bacardi, United Airlines, American Airlines, Virgin Atlantic, Delta, and Continental.

Mona has lived on three continents and is proficient in six languages. She has been quoted by CNBC, NPR/WBEZ, Microsoft, Bloomberg, Crain's Chicago, and Entrepreneur.com, and interviewed by other media on global issues and strategies. She is a frequent speaker at global-related conferences and is the author of the book *Grow Globally: Opportunities for Your Middle-Market Company Around the World.* Mona is an adjunct professor at DePaul University, teaching International Business, as well as a guest lecturer in executive MBA programs around the world.

Mona authors a column on current global competitiveness issues in *Manufacturing Today* and *Management Today* magazines, and publishes in other business-related magazines.

Michael S. Roberts is a corporate attorney and one of the founders of the law firm of Roberts McGivney Zagotta, LLC, in Chicago, Illinois. He is also a certified public accountant. Michael has extensive experience in corporate and securities transactions, mergers and acquisitions, venture capital, and other financing transactions, and international outsourcing deals. He has represented private and public companies, entrepreneurs, private equity funds, and software, technology, manufacturing, and retail companies in a wide variety of transactions, including mergers, acquisitions, dispositions, joint ventures, private placements of debt and equity, and financings. Michael obtained an undergraduate degree in accounting from Northern Illinois University and received his law degree from the DePaul College of Law. Michael is a frequent guest speaker on topics involving corporate transactions.

Michael P. Saber is a partner of Smith, Anderson, Blount, Dorsett, Mitchell & Jernigan, LLP, in Raleigh, North Carolina, practicing corporate law with an emphasis on the formation, financing, and general representation of public and private growth and technology companies and closely held businesses, and the representation of entrepreneurs, investors, shareholders, and institutions involved with such companies. He represents clients in a variety of corporate activities, including venture capital transactions, mergers and acquisitions, commercial contracts, capital raising, and strategic licensing and collaborations. Smith Anderson is the largest law firm based in Research Triangle Park and one of the largest in the state of North Carolina.

Mike has been recognized as a Legal Elite lawyer in North Carolina, named to the list of Best Lawyers in America, and named a Superlawyer. He practiced corporate law at Blank Rome, LLP, in Philadelphia before he joined Smith Anderson in 1996.

William H. Stewart, CFA, is a senior private equity investment executive with more than 22 years of successful, diverse, and progressive experience in private equity investing and institutional investment management. In his present position as managing partner of Navigator Partners, he leads a private equity investment group dedicated to investing in profitable businesses in the lower middle market. Before joining Navigator, Bill was a managing director with Nassau Capital, an independent firm which managed the private equity, real estate and energy assets of Princeton University's $12 billion endowment. Concurrently, between 2000 and 2005, Bill performed as the chief financial officer of KMC Telecom Holdings, Inc., America's largest privately-held Competitive Local Exchange Carrier (CLEC), with over $1.8 billion in invested capital, $565 million in annual revenue and $270 million in EBITDA. His career began at the Bank of New York, where he was an assistant vice president.

Bill's background includes working with leading fund investors and institutions in control buyouts, growth equity transactions, and distressed turnaround situations. He sources, analyzes, evaluates and executes investments. Bill also serves on several corporate boards including Firstlight Homecare.

His education includes a Master of Business Administration in Finance, awarded cum laude from New York University's Leonard N. Stern School of Business in 1994. His undergraduate work was done at Villanova University, where he received a cum laude degree in economics.

Amalie Tuffin is an attorney who has spent more than 15 years specializing in mergers and acquisitions, venture capital transactions, general corporate law, and related tax matters. She is a partner in the Raleigh, North Carolina, law firm of Whitmeyer Tuffin, PLLC. Amalie previously spent four years at Hutchison Law Group; prior to that she practiced at the Research Triangle Park technology law firm of Daniels Daniels & Verdonik and the Boston firm of Peabody & Arnold. Amalie frequently writes on corporate and tax law issues relevant to emerging-growth companies.

Amalie graduated from the University of California's Hastings College of the Law in 1992, and received her LL.M in tax from Boston University's Graduate Tax program in 1996. Amalie received her undergraduate degree from Harvard University in 1989, where she graduated with honors. Amalie is admitted to practice law in North Carolina, Florida, and Massachusetts.

John C. Watts, CM&AA, is a director of business development at Curtiss-Wright Controls, a division of Curtiss-Wright Corporation (NYSE: CW). Curtiss-Wright is a $2 billion (sales) diversified aerospace company; Curtiss-Wright Controls' sales are approximately $650 million annually. Prior to Curtiss-Wright, John served in business development and operational roles in General Dynamics Advanced Information Systems and as a commissioned officer in the United States Army.

Since joining Curtiss-Wright Controls, John has led the corporate development activities of the division, including mergers, acquisitions, divestitures, and strategic planning. His M&A responsibilities include the range of process tasks from initial target identification through closing: specifically, strategic fit analysis, seller contact, valuation, LOI/offer generation and negotiation, due diligence team organization and leadership, purchase agreement negotiation (in concert with counsel), closing mechanics, and internal documentation and approvals. Averaging three completed transactions annually, Curtiss-Wright Controls submits approximately 30 indication letters each year. John has executed transactions in the United States, England, Scotland, Ireland, and Norway, and has substantially progressed transactions in France and Germany as well.

A member of the Association of Corporate Growth (ACG) and the Association of Merger & Acquisition Advisors (AM&AA), John is a Certified M&A Advisor. He earned a Bachelor of Arts degree from Furman University and a Masters in Business Administration degree from Duke University.

Index